Sufism

Sufism
The Formative Period

AHMET T. KARAMUSTAFA

University of California Press
Berkeley Los Angeles

University of California Press, one of the most distinguished university presses in the United States, enriches lives around the world by advancing scholarship in the humanities, social sciences, and natural sciences. Its activities are supported by the UC Press Foundation and by philanthropic contributions from individuals and institutions. For more information, visit www.ucpress.edu.

University of California Press
Berkeley and Los Angeles, California

First published in the UK by
Edinburgh University Press Ltd, 22 George Square, Edinburgh.

Library of Congress Cataloging-in-Publication Data

Karamustafa, Ahmet T., 1956–.
Sufism : the formative period / Ahmet T. Karamustafa.
p. cm.
Includes bibliographical references and index.
ISBN-13: 978-0-520-25268-4 (cloth : alk. paper)
ISBN-13: 978-0-520-25269-1 (pbk. : alk. paper)
1. Sufism—History. I. Title.

BP188.5.K37 2007
297.409′02—dc22 2006051406

Manufactured in Great Britain

16 15 14 13 12 11 10 09 08 07
10 9 8 7 6 5 4 3 2 1

The paper used in this publication meets the minimum requirements of ANSI/NISO Z39.48-1992 (R1997) (*Permanence of Paper*).

Contents

CONTENTS

Preface

'Mysticism' has been a highly popular category in the academic study of religion since the beginning of the twentieth century. During the last few decades, however, the category has come under widespread criticism for its essentialist assumptions. The claim that mystical experiences are at once private, unmediated and ineffable yet universally present in all human religiosity has been exposed as a modern Euro-American construction with a peculiar history of its own, and 'mysticism was returned to the conditioning webs of history, culture, and language' by its new critics.[1] More recently, the same criticism was also extended to 'spirituality', the category that has come to enjoy widespread popularity during the last quarter-century.[2] As a result, any historically uncontextualised use of mysticism or spirituality as if these were self-evident, uncontested, and universally applicable categories now appears problematic and even unwarranted, if not downright naive.

But if it is no longer possible to view mysticism and spirituality as general analytical categories abstracted from historical and cultural context, what can be said about the study of the 'mystical and spiritual dimensions' of individual religious traditions? What is the relevance of the historicist criticism for the academic scrutiny of religion-specific mysticisms and spiritualities? The answer lies in acknowledging the primacy of the 'conditioning webs' of history and culture also at this level. Each religious tradition can certainly be said to contain mystical and spiritual dimensions, yet the exact content and meaning of these dimensions should not be conceived as unchanging essences; instead, the mystical and the spiritual need to be discovered, described and analysed in particular contexts.

In the study of Sufism, often described as the major mystical tradition within Islam, essentialising approaches that postulate an unchanging core to all Sufi phenomena have certainly occupied a prominent place, yet historical and philological approaches that direct proper attention to historical context have been in place long before the onset of historicist and constructivist criticism and can hardly be characterised as marginal.[3] In other words, while some trends in existing scholarship on Sufism certainly remain vulnerable to charges of essentialism, others are only vindicated and invigorated by the new historicist critique. The present work, written in the historicist mode, is intended as a contribution to the ongoing attempt to situate Sufism in its proper historical context. It was born out of the realisation that although Sufism, as a whole or in part, has been the subject of many scholarly surveys during the past half century, the earliest phase of Sufi history, roughly from the third/ninth to the sixth/twelfth century, has not yet received sustained treatment in the form of a book-length monograph.[4] The need for a detailed and analytically-oriented historical overview of the early period is acute since this 'classical' phase provides the foundation for the study of all subsequent phases of the history of Sufism in its various aspects, and a firm grounding in this foundation is a natural desideratum for all students of Sufism. Moreover, during the past few decades, there have been significant advances in our understanding of the early period, and, while there remains much spadework to be done, the time is ripe for a provisional synthesis of existing scholarship on the subject in different languages.[5] *Sufism: The Formative Period* is an attempt to meet this need for comprehensive and up-to-date contextualisation of the early history of Sufism.

The study is in the form of an historical overview that is at once synthetic and analytical. It is synthetic in its integration of excellent recent works on individual figures and particular themes into a unified narrative of the emergence and development of Sufism as a major mode of piety in early Islamic history.[6] When in-depth examinations of specific aspects of early Sufi history are synthesised with care, it becomes possible to draw the contours of Sufism with considerable clarity. *Sufism: The Formative Period* is, however, also analytical in building a new framework for tracing the historical trajectory of early Sufism. When one steps back and attempts to take stock of focused case-studies, new questions arise concerning issues of emergence, development, spread and blending among the different mystical trends in early Islamic history, and it becomes possible to detect new patterns of change and continuity on both social and intellectual levels.

The book is divided into six chapters. A significant number of Muslims in the third/ninth century attempted to explore reality through the prism of the human soul, and initially there were several distinct mystical groups in the different cultural regions of Islamdom. Chapter 1 is devoted to historically the most consequential of these mystical circles, the Sufis of Baghdad. It examines the emergence of Baghdad Sufism as a distinct mode of piety during the second half of the third/ninth century and draws a complete social and intellectual profile of this movement after presenting individual portraits of three of its most prominent representatives: Kharrāz, Nūrī and Junayd. Chapter 2 reviews major mystical figures and trends during the same time period outside Baghdad – in lower Iraq (Tustarī), in north-eastern Iran (the Malāmatīs), in Central Asia

(Tirmidhī) – and demonstrates the vibrancy of mystical thought and practice in these different regions. Chapter 3 traces the spread of Baghdad Sufism to other areas including Iberia, and documents the process of its fusion with indigenous mystical trends during the course of the fourth/tenth century, a process that ultimately led to the ascendancy of 'metropolitan' Baghdad Sufism over its 'provincial' counterparts. Chapter 4 examines the formation of a self-conscious Sufi tradition in the form of a specialised Sufi literature, first in Arabic, then, from the fifth/eleventh century onward, also in Persian, and suggests that the emergence of the Sufi literary tradition can be understood as an attempt on the part of fourth/tenth and fifth/eleventh-century mystics to delineate the boundaries of 'normative' Sufism. The chapter also demonstrates that while this normative Sufi tradition was certainly constructed in the image of the Baghdad masters, the Sufi authors of the period were not united in their understanding of Sufi norms, and they situated themselves and their perceptions of the Sufi tradition in rather different ways in the rapidly-evolving matrix of Islamic thought and practice of the era. In a nutshell, traditionalist Sufis did not see eye to eye with their more academically-minded counterparts. Chapter 5 approaches the issue of tradition-building from the perpective of social history and narrates the story of the formation of Sufi communities around powerful training masters in Sufi lodges. The chapter also argues that the rise of such tightly-knit communities of mystics was intertwined with another equally seminal social development, that is, the emergence of saints cults. Chapter 6 then traces the spread of Sufism to all levels of social and cultural life in both urban and rural environments during the fifth/eleventh and sixth/twelfth centuries and revisits the issue of normativity from the perspective of antinomian and conformist elements within Sufism. The conclusion provides a succinct presentation of the major findings of the study.

Although this book casts a wide net to cover most major issues in the history of early Sufism, there are, naturally, some questions that are not properly addressed here. Perhaps most conspicuous for its omission is the issue of the influence of earlier religious traditions on Sufism. The extent to which Islamic mystical trends developed as fresh syntheses of patterns of mystical thought and practice that were already current in the broader religious environment of the Near East and North Africa as well as Western and South Asia prior to the rise of Islam has been a contested issue in the academic study of Sufism. If the question of influence is omitted from discussion in the present study, this is not out of a desire to belittle its significance but is occasioned by the conviction that the secondary literature on the subject continues to be thin in volume and conjectural in substance.[7] Adequate consideration of the topic would have necessitated new, in-depth research into primary and secondary sources in many languages on related issues in a wide array of religious traditions, which, however, clearly fell beyond the scope of this book project.[8] Given the renewed interest in the question of Islamic origins during the last decade, it is hoped that new scholarly vistas will become available in the near future on the issue of continuity and discontinuity in mystical thought and practice among the different religious traditions of Late Antiquity.[9]

Another topic that deserves close attention but had to be excluded from the study is the thorny question of the relationship between Shīʿism and Sufism in the early period. Although no Shīʿīs were to be found among Sufi ranks, there were affinities between Shīʿī and Sufi thought, especially in their respective theories of divine selection (*wilāya/walāya*) and their interiorising approaches to Qur'ān interpretation.[10] Although our understanding of early Shīʿism has advanced significantly over the last few decades, no substantive comparative examination of Sufism and Shīʿism in the early period has appeared recently.[11] It did not seem wise to tackle a subject on which reliable scholarship is meagre.

No doubt, there are other areas in which the coverage of the present work will appear thin or even deficient to some readers. It is hoped, nevertheless, that the historical overview offered here will serve as the obvious gateway into early Sufism for all who are interested in this fascinating subject.

Note on presentation

All Arabic and Persian terms are transliterated except for the following commonly-used place names: Baghdad, Basra, Nishapur, Isfahan, Shiraz, Herat, Mecca and Medina. The transliteration system used is that of the *Encyclopaedia of Islam*, with modifications customary for works published in English. The Arabic definite article 'al-' is used only when all proper names are introduced in full for the first time in the text; it is dropped in all other appearances of the same name in the text as well as in the notes and the bibliography (for instance, 'Sarrāj' rather than 'al-Sarrāj' except in the first full mention of his name). All transliterations in quotations (though not in notes or bibliography) are standardised for uniformity.

Dates are given in the Islamic lunar Hijrī (and for books published in Iran, Islamic solar Shamsī) years first, followed by their common-era equivalents.

Only two abbreviations are used in the notes: EI for the *Encyclopaedia of Islam* (the second edition is used), and EIr for the *Encyclopaedia Iranica*.

Unless otherwise indicated, all translations are by the author.

Notes

1 See the deft summary in Leigh Eric Schmidt, 'The Making of Modern "Mysticism"', *Journal of the American Academy of Religion* 71 (2003): 273–4; the quote is from 274.
2 Jeremy R. Carrette and Richard King, *Selling Spirituality: The Silent Takeover of Religion* (London: Routledge, 2005), esp. 2–6. Carrette and King write: 'There is no view from nowhere ... from which one could determine a fixed and universal meaning for the term "spirituality"' (p. 3).
3 The prominence of the former approach is demonstrated, for instance, by the continuing popularity of the works of Annemarie Schimmel, most notably her *Mystical Dimensions of Islam* (Chapel Hill: University of North Carolina Press, 1975), while the latter is best exemplified by the *oeuvre* of Fritz Meier.
4 Recent overall surveys of Sufism in English include Julian Baldick, *Mystical Islam: An Introduction to Sufism* (New York: New York University Press, 1989); William C. Chittick, *Sufism: A Short Introduction* (Oxford: Oneworld, 2000); Carl W. Ernst, *The Shambhala Guide to Sufism* (Boston, MA: Shambhala, 1997); Alexander Knysh, *Islamic Mysticism: A Short History* (Leiden: Brill, 2000); John Renard, *Seven Doors to Islam: Spirituality and the Religious Life of Muslims* (Berkeley: University of California Press, 1996); and Mark J. Sedgwick, *Sufism: The Essentials* (Cairo: American University in Cairo Press, 2000). For an extensive, up-to-date bibliography on Sufism that includes most major recent publications on Sufism in western European languages, conveniently organised into five major categories (general and comparative studies; primary sources; focused studies; historical studies by geographical region; society; politics, the arts and gender), see John Renard, *Historical Dictionary of Sufism* (Lanham, MD: Scarecrow Press, 2005), 279–349.
5 The new advances are represented especially in the publications of Böwering, Chabbi, Gramlich, Melchert, Nwyia, Pūrjavādī, Radtke, Renard, Sells, Sobieroj and Sviri listed in the bibliography.
6 Recent scholarship on individual mystics is best exemplified, to cite only books, by works such as Gerhard Böwering, *The Mystical Vision of Existence in Classical Islam: The Qur'ānic Hermeneutics of the Ṣūfī Sahl at-Tustarī (d. 283/896)* (Berlin: De Gruyter, 1980); Richard Gramlich, *Alte Vorbilder des Sufitums* (Wiesbaden: Harrassowitz, 1997); and the many publications of Bernd Radtke on Tirmidhī. Among thematic studies, one can mention Benedikt Reinert, *Die Lehre vom* tawakkul *in der klassischen Sufik* (Berlin: De Gruyter, 1968); Naṣr Allāh Pūrjavādī, *Ru'yat-i māh dar āsumān: barrasī-yi tārīkhī-yi mas'ala-i liqā' Allāh dar kalām va taṣavvuf* (Tehran: Markaz-i Nashr-i Dānishgāhī, 1375/1996); and Kristin Sands, *Sufi Commentaries on the Qur'an in Classical Islam* (London: Routledge, 2005).
7 For the most recent attempt to demonstrate eastern Christian and Indian influences on the formation of Sufism as well as an overview of the state of scholarship on the issue of influence in general, see Baldick, *Mystical Islam*, esp. 15–24; but see the cautionary remarks of Bernd Radtke on this issue in his review of Baldick's book in *Religious Studies* 29 (1993): 267.
8 As an example of the kind of scholarly study that is needed on this front, one can point to Bernd Radtke, 'Iranian and Gnostic Elements in Early *Taṣawwuf*: Observations Concerning the *Umm al-Kitāb*', in *Proceedings of the First European Conference*

of Iranian Studies Held in Turin, September 7th-11th, 1987 by the Societas Iranologica Europaea, ed. Gherardo Gnoli and Antonio Panaino (Rome: Istituto italiano per il Medio ed Estremo Oriente, 1990), 519–30.

9 A collection of essays that exemplifies recent scholarly interest in the study of early Islam in its broader cultural milieu is Herbert Berg (ed.), *Method and Theory in the Study of Islamic Origins* (Leiden: Brill, 2003); this volume does not include an article on Sufism.

10 For concise treatments, see 'Walāyah', *Encyclopedia of Religion*, 2nd edn, ed. Lindsay Jones (Detroit : Macmillan Reference USA, 2005), 14: 9656–62 (Hermann Landolt); 'Wilāya, 2. In Shīʿism', EI 11: 208b–9b (Paul E. Walker); and 'Ta'wīl', EI 10: 390a–2a (Ismail Poonawala).

11 For a sampling of recent scholarship on early Shīʿism, see Etan Kohlberg (ed.), *Shi'ism* (Burlington, VT: Ashgate, 2003). The most extensive comparative treatment of Sufism and Shīʿism continues to be Kamil M. Al-Shaibi, *Sufism and Shiism* (Surbiton: LAAM, 1991), which was originally published in Arabic as *al-Ṣila bayna al-taṣawwuf wa al-tashayyuʿ* in 1382/1963; this work, however, is not particularly helpful for the early period.

Acknowledgements

I would not have written this book had Carole Hillenbrand not invited me to contribute a volume on the history of Sufism to Edinburgh University Press' publications on Islamic Studies, and I would like to thank her for initiating this project.

Most of the book was written during a year-long leave of absence from Washington University in St Louis during the calendar year 2005. One semester of this leave was made possible by the Annemarie Schimmel Award granted to me by the Institute of Ismaili Studies, London, UK, and I am grateful to the Institute for this prestigious award. Even though my approach to the history of Sufism differs considerably from that of the late Professor Schimmel, I would like to think that she would have been pleased with the work had she lived to see it. I myself feel gratified that her name is associated with this project through this award.

Several colleagues generously read draft versions of the book, in whole or in part, and it is a genuine pleasure to acknowledge their support and assistance here: Carl Ernst (University of North Carolina, Chapel Hill), Peter Heath (American University of Beirut), Hermann Landolt (McGill University and the Institute of Ismaili Studies), John Renard (St Louis University), Omid Safi (University of North Carolina, Chapel Hill), and Laury Silvers (Skidmore). My indebtedness to a much broader circle of colleagues without whose contributions to the study of early Sufism this work could not have been written should be more than evident in the notes and the bibliography. Naturally, I alone am responsible for any errors or shortcomings that may have remained in the work.

Although many a Sufi chose to remain celibate, as will become obvious to the readers of this book, as a student of Sufism I myself feel blessed to have a life-companion whose presence illuminates all aspects of my life. I thank my wife Fatemeh Keshavarz for her unfailing support for this project as with all the others.

Finally, it was a rare privilege to be able to spend hours on end trying to trace the legacy of early Muslim mystics of all types, and it is to their living memory that this book is dedicated.

Acknowledgments

1

The Sufis of Baghdad

Sufism, the major mystical tradition in Islam, emerged from within renunciatory modes of piety (*zuhd*) during a period that extended from the last decades of the second/eighth to the beginning of the fourth/tenth century. The earliest mystical approaches appeared in the first half of this period, but these were likely disparate and heterogeneous in nature and, more significantly, they remain obscure to modern researchers owing to sparse documentation. From the mid-third/ninth century onwards, however, Sufis of Baghdad came into full view as members of a distinct mode of mystical piety. In the same time period, other mystical movements took shape elsewhere, notably in lower Iraq, northeastern Iran, and Central Asia. Mystics who belonged to these latter movements were not initially known as Sufis, and in their thought and practice, they differed from Baghdad Sufis and from each other in many ways, but they gradually blended with the Baghdad mystics, and in time, like them, they too came to be identified as Sufis.

Renunciants, the inward turn and the term *ṣūfī*

During the first century of ʿAbbāsid rule, renunciation was a widespread form of piety in Muslim communities.[1] Renunciants (*zāhid*) and pietists (*ʿābid, nāsik*) of this period were not organised into a single homogeneous movement but came in different colours and stripes. Some, like the early figure Ibrāhīm ibn Adham al-Balkhī (d. 161/777–8), had a 'radical aversion' to mainstream social life, voluntarily adapted the life of poverty characterised by 'a search for exteme purity, especially in dietary matters', and literally moved to the margins of society by living at the frontiers, where they engaged in warfare.[2] Others, scholar-ascetics who cultivated Qur'ān and *ḥadīth* studies, spent time at a special retreat (*ribāṭ*) in ʿAbbādān (then an island close to Basra on the river Tigris) founded by disciples of the famous preacher Ḥasan al-Baṣrī (d. 110/728), perhaps around ʿAbd al-Wāḥid ibn Zayd (d. c. 150/767).[3] Some, specifically identified as 'wool-wearers', were social activists associated with the practice of *al-amr bi'l-maʿrūf wa nahy ʿan al-munkar*, 'commanding right and forbidding wrong'.[4] Still others, like Fuḍayl ibn ʿIyāḍ (d. 188/803) and Bishr ibn al-Ḥārith al-Ḥāfī (c. 152–227/c. 766–841), were scholars who turned into renunciants and gave up scholarship.[5] Some renunciants of all these types are known to have worn wool (*ṣūf*).

In this same period, a remarkable development was underway among renunciants. Whatever their approach to renunciation and to the question of how far to detach themselves from mainstream social life, some prominent renunciants and the renunciant communities that formed around them began to direct their energies increasingly to the cultivation of the inner life. This inward turn manifested itself especially in new discourses on spiritual states, stages of spiritual development, closeness to God, and love; it also led to a clear emphasis on 'knowledge of the interior' (*ʿilm al-bāṭin*) acquired through ardent examination and training of the human soul. The proponents of the inward turn explored the psychological aspects of the standard renunciant themes of repentance and turning toward God (*tawba*) and placing one's trust in God (*tawakkul*) through scrupulous observation of the divine commands (*waraʿ*), and they reached the conclusion that true repentance could not be achieved without a rigorous examination of the conscience and the soul. For these 'interiorising' renunciants, the major renunciatory preoccupation of eschewing this world (*dunyā*, literally, 'the lower, nearer realm') in order to cultivate the other world (*ākhira*, 'the ultimate realm') was transformed into a search for the other world within the inner self.[6]

Interestingly, the 'discovery' and cultivation of the inner dimensions of the human person was concomitant with a similar inward reorientation among the same circles of renunciants in the attempt to achieve a true understanding of the divine revelation. The concern with attaining knowledge of the inner self was evidently accompanied by a parallel effort to discern the inner meaning of the Qur'ān and the Sunna, a 'method of interpretation from within ... often described as *istinbāṭ* (inference)'. Moreover, in a further intriguing twist, these interiorising epistemic developments were gradually also bundled up with a certain doctrine of selection, whereby knowledge of the soul as well as understanding of the inner meanings of divine speech and prophetic example were thought to be 'God-given' as opposed to being the fruit of human effort. According to this increasingly conspicuous doctrine, only God's elect, designated most notably as 'friends' and 'protégés' of God (*walī*, pl. *awliyā'*), could attain ultimate self-knowledge and thus have access to aspects of divine knowledge. This idea of divine selection in the post-prophetic era, later normally expressed by the term *walāya/wilāya*, was most prominent among Shīʿīs, but it seems to have been in circulation also among proto-Sunnīs, especially in the form of *ḥadīth* reports about various categories of God's *awliyā'*, often designated by terms such as *abdāl* (literally 'substitutes' but exact derivation is not clear) and *ṣiddīqūn* ('righteous ones').[7]

The exact origin and trajectory of these trends are obscure, but some of the pioneering figures in this process – some of them not renunciants – can be identified: the female renunciant Rābiʿa al-ʿAdawiyya (d. 185/801) in Basra, Shaqīq al-Balkhī (d. 194/810) in northern Khurāsān, Abū Sulaymān al-Dārānī (d. 215/830) in Syria, Dhu'l-Nūn al-Miṣrī (d. 245/860) in Egypt, al-Ḥārith al-Muḥāsibī (d. 243/857) in Baghdad, Yaḥyā ibn Muʿādh al-Rāzī (d. 258/872) in central Iran, and Bāyazīd Ṭayfūr ibn ʿĪsā al-Basṭāmī (d. 234/848 or 261/875) also in Khurāsān.[8] Since the historical record on these figures is particularly difficult to disintentangle, it is not always possible to establish associations between particular trends and specific figures. Nevertheless, we can be more specific about the legacy of some of these 'interiorising' renunciants and early mystics. By way of illustration, let us review briefly the cases of Rābiʿa, Bāyazīd (a contraction of 'Abū Yazīd') and Muḥāsibī.

Rābiʿa al-ʿAdawiyya al-Qaysiyya (perhaps d. 185/801) was one of the numerous female renunciants of this early period, but she achieved greater fame in posterity than her counterparts.[9] Even though she most certainly existed as a historical figure, her personality is wrapped in later stories that are impossible to substantiate.[10] The earliest writer to mention her, the famous *littérateur* al-Jāḥiẓ (160–255/776–868/9), gave no details of her biography and simply referred to her among renunciants of Basra, reproducing two statements of hers that demonstrate her asceticism as well as her irrepressible fear of God. Upon being told, 'If you were to speak to the men of your family, they would buy a servant for you, and he would save you the trouble of your housework', Rābiʿa replied, 'I should be ashamed to ask for this world from Him to Whom it belongs, so how should I ask for it from him to whom it does not?'[11] And when she was asked 'Have you ever performed any act that you think will be accepted [by God]?' she responded by saying 'If there was any such [act], I would still fear that it would be rejected!'[12] After al-Jāḥiẓ, there is a century-long period of silence on Rābiʿa in the sources that is broken only in the second half of the fourth/tenth century with several notices on her in works composed by Sufi authors. It is clear that by that time the spiritual portrait of Rābiʿa had been almost fully drawn, at least partly under the influence of legends of 'early Christian penitent courtesans'. The evolution of her hagiographical profile was rendered even more complicated by a certain degree of confusion between her and other Rābiʿas, most notably her contemporary Rābiʿa bint Ismāʿīl of Syria. The historical life of this latter, said to be the wife of the prominent renunciant Aḥmad ibn Abi'l-Ḥawārī, is even more obscure than her more famous namesake from Basra, and it appears that the stories about the two women were sometimes blended together.[13]

In the later accounts about her, Rābiʿa of Basra was depicted most commonly as a pious woman who rose from slavery to become a saintly figure. Her unswerving devotion to God was exemplified by her saying 'First the neighbour, then the house' ('*al-jār thumma al-dār*'), which was normally interpreted to mean that God deserved worship for His own sake and that Paradise and, by extension, Hell were secondary. Her relentless focus on God reportedly took the form of love (*maḥabba*) and intimacy (*uns*). Even though it has been proven that some verses about love that were attributed to her in these sources are in fact from an originally secular love poem, it is possible that she was one of the first 'to teach the doctrine of Pure Love, the disinterested love of God for His own sake alone, and one of the first also to combine with her teaching on love the doctrine of *kashf*, the unveiling, to the lover, of the Beatific Vision.'[14]

Little is known about the biography of Bāyazīd, who seems to have spent his life as a celibate in his native Basṭām, to the east of Nishapur.[15] He was the earliest mystic to have left behind a substantial number of 'ecstatic utterances' (*shaṭḥ*), most famously 'Glory be to Me! How great is My majesty!' (*subḥānī! mā aʿẓama sha'nī!*) and 'I am He' (*anā huwa*). How he thought God could talk through him in such fashion was explained by him in the following words:

> Once He raised me up and caused me to stand before Him and said to me, 'O Abū Yazīd, My creatures desire to behold you.' I answered, 'Adorn me with Your unity and clothe me in Your I-ness and raise me to your Oneness, so that when Your creatures behold me they may say that they behold You, and that only You may be there, not I.'[17]

Bāyazīd evidently thought that this request was granted, since many of the sayings attributed to him evince complete erasure of his human subjectivity and its total replacement with God, conceived as the absolute 'I', the only true subject in existence. In an early Arabic text of uncertain attribution, Bāyazīd reportedly recounted his 'heavenly ascent' (*miʿrāj*, thus paralleling the celebrated night journey and ascent of Muḥammad) through the seven heavens to the divine throne where he experienced such intimacy with God that he was 'nearer to him than the spirit is to the body.'[18] His often shocking, even outrageous, utterances became the subject of commentary by later mystics, who considered them to be verbal overflow of experiential ecstasy.[19] Departing from Qur'ānic usage, where reciprocal love between God and humans is expressed by the word *maḥabba* (Qur'ān 5 [al-Mā'ida]: 59), Bāyazīd characterised the relationship of love between the mystic and God as *'ishq* ('passionate love'), a term normally used for love between humans. Through his powerful expressions of love for God, Bāyazīd later came to symbolise the insatiable, intoxicated lover:

> Yaḥyā ibn Mu'ādh [al-Rāzī, d. 258/872] wrote to Abū Yazīd [Bāyazīd], 'I became intoxicated by the volume that I drank from the cup of his love.' Abū Yazīd wrote to him in his reply, 'You became intoxicated and what you drank were mere drops! [Meanwhile] someone else has drunk the oceans of the heavens and the earth and his thirst has still not been quenched; his tongue is hanging down from thirst and he is asking, 'Is there more?'[20]

We possess no clues as to how Bāyazīd achieved his experiences of proximity to God; reportedly, he was scrupulous in his observance of regular Islamic rituals, but he apparently rejected renunciation as an option (he said, 'This world is nothing; how can one renounce it?'), and advocated inner detachment from everything other than God instead.[21] In spite of the obscurity that surrounds his thought and practice, Bāyazīd achieved lasting fame as the clearest example of the possibility of direct, albeit mystical, communication with God even after the completion of the mission of Muḥammad.[22]

Muḥāsibī too was a key figure in the development of early Islamic thought.[23] His imprint was in the area of 'introspection', a rigorous inner probing and examination of the conscience (*muḥāsabat al-nafs*, from which his name Muḥāsibī was derived), especially as articulated in his work *Kitāb al-riʿāya li-ḥuqūq Allāh* (*The Book on the Observance of God's Rights*). This introspection took the form of detailed psychological analysis of the various forms of egoism originating from the lower self (*nafs*) – these included 'egoistic self-display' (*riyā'*), 'pride' (*kibr*), 'vanity' (*ʿujb*) and 'self-delusion' (*ghirra*) – and the ways in which such egoism stood in the way of fulfilling the terms of 'what is due to God'(*ḥuqūq Allāh*).[24] Muḥāsibī thought that the lower self, 'the seat of the appetites and of passion', blocked the functioning of the heart, which he regarded as the core of human self-consciousness. The resolution of this conflict came through intense self-examination conducted with the light of reason, a 'natural disposition or instinct (*gharīza*) bestowed by God upon His creatures' that served to orient humans towards God by discerning what God loved and what He detested.[25] Significantly, Muḥāsibī did not argue that reason could discern the principles of morality as such; reason had no moral autonomy, and its role was to adhere to the moral code contained in the revelation.[26] But reason was capable of exposing the tricks of the lower self through intellectual meditation on the Qur'ān and the Sunna and thus of orienting the heart to God. Muḥāsibī's distinctive introspective gaze was thus focused on disentangling and taming the lower self, and his theological psychology was elegant testimony to the depth and sophistication of the examination of the human soul that had become increasingly conspicuous during the first half of the third/ninth century.

Although similar portraits can be drawn for each of the other 'interiorising' figures listed above, here it will be sufficient to point to their connection with the major themes of the 'inward turn' identified above. The tradition of examining the soul seems to have been especially strong in Basra among the followers of Ḥasan al-Baṣrī, especially ʿAbd al-Wāḥid ibn Zayd, and it culminated in the thought of Muḥāsibī in Baghdad (Muḥāsibī was originally from Basra). The attempt to fathom the inner meaning of the Qur'ān also had deep roots in Basra among the same circles, but it was cross-fertilised by similar trends originating from the sixth Shīʿī *imām* Jaʿfar al-Ṣādiq (d. 148/765) in Medina and perhaps further developed by Dhu'l-Nūn.[27] The idea of spiritual states and of a spiritual path consisting of different stages was nurtured by Dārānī in Syria, Shaqīq in Khurāsān, and by Dhu'l-Nūn in Egypt. Rābi'a al-'Adawiyya in Basra, also Bāyazīd, exemplified love of God as a central preoccupation. Moving outside the boundaries of 'sober' renunciation, Yaḥyā ibn Mu'ādh epitomised joyfullness as an outcome of reliance on God's mercy. Experiences of closeness to God were, as noted above, famously verbalised in the ecstatic utterances of Bāyazīd. The idea that God appoints special agents from amongst the believers is not unambiguously connected with any early renunciant or mystic of this period.

While the trends of inner knowledge and divine selection of *awliyā'* were certainly in the air and were cultivated especially by some eminent renunciants and early mystics of the first half of the third/ninth century, they did not form a coherent and unified whole but could only be found as correlated and occasionally intertwined strands of piety. In the second half of that century, however, and especially in Baghdad, which had emerged after its foundation in the mid-second/eighth century as the indisputable cultural capital of the 'Abbāsid domains, they coalesced with several other elements of religiosity to form a distinct type of piety that became the foundation of what would prove to be one of the most durable pietistic approaches in Islam. Furthermore, for reasons that remain obscure, the members of this Baghdad-centred movement came to be known as *ṣūfīs* and the new movement itself was given the name *ṣūfiyya*.

Both 'Sufi' and 'Sufism' are terms adopted from Arabic. In Arabic texts dating from the first few centuries of Islam, especially in the earliest major manuals of Sufism composed during the fourth and fifth/tenth and eleventh centuries, we come across the terms *ṣūfī* and *mutaṣawwif* (pl. *ṣūfiyya* and *mutaṣawwifa*) that refer to devotees of a particular type of piety. This mode of pious living was most commonly referred to by the name *taṣawwuf*, which is the Arabic equivalent of the modern English name Sufism. There was controversy over the origins of the term *ṣūfī* among the authors of these early texts, and even though modern scholars have reproduced this controversy at different levels in their own writings, there is considerable agreement among both early authors and modern scholars that the word *ṣūfī* most probably comes from *ṣūf*, the Arabic word for 'wool' and that it was originally used to designate 'wearers of woolen garments'.[28]

The word *ṣūfī* was first coined as early as the second/eighth century to refer to some renunciants and pietists who wore wool as opposed to other renunciants and the majority of Muslims who wore linen and cotton.[29] The practice of wearing wool, a form of 'self-deprivation and self-marginalization as moral and political protest', was most certainly bound up with social and cultural negotiations that took place around the concepts of renunciation (*zuhd*), earning a living (*kasb*) and trust in God (*tawakkul*) that were prevalent especially during the second half of the second/eighth century among Muslims.[30] The details are hard to assemble, but it appears that some interiorising renunciants who can be described as mystics expressed their special form of piety by wearing wool, and hence the word 'wool-wearer' came to carry the connotation of 'devoted, radical renunciant/mystic'. However, the words *zāhid*, *nāsik*, and *'ābid* continued to be the primary signifiers of renunciation.[31] In the second/eighth and roughly the first half of the third/fourth century, then, the term *ṣūfī* designated 'nascent mystics' who were commonly viewed as 'radical renunciants'. In as much as the collective term *ṣūfiyya* is attested for this period, it designated not one distinct social group but several different social types, or, more properly, it was the name of a particular orientation towards piety marked by the socially unconventional, and thus remarkable, habit of donning woollen garments.[32]

However, from the middle of the third/ninth century, the term *ṣūfī* came to be used increasingly as a technical term to designate a group of people who belonged to a clearly identifiable social movement in Baghdad that was based on a distinct type of piety. The process through which the earlier term *ṣūfī* became the preferred name for Baghdad mystics remains obscure, though one can speculate that the term *ṣūfī* had a certain 'avant-garde' or 'cutting-edge' resonance among both renunciants and others, and that this 'hip' quality facilitated its application to the new movement. Also, unlike the other terms commonly used to designate renunciants such as *zāhid* and *nāsik*, which could hardly be dissociated from renunciation as a form of piety, the term *ṣūfī* was of more recent coinage and could be redeployed to point to a new cultural development. In time, the Baghdad Sufis themselves adopted this name and began to use it for themselves, and the word no longer signified 'wool-wearing radical renunciant/mystic' but came to be applied exclusively to the members of this new group. In this way, an epithet that had been the name of some mystical trends of renunciatory origins now became the name of a distinctive form of pious living that could no longer be characterised simply as renunciation.[33]

Prominent Sufis of Baghdad

In order to identify the salient themes and features of Sufism after its emergence as a full-fledged movement in the 'Abbāsid capital, let us first review some of its prominent representatives whose views are preserved for us in their own works that have survived to this day.

Kharrāz (d. 286/899 or a few years earlier)

Abū Sa'īd al-Kharrāz was one of the best-known members of the Sufi circles in Baghdad during the middle decades of the third/ninth century. We know practically nothing about his life beyond a few details: he travelled extensively, including to Basra, Jerusalem, Mecca, Egypt as well as Qayrawān in present-day Tunis; he had to leave his native Baghdad and later also Mecca because of unspecified conflicts with some local scholars concerning his teachings; and, if his name was indicative of his profession, he may have been a cobbler at some point in his life. Several of his writings are extant, and they make it possible for us to capture some aspects of Kharrāz's thought.[34]

The Book of Truthfulness (*Kitāb al-ṣidq*), possibly addressed to disciples of Kharrāz, is a decription of the stations on the Sufi path. Kharrāz starts by linking the concept of truthfulness to sincerity and patience; he then proceeds to discuss the following stations that God-seekers traverse: repentance, knowledge of the lower soul, knowledge of the devil, scrupulousness, knowledge of God's commands and interdictions, renunciation of the world, trust in God, fear, shame, knowledge of God's bounties and gratitude, love, acceptance, desire and intimacy.[35] The seeker's mount on the path is recollection of God, and when he succeeds in rendering this recollection into a perpetual act, then

> his heart gains a quick understanding, and his thoughts become clear, and light lodges in his heart: he draws near to God, and God overwhelms his heart and purpose. Then he speaks, and his heart surges with the recollection of God: the love of God lurks deeply hidden in his inmost heart, cleaving to his mind, and never leaving it. Then his soul is joyfully busied with secret converse with God.[36]

We get a better view of this state of intimacy in five short epistles of Kharrāz that have survived in a single manuscript.[37] In the *Book of Light* (*Kitāb al-ḍiyā'*), Kharrāz characterises the advanced seekers who come face to face with the essence of divine reality (*'ayn al-'ayn*) and are thus possessed by an absolute confoundment of spirit as 'people of bewilderment and perplexitude' (*ahl tayhūhiyya wa-ḥayrūriyya*). Kharrāz classifies these into seven groups: (1) *ahl al-ishārāt*: these search God through 'allusions and signs'; (2) *ahl al-'ilm*: these search God through 'discursive knowledge'; (3) *ahl al-mujāhada*: these practise 'spiritual combat', and their states are subject to change (*talwīn*); (4) *ahl al-khuṣūṣiyya*: these come to God through God by being 'specially' pulled by Him; (5) *ahl al-tajrīd*: these are 'isolated' from everything other than God; (6) *ahl istīlā wa-tamkīn*: these are 'masters' of their own states, who achieve 'permanence' in the state of being absent to the sensible world and present to the unknowable world; and (7) *ahl al-muḥābāt* 'people of courtesy': these are the special elect, who, moreover, know their special status. They are taken by God to where 'there is no "where"' (*min ḥaythu lā ḥaythu*) or taken by Him in a placeless manner. They lose all their attachments and their own attributes. Significantly, Kharrāz makes it clear that while the first six groups are all temporally limited, in that even though they all achieve intimacy with God they always 'return' (*rujū'*) from such a state, the people of courtesy remain perpetually absorbed in God's majesty.

Kharrāz addresses the last stage of intimacy in greater detail in the *Book of Serenity* (*Kitāb aṣ-ṣafā'*), which is squarely about the notion of proximity (*qurb*).[38]

He introduces his topic with a fourfold classification of humankind according to their response to God's call. First are those who choose this world over the next; they will depart from this life in a sorry state. Second, there are those who heed God's commands and interdictions, but since their eyes are firmly fixed on the promised rewards of obedience, they are veiled from God and cannot begin to love Him. Third are the sincere ones who orient their spirits toward God and, in return, have been granted certainty by Him. Yet, they remain preoccupied by talk of 'stations' on the path (*maqāmāt*) and are thus veiled and distracted from the Truth (*al-Ḥaqq*). Only the fourth group achieve true proximity to God. This latter is a problematic state, since God's direct self-manifestation is destructive, as it is explicitly expressed in the Qur'ān 7 [al-Aʿrāf]: 143, where God, in response to Moses' plea to show Himself to him, manifests Himself to the mountain, which is pulverised and annihilated. This is why God does not gaze at his friends (*awliyā'*) directly but cloaks his gaze with a veil (*ḥijāb*) in order to protect them from total destruction. Now, some who are granted proximity are yet not bestowed knowledge of this privilege and enjoy the fruits of this blessing behind the veil of 'stations', while others, the strongest ones, proceed beyond stations, beyond the path, so to speak, and are plunged into 'ecstacy', or, better yet, 'pure being' (*wajd*, but *wajada* in Arabic means 'to be, to exist'). This ecstatic state is simultaneously a state of 'finding' (*wajada* also means 'to find') where those who are rendered close to God (*muqarrabūn* – Qur'ān 56 [al-Wāqiʿa]: 11 and 88) are granted a firm understanding and pure knowledge of God's intimacy. The door between these ecstatic ones and God is forever open, and the 'close ones' remain in perpetual perplexitude and stupefaction (*dahsha*), which is caused by the onslaught of God's majesty. Blinded to themselves by the overwhelming power of God's nearness, they lose all self-consciousness:

> If you ask one who is in this state 'What do you want?' he responds 'God'; and if you ask him 'What do you say?'he replies 'God'; if you ask him 'What do you know?' he replies 'God'; and if his limbs could speak, they would say 'God', since his limbs and his joints are full of God's light. He knows nothing but God, and all his knowledge is of God; he is of God, by God, for God and with God; he has lost his identity and has no bearings. If you ask him 'Who are you?' he cannot even reply 'I, myself' because of the domination of divine secrets on him. Such is the reality of ecstacy/finding (*wajd*). When he attains the zenith of proximity, he can no longer say even 'God.'[39]

This is the point of the coincidence of opposites when the terms of opposition (God-servant and God) become blurred, and the one who is rendered close is left speechless. The friends of God who are blessed with such proximity never 'recover' from this experience of intimacy. Kharrāz concludes the epistle with the assertation that the 'friends' are chosen for this honour directly by God.

In the *Book of Surrender* (*Kitāb al-farāgh*), Kharrāz examines the issue of human subjectivity through the prism of the doctrine of God's unity, *tawḥīd*, and reaches the conclusion that God is the only true subject of human history. Indeed, 'saying "I" is the sole prerogative of God', and 'whoever else says "I" remains veiled from [true] knowledge.'[40] The consequence of God's oneness is the erasure of any lingering feeling of subjectivity on the part of human individuals. This same principle also applies to all other would-be subjects, most notably the angels and the Devil, who remain cloaked in false subjectivity (see Qur'ān 7 [al-A'rāf]: 12, where the Devil says of Adam 'I am better than he'; and Qur'ān 2 [al-Baqara]: 30, where the angels speak of themselves in the first-person plural), and, as a chastisement for their inappropriate claims to being subjects, are asked by God to prostrate themselves in front of Adam (for instance, Qur'ān 2 [al-Baqara]: 34). In short, the words 'I', *anā*, and the Truth, *al-Ḥaqq*, in so far as this latter refers to God, are ontologically linked and inseparable from one another. As a consequence, if a Sufi says 'I' – as did Ḥallāj, as we will see – he can only mean God.

But how is it that the 'friends of God' can have the experience of erasing their own identity in the face of God's majesty because they are pulled near God by God Himself, while all others remain wrapped in the darkness of false subjectivity? In this context, Kharrāz refers back to the Day of Covenant, when all human beings, in spirit, stood witness to God's Lordship (Qur'ān, 7 [al-A'rāf]: 172). There is, therefore, an essential link between human spirits and knowledge of God's unity. However, once human spirits, *rūḥ*, are coupled with lower souls (*nafs*) and instincts (*ṭab'*) after the creation, unbelievers, whose spirits are created from the place of darkness, forget this link, while the believers, whose spirits are created from the place of light, continue to hanker after the experience of witnessing God's unity. Nonetheless, most believers too remain veiled from God's majesty on account of false subjectivity, and only the spiritual elect, the friends of God, driven by the desire (*shawq*) and love (*maḥabba*) of God, overcome the veils imposed by their lower souls and intincts and achieve proximity to the Divine.

In both the *Book of Surrender* and another treatise titled the *Book of Unveiling and Exposition* (*Kitāb al-kashf wa'l-bayān*), Kharrāz comments further on the status of God's friends (*awliyā'*), this time raising the thorny issue of the relationship between them and the prophets (*nabī*, pl. *anbiyā'*). He rejects the view that the friends rank higher than the prophets on the grounds that while all prophets are also friends, not all friends are prophets. The distinction between them is that the prophets are charged with the task of conveying God's commands while the friends serve to remind believers of God. Kharrāz also deals with the questions of whether the friend of God can receive inspiration from God (*ilhām*), and the difference between the miracles of the prophets (*āyāt*) and those of the friends (*karāmāt*).[41]

Abu'l-Ḥusayn (or al-Ḥasan) al-Nūrī (d. 295/907–8)

> Know that God created a house inside the believer called the heart. He then sent a wind of His magnanimity and cleansed this house of idolatry, doubt, hypocrisy and discord. Afterwards, he directed clouds of His favor to rain over the house, and there grew in it all kinds of plants such as certainty, trust, sincerity, fear, hope and love. Then he placed in the center of the house a couch of unity and covered it with the rug of contentment. And He planted the tree of knowledge opposite the couch, with its roots in the heart and its branches in the sky (Qur'ān 14 [Ibrāhīm]: 24), below the throne. He also placed on the right and left sides of the couch armrests of his laws. Then He opened a door to the garden of His mercy and sowed there many kinds of fragrant herbs of praise, glorification, exaltation and commemoration. He made waters of the ocean of guidance flow to these plants through the river of kindness. He hung a lamp of grace high on the door and lighted it with the oil of purity and the light of the lamp gleamed with the light of piety. Then He locked its door in order to keep out the wicked. He held on to its key and did not entrust it to any of his creatures, neither Gabriel, nor Michael, nor Seraphiel, nor others. He then said: 'This is My treasure on My earth, the mine of My sight, the home of My unity and I am the resident of this dwelling.' What an excellent resident and what a wonderful residence![42]

This is how Abu'l-Ḥusayn Aḥmad ibn Muḥammad al-Nūrī describes the heart in his treatise *Stations of the Heart* (*Maqāmāt al-qulūb*). Born and raised in Baghdad, Nūrī spent his whole life – except for a number of years of exile in Raqqa – in the 'Abbāsid capital, where he became one of the most prominent Sufis of his time.[43] It is likely that his name Nūrī, 'of light', was given to him by fellow Sufis on account of the luminosity of his person and his piety. Later sources also record other titles he held as 'the commander of hearts' (*amīr al-qulūb*) and 'the moon of the Sufis' (*qamar al-ṣūfiyya*). It is not possible to reconstruct the different stages of his life with certainty, but according to one tradition, he was a petty merchant or artisan in the early part of his life:

> Every day he would set out from home and take bread with him. On his way, he gave the bread away as alms, went into a mosque and prayed there till shortly before midday. Then he left the mosque, opened his shop and fasted. His family thought he ate at the market, and people of the market thought he ate at home. He maintained this practice for twenty years in his early life.[44]

The proclivity for 'ascetic hunger' described in this report appears to have stayed with him throughout his life. Before his departure for Raqqa, he was associated with the circle of Junayd (see below), but generally he kept himself aloof. In 264/877, he was interrogated on charges of heresy (*zandaqa*) brought against him and other Sufis, seventy-odd in number, by the traditionalist preacher Ghulām Khalīl (d. 275/888).[45] The Sufis were reportedly taken to the caliph, whose summary judgment against them was death by decapitation. Hearing the judgment, Nūrī rushed towards the executioner, who asked him why he was in such a hurry. Nūrī's reply, that the lives of his companions were dearer to him than his own even for such a short period of time, caused the headsman to cancel the execution, and the matter was taken to court. There, the judge Ismā'īl ibn Isḥāq al-Ḥammādī (d. 282/896) questioned the Sufis, especially Nūrī, about matters of ritual purity and prayer and was impressed by their answers. Nūrī closed the proceedings by saying 'God has servants who hear by God, see by God, go by God, and come by God, eat by God and are clothed by God.' Moved to tears by these words, the judge acquitted the Sufis and reported to the caliph: 'If these people are heretics, then there is not a single monotheist on earth!'

There are anomalies in this story, like the summary judgment of death issued for a high number of well-known figures without a trial and the cancellation of the execution by the executioner himself, that suggest some gradual embellishment of the event in the Sufi tradition to throw Nūrī's portrait into greater relief. A similar process might have been at work in the development of some other 'interrogation' narratives around Nūrī, such as this one that is clearly linked with the trial of 264/877, since it is known that Ghulām Khalīl objected to talk of passionate love for God:

> When Nūrī was called on to explain his saying 'I love (*a'shuqu*) God and He loves me (*ya'shuqunī*)', he replied 'I have heard God – His rememberance is exalted – say, "He loves them and they love Him (*yuḥibbuhum wa yuḥibbūnahu*) (Qur'ān 5 [al-Mā'ida]: 59)", and passionate love (*'ishq*) is not greater than serene love (*maḥabba*), except that the passionate lover (*'āshiq*) is kept away, while the serene lover (*muḥibb*) enjoys his love.'[46]

Nūrī was also asked to explain some puzzling utterances he made: once, when he heard the muezzin utter the call to prayer, he said 'Stab and poison him!' On another occasion, he heard a dog bark and exclaimed, using an expression normally directed only towards God, 'Here I am! At your service!' Yet another time, he said 'Last night I was in my house with God.' Finally, there is the amusing intervention he made when he once saw a man stroking his beard during prayer: 'Take your hand off of God's beard!' In the reports we have about these questionings, Nūrī is able to explain every one of these provocative statements, mostly by citing relevant verses from the Qur'ān. Yet, since our sources do not provide any social context, it is impossible to know if these were associated with real interrogations by political authorities in Baghdad or if they are to be viewed simply as narrative devices that grew around the one major trial of Baghdad Sufis in 264/877, though the latter scenario seems more plausible.[47] In any case, it is certain that Nūrī had a proclivity for verbal trespass that shocked some like Ghulām Khalīl. He also had a habit of trampling social convention or at least engaging in shocking behaviour, as when he threw 300 dinars that he had earned from the sale of a piece of land into the river from the Ṣarāt bridge, one coin at a time, saying 'My Lord, do you want to deceive me into turning away from you with these?'[48]

Following his acquittal at the trial of 264/877, Nūrī left Baghdad for Raqqa (today in Syria), where he stayed for a good number of years, perhaps as many as fourteen. It is probable that in this period of his life he grew into more of a recluse: he shunned people, frequented the ruins around town, avoided settlements, and appeared in town only to attend Friday prayers. Eventually, after the death of caliph al-Muʿtamid (d. 279/892), he returned to Baghdad. Melancholic and dreamy, he stayed aloof, and on the one occasion he visited the circle of Junayd, he refused to join the conversation on the grounds that he was not familiar with the expressions they used.[49] However, he continued to be prominent among the Sufis of Baghdad and was well-known at the court of caliph al-Muʿtaḍid (r. 279–289/892–902). In a famous incident, Nūrī broke jars of wine belonging to the caliph, and when questioned about this by al-Muʿtaḍid himself, he claimed to be the *muḥtasib*, the officer charged with the supervision of public morality, especially in the market place. When the caliph asked him 'Who appointed you?' Nūrī replied 'He Who appointed you caliph!'[50] The caliph's vizier too knew Nūrī well, to judge by a report that he gave Nūrī some money for him to distribute among the Sufis of Baghdad, which Nūrī did.[51] Although he habitually lived right at the edge of social propriety and had no qualms about stepping on the toes of political powers, Nūrī's death was reportedly caused by another kind of 'trespassing' that had characterised his approach to God throughout his life: hearing a verse on love, he went into a trance and wandered into a freshly-cut reedbed. The sharp reed-ends slashed his bare feet and he died from the wounds soon after the incident.[52]

According to Nūrī, humankind was created in order to know God, and intimate knowledge of God was the first obligation of humans toward God:

> He was asked about the first obligation that God laid upon his servants, and he said, 'Experiential knowledge (*maʿrifa*), as God said "I created the jinn and humankind so that they might worship Me" (Qur'ān 51 [al-Dhāriyāt]: 56) – and Ibn ʿAbbās [companion of Muḥammad and commentator, d. 68/687] said, "So that they might know me experientially" (*yaʿrifūnī*).'[53]

Such intimate knowledge of God is the goal of the Sufis, but ultimately only God can take one to this goal, not human effort:

> His Greatness is higher than that there should be a way to Him other than by Him or that He could be changed by what He created. No, there is no guide to God except Him and nothing has any effect on Him since it was He Who created all effects.[54]

The intellect by itself cannot lead to God:

> They said to Nūrī: 'By what means did you know God?' He replied 'By God.' They said: 'How about reason?' He replied 'Reason is weak and can only lead to something that is weak like itself. When God created reason He said to it "Who am I?" and it

> remained silent. Then He rubbed it [its eyes] with the light of [His] singleness and it said "Your are God". So reason cannot know God except by God.'[55]

> 'Someone asked Abu'l-Ḥusayn an-Nūrī, God be compassionate with him, 'How is it that intellects cannot reach God while God can be known only through the intellect?' He replied 'How can a being with temporal limits comprehend one who has no such limits? How can a being beset with frailties comprehend one who has no weakness or infirmity? Or how can one whose being is conditional know the one who has fashioned conditionality itself? Or how can one whose being presumes a "where" know the one who has given "where" a place and named it "where"?[56]

The only way is to turn the reins over to God:

> To the question 'by what [means] did you come to know God' he replied 'By omission/lack of all determination. Whatever I thought and contemplated about happened otherwise. And whatever I did He ruined.'[57]

Since God is humankind's best friend, there is little need for believers to be concerned with questions about their ultimate destiny or about matters of predestination; for their part, all they need to do is to choose God over everything else: 'Temptation is being occupied with something other than God.'[58] Clearly, the body is one source of temptation: 'The body necessarily leads [one] to oppose God under all circumstances, [since] it covets what is harmful in desiring this world.'[59] Wealth too leads away from God, and the believer should choose poverty. But poverty extends to and merges with altruism: 'The description of the poor man is that he should be quiet when he possesses nothing and generous and unselfish when he possesses something.'[60] The mark of true poverty, however, is joy: 'You recognise them [the poor] by their characteristic of having joy in their poverty and their composure on occasions when misfortune visits them.'[61] Such joy is the result of being oriented towards God at all times instead of being bogged down by one's attachments to everything other than God: 'The highest station of the people of realities is the severance of all attachment.'[62]

Continuous orientation towards God takes the form of an intense 'watchfulness' (*murāqaba*) of God's action on earth; in an amusing anecdote, Nūrī tells fellow Sufi Shiblī that he learned such vigilance from a cat lying in ambush in front of a mousehole.[63] Nūrī's favourite medium of vigilance was, however, 'hearing' (*samā'*). By 'hearing', Nūrī meant not so much an 'audition', an active act of listening to a recitation of poetry or a song, but keeping his ears open for detecting mystical meanings that lay behind the level of sound. One who learned to listen in this manner ultimately 'heard' and was moved to answer: 'He whose ear is opened to hearing, his tongue is moved to answer.'[64] This ability to lend an ear to God and the urge to answer Him was no doubt what took Nūrī to the edges of acceptable speech on many occasions ('verbal trespass') and also turned him into a poet, with many verses preserved in his name.[65] Such moments of response to God were moments of 'finding' and 'ecstasy' (*wajd*, with both meanings), though for Nūrī ecstasy could never become a pretext for improper behaviour: 'He who does not observe propriety in his moments [of finding/ecstasy], his is [a moment of] detestation.'[66] In the attempt to be oriented towards God, the Sufi turned away from everything other than God, turned himself over to God and remained attentive to His call. The path that led to God actually was to be found in the heart.

Intimate knowledge of God is located in the heart. The heart, created by God as the locus of the human encounter with Himself, is composed of four layers: breast (*ṣadr*), heart proper (*qalb*), inner heart (*fu'ād*) and heart's core (*lubb*). These four layers harbour, respectively, Islam, faith (*imān*), intimate knowledge (*ma'rifa*) and unification (*tawḥīd*). Islam activates the outer layer, and correct practice leads to the activation of the level of faith, and this process of a deepening spiritual awakening continues until only God's love remains in the heart:

> The first thing created by God in the heart of one for whom He wishes happiness is light. Then this light becomes brightness, then rays, then a moon, then a sun. And when the light appears in the heart, this world and what is in it grows cold to his heart. And when it [the heart] becomes a moon he renounces the next world and what is in it. And when it becomes a sun he sees neither the world and what is in it nor the next world and what is in it: he knows nothing but God. And his body is light and his heart is light and his speech is light, 'Light upon light, God guides whom He will to his light' [Qur'ān 24 (al-Nūr): 35].[67]

Once the heart is taken over with God's light, the stage of 'unification' (*jam'*) sets in and the Sufi arrives at God Himself. This is more a continuous game of finding and losing than a losing of the self in God: 'For twenty years I have been between finding and losing. When I find my Lord, I lose my heart, and when I find my heart, I lose my Lord.'[68] But the seeker does not cease to hope that he might just merge with God: 'Common people don the shirt of obedience; the elite the shirt of [acknowledging God's] lordship and do not pay heed to obedience; but the chosen ones God pulls to Himself and effaces them from themselves.'[69]

Junayd (d. 298/910)

Abu'l-Qāsim al-Junayd ibn Muḥammad al-Khazzāz, a silk merchant of Baghdad who excelled in the study of law early in life, was by common consensus of both pre-modern and modern authorities one of Sufism's major architects. He was born and raised in the 'Abbāsid capital, which he seems to have left only once in his life on pilgrimage to Mecca. In his youth, he was a prodigious student of jurisprudence under the eminent jurist Abū Thawr (d. 240/855), and he continued to cultivate legal science into his adult years, since he could escape the round-up of Sufis during the inquisition of Ghulām Khalīl by declaring himself to be a jurist.[70] Several of his treatises of various lengths as well as a number of letters that he wrote to some of his companions are extant in a single manuscript, and other fragments of his writings are preserved in later Sufi works.[71] A perusal of Junayd's works reveals that his thought revolved around the following pillars.

Deep meditation on the meaning of God's unity

No fewer than eight of Junayd's short treatises are on the question of *tawḥīd*, literally 'unification'. In focusing on this central concept, Junayd was operating firmly within mainstream Islamic thought of his time. Already by the beginning of the third/ninth century, the exact meaning of God's unity and uniqueness had become a major bone of contention among a growing number of specialists in the intellectual and confessional foundations of Islam.[72] Junayd's definition of *tawḥīd* as *ifrād al-qidam 'an al-ḥadath*, 'the isolation of the Eternal from the created', was exemplary and garnered much praise for him from posterity.[73] What set him apart from others, however, was his assertion that the attempt to attain true unification could succeed only if the individual abandoned any pretence to having powers of intellection and intuition in understanding the issue of God's uniqueness and turned himself over completely to God's hands: 'Know that you are veiled from Him through yourself, and that you do not reach him through yourself but that you reach Him through Him.'[74] In other words, the realisation of divine unity required the annihilation of human agency and denied the possibility of individuality to all but God Himself. Junayd's insistence on divine agency to the exclusion of all human agency led him to elaborate the peculiar notion of *fanā'*.

Fanā', 'the passing away of self-consciousness'

Junayd thought that when the human individual approached God with his customary sense of being a self-contained, separate entity, it proved impossible for him to affirm God's unity since his own self-consciousness imprisoned him in himself. The only solution was for him to 'pass away from his sense of self', *fanā'*, and thus to arrive at God's presence denuded of his own individuality. Only when all awareness of self disappeared through a total annihilation of self-consciousness was it possible to talk of 'affirmation of God's unity' or *tawḥīd*. In order to exemplify this state, Junayd referred to a well-known *ḥadīth qudsī*, an 'extra-Qur'ānic divine saying':

> My servant draws near to Me by means of nothing dearer to Me than that which I have established as a duty for him. And My servant continues drawing nearer to Me through supererogatory acts until I love him; and when I love him, I become his ear with which he hears, his eye with which he sees, his hand with which he grasps, and his foot with which he walks.[75]

Moreover, Junayd conceptualised such dissolution of self-consciousness not as a new existential state but as a 'return' to a primordial state that human beings had before the creation on the Day of the Covenant.

Mīthāq, 'the Primordial Covenant'

'When your Lord brought forth offspring from the children of Adam, from their loins, and had them testify regarding themselves: "Am I not your Lord?" They said: "Oh yes, we so testify." Lest you say on Judgment Day "We were unaware of this!"' (Qur'ān, 7 [al-Aʿrāf]: 172). According to Junayd, this primordial covenant recorded in the Qur'ān marked the true and perfect type of human existence as selfless existence in God, presumably as non-individualised spiritual entities in God's mind:

> In this verse God tells you that He spoke to them at a time when they did not exist, except so far as they existed in Him. This existence is not the same type of existence as is usually attributed to God's creatures; it is a type of existence which only God knows and only He is aware of. God knows their existence; embracing them he sees them in the beginning when they are non-existent and unaware of their future existence in this world.[76]

Thus initiated by God as divine ideas, humans are then created as individual spirits wrapped in a body and placed on earth. But the memory of their divine, completely spiritual existence on the Day of the Covenant haunts them and lures them into the experience of *fanā'*, which is literally a re-enactment of the primordial covenant. Passing away from consciousness of earthly existence, however, is not total annihilation of the individual since even after *fanā'*, the self survives in a transformed fashion.

Ṣaḥw, 'sobriety'

Those who experience *fanā'* do not subsist in that state of selfless absorption in God but find themselves returned to their senses by God. Such returnees from the experience of selflessness are thus reconstituted as renewed selves:

> He is himself, after he has not been truly himself. He is present in himself and in God after having been present in God and absent in himself. This is because he has left the intoxication of God's overwhelming *ghalaba* (victory), and comes to the clarity of sobriety, and contemplation is once more restored to him so that he can put everything in its right place and assess it correctly. Once more he assumes his individual attributes, after *fanā'*. His personal qualities persist in him and his actions in this world; when he has reached the zenith of spiritual achievement vouchsafed by God, he becomes a pattern for his fellow men.[77]

It turns out, therefore, that those who transform their earthly selves through the experience of passing away from self-consciousness and reclaim their primordial states as witnesses of God's lordship by re-enacting the Day of the Covenant are not only returned to their earthly existence but are given the special mission of guiding others to God.

The spiritual elect

While the struggle to affirm God's uniqueness by erasing the sense of self might be seen as a serious blow to any conception of human agency, for the select few who are picked by God specially for this purpose, *fanā'* and the return from it lead in fact to the formation of new or 'reclaimed' selves reconstituted in God's image. Such reconstituted individuals, now operating as God's instruments on earth, serve to shepherd the community towards God. It is clear that Junayd's doctrines of the covenant, passing away, and sobriety apply only to the spiritual elect, and not to the generality of humankind.[78] The elect are a tightly-knit group of 'brethren' that Junayd designates by such phrases as 'the choice of believers' (*ṣafwa min 'ibād*) or 'the pure ones' (*khulaṣā' min khalq*). They play significant roles in the community of believers:

> God has made them unfurled flags of truth, lighthouses erected for guidance, beaten paths for humanity. These are indeed the scholars among the Muslims, the truly trusting among the faithful, the noblest of those who are pious. They are those who guide in the crises of religion, and theirs is the light which leads in the darkness of ignorance; the brilliance of their knowledge shines through darkness. God has made them the symbol of His mercy for His creatures, and a blessing for whom He chooses. They are the instruments whereby He instructs the ignorant, reminds the negligent, guides the seeker aright ... The brilliance of their light shines clearly for their fellow creatures ... He who follows in their footsteps is guided on the right path, he who follows their mode of life will be happy and never depressed.[79]

Junayd, then, viewed Sufis as a select company of companions who were privileged with the God-given ability of truly affirming God's oneness by blotting out their earthly identities but who also bore the responsibility of acting as guides to humankind in all aspects of life. Indeed, all of Junayd's writings belong to the category of correspondence with fellow Sufis, and he clearly intended these letters solely for the internal consumption of the spiritual elect, and not for the general public. It is reported that when fellow Sufi Abū Bakr al-Shiblī (d. 334/946) wrote him a letter that he considered too explicit, Junayd sent the letter back to Shiblī with the following note: 'Oh, Abū Bakr, be careful with the people. Always we devise some means of camouflaging our words, splitting them and discussing them between ourselves, yet here you come along and tear away the veil!'[80] Daring in his spiritual vision and learned in the science of law, Junayd was a cautious figure in public life, who sat on the fence between private, inner devotion and public piety.[81]

Major characteristics of the Sufis of Baghdad

On the basis of the preceding review of some undisputed Sufi masters of Baghdad, it is now possible to draw a portrait of early Sufism as a distinct mode of Islamic piety. Clearly, these early Sufis were most concerned with obtaining experiential knowledge (*ma'rifa*) of God's unity, with distilling the reality of the Islamic profession of faith 'There is no god but God' into their daily lives. Human life presented itself to them as a journey towards the ever-elusive goal of achieving true 'God-consciousness', as an on-going attempt to draw near God. In Sufi perspective, human beings, viewed as God-servants, had experienced such proximity to their Lord before the beginning of time when God granted them an audience on the Day of the Covenant, and they were promised an even more intimate closeness to Him at the end of time in paradise. While on earth, however, they had to strive to preserve and renew the memory of their primordial proximity to their creator by turning their backs on everything other than God and by living their lives in constant recognition of His presence.

In practice, this meant training and domestication of the lower self through appropriate measures that included continuous cultivation of the heart and, for many but not all Sufis, asceticism as well as seclusion and poverty. The heart was understood as the spiritual organ of God's presence in the human person, and its chief sustenance was 'recollection and invocation' of God (*dhikr*) and perceiving God's activity on earth through 'hearing and vigilant observation' (*samā'* and *murāqaba*). Paradoxically, the journey (*sulūk*) towards the Lord started and continued only when the Sufi realised his own weakness as an agent and acknowledged God as the only true actor in the universe. Only when the reins were turned over to God did the human individual become a wayfarer (*sālik*) and begin the journey towards the goal of achieving proximity to the Creator.

This journey was normally envisaged as a path (*ṭarīq* or *ṭarīqa*) marked by various stopping places (*manzil*, pl. *manāzil*), stations (*maqām*, pl. *maqāmāt*) and states (*ḥāl*, pl. *aḥwāl*) that the wayfarer passed through, even though at this earliest stage of Sufism there was no systematic thinking, let alone any agreement, on the number, nature and order of these stages among the early Sufis. Nor was there a consensus on the destination of the journey. Everyone agreed that closeness to God normally entailed a sharp turn from lower concerns of this world (*dunyā*) towards the realm of ultimate matters (*ākhira*), a movement away from the lower self (*nafs*) towards the inner locus of God's presence (*qalb*), but it proved difficult to characterise the final encounter with God located at the end of the journey. While some, like Kharrāz and Nūrī, described the highest stage of intimacy with God as the dissolution of all self-consciousness, others like Junayd viewed the ultimate goal as a 'reconstituted' self, a human identity recomposed in the image of God after being thoroughly deconstructed during the Sufi journey. All agreed, however, that the ultimate Sufi experience was to be viewed as the passing away or re-absorption of the created human being into the only true/real (*ḥaqq*) being of God, and, most emphatically, not as a divinisation of the human. More generally, the encounter between the Sufi and God was a 'unidirectional merger' whereby the former was thought to flow into the latter but movement in the other direction was off limits or, at the very least, extremely limited, since such a flow from the divine into the human could pave the way to divinisation of the human and thus lead to the suspect, even heretical, doctrines of incarnation and inherence (*ḥulūl*).

No matter what their approach to the thorny issue of encounter with the Divine, those who shared the common aim of drawing close to God through experiential knowing enjoyed a special camaraderie with one another in the form of circles of fellowship, mutual mentoring and relationships of master and disciple. Not all human beings ever became wayfarers, let alone grew close to God: that privilege was, it seems, reserved for the few 'friends of God' (*awliyā'*) who were highly conscious of their special status and viewed themselves as the spiritual elect. Many friends, much like the prophets, saw themselves as God's special agents among humans, rendered distinct by their special status as intermediaries between the divine and human planes of being. In their view, they channelled God's mercy to humankind and served to increase God-consciousness among the otherwise heedless, self-absorbed human race through their personal example and their tireless advocacy of God's cause in human affairs.

The special status of the friends manifested itself in a number of practices that simultaneously underscored their distinctness from the common believers (*'awāmm*) and served to forge bonds of fellowship, loyalty and mutual allegiance among the spiritual elect (*khawāṣṣ*). They began to assemble in certain places of congregation (the Shūnīziyya mosque for the circle around Junayd) and to travel in groups, they developed distinctive prayer rituals in the form of the invocation (*dhikr*) and the audition to poetry and music (*samā'*) that frequently led to rapture or ecstasy (*wajd*), and they adopted special initiation practices, notably the investiture with the white woollen robe (*khirqa*) and the clipping of the moustache.[82] It seems likely, though difficult to verify, that other initiatic acts that came to be characteristic of Sufism, such as the handclasp (*muṣāfaḥa*, *bay'a*), the bestowal with the rosary (*subḥa*), and the entrusting of the initiate with the *dhikr* formula, were also practised by the first Sufis of Baghdad.[83]

This inward-looking portrait of the initial phase of full-fledged Sufism needs to be viewed in its proper historical and social context. The Ṣūfiyya developed as a convergence of many disparate ideas and practices into a distinct movement in Baghdad in the second half of the third/ ninth century. Most prominent among its members were the following figures: Abū Ḥamza al-Baghdādī (d. 269/882–3 or 289/902), Abū Sa'īd al-Kharrāz (d. 286/899 or a few years earlier), 'Amr ibn

'Uthmān al-Makkī (d. 291/903–4), Abū'l-Ḥusayn al-Nūrī (d. 295/907), Junayd al-Baghdādī (d. 298/910), Ruwaym ibn Aḥmad (d. 303/915–16), Ibn 'Aṭā' (d. 309/921–2 or 311/923–4), Khayr al-Nassāj (d. 322/934) and, a generation later, Abū Bakr al-Shiblī (d. 334/946), al-Jurayrī (d. 311/923–4), Abū 'Alī al-Rūdhbārī (d. 322/933–4), and Ja'far al-Khuldī (d. 348/959).[84] Even allowing for some embellishment of their learning by the later Sufi tradition, these first Sufis clearly formed an intellectual elite who were highly literate and learned in the Qur'ān, the *ḥadīth* and much else besides. However, since they looked askance at the use of human reason in the attempt to attain knowledge of God, the Sufis were at best sceptical, and at worst dismissive, of scholarly pursuits other than study of the Qur'ān and the *ḥadīth* such as jurisprudence (*fiqh*), rational speculation on the foundations of Islam (*kalām*), and even *belles lettres* (*adab*). It is true, for instance, that Junayd had studied jurisprudence under Abū Thawr (d. 240/855) and later in his life made use of his scholarly credentials to avoid the inquisition started by Ghulām Khalīl (he claimed to be a jurist, not a Sufi), but his own extant writings do not evince any fondness for scholarship, legal or otherwise, let alone any reliance on human reason as a tool to attain proximity to God.

On the other hand, the decidedly distanced attitude of the Sufis towards the nascent legal and theological scholars of their time was not the result of a denial or condemnation of God's law (*sharī'a*). Enthusiastic and total acceptance and implementation of God's commands formed the foundation of the whole Sufi enterprise, and the idea that the divine stipulations could somehow prove to be irrelevant to the endeavour to become true God-servants would have been alien to the Sufis. In maintaining their distance from the representatives of discursive scholarship, the Ṣūfiyya were, rather, motivated by the conviction that scholarly knowledge of God's laws could only be the beginning, and not the end-goal, of servanthood to God (*'ubūda*/*'ubūdiyya*) and that the *sharī'a* was not and could not be the sole or even the primary aspect of the broader relationship between God and His human servants. The bond between the Creator and the creation was, instead, one of intimacy, for some even love, and while the *sharī'a* laid the foundation for the house of God's presence in the heart of the believer, it could not build it by itself.[85] The Sufis thus directed their energies to the cultivation of the heart, and to the extent that preoccupation with legal and theological scholarship tended to distract one from this central exercise, it was inevitable that they would view the increasingly 'professional' scholarly enterprises with a mixture of caution, suspicion, alarm and, at times, even disdain. Indeed, no Sufi participated in the burgeoning, interconnected fields of *kalām* and *uṣūl al-fiqh* ('principles of jurisprudence'); quite the contrary, the advocates of experiential knowledge assumed an antagonistic posture towards representatives of the theoretical disciplines, and to judge by evidence from the early fourth/tenth century they were especially critical of the theological disputations of the rationalist Muʿtazila.[86] On the professional side too, the Sufis apparently held the practical dimensions of the juristic enterprise in low esteem. Junayd was incensed at fellow Sufi ʿAmr al-Makkī's decision to accept the title of the *qāḍī* of Jidda and later refused to preside over his funeral for this reason. He was equally displeased with Ruwaym when the latter became a deputy to the chief *qāḍī* of Baghdad, Ismāʿīl ibn Isḥāq (the same judge who had acquitted Nūrī and the other Sufis, including Ruwaym himself, from the charge of heresy).[87]

For their part, the scholars and lawyers maintained a variety of attitudes towards the Sufis that ranged from curious, and at times sympathetic, observation to scepticism and even contempt. The Mālikī chief judge Ismāʿīl ibn Isḥāq was clearly accommodating towards them, while Ibn Surayj (d. 306/918), perhaps the leading Shāfiʿī jurist of the day, who visited a session of Junayd out of curiosity and refrained from issuing a *fatwa* about Ḥallāj 'declaring himself ignorant of his [Ḥallāj's] source of inspiration', may have been favourably disposed towards the mystics.[88] However, the Muʿtazila, and possibly most Ḥanafīs, were dismissive of the Sufis, whom they criticised as antirational obscurantists at best and ignorant imposters as worst. They were especially irritated by miracles attributed to the Sufis by the populace and tended to view these as plain sorcery (*siḥr*).[89] Neither the Sufi approach to knowledge nor the Sufi doctrine of selection, not to mention esoteric Qur'ān interpretation, could have pleased full-fledged rationalists in *kalām* or *fiqh*.

On the other hand, in their scepticism toward the use of human reason in the matters of God, the first Sufis were aligned with the 'traditionalists' who had formed especially around the example of Aḥmad ibn Ḥanbal (164–241/780–855). These latter, like the Sufis, were opposed to the utilisation of common sense and reason (*ra'y*) in legal and theological issues and honoured only scriptuary evidence (inclusive of *ḥadīth* reports) on this front. However, Sufi scepticism towards reason did not extend as far as to denounce 'semi-rationalism' in law, as evidenced by the fact that many Sufis were affiliated with the nascent semi-rationalist schools of law (*madhhab*, pl. *madhāhib*): Junayd was a follower of Abū Thawr (d. 240/854); ʿAmr ibn ʿUthmān and Abū ʿAlī al-Rūdhbārī were Shāfiʿīs; Shiblī was a Mālikī; and Ruwaym was a Ẓāhirī. On the other hand, only one Sufi, Ibn ʿAṭā', adhered to the more traditionalist Ḥanbalī school, and there was even one Sufi, Jurayrī, who belonged to the more rationalist Ḥanafī school.[90] For their part, the traditionalists did not approve of the nascent schools of law, most of which had allowed the use of reason at various levels in law and theology (Ḥanafīs were mostly rationalists, and Abū Thawrīs, Shāfiʿīs, Mālikīs, and, to a lesser extent, Ẓāhirīs were semi-rationalists), and the affiliations of the Sufis with the schools might have been sufficient to make them into targets of traditionalists' ire. In the event, the shared ground between the traditionalists and the Sufis, especially the cultivation of the *ḥadīth* as a form of strong opposition to rationalism, proved to be substantial, and there were few clashes between them, with the inquisition of Ghulām Khalīl as the major example. This incident, we have seen, was most likely prompted by Nūrī's use of the non-Qur'ānic verb *'ashiqa* instead of the Qur'ānic *ḥabba* (both mean 'to love') with respect to God, a usage that in the eyes of Ghulām Khalīl must have amounted to a 'departure from sanctioned belief and practice' (*bid'a*), which was worthy of supression. But, there are vague signs that Ghulām Khalīl's ire was raised by talk of sexual promiscuity at Sufi meetings, possibly caused by intermixing between genders and association of adult males with male adolescents at these gatherings. Sumnūn ibn Ḥamza (or 'Abd Allāh) al-Muḥibb (d. 298/910–11), one of the Sufis charged in Ghulām Khalīl's inquisition, and Kharrāz had female disciples, and even though teacher-pupil relationships between males and females did not by any means constitute a clear departure from the Sunna, allegations of sexual misconduct between the sexes among the Sufis would certainly have caught Ghulām Khalīl's attention.[91] Whatever the real cause of this latter's persecution of the Sufis, the suspicion of *bid'a* remained, equally during the second half of the third/ninth century and the following centuries, the fault-line between the traditionalists and the later Ḥanbalīs on the one hand and the Sufis on the other hand, but it is important to note that the relationship between them was not necessarily confrontational and was, instead, frequently quite cordial.

The Ṣūfiyya was a distinctly urban phenomenon, and although our information on the social backgrounds of its members is admittedly rather thin, they seem to have been middle-class urbanites of artisanal and merchant origins. Upper classes were also represented: Shiblī was a high-ranking official of the caliph before his conversion to the Sufi path, and there certainly were wealthy Sufis, of whom Ruwaym and Ibn 'Aṭā' were prominent, if rare, examples.[92] Of respectable social origins, the Sufis by and large also appear to have remained within the boundaries of mainstream social life. Nevertheless, they were clearly too close to the borderline on many an issue, and there were always some Sufis who crossed the line into unconventional, if not downright shocking, social comportment. Nūrī and in particular Shiblī, for instance, were well-known for their transgressions in social behaviour. Others were not that idiosyncratic in public conduct, yet many of them – including Junayd, Nūrī, and Abū Ḥamza Baghdādī – appear to have opted out of the mainstream social practices of marriage and earning a living, though some, like Ibn 'Aṭā' and Ruwaym, were gainfully employed and married with children.[93] It may indeed be appropriate to characterise their attitude towards family and economic activity as a principled refusal to condemn marriage as well as work, combined with a distinct preference for celibacy and avoidance of active search for sustenance.[94] Their stance on earning a living is exemplified in the following report about Junayd:

> A group of people approached Junayd and asked, 'Where should we seek our sustenance?' He said, 'If you know where it is, go seek it there!' They said, 'Should we ask God for it?' He answered, 'If you know that He has forgotten you, then request it from Him!' They said, 'Should we stay home and place our trust in Him?' He replied, 'To test [God] would mean doubt!' They said, 'What is the solution, then?' He answered, 'To abandon [the idea of] a solution!'[95]

Significantly, this 'fence-sitting' on the key social issues of having a family and holding a job did not translate into a total rejection of human social life and its basic principles by the Sufis. Hermetic seclusion and isolation from social life, though partially practised by Nūrī and possibly by some others, were generally shunned. By and large they did not practise itinerant mendicancy and group withdrawal from society, traits that were, or could be, characteristic of renunciants who were so prevalent in the first three centuries of Islamic history. In contrast to these and other approaches located beyond the boundaries of mainstream urban life, the Sufis planted themselves firmly into the social fabric of Baghdad, although they occupied the 'grey areas' on many social fronts. In this, their rootedness within urban society, they resembled the majority of the scholars, the *'ulamā'*, who occupied the social centre of major towns in Islamic polities of the time. In brief, the Ṣūfiyya, like scholars of discursive knowledge, took shape at the very heart of 'Abbāsid urban culture in Baghdad, and put forward their claim to be central players on the main stage in the unfolding drama of authority in urban Muslim communities.

In comparison to the more extremist renunciants, all traditionalists, of the first century of 'Abbasid rule (mid-third/ninth to mid-fourth/tenth century), who tended to be severely critical of the social mainstream and the political status quo, the Baghdad Sufis were firmly 'centrist' in their social and political orientation. Apart from an activist streak characterised by willingness to 'command right and forbid wrong' (exemplified in Nūrī's provocative act of smashing wine jars that belonged to the caliph), which they may have interited from the early ascetic Mu'tazilīs, the Baghdad Sufis were as a rule politically inactive and quietist.[96] Shiblī, for instance, quit politics upon his conversion to Sufism at around the age of forty, even though he was a high-level government official earlier in life and continued to have connections in the upper echelons of government until his death. As a Sufi, he incurred the criticism of his mentor Junayd, who, probably because of his preference for quietism, disapproved of Shiblī's preaching in public.[97] Nevertheless, a few Sufis, like 'Amr and Ruwaym, did not hesitate to step into politically sensitive legal positions, though they did not participate in the making of politics as such. In accepting posts as judges, they may have been motivated by their desire to uphold God's law, the *sharī'a*. For their part, politicians were certainly aware of the Sufis, and some of them even paid special attention to the mystics in the form of charity, but they clearly saw no need to monitor this pious group unless charges of heresy were brought against them by politically influential figures. The Sufis did not constitute a political threat; indeed, they were neither an asset nor a liability for political powers at this stage. There was, however, one figure associated with the Sufis who became entangled in political power struggles at the highest levels and whose grisly execution at the orders of an ʿAbbāsid vizier, Ḥāmid ibn al-ʿAbbās (d. 311/924), cast a long shadow over the whole course of subsequent Sufi history. That figure was al-Ḥusayn ibn Manṣūr al-Ḥallāj (d. 309/922).

Ḥallāj was a controversial figure throughout his life. His Sufi affiliation is clear: originally tutored in Tustar by Sahl al-Tustarī (discussed below) for two years in his early youth, he was later initiated into Baghdad Sufism by ʿAmr al-Makkī in Basra and is said to have met this latter's teacher Junayd in the early period of his life. Yet, neither is there any doubt about his clean break with ʿAmr and Junayd within a decade of his induction into Sufism, a rupture evidently brought about by Ḥallāj's emergence in the mature, adult phase of his life as a relentless social and political activist, a transformation that proved to be unacceptable to his Sufi masters. During the 270s/880s and 280s/890s, Ḥallāj travelled widely as a popular preacher and a thaumaturge and acquired a considerable following in the lands he visited, including Khurāsān, Transoxania, and India. The exact nature of the ideas that fuelled his activism remains the subject of scholarly controversy, especially about whether or not extremist Shīʿī themes coloured his preaching. Ḥallāj spent the last two decades of his life mostly in Baghdad, where he became an intensely controversial figure with a high number of supporters and detractors. Significantly, his friends in the capital included two prominent Sufis, Shiblī and Ibn ʿAṭāʾ, who continued to befriend him until the bitter end. After nine years of house arrest at the court and an extended power struggle between his political enemies and allies, Ḥallāj was brutally put to death in 309/922 on the charge that he had advocated the substitution of the ritual obligation of pilgrimage (*ḥajj*) with a private pilgrimage performed around a replica of the Kaʿba that he had built in his yard. His miracle-mongering may have also been among the charges. Shortly before having Ḥallāj executed, the vizier Ḥāmid ibn al-ʿAbbās interrogated the Sufi Ibn ʿAṭāʾ on his views about Ḥallāj, and when this latter publicly denounced the vizier's policies instead, he had Ibn ʿAṭāʾ beaten to death. No other Sufi, including Shiblī, rose to defend Ḥallāj, while Jurayrī, who had assumed the mantle of Junayd, is said to have agreed with the death sentence against him.[98]

Was Ḥallāj a Sufi? Clearly, he absorbed and internalised Sufi ideas and practices early in life, but it is equally obvious that he forged his own unique mode of piety that went well beyond the domain of the thinking and behaviour of the Baghdad Sufis.[99] The fact that he stood with one foot inside and the other outside Baghdad Sufism, coupled with his firm friendship with two highly prominent Sufis until the end of his life, meant that he remained a controversial figure for later generations of Sufis. Was Ḥallāj's trial and execution an unmistakable example of persecution of Sufis by political authorities *because* of their Sufi views and practices? This question is complicated by the existence of a legend, extremely popular among later Sufis, that Ḥallāj was executed because of his explosive utterance 'I am the Truth' (*anā' l-ḥaqq*). According to this account, Ḥallāj suffered the consequences of exposing the secret of the 'union' or 'merger' between God and the Sufi at the highest level of experiential knowledge. Unable to comprehend the subtleties of the complete meltdown of human self-consciousness that takes place when the human comes too close to the Divine, the political authorities mistook Ḥallāj's statement 'I am the Truth' as a claim of incarnationism (*ḥulūl*) and condemned him to death. As this legend would have it, therefore, Ḥallāj was executed as a Sufi by the political establishment because he had attempted to reveal the shocking truth at the heart of Sufi thought and practice to those who could not have possibly understood it.[100]

This legendary account is clearly inaccurate and anachronistic. Ḥallāj's involvement in high Baghdad politics was uniquely personal and did not revolve around his identity as a Sufi. More significantly, there is no evidence that Ḥallāj ever uttered the statement 'I am the Truth' which is attributed to him in later sources. Even if he had, there is the fact that most Baghdad Sufis do not seem to have viewed the loss of self-consciousness at the threshold of the divine realm as complete identification of the human with the Godhead, so that if Ḥallāj actually said 'I am the Truth' and meant it in the sense of divinisation of the human, then he had departed from the 'mainstream' Sufi perpectives on proximity to God and, to that extent, was not representative of this mainstream.[101] Finally, no Sufi other than Ibn 'Aṭā' was embroiled in the Ḥallāj affair, and Ibn 'Aṭā', as we have seen, was killed not because of his Sufi views but because of his willingness to rebuke the vizier for his usurious policies. Indeed, the Sufis of Baghdad continued to thrive even after the execution of Ḥallāj, under the leadership of Jurayrī. It is, therefore, an error to view Ḥallāj's grueling ordeal as an instance of the persecution of Sufis by political and religious authorities hostile to Sufi ideas.[102]

In summary, the case of Ḥallāj does not invalidate our earlier observation about the centrist orientation of Baghdad Sufis in social and political matters. The plight of Ḥallāj deeply wounded Shiblī and moved Ibn 'Aṭā' to take a stance against the cruel and unscrupulous vizier Ḥāmid, which proved to be a fatal step, but Ḥallāj's trial and execution was not a trial and condemnation of the Sufis, who were neither radicalised nor driven underground as a result of that event. Having successfully inserted themselves into the midst of mainstream intellectual elites of Baghdad, in between the rationalist and semi-rationalist legalists and theologians on the one hand and the conservative traditionalists on the other, with one foot in each camp, the Sufis had arrived to stay.[103]

Notes

1 The most comprehensive survey of *zuhd* in this period is Richard Gramlich, *Weltverzicht: Grundlagen und Weisen Islamischer Askese* (Wiesbaden: Harrassowitz, 1997). Individual portraits of many prominent early renunciants appear in Gramlich, *Alte Vorbilder*.

2 Michael D. Bonner, *Aristocratic Violence and Holy War: Studies in the Jihad and the Arab-Byzantine Frontier* (New Haven, CT: American Oriental Society, 1996), 125–30; the quotes are from pages 126 and 128; and Deborah Tor, 'Privatized jihad and public order in the pre-Seljuq period: the role of the *mutatawwi'a*', *Iranian Studies* 38 (2005): 555–73. Major primary sources on Ibn Adham are listed in Gerhard Böwering, 'Early Sufism between persecution and heresy', in *Islamic Mysticism Contested: Thirteen Centuries of Controversies and Polemics*, ed. Frederick de Jong and Bernd Radtke (Leiden: Brill, 1999), 46, n. 1, and these are used fully in Gramlich, *Alte Vorbilder*, 135–282.

3 Böwering, *Mystical Vision*, 47; Louis Massignon, *Essay on the Origins of the Technical Language of Islamic Mysticism*, trans. Benjamin Clark (Notre Dame, IN: University of Notre Dame Press, 1997), 106–7, esp. note 103. Sources on 'Abd al-Wāḥid ibn Zayd are listed in Bernd Radtke, 'How can man reach the mystical union: Ibn Ṭufayl and the divine spark', in *The World of Ibn Ṭufayl*, ed. Lawrence I. Conrad (Leiden: Brill, 1996), 190, n. 221, and Josef van Ess, *Theologie und Gesellschaft im 2. und 3. Jahrhundert Hidschra: Eine Geschichte des religösen Denkens im frühen Islam* (Berlin: De Gruyter, 1991–7), 2: 96ff; see ibid., 102ff on 'Abbādān; also Knysh, *Short History*, 16–18.

4 Christopher Melchert, 'The Ḥanābila and the early Sufis', *Arabica* 58 (2001): 354–55; cf. Fritz Meier, *Abū Sa'īd-i Abū l-Ḫayr (357–440/967–1049): Wirklichkeit und Legende* (Tehran: Bibliothèque Pahlavi, 1976), 300–1. For the 'Sufis of the Mu'tazila', see Ess, *Theologie*, 3: 130–33; and Florian Sobieroj, 'The Mu'tazila and Sufism', in *Islamic Mysticism Contested*, ed. Jong and Radtke, 68–70.

5 Jacqueline Chabbi, 'Fuḍayl b. 'Iyāḍ, un précurseur du ḥanbalisme', *Bulletin d'Études Orientales de l'Institut Français de Damas* 30 (1978): 331–45, and Michael Cooperson, *Classical Arabic Biography: The Heirs of the Prophets in the Age of al-Ma'mūn* (Cambridge: Cambridge University Press, 2000), 154–87. Cf. Böwering, 'Early Sufism', p. 48, notes 5 and 6.

6 For a pithy discussion of the theme of *tawba* among early renunciants, see Böwering, 'Early Sufism', 45–50; on *tawakkul*, see the detailed survey Reinert, *Lehre*.

7 The clustering of the themes of 'inner life', 'inner meaning of the Qur'ān', and 'doctrine of selection' is suggested by Bernd Radtke in 'Bāṭen', EIr 3: 859–61 (quote on 860). For the earliest phase of the search for inner meaning of the Qur'ān, see Gerhard Böwering, 'The Qur'ān commentary of al-Sulamī', in *Islamic Studies Presented to Charles J. Adams*, eds Wael B. Hallaq and Donald P. Little (Leiden: Brill, 1991), 41–56, and Gerhard Böwering, 'The major sources of Sulamī's minor Qur'ān commentary', *Oriens* 35 (1996): 35–56. A comprehensive new treatment is Sands, *Sufi Commentaries*. For concise but comprehensive surveys on the idea of divine selection as expressed by the terms *walāya/wilāya*, see 'Walāyah', *Encyclopedia of Religion*, 2nd edn, ed. Lindsay Jones (Detroit: Macmillan Reference USA, 2005), 14: 9656–62 (Hermann Landolt); 'Walī, 1. General Survey', EI 11: 109a–111b (B.

Radtke); Michel Chodkiewicz, 'La Sainteté et les saints en Islam', in *Le Culte des saints dans le monde musulman*, ed. Henri Chambert-Loir and C. Guillot (Paris: École française d'Extrême Orient, 1995), 13–22; and Michel Chodkiewicz, *Seal of the Saints: Prophethood and Sainthood in the Doctrine of Ibn Arabi* (Cambridge: Islamic Texts Society, 1993), 17–46. Two more recent treatments are Gerald Elmore, *Islamic Sainthood in the Fullness of Time: Ibn al-ʿArabī's Book of the Fabulous Gryphon* (Leiden: Brill, 1999), 109–30; and Richard J. A. McGregor, *Sanctity and Mysticism in Medieval Egypt: The Wafāʾ Sufi Order and the Legacy of Ibn ʿArabī* (Albany: State University of New York Press, 2004), 8–26. 'Abdāl', EIr 1: 173–4 (J. Chabbi) is somewhat sketchy.

8 This is not meant to be a complete list. For a recent discussion of the first four of these figures, see Knysh, *Short History*, chs 1–2; his references should be supplemented by the following: Gramlich, *Alte Vorbilder*, 2: 13–62 (on Shaqīq); Sarah Sviri, 'The self and its transformation in Ṣūfism, with special reference to early literature', in *Self and Self-Transformation in the History of Religions*, ed. David Shulman and Guy G. Stroumsa (Oxford: Oxford University Press, 2002), 195–215 (partly on Shaqīq); Richard Gramlich, 'Abū Sulaymān ad-Dārānī', *Oriens* 33 (1992): 22–85; 'D̲u'l-Nūn Meṣrī', EIr 7: 572–3 (G. Böwering); and Josef van Ess, 'Der Kreis des Dhu'l-Nūn', *Die Welt des Orients* 12 (1981): 99–105. On Yaḥyā ibn Muʿādh, see Meier, *Abū Saʿīd*, 148–84. Bāyazīd is discussed below.

9 Female renunciants of this early period were recorded by Abū ʿAbd al-Raḥmān al-Sulamī (d. 412/1021) in his biographical notices on women devotees and Sufis, and later, by Ibn al-Jawzī (d. 597/1201), in his *Ṣifat al-ṣafwa*; see complete text of the former work and selections from the latter in Abū ʿAbd al-Raḥmān Muḥammad ibn al-Ḥusayn Sulamī, *Early Sufi Women: Dhikr an-niswa al-mutaʿabbidāt aṣ-ṣūfiyyāt*, ed. and trans. Rkia Elaroui Cornell (Louisville, KY: Fons Vitae, 1999); for a concise but comprehensive treatment, see Laury Silvers-Alario, 'Women, gender, and early Sufi women', forthcoming in *Encyclopedia of Women and Islamic Cultures*, 6 vols (Leiden: Brill, 2003–7).

10 The most comprehensive treatment of Rābiʿa is Margaret Smith, *Rabiʿa: The Life and Work of Rabiʿa and Other Women Mystics in Islam* (Oxford: Oneworld, 1994) [1928]), though this does not include the valuable discussion of Sulamī recovered much more recently: Sulamī, *Early Sufi Women*, 276–83. See also ʿAbd al-Raḥmān Badawī, *Shahīda al-ʿishq al-ilāhī Rābiʿa al-ʿAdawiyya* (Cairo: Maktaba al-Nahḍa al-Miṣriyya, 1962), and for a concise treatment, 'Rābiʿa al-ʿAdawiyya al-Ḳaysiyya', EI 8: 354b–356a (M. Smith [Ch. Pellat]).

11 Julian Baldick, 'The Legend of Rābiʿa of Baṣra: Christian antecedents, Muslim counterparts', *Religion* 19 (1990): 234, translating from *al-Bayān wa al-tabyīn*, ed. ʿAbd al-Salām Muḥammad Hārūn, 3rd edn (Cairo, 1388/1968), 3: 127. Cf. Sulamī, *Early Sufi Women*, 276–7.

12 Also from *al-Bayān wa al-tabyīn*, (Cairo, 1332), 3: 85, translating from the Arabic as reproduced in Badawī, *Shahīda al-ʿishq*, 137; cf. Sulamī, *Early Sufi Women*, 278–9. Smith's reading of this statement as being about miracles is forced: Smith, *Rabiʿa*, 107–8.

13 On Rābiʿa bint Ismāʿīl of Syria, see Smith, *Rabiʿa*, 170–3; and Sulamī, *Early Sufi Women*, 138–41, also 63–5 of Cornell's introduction. Sources on Aḥmad ibn Abi'l-

Ḥawārī are listed in Gramlich, *Weltverzicht*, 261, note 338. For other Rābiʿas, see Baldick, 'Legend of Rābiʿa', who thinks that Rābiʿa of Syria did not exist (p. 237).

14 'Rābiʿa al-ʿAdawiyya al-Ḳaysiyya', EI 8: 355b (M. Smith [Ch. Pellat]); in addition to the sources mentioned there, now see also Abu'l-Ḥasan ʿAlī ibn Muḥammad Daylamī, *A Treatise on Mystical Love*, Joseph Norment Bell and Hassan Mahmood Abdul Latif Al Shafie (Edinburgh: Edinburgh University Press, 2005), 112 (I owe thanks to Hermann Landolt for bringing this publication to my attention).

15 'Besṭāmī (Basṭāmī), Bāyazīd', EIr 4: 183–6 (Gerhard Böwering), and more recently Muḥammad Riżā Shafīʿī-Kadkanī, *Daftar-i rawshanāyī: az mīrāṣ-i ʿirfānī-i Bayazīd-i Basṭāmī* (Tehran: Intishārāt-i Sukhan, 1384/2005), esp. 67–73; I owe thanks to Muḥammad Riẓa Shafīʿī-Kadkanī for generously sending me a copy of this book as well as copies of his two recent works on Kharaqānī and Abū Saʿīd. *Daftar-i rawshanāyī* is a complete Persian translation of Abu'l-Faḍl Muḥammad ibn ʿAlī Sahlagī's (d. 477/1084) Arabic work, *Kitāb al-nūr min kalimāt Abī Ṭayfūr*, which is the most detailed biography of Bāyazīd available. *Kitab al-nūr* was edited by A. R. Badawī (Cairo, 1949), but Shafīʿī-Kadkanī has based his Persian translation on his own new edition of the Arabic original soon to be published in Beirut, see *Daftar-i rawshanāyī*, 14. A useful compilation of information on Bāyazīd in primary sources is ʿAbd al-Rafīʿ Ḥaqīqat, *Sulṭān al-ʿārifīn Bāyazīd-i Basṭāmī* (Tehran: Intishārāt-i Āftāb, 1361/1982). There is also a doctoral dissertation on him that I have not seen: Diana Tehrani, 'Bayazid Bistami: an analysis of early Persian mysticism' (Columbia University, 1999).

16 'Shaṭḥ', EI 9: 361b (Carl Ernst); in-depth treatment: Carl Ernst, *Words of Ecstasy in Sufism* (Albany: State University of New York Press, 1985).

17 Abū Naṣr ʿAbd Allāh ibn ʿAlī Sarrāj, *Kitāb al-lumaʿ fi'l-taṣawwuf*, ed. Reynold A. Nicholson (London: Luzac & Co., 1914), 382 / *Schlaglichter über das Sufitum*, trans. Richard Gramlich (Stuttgart: F. Steiner, 1990), 522 (124.1); this passage trans. by Nicholson in the English section, 102 (with minor changes).

18 Reynold A. Nicholson, 'An early Arabic version of the miʿraj of Abu Yazid al-Bistami', *Islamica* 2 (1926): 403–8, translated in Michael A. Sells, *Early Islamic Mysticism: Sufi, Qur'an, Miʿraj, Poetic and Theological Writings* (New York: Paulist Press, 1996), 244–50; the quote is from 249.

19 For the earliest of such commentaries, most notably by Junayd (d. 298/910), see Sarrāj, *Lumaʿ*, 380–95 / *Schlaglichter*, 520–34 (chs 123–7); translated in Sells, *Early Islamic Mysticism*, 214–31. Sells also translates (234–42) sayings of Bāyazīd found in Abū ʿAbd al-Raḥmān Muḥammad ibn al-Ḥusayn Sulamī, *Ṭabaqāt al-ṣūfiyya*, ed. Nūr al-Dīn Shurayba (Cairo: Maktaba al-Khānjī, 1406/1986 [1372/1953]), 67–74; and in ʿAbd al-Karīm ibn Hawāzin Qushayrī, *al-Risāla al-Qushayriyya*, ed. ʿAbd al-Ḥalīm Maḥmūd and Maḥmūd ibn al-Sharīf (Cairo: Dār al-Kutub al-Ḥadītha, 1375/1956), 88–91/ *Das Sendschreiben al-Qušayrīs über das Sufitum*, trans. Richard Gramlich (Wiesbaden: F. Steiner, 1989), 50–2 (1.10).

20 Aḥmad ibn ʿAbd Allāh Abū Nuʿaym al-Iṣfahānī, *Ḥilyat al-awliyā' wa-ṭabaqāt al-aṣfiyā'* (Cairo: Maktaba al-Khānjī, 1932–8), 10: 40; translation reproduced, with minor omissions, from Jawid A. Mojaddedi, *The Biographical Tradition in Sufism: The Ṭabaqāt Genre from al-Sulamī to Jāmī* (Richmond, Surrey: Curzon, 2001), 54; this report is repeated in later sources such as ʿAlī ibn ʿUthmān Hujwīrī, *Kashf al-Maḥjūb*,

ed. Valentin Zhukovsky (Tehran: Kitābkhāna-i Ṭahūrī, 1378/1999), 233 / *Revelation of the Mystery (Kashf al-Mahjub)*, trans. Reynold A. Nicholson (Accord, NY: Pir Press, 1999), 187; and Abu'l-Faḍl Muḥammad ibn 'Alī Sahlagī, *Kitāb al-nūr min kalimāt Abī Ṭayfūr*, ed. A. R. Badawī (Cairo, 1949), 136.

21 'Besṭāmī (Basṭāmī), Bāyazīd', EIr 4: 184 (Gerhard Böwering). Cf. his statements reported by Sulamī, *Ṭabaqāt*, 74, translated in Mojaddedi, *Biographical Tradition*, 21, in which he distinguishes experiential knowledge of God from renunciation; also see p. 26 for Mojaddedi's own comments on Sulamī's portrayal of Bāyazīd as an *'ārif*.

22 The evolution of Bāyazīd's image in the Sufi biographical tradition is traced in detail in Mojaddedi, *Biographical Tradition*.

23 Ess, *Theologie*, 4: 195–209. Major monographic treatments include Josef van Ess, *Die Gedankenwelt des Ḥāriṯ al-Muḥāsibī* (Bonn: Selbstverlag des Orientalischen Seminars der Universität Bonn, 1961); Margaret Smith, *Al-Muḥasibī: An Early Mystic of Baghdad* (London: The Sheldon Press, 1935); and Yolande de Crussol, *Le rôle de la raison dans la réflexion éthique d'al-Muḥāsibī: 'aql et conversion chez al-Muḥāsibī, 165/243–782/857* (Paris: Concep, 2002). Massignon, *Essay*, 161–71 is still useful for his connection to Sufism.

24 Selections from *The Book on Observance of God's Rights* are translated into English in Sells, *Early Islamic Mysticism*, 171–95; for the forms of egoism, see p. 172.

25 Smith, *Muḥasibī*, 87–93.

26 Crussol, *Le rôle de la raison*, 365–70. De Crussol gives a comparison of Muḥāsibī and Junayd, 345ff.

27 Paul Nwyia, *Exégèse coranique et langage mystique: nouvel essai sur le lexique technique des mystiques musulmans* (Beirut: Dar el-Machreq, 1970), 156–208; Arabic text of commentary attributed to Ja'far is in Paul Nwyia, 'Le tafsīr mystique attribué àĞa'far Ṣādiq: éditions critique', *Mélanges de l'Université Saint-Joseph* 43 (1968): 181–230; selections in English: Sells, *Early Islamic Mysticism*, 75–89.

28 For a synopsis, see Baldick, *Mystical Islam*, 30–2; for focused discussion, Göran Ogén, 'Did the term 'ṣūfī' exist before the Sufis?', *Acta Orientalia* 43 (1982): 33–48; still indispensable is Massignon, *Essay*, 104–6. For other derivations and a total of seventy-eight definitions of Sufism, see Reynold A. Nicholson, 'An historical enquiry concerning the origin and development of Sufism', *Journal of the Royal Asiatic Society* 38 (1906): 303–48.

29 The earliest use of the term is said to be with respect to a certain Abū Hāshim of Kūfa (d. 150/767–68), and it was definitely in circulation during the first half of the third/ninth century, see Massignon, *Essay*, 105. On Abū Hāshim, see 'Abd Allāh ibn Muḥammad Anṣārī al-Harawī, *Ṭabaqāt al-ṣūfiyya*, ed. 'Abd al-Ḥayy Ḥabībī (Tehran: Intishārāt-i Furūghī, 1942/1963), 7; cf. Mojaddedi, *Biographical Tradition*, 71; an English translation of this notice on Abū Hāshim is in A. G. Ravān Farhādī, *'Abdullāh Anṣārī of Herāt (1006–1089 C.E.): An Early Ṣūfī Master* (Richmond, Surrey: Curzon, 1996), 47–9; further references in Ess, *Theologie*, 1: 228, note 5.

30 The quote is from Michael Bonner, 'Poverty and charity in the rise of Islam', in *Poverty and Charity in Middle Eastern Contexts*, ed. Michael Bonner, Mine Ener, and Amy Singer (Albany: State University of New York Press, 2003), 25. For the meaning of wearing wool during the second/eighth century, see Ess, *Theologie*, 2: 88. On *zuhd*, see Leah Kinberg, 'What is meant by *zuhd*?' *Studia Islamica*, 61 (1985): 27–44 and 'Zuhd',

EI 11: 559b (Geneviéve Gobillot); on questions of poverty and wealth, see Leah Kinberg, 'Compromise of commerce: a study of early traditions concerning poverty and wealth', *Der Islam* 66 (1989): 193–212, and on *tawakkul*, see Reinert, *Lehre*.

31 Bernd Radtke, *Neue kritische Gänge: Zu Stand und Aufgaben der Sufikforschung* (Utrecht: Houtsma, 2005), 259–80, presents systematically the evidence for these earliest *ṣūfīs*; in this study, Radtke announces a forthcoming publication titled *Materialien zur alten islamischen Frömmigkeit und Mystik*, which will presumably include even more new evidence on the prehistory of Sufism. Precisely what differentiated 'wool-wearer' renunciants from their renunciant counterparts is difficult to identify; for an excellent discussion, see Christopher Melchert, 'Baṣran origins of classical Sufism', *Der Islam* 82 (2005): 221–40.

32 The first appearance of the collective noun *ṣūfiyya* in the sources appears to be in al-Kindī, *The Governors and Judges of Egypt*, ed. Rhuvon Guest (London, 1912), 162, as noted by Massignon, *Essay*, 107, note 103 and Melchert, 'Ḥanābila', 354, note 10; now freshly translated in Bernd Radtke, *Kritische Gänge*, 278–9. For a catalogue of the ascetics of the second/eighth century, see Massignon, *Essay*, 113–19; for longer treatments, see ibid., 147–60; Ignác Goldziher, *Introduction to Islamic Theology and Law*, trans. Andras Hamori and Ruth Hamori (Princeton: Princeton University Press, 1981), 116–34; Tor Andrae, *In the Garden of Myrtles: Studies in Early Islamic Mysticism* (Albany: State University of New York Press, 1987), 33–54; and Ess, *Theologie*, 2:87–121.

33 The most comprehensive recent treatments of the issue of the 'pre-history' of Sufism are Melchert, 'Baṣran origins', which supercedes Melchert's earlier article on the same topic ('The transition from asceticism to mysticism at the middle of the ninth century C.E.', *Studia Islamica* 83 [1996]: 51–70), and Bernd Radtke, *Kritische Gänge*, 251–91, esp. 280–5, which is also a criticism of Melchert's 1996 article.

34 Fuat Sezgin, *Geschichte des arabischen Schrifttums* (Leiden: Brill, 1967–2000), 1:646; a short but comprehensive bibliographic essay is Maryam Sha'bānzāda, 'Abū Sa'īd-ī Kharrāz', *Ma'ārif* 19, no 1 (2002): 131–44. On his life, see 'Abū Sa'īd al-Kharrāz', EI 4: 1083–4 (W. Madelung). There is also a PhD dissertation on him by Nada Saab, 'Mystical language and theory in Sufi writings of al-Kharrāz' (Yale University, 2004); I have not seen this work.

35 Baldick, *Mystical Islam*, 40.

36 Abū Sa'īd Kharrāz, *The Book of Truthfulness (Kitāb al-ṣidq)*, Arthur J. Arberry (London: Oxford University Press, 1937), 66.

37 The following coverage of al-Kharrāz's epistles is based on Nwyia, *Exégèse coranique*, 234–70.

38 Nwyia, *Exégèse coranique*, 234ff, which includes a complete translation of this work (256–67), reads *ṣifāt*, as does Sezgin, GAS, 1: 646, relying on A. Ateş in *Oriens* 5 (1952): 29, but Sāmarrā'ī's edition has it as *ṣafā'*, which makes better sense. Gören Ogén, 'Religious ecstasy in classical Sufism', in *Religious Ecstasy Based on Papers Read at the Symposium on Religious Ecstasy Held at Åbo, Finland, on the 26th–28th of August 1981* (Stockholm: distributed by Almqvist & Wiksell International, 1982), 230, also opts for the reading *ṣafā'*.

39 Nwyia, *Exégèse coranique*, 262–3. As Nwyia notes, a version of this passage was apparently contained in a lost epistle of Kharrāz (*Kitāb as-sirr*) and reproduced by some

later Sufi writers (Sarrāj, Sulamī and ʿAttār). Cf. the translation in Ogén, 'Religious ecstasy', 234.

40 Paul Nwyia, 'Textes mystiques inédits d'Abū-l-Ḥasan al-Nūrī (m. 295/907)', *Mélanges de l'Université Saint-Joseph* 44 (1968): 248.

41 Bernd Radtke, 'The concept of *wilāya* in early Sufism', in *Classical Persian Sufism from Its Origins to Rumi*, ed. Leonard Lewisohn (London: Khaniqahi Nimatullahi Publications, 1993), 485–6. The view that the *awliyā'* were superior to the prophets was apparently held by Abū Sulaymān al-Dārānī (d. 215/830), the premier disciple of ʿAbd al-Wāḥid ibn Zayd, as well as Dārānī's own disciple Aḥmad ibn Abi'l-Ḥawārī (d. 230/844–5); see Massignon, *Essay*, 152–4, now to be read in conjunction with Gramlich, 'Abū Sulaymān ad-Dārānī', who, however, is silent on this issue; for ibn Abi'l-Ḥawārī, see Gramlich, *Alte Vorbilder*, 1: 382. But Kharrāz's criticism might have been also directed at Tustarī, discussed in Chapter 2 below.

42 Nwyia, 'Textes mystiques', 131–2. Cf. *A Treatise on the Heart* attributed to Tirmidhī (who is discussed in Chapter 2 below) that appears in Abū ʿAbd al-Raḥmān Muḥammad ibn al-Ḥusayn Sulamī and al-Ḥakīm al-Tirmidhī, *Three Early Sufi Texts*, trans. Nicholas Heer and Kenneth Honnerkamp (Louisville, KY: Fons Vitae, 2003), 11–56, which may instead be a work of Nūrī, as noted by Nicholas Heer on p. 57.

43 Gramlich, *Alte Vorbilder*, 1: 381–446 is the most detailed and up-to-date account on Nūrī. Also see Annemarie Schimmel, 'Abu'l-Ḥusayn al-Nūrī: "Qibla of the Lights"', in *Classical Persian Sufism from Its Origins to Rumi*, ed. Leonard Lewisohn (London: Khaniqahi Nimatullahi Publications, 1993), 59–64. An account of his trials in English is found in Ernst, *Words of Ecstasy*, 97–101.

44 Qushayrī, *Risāla*, 123 / *Sendschreiben*, 70 (1.25). Other sources that contain this report are listed in Gramlich, *Alte Vorbilder*, 1: 382, n. 19. However, earning a living in order to spend it on the poor while one is secretly fasting seems to have been either a common practice or, more likely, a 'floating literary motif'; see, for instance, Abū al-Faraj ʿAbd al-Raḥmān ibn ʿAli Ibn al-Jawzī, *Talbīs Iblīs*, eds. ʿIṣām Ḥarastānī and Muḥammad Ibrāhīm Zaghlī (Beirut: Al-Maktab al-Islāmī, 1994), 202, where this same report is attached to Dāwud ibn Abī Hind, an earlier figure. Ibn al-Jawzī gives another variation of this theme about Abū Ḥafṣ Ḥaddād on p. 471.

45 This event occurred under the caliph al-Muʿtamid (256–79/870–92), though the real ruler was his brother the regent al-Muwaffaq (d. 278/891). For the dating, see Melchert, 'Ḥanābila', 360. On Ghulām Khalīl, see, most comprehensively, Maher Jarrar and Sebastian Günther, 'Ġulām Ḫalīl und das *Kitab Šarḥ as-sunna*: Erste Ergebnisse einer Studie zum Konservatismus hanbalitischer Färbung im Islam des 3./9. Jahrhunderts', *Zeitschrift der Deutschen Morgenländischen Gesellschaft* 153 (2003): 6–36, esp. 23–6 on his 'inquisition'; also Melchert, 'Ḥanābila', 360–2; Josef van Ess, 'Sufism and its opponents: reflections on topoi, tribulations, and transformations', in *Islamic Mysticism Contested: Thirteen Centuries of Controversies and Polemics*, ed. F. de Jong and Bernd Radtke (Leiden: Brill, 1999), 26–8; and Ess, *Theologie*, 4: 281f.

46 Ernst, *Words of Ecstasy*, 98, citing from A. J. Arberry, *Pages from the Kitāb al-lumaʿ* (London, 1947), 5 / *Schlagrichter*, 549 (132.1). This saying of Nūrī was actually a *ḥadīth qudsī*, 'divine saying' (*ʿashiqanī wa ʿashiqtuhu*) narrated from ʿAbd al-Wāḥid ibn Zayd with an attribution to al-Ḥasan al-Baṣrī; see Massignon, *Essay*, 88 and Ess, *Theologie*, 2: 98.

47 Gramlich, *Alte Vorbilder*, 1: 384 thinks these may have been separate incidents; Ernst, *Words of Ecstasy*, 99, suggests that several of these incidents may be unauthentic; and Böwering, 'Early Sufism', 55, does not comment on whether the accusations were related to the inquisition of Ghulām Khalīl. The first four of the five reports are from A. J. Arberry, *Pages from the Kitāb al-luma'* (London, 1947), 5 / *Schlaglichter*, 549–50 (131.1–2), while the last is by Ibn al-Jawzī and 'Aṭṭār; see note 28 in Gramlich, *Alte Vorbilder*, 1: 384.

48 Sarrāj, *Luma'*, 193–4/ *Schlaglichter*, 400–1 (77.3). For more infromation on and criticism of Nūrī's shocking behaviour, see especially Ibn al-Jawzī, *Talbīs*, 468–72.

49 Gramlich, *Alte Vorbilder*, 1: 385–6, based on a long report by Ibn al-A'rābī (d. 341/952), who had seen Nūrī in Raqqa in 270, about this latter's return to Baghdad (as reported by Dhahabī, *Siyar a'lām al-nubalā'*, 14: 74–5).

50 Gramlich, *Alte Vorbilder*, 1: 387 [relying on Dhahabī, *Siyar*, 14:76]; and Ernst, *Words of Ecstasy*, 99 [from Ghazālī, *Iḥyā'*]. The rest of the conversation between Nūrī and the caliph, which is about how Nūrī refrained from breaking one last jar when he detected a growing sense of complacency in his lower soul, might actually contain a later Sufi critique of unbridled moral activism.

51 Sarrāj, *Luma'*, 195 / *Schlaglichter*, 299 (77.5). Nūrī allowed the Sufis to take as much money as they wanted and once it was all gone, he remarked, 'Your distance from God is to be measured by the amount of money you have taken and your closeness to Him by your avoidance of it!'

52 Sarrāj, *Luma'*, 210, 290 / *Schlaglichter*, 323–4 (88.4) and 418 (102.5). Other reports about Nūrī's death, with conflicting information, are listed in Gramlich, *Alte Vorbilder*, 1: 388–9; cf. Meier, *Abū Sa'īd*, 17.

53 Sarrāj, *Luma'*, 63 / *Schlaglichter*, 81 (18, 1).

54 Commentary on Qur'ān 72 [al-Jinn]: 3, reproduced in Arabic in Nwyia, 'Textes mystiques', 147; Abū 'Abd al-Raḥmān Muḥammad ibn al-Ḥusayn Sulamī, *Ḥaqā'iq al-tafsīr*, ed. Sayyid 'Imrān (Beirut: Dār al-Kutub al-'Ilmiyya, 1421/2001), 2: 353.

55 Sarrāj, *Luma'*, 63 / *Schlaglichter*, 81 (18, 1). See Abū Bakr Muḥammad ibn Ibrāhīm Kalābādhī, *al-Ta'arruf li-madhhab ahl al-taṣawwuf*, ed. Aḥmad Shams al-Dīn (Beirut: Dār al-Kutub al-'Ilmiyya, 1993), 71 / *The Doctrine of the Ṣūfis*, trans. A. J. Arberry (Cambridge: Cambridge University Press, 1989), 49–50, where this report about the intellect is narrated from a certain Abū Bakr al-Sabbāk.

56 Sarrāj, *Luma'*, 58 / *Schlaglichter*, 76 (16.6), translation reproduced from John Renard, *Knowledge of God in Classical Sufism: Foundations of Islamic Mystical Theology*, trans. John Renard (New York: Paulist Press, 2004), 86.

57 Anṣārī, *Ṭabaqāt*, 544.

58 Commentary on Qur'ān 24 [al-Nūr]: 63, reproduced in Arabic in Nwyia, 'Textes mystiques', 146; Sulamī, *Ḥaqā'iq*, 2: 57.

59 Commentary on Qur'ān 4 [al-Nisā']: 128, reproduced in Arabic in Nwyia, 'Textes mystiques', 145; Sulamī, *Ḥaqā'iq*, 1: 163.

60 Kalābādhī, *Ta'arruf*, 112 / *Doctrine*, 86, Arberry's translation preserved.

61 Commentary on Qur'ān 2 [al-Baqara]: 273, reproduced in Arabic in Nwyia, 'Textes mystiques', 144; Sulamī, *Ḥaqā'iq*, 1: 83.

62 Commentary on Qur'ān 2 [al-Baqara]: 29, reproduced in Arabic in Nwyia, 'Textes mystiques', 144; Sulamī, *Ḥaqā'iq*, 1: 54.

63 Gramlich, *Alte Vorbilder*, 1: 409.

64 Commentary on Qur'ān 6 [al-An'ām]: 36, reproduced in Arabic in Nwyia, 'Textes mystiques', 145; Sulamī, *Ḥaqā'iq*, 1: 197.
65 See, for instance, Kalābādhī, *Ta'arruf*, index, where Nūrī is one of the most cited poets among Sufis.
66 Qushayrī, *Risāla*, 563/ *Sendschreiben*, 396 (42.11).
67 Nwyia, 'Textes mystiques', 138, ch. 12.
68 Qushayrī, *Risāla*, 217–18/ *Sendschreiben*, 116 (2.6).
69 Commentary on Qur'ān 3 [Āl 'Imrān]: 152, reproduced in Arabic in Nwyia, 'Textes mystiques', 144; Sulamī, *Ḥaqā'iq*, 1: 123.
70 Qushayrī, *Risāla*, 503/ *Sendschreiben*, 345 (36.3); also cited in Ali Hassan Abdel-Kader, *The Life, Personality and Writings of al-Junayd* (London: Luzac, 1962), 38.
71 Sezgin, *Geschichte*, 1: 647–50.
72 For instance, *tawḥīd* was one of the five principles of the Mu'tazila, the rationalist theological movement that was especially prominent in the third and fourth/ninth and tenth centuries; see 'Mu'tazila', EI 7: 783a–793a (D. Gimaret).
73 The citation of this saying at the very beginning of possibly the most popular handbook of Sufism must have contributed to its popularity; see Qushayrī, *Risāla*, 28–9/ *Sendschreiben*, 25 (0.8).
74 Abdel-Kader, *Junayd*, Arabic 54, English 175; Süleyman Ateş, *Cüneyd-i Bağdâdî: Hayatı, Eserleri ve Mektupları* (Istanbul: Sönmez Neşriyat, 1969), Arabic 57, Turkish 154.
75 Abdel-Kader, *Junayd*, Arabic 33, English 154; Ateş, *Cüneyd*, Arabic 36, Turkish 136. The English translation is from William A. Graham, *Divine Word and Prophetic Word in Early Islam: A Reconsideration of the Sources, with Special Reference to the Divine Saying or Hadīth Qudsī* (The Hague: Mouton, 1977), 173–4 (saying 49), with full text and ample references to other occurrences, including the *ḥadīth* collections of Bukhāri and Aḥmad ibn Ḥanbal, to which one can add Badī' al-Zamān Furūzānfar, *Aḥādīs̱-i Mas̱navī* (Tehran: Amīr Kabīr, 1361/1982), 18–19 (no. 42).
76 Abdel-Kader, *Junayd*, Arabic 41, English 76; Ateş, *Cüneyd*, Arabic 44, Turkish 141–2.
77 Abdel-Kader, *Junayd*, Arabic 52, English 172 (retained here); Ateş, *Cüneyd*, Arabic 55, Turkish 150.
78 The case for Junayd's doctrine of selection is made in Ahmet T. Karamustafa, 'Walāyah according to al-Junayd', in *Reason and Inspiration in Islam: Theology, Philosophy and Mysticism in Muslim Thought, in Honor of Hermann Landolt*, ed. Todd Lawson (London: I. B. Tauris in association with the Institute of Ismaili Studies, 2005), 64–70. Louis Massignon, *The Passion of al-Hallāj, Mystic and Martyr of Islam*, trans. Herbert Mason (Princeton: Princeton University Press, 1982), 1: 76 sees evidence of predestinarianism in Junayd's thinking about sanctity.
79 Abdel-Kader, *Junayd*, Arabic 23, English 143–4 (reproduced here with one revision); Ateş, *Cüneyd*, Arabic 25, Turkish 124.
80 Sarrāj, *Luma'*, 233–4, as translated by Abdel-Kader, *Junayd*, 51 / *Schlagrichter*, 356 (90.3). On Junayd's esoterism, see ibid., 35–6. For references on Shiblī, a very prominent figure in his own right, see note 92 below.
81 For in-depth treatment of Junayd's image in the Sufi biographical tradition, see Mojaddedi, *Biographical Tradition*.

82 On the Shūnīziyya mosque as a gathering place, see Gramlich, *Alte Vorbilder*, 2: 576, s.v. 'Šūnīzīyamoschee', with multiple references to episodes in the lives of Nūrī and Ruwaym; on travelling in bands, see Meier, *Abū Sa'īd*, 296–9; on the robe and initiation, see Massignon, *Passion*, 1: 72 and 103; on the earliest phase of Sufi prayer practice, see 'Dekr', EIr 7: 230, col. ii (Gerhard Böwering), and on *samā'*, see esp. Sarrāj, *Luma'*, 267–300 / *Schlagrichter*, 389–428 (chapters 95–106), which is discussed in detail in Kenneth S. Avery, *A Psychology of Early Sufi Samā': Listening and Altered States* (London: Routledge Curzon, 2004). Massignon, *Passion*, 3: 226–8 contains a very useful, albeit brief, catalogue of rituals peculiar to the Sufis, many of which must have been practised by the Baghdad Sufis.

83 By contrast, the use of the prayer rug, *sajjāda*, and its use as investiture, does not seem to date back to the third/ninth century; the earliest attestation of the use of the *sajjāda* by Sufis, as noted by Hermann Landolt, 'Gedanken zum islamischen Gebetsteppich', in *Festschrift Alfred Bühler*, ed. Carl August Schmitz (Basel: Pharos Verlag, 1965), 247, is a passing reference in the *Kitāb al-luma'* of al-Sarrāj who died in 378/988; see Sarrāj, *Luma'*, 201 / *Schlagrichter*, 308 (81.1). For a depiction of Junayd with a rosary, see Qushayrī, *Risāla*, 119 / *Sendschreiben*, 68 (1, 24).

84 This list is reproduced, with minor changes, from Knysh, *Short History*, 67.

85 On the relationship between the Sufis and the *sharī'a*, see Bernd Radtke, 'Warum ist der Sufi orthodox?', *Der Islam* 71 (1994): 302–7.

86 Sobieroj, 'Mu'tazila and Sufism', 87–9.

87 On 'Amr and Junayd, see Florian Sobieroj, *Ibn Ḫafīf aš-Šīrāzī und seine Schrift zur Novizenerziehung (Kitāb al-Iqtiṣād)* (Beirut: Orient-Institut der Deutschen Morgenländischen Gesellschaft im Kommission bei F. Steiner Verlag Stuttgart, 1998), 257, citing al-Khaṭīb al-Baghdādī, *Tarīkh Baghdād* (Cairo, 1349/1931) 12: 224. 'Amr was a *muḥaddith* and author of treatises that did not survive; he apparently denied the value of inner states, see Massignon, *Passion*, 1: 72–5, and Sobieroj, ibid., 51–3. On Ruwaym and Junayd, see Abū Nu'aym al-Iṣfahānī, *Ḥilyat al-Awliyā'*, 10: 268, cited in Sobieroj, ibid. (see 257–9 for more information on this topic).

88 'Ibn Suraydj, Abu'l-'Abbās Aḥmad ibn 'Umar', EI 3: 949a (J. Schacht); Sobieroj, *Ibn Ḫafīf*, 103–4. On his opinion of Ḥallāj, see also Ibn al-Jawzī, *Talbīs*, 224, where he is quoted as saying 'I do not understand what he [Ḥallāj] says'; and Ernst, *Words of Ecstasy*, 102–3. Cf. Abdel-Kader, *Junayd*, 5; the later sources used by Abdel-Kader (Subkī and Ibn al-Kathīr) seem to have portrayed the relationship between Junayd and Ibn Surayj as a much closer one than it probably was.

89 Mu'tazilī attitudes towards the Sufis are documented in Sobieroj, 'Mu'tazila and Sufism'. In this article, Sobieroj reproduces the details of the Mu'tazilī writer Abū 'Alī Muḥassin ibn 'Alī al-Tanūkhī's (329–84/941–94) criticism of Sufis, in particular of Ibn Khafīf, Shiblī, Ruwaym and Hallāj. His charge against Ibn Khafīf, which was that the latter encouraged sexual promiscuity among his followers, is one of the earliest attestations for this accusation that becomes a standard component of criticism of Sufis.

90 Christopher Melchert, 'The adversaries of Aḥmad Ibn Ḥanbal', *Arabica* 44 (1997): 250–1; Melchert overlooks the cases of Ibn 'Aṭā' and Jurayri when he states that no Sufis adhered to the Ḥanbalī and the Ḥanafī schools; for the *madhhab* of Jurayrī, see Massignon, *Passion*, 1: 78. The term 'semi-rationalist' is Melchert's. For the term

'traditionalist', as well as 'rationalist' in this context, see Binyamin Abrahamov, *Islamic Theology: Traditionalism and Rationalism* (Edinburgh: Edinburgh University Press, 1998), ix–xi.

91 Since the exact reason for Ghulām Khalīl's anger against the Sufis is not known, admittedly all speculation about this incident is conjectural, but see Ess, 'Sufism', 27–8. On Sumnūn, see 'Sumnūn', EI, new edition, 9: 873a–b (B. Reinert); his role in the inquisition is described in A. J. Arberry, *Pages from the Kitāb al-luma'* (London, 1947), 8 / *Schlaglichter*, 554 (134.3); summarised in Abdel-Kader, *Junayd*, 39. Two female disciples of Kharrāz are included in Sulamī, *Early Sufi Women*, 154–5, 172–3.

92 On Shiblī, see 'Shiblī, Abū Bakr Dulaf b. Djaḥdar', EI 9: 432a-b (Florian Sobieroj) and Gramlich, *Alte Vorbilder*, 1: 513–665; Sobieroj has written an unpublished 'Habilitationsschrift' titled 'Abu Bakr al-Shibli: Dichtung, tafsir und Aspekte der Überlieferung' (I have not seen this work). On Ibn 'Aṭā', see Massignon, *Passion*, 1: 93 and Richard Gramlich, *Abu l-'Abbās b. 'Aṭā': Sufi und Koranausleger* (Stuttgart: Deutsche Morgenländische Gesellschaft Kommissionsverlag, F. Steiner, 1995), and on Ruwaym, see Gramlich, *Alte Vorbilder*, 1: 447–82.

93 Junayd, Nūrī, and Abū Ḥamza Baghdādī possibly lived as celibates and reportedly all shared the same female servant, Fāṭima nicknamed 'Zaytūna'; see Sulamī, *Early Sufi Women*, 158–61; also Abdel-Kader, *Junayd*, 50, with further references. The status of celibacy was a debated, and therefore open, issue at this time, with attention focused on the Qur'ānic term *rahbāniyya* (Qur'ān 57 [al-Ḥadīd]: 27) and, later, on the non-cannonical *ḥadīth 'lā rahbāniyyata fi'l-islām'*, 'there is no monkery in Islam', see Massignon, *Essay*, 98–104; 'Rahbāniyya', EI 8: 396b (A. J. Wensinck); and Sarah Sviri, 'Wa-rahbāniyyatan ibtada'ūhā: An analysis of traditions concerning the origin and evaluation of Christian monasticism', *Jerusalem Studies in Arabic and Islam* 13 (1990): 195–208.

94 For a discussion of the issue of refraining from earning a living among renunciants, which provided the background for the distinct approach of the Baghdad Sufis, see Reinert, *Lehre*, 170–90, 252–62, and 272–84. For further confirmation of the Sufi attitude to earning a living and having a family, see especially the relevant chapters in Sarrāj, *Luma'*, 195–7 (earning a living) and 199–200 (family) / *Schlaglichter*, 300–2 (78) and 305–7 (80).

95 Qushayrī, *Risāla*, 427 / *Sendschreiben*, 244 (19.18).

96 On early wool-wearers who 'commanded right and forbade wrong', see Melchert, 'Ḥanābila', 354. These activist wool-wearers might have been 'the Sufis of the Mu'tazila', who were otherwise known for forbidding gainful employment (*taḥrīm al-makāsib*) and denied the need for a single political ruler; see Ess, *Theologie*, 3: 130–3; cf. Sobieroj, 'Mu'tazila and Sufism', 69–70.

97 Gramlich, *Alte Vorbilder*, 1: 519–22 (on his conversion), 555–60 (on his relations with Junayd); see also 'Shiblī, Abū Bakr Dulaf b. Djaḥdar', EI 9: 432a–b (F. Sobieroj).

98 See Massignon, *Passion*, in four volumes, but also available in an abridged edition (Princeton: Princeton University Press, 1994). For condensed treatments, see Herbert Mason, *Al-Hallaj* (Richmond, Surrey: Curzon, 1995) and 'Ḥallāj', EIr 11: 589–92 (Jawid Mojaddedi). On the question of his miracles, see Ess, 'Sufism', 30–3. On Ibn 'Aṭā''s death and Jurayrī's stance, see Massignon, *Passion*, 1: 527–32. Ibn 'Aṭā''s support of Ḥallāj may have been in part occasioned by his Ḥanbalī allegiance, since

a group of Ḥanbalīs defended Ḥallāj; favourable attitudes to him among Ḥanbalīs are seen later, as evidenced, for instance, by the fact that Ibn ʿAqīl (431–513/1040–1119) wrote a treatise in defence of Ḥallāj's miracles in his youth, see George Makdisi, 'The Hanbali school and Sufism', *Humaniora Islamica* 2 (1974): 67.

99 See the penetrative remarks of Meier about Ḥallāj in Fritz Meier, 'An important manuscript find for Sufism', in *Essays on Islamic Piety and Mysticism*, trans. John O'Kane (Leiden: Brill, 1999), 184–5.

100 This perspective reaches its culmination in the works of the Persian poet Farīd al-Dīn ʿAttar (d. after 618/1221–2), see 'Ḥallāj', EIr 11: 591 (Jawid Mojaddedi), and Ernst, *Words of Ecstasy*, 130–2.

101 See Bernd Radtke, 'Mystical union', 185–94, which surveys Sufi approaches to the question of 'mystical union' with God.

102 For a concise yet comprehensive discussion of his trial, largely on the basis of Massignon's *oeuvre* on Ḥallāj, that comes to this conclusion, see Ernst, *Words of Ecstasy*, 102–10.

103 There seems to be precious little information on the relationship, if any, between the Sufis and other groups of intellectuals such as the nascent philosophers (*falāsifa*), the government secretaries (*kuttāb*) and the litterateurs (*udabāʾ*), but for some leads, see Sobieroj, *Ibn Ḫafīf*.

2

Mystics outside Baghdad

While the Ṣūfiyya was taking shape in Baghdad, individuals and social groups with similar views and practices were to be found among Muslim communities in other locations, even though these latter were not generally known as Sufis. There is evidence that these separate communities had some contacts with one another. Over time, such contacts grew into real networks, which, in the long run, led to the application of the term Sufi to all such interconnected mystical groups.

Lower Iraq: Sahl al-Tustarī

Abū Muḥammad Sahl ibn ʿAbd Allāh (c. 203/818–283/896), a native of the town Tustar in south-west Iran, was without doubt one of the prominent personalities of early Islamic religiosity. From a very early age, he began to lead a life of ascetic piety marked by severe fasting, training in the Qur'ān and the *ḥadīth*, and the yearning to draw near to God through constant remembrance of His presence. This latter took the form of a special prayer formula that he learned from his maternal uncle:

> One day my maternal uncle said to me, do you not remember God who created you? I replied, how shall I remember Him? He told me, when you change into your bedclothes, say three times in your heart without moving your tongue: God is with me, God watches over me, God is my witness … For years I did not cease to practise this, and I experienced a sweetness in my innermost being because of it.[1]

Motivated by the urge to draw close to God, the young Sahl spent a good few of his adolescent years travelling in search of spiritual and practical guidance. His travels took him to the regional urban centres of Basra and Kūfa as well as Mecca for the pilgrimage and possibly also Egypt, where (or in Mecca) he may have met the Egyptian sage Dhu'l-Nūn (d. 245/860), who is regularly cited in later sources as his spiritual forebear. He also went to the retreat, *ribāṭ*, at ʿAbbādān frequented by ascetics and scholars, where he not only found the answer to a spiritual question that had occupied him for some time but also had a formative visionary experience in which he saw the greatest name of God written across the sky in large green letters.[2] After this initial phase of training and travel in search of knowledge, Tustarī returned to his native town and settled into a life of seclusion and introspection marked by austere asceticism, especially systematic hunger, with continuous recollection of God as his main sustenance. This period of private austerities likely included intense contemplation on the Qur'ān, since one of his two major extant works is a Qur'ānic exegesis compiled by his disciples.[3] To judge by reports about him as a visionary, it is probable that many of his interpretative exercises were facilitated by experiences of the following type:

> [Commenting on Qur'ān 2 (al-Baqara): 25, a description of paradisiac bliss] Sahl said, truly I know a man from among the friends (*awliyā'*) who, in this world, saw a pomegranate, the biggest that there ever was, before a man on the shore of the sea. The friend (*walī*) said to him, what is this before you? He answered, it is a pomegranate which I saw in paradise. I desired it and God gave it to me. But when He put it before me, I felt remorse about my haste to have it in this world. That man (i.e., the *walī*) asked him, may I eat from it? The man replied, if you are foreordained to (eat from) it, then do so. He (the *walī*) grabbed it with his hand and ate most of it ... Only one who belongs to the people of paradise eats from the food of paradise in this world.[4]

After about two decades of this intense private probing, Tustarī emerged from his seclusion – curiously at about the same time as the death of Dhu'l-Nūn of Egypt at 245/860 – as a teaching master surrounded by a circle of disciples.[5] He lived the rest of his life as a public figure of considerable renown and controversy, first in his native Tustar and later, when he was compelled to leave his home town at about 263/877, in Basra. The controversy that surrounded him in the public phase of his life had to do with his claim to be the 'proof of God', *ḥujjat Allāh*: 'Tustarī used to say: I am the proof of God for the created beings and I am a proof for the saints (*awliyā'*) of my time.'[6] In all likelihood, this provocative claim should be understood as evidence for Tustarī's conviction of his own status as a special friend of God, *walī*. Collectively, the friends formed a select company of God's protégés who were in direct contact with the divine power at all times, and Tustarī was clearly persuaded that he himself occupied an elevated rank among the spiritual elect. Such claims of direct rapport with God appear to have aroused the suspicion of at least some legal scholars in Tustar and Basra, who, quite accurately, may have seen in Tustarī's talk of unmediated access to God a clear challenge to the scope and efficacy of their own legal scholarly authority. This was, after all, the formative period of Islamic legal sciences and of the legal schools (*madhhab*), and the proponents of the legal interpretation of Islam were negotiating their place within Muslim polities through charged encounters with, on the one hand, holders of political power and, on the other, other claimants to special authority among Muslims such as scholars of various stripes (most notably, *ḥadith* experts), ascetics, pious warriors, messianic and millenarian figures and the Shīʿa.

The controversy around Tustarī's claim to an authoritative status among Muslims demonstrates that by the time Tustarī embarked on the public phase of his career as a teaching master of spiritual realities, the friends of God, *awliyāʾ*, had emerged as major players in the on-going tug of war among Muslims for special authority. Tustarī, for his part, managed to keep himself and his circle of followers clear of any major social and political conflict, even though he may have harboured some sympathy for political opponents of the reigning ʿAbbāsid caliphs such as the Ṣaffārids and the Zanj.[7] In negotiating the turbulent terrain of public authority, Tustarī was no doubt helped by his 'restrained attitude' in matters of devotion and ecstasy, as evidenced by his saying: 'Every ecstatic experience (*wajd*) to which the Book and the *Sunna* do not bear witness is false.'[8] One of his most devoted followers stated: 'I served Sahl for sixty years, yet I did not see him change while listening to (a repetitive formula of God's) commemoration (*dhikr*), to Qur'ān recital, or any other recitation.'[9]

Tustarī's attitude towards stories of miracle mongering was similarly cold: 'One day [one of his disciples] said to Sahl: Abū Muḥammad, sometimes when I perform the ablution for ritual prayer, the water flows from my hands and forms into a rod of gold and a rod of silver. Sahl said to him: 'My friend, you know that boys when they weep are given a rattle to keep them busy. So watch out what you are doing.'[10] He reacted equally negatively to miraculous stories people told about him during his own lifetime: 'When people credited him with walking on water without his feet being so much as moistened, he simply referred them to the muezzin of the mosque, who one morning spotted Tustarī as he fell into a pool and rescued him from drowning.'[11] However, his measured rejection of miracle stories did not prevent his own disciples from recording reports of his miraculous feats even in their compilation of his exegetical work.[12] This appears to have been a tightly-knit group of disciples bound by their loyalty to their master, who guided them in both doctrinal and practical matters such as concern and proper method for eating only lawful food and regulation of daily diet through moderate vegetarianism.[13] Tustarī, who seems to have shed his intense asceticism in the later phases of his life, died of chronic haemorroids at about age eighty in Basra, as a popular spiritual master of considerable public acclaim.

Tustarī's thought and practice unfolded in a field defined by the tension between God's utter transcendence and His mysterious immanence within the innermost secret of human beings. In his view, the affirmation of God's unity, *tawḥīd*, entailed an unbridgeable distinction between God and His creation, yet, at the same time, the presence of God in human experience was most palpable. Human life at both ends of time, before the creation and after the resurrection, was marked by divine self-manifestation to humanity. At one end, there was the primordial Day of Covenant recorded in Qur'ān, 7 [al-A'rāf]: 172. On this pre-existential day, human beings had stood witness, in the form of specks of light, to God's Lordship, thus acknowledging their standing vis-à-vis God as servants. This intimate colloquy between the Lord and humankind as God-servants was to be re-enacted after the Day of Resurrection, when the believers would be rewarded by direct and full vision of God in a fulfillment of their faithful service to Him. In their phenomenal existence on earth, however, suspended as they were between a vague, ever-fading memory of their witnessing of God on the Day of Covenant on the one hand and anxious anticipation of His vision after the Day of Judgment on the other, human beings lived in the charged space delimited by God's commands and interdictions.

Life on earth developed as a struggle between two antagonistic forces: 'a positive force, the heart (*qalb*), which turns man towards God, and a negative force, the lower self (*nafs*), which induces man to turn toward his own ego.'[14] Tustarī envisaged both the heart and the lower self as subtle substances (*laṭīf*) that combined to form the human person. The former was the spiritual vital force defined as the locus of colloquy between the human individual and God, and it was sustained by constant recollection of God (*dhikr*), without which the heart would not be alive. The latter was the carnal vital force acting as the interface between the heart and this earth, and its sustenance was eating, drinking, and enjoyment. The heart, always oriented towards God, re-enacted the witnessing on the Day of the Primordial Covenant through constant recollection of God, and yearned for a complete vision of God after the Day of Judgment. The lower self, however, was busy orienting the human person away from God and towards itself, claiming itself as the centre of human existence.

In the struggle between the heart and the lower self, the stakes were high, and the heart had to be vigilant: 'If a man closes his eyes to God [said Tustarī] but the twinkling of an eye, he will not be guided for the length of his life.'[15] It was best to constrict the life sphere of the lower self by cutting its life lines through systematic hunger, vegetarianism and seclusion (but apparently not celibacy, since Tustarī may have been married) and to cultivate the 'house of affirmation of God's unity', that is, the heart, through constant turning to (*tawba*, 'repentance') and recollection of God (*dhikr*).[16] Ultimately, however, it became clear to the recollector that the true agent of recollection was not the believer engaged in recollection but God Himself, who commemorated Himself in the heart of the believer. This realisation of God's control over the heart led the believer to the state of complete trust in the Divine, which Tustarī described in a famous saying as follows: 'The first stage in trust is when the servant is in the hands of God like the corpse in the hands of the washer, turning him as he wishes while he has neither motion nor control.'[17] This state of trust, which signalled the triumph of the heart over the lower self and meant final relief from the struggle between the two antagonistic forces, marked the climax of human life on earth.

Tustarī's sweeping vision of the human condition on earth had a cosmic framework. He conceived God and Muḥammad as cosmic entities composed of light: 'When God willed to create Muḥammad, He made appear a light from His light. When it reached the veil of Majesty it bowed in prostration before God. God created from its prostration a mighty column like crystal glass of light that is outwardly and inwardly translucent.'[18] It was from this column of light that God created everything else, first the spiritual prototypes of His prophets, His friends (*awliyā'*), and the rest of humankind, then their material forms. The primordial light of Muḥammad absorbed the light of God like a crystal and projected it eternally on to the rest of His creation in the form of the Qur'ān. In this scheme, the prophets and the friends occupied a special place: they were the spiritual elect, the objects of God's desire (*murād*, 'desired'), while the rest of humankind, engaged in a quest for God's countenance, were characterised as 'God-seekers' (*murīd*, 'desiring'). The elect never forgot their witnessing of God's Lordship on the Day of Covenant, while the common people clearly suffered from an amnesia about this key event. The elect, chosen by God, enjoyed special privileges: they were granted entry into Paradise without having to account for their actions on earth; they received revelations of God's signs (which, for the prophets, meant 'miracles', *mu'jizāt*, and for the friends 'charismatic gifts', *karāmāt*), and they were endowed with the gift of understanding the Qur'ān. Between the two types of elite, the prophets had a clear superiority to the friends: 'the last of the ranks of the righteous [read 'friends'] is the first of the states of the prophets.'[19] The prophets had the duty of propagating the faith while the friends were charged with being God's reminders and directing believers to Him. If there is any validity to a statement attributed to him in his Qur'ān commentary, Tustarī appears to have had a hierarchical notion of the friends: 'I met 1,500 righteous (*ṣiddīq*), among them forty substitutes (*budalā'*) and seven pegs (*awtād*). Their path (*ṭarīqa*) and their way (*madhhab*) is the same as mine.'[20] It was against this background that some, perhaps including Tustarī himself, understood his statement 'I am the proof of God' to mean that he claimed to be the spiritual axis of the world, that is the pole (*quṭb*) at the summit of the saintly hierarchy.

Clearly, there was considerable overlap between the thought and practice of Tustarī and the Baghdad Sufis. The stress on the necessity of a permanent re-orientation of the human individual towards God in the form of repentance (*tawba*), the assumption of a fierce antagonism between the lower self (*nafs*) and the heart (*qalb*), the acceptance of human weakness and the recognition of God as the only true agent and saviour, the invocation (*dhikr*) as the sure link between

God and His chosen servants, the idea of a primordial covenant, the belief in the existence of a spiritual elect, and friction with other intellectual elites: in all these areas of overlap, it is plausible to see signs of mutual influence between the circle around Tustarī in Basra and the Sufis of Baghdad, even though it is not always possible to verify them in the sources. Actual linkages between the two groups did indeed exist. Although he eventually chose his own individual path, Ḥallāj started out as a disciple of Tustarī but then became a follower of Junayd's disciple and associate ʿAmr al-Makkī, thus linking the two circles. More directly, some of Tustarī's disciples left Basra upon the death of their master in 283/896, relocated to Baghdad, and became direct disciples of Junayd. These included al-Muzayyin 'the Younger' and Jurayrī, who, significantly, emerged as the leader of the Sufi circle of Junayd after this latter's death.[21] While the Basran followers of Tustarī and the Baghdad Sufis were thus clearly linked and had shared beliefs and practices, the overlap between them was by no means comprehensive. Certain aspects of Tustarī's thought and practice – such as vegetarianism, the proclivity for having 'visions', his peculiar 'light' cosmology centred on the idea of 'the light of Muḥammad', and the conviction that he could access the 'inner meaning' of the Qur'ān – did not have clear parallels among his Sufi contemporaries in Baghdad, and they should be seen as particular to the Basran milieu and lower Iraq in general. There were also points of disagreement: when Junayd was told that the followers of Sahl fasted during the day and ate food saved in their baskets at night, he expressed regret that the Basrans did not forgo reliance on saved food.[22] Tustarī endorsed work as prophetic example (*sunna*), while Junayd preferred complete reliance on God (*tawakkul*) unadulterated with search for sustenance.[23]

While Tustarī was a seminal figure in Basra, he was, most likely, not the only influential paragon of piety in town whose thought and practice evinced affinities with Baghdad Sufism. Abū Ḥātim al-ʿAṭṭār (d. 260s/874–84) was another figure whose pietistic approach may have resembled that of Junayd. Critical of renunciatory display, Abū Ḥātim denounced the wearing of wool, and he seems to have advocated earning a living. Although his historical personality remains obscure, he and his disciples provide other examples of links between renunciatory and mystical circles in Basra on the one hand and Baghdad Sufis on the other.[24]

Iran and Central Asia

Even while Sufism was taking shape in central and lower Iraq, modes of piety similar to it were in evidence further east, in particular in Khurāsān and Transoxania, even though the term Sufi had not yet not travelled that far.

Tirmidhī (d. probably between 295/905 and 300/910) and the sages of the north-east

It is likely that Abū ʿAbd Allāh Muḥammad ibn ʿAlī al-Ḥakīm al-Tirmidhī spent most of his life in his native Tirmidh in present-day Uzbekistan. The silence of contemporary sources on him is amply compensated, most remarkably, by his extant autobiography, which is one of the earliest examples of this genre in Arabic, as well as by his numerous surviving works, possibly as many as eighty, which makes him by far the most prolific early Muslim mystic author.[25] According to his autobiography, which reads like a 'spiritual itinerary', he began to study *ḥadīth* and Ḥanafī jurisprudence from an early age sometime in the first few decades of the third/ninth century, but did not have any mystical inclinations until he had a decisive experience of repentance while on pilgrimage at around the age of twenty-seven.[26] Upon returning home, he memorised the Qur'ān, began to fast and pray intensively, and searched in vain for spiritual guides in the region. He found some guidance for disciplining his lower soul in a book but otherwise continued his spiritual training on his own in seclusion.[27] He soon began to have dreams and visions that provided clear evidence of his increasing proximity to God, which only fuelled his efforts to tame his lower soul and his zeal for prayer. In the meantime, he began to reveal his experiences to others in what appears to have been nightly *dhikr* sessions, but this led to charges of heresy, brought about by 'those who purport[ed] to be possessed of religious learning' on account of Tirmidhī's discourse of love, and he was summoned to Balkh by the governor and ordered to desist from such talk.[28] Ironically, this experience of humiliation actually helped Tirmidhī finally to overcome his lower self, and through increased practice of *dhikr* he began to feel close to God's throne. In time, he confronted and bested his detractors in public debate, and became a popular public preacher with a following. He was not alone in his spiritual journey, and remarkably, his closest spiritual companion may have been his wife, since he seems to have in part relied on her dreams for confirmation of his own spiritual status. In his autobiography, Tirmidhī gives detailed descriptions of his wife's dreams, which on occasion contain short sections in Persian, and these reveal his wife to have been a spiritual visionary of a high rank in her own right; but they also depict Tirmidhī – as do dreams of several other companions also narrated by him – as having attained the highest level of friendship with God.

In several clearly related treatises – two prominent examples are a substantial work entitled *The Life of the Friends of God* (*Kitāb sīrat al-awliyā'*) or *The Seal of Friendship / of Friends* (*Kitāb khatm al-walāya / al-awliyā'*), and another *The Difference between the Miracles of Prophets and the Miracles of Friends* (*al-Farq bayn al-āyāt wa'l-karāmāt*) – Tirmidhī gave one of the most systematic treatments of the concept of 'friendship with God' (*walāya*) in Islamic thought.[29] The idea of a spiritual elect appointed by God was known and discussed in some detail in third/ninth-century Iraq, not only by Baghdad Sufis like Kharrāz in his *Book of Unveiling and Exposition*, as seen above, but also by traditionalists such as Ibn Abi'l-Dunyā (d. 281/894) in his *Book of God's Friends* (*Kitāb al-awliyā'*). Tirmidhī's elaboration of this idea, however, was not only more systematic but also clearly embedded in a highly-developed world-view composed of a distinct combination of anthropology and cosmology, in which the human being and the cosmos were seamlessly integrated into a single whole. In this view, God was unknowable in His essence, but could be known by certain created beings through His attributes and His names.

Tirmidhī conceived the divine attributes in the form of realms of light above God's throne. Beneath the celestial throne was found the created world: the earths were held up by an angel who stood on a paradisal rock, which rested on the three horns of a bull that itself stood on a fish afloat on a deep ocean held in place by the world-ground. The supports of the celestial throne themselves stood on this world-ground, presumably enveloping the whole of creation, and the throne marked the boundary between the eternal divine world above it and the world of creation below.[30] The divine attributes above the throne were thus eternal, not created, and, indeed, they played a key role in the origination and making of the created world. The creation started with the spirit (*rūḥ*) and ended with Adam. This latter was a composite being, with three centres: the head, the heart or breast, and the belly. The head was the seat of reason, the faculty of discernment and differentiation, and spirit, the principle of life, while the belly housed the carnal soul, with its principal force lust (*shahwa*) and all the lower instincts (*hawā*), which arose directly from Hell and were fanned by Satan himself. The heart (*qalb*) was the repository of the knowledge of God (*ma'rifa*), which shone forth in the form of the light of divine attributes from the heart into the breast (*ṣadr*). The light of the heart in the breast was, however, normally clouded over by the smoke generated by hot winds originating from the carnal soul, which formed a screen that made it impossible for reason's light to discern the light of the heart and thus to know God, unless the carnal soul's activities were countered and subdued by strict observance of what was 'due to God' (*ḥaqq Allāh*), that is, fulfilling God's commands as contained in His laws.

Tirmidhī characterised those who succeeded in turning to God through continuous struggle with their carnal souls by following God's laws as 'friends of what is due unto God' (*awliyā' ḥaqq Allāh*). Such people could travel through the seven different stages (*manāzil*) of the mystic path and rise all the way to God's throne, to the upper limits of the created world.[31] They could not, however, step into the divine realms of light above the throne, since they remained tied down by their indispensable preoccupation with the carnal soul, which they could not transform but could only contain, no matter how rigorous their efforts were to subdue it. Nevertheless, when some friends of what is due unto God, who were thoroughly flustered by their inability to crush their carnal souls, turned in desperation to God and solicited His help, God answered their call and through His mercy and grace released them from slavery to the carnal soul and allowed them entry into the divine realms of his attributes. Tirmidhī identified this select company as the 'friends of God' (*awliyā' Allāh*) and referred to them as the 'noble free' ones (*al-aḥrār al-kuramā'*). Not all of these were elevated to this high position from among the lower rank of 'friends of what is due unto God'; some were born free from slavery to the carnal soul and were never constrained by it or they were set free later in life directly by God when He decided to draw them to close to Himself. The friends of God were hierarchically organised and occupied special positions in the celestial realms according to their proximity to God, with the highest layers consisting of the forty 'substitutes' (*abdāl*) or 'sincere/righteous ones' (*ṣiddīqūn*), above them an unspecified number of 'trustworthy' or 'strong' ones (*umanā'*, *aqwiyā'*), and, finally, at the zenith, a 'seal of friendship' (*khatm*, *khātim* or *khātam al-walāya*), also known as the 'singular one' (*munfarid*, *mufrad*).

Tirmidhī provided detailed information about the friends of God and their status in comparison to that of the prophets. The friends ranked right below the prophets, to whom they were clearly inferior, yet they shared with them many of their characteristics. Upon the prophets was bestowed divine speech (*kalām*) in the form of revelation (*waḥy*) accompanied by a spirit from God (*rūḥ*); correspondingly, the friends possessed 'supernatural speech' (*ḥadīth*) in the form of inspiration (*ilhām*) accompanied by peace of mind (*sakīna*). Like the prophets, the friends had knowledge of the primordial beginnings, the divine decrees, the divine covenant and the inner meaning of the letters of the alphabet, and like the prophets, they performed miracles, though with some differences (the miracles of the prophets were known as *mu'jizāt* or *āyāt* while those of the friends were called *karāmāt*). These included clairvoyance, travelling with great speed (literally 'folding the earth', *ṭayy al-arḍ*) and walking on water. Just as neglect or ignorance of prophetic messages led people to perdition, so neglect or heedlessness with respect to the friends' words inevitably brought misfortune. Prophets and friends equally were assured of salvation, but, unlike the prophets who were sinless, the friends were not protected from sin lest they succumb to arrogance. All in all, while Tirmidhī repeatedly declared that the prophets were superior to the friends, the differences that he identified between these two classes of holy people were fairly minimal. More significantly, it was clear that in the post-prophetic era after the death of Muḥammad, who was the seal of prophets, Tirmidhī viewed the friends as the successors to the Prophet and assigned to them, in particular to the seal of the friends, the task of protecting and leading the community of believers. It was also patently obvious that Tirmidhī claimed the key role in the hierarchy of the friends, the seal of friendship with God, for himself.

There is much overlap between the thought of Tirmidhī and Tustarī, in particular in their hierarchical conception of the *awliyā'* and the place they both assign to 'light' in cosmic matters. While this commonality may be attributed at least in part to the possible exposure of Tirmidhī to the Basran milieu during the pilgrimage that led to his 'conversion' to mystic life, it is clear that Tirmidhī developed his views on his own, with no detectable contact either with lower Iraq or with the Sufis of Baghdad, in the different cultural environment of Khurāsān and Transoxania. In these north-eastern regions of the Muslim polity, there seems to have been a particular social type known as *ḥakīm*, 'sage' who combined in his person several different areas of learning, such as Ḥanafī jurisprudence, *kalām*, Qur'ānic exegesis, *ḥadīth*, and, most notably for our purposes, also 'experiential', spiritual knowledge.[32] Tirmidhī was dubbed a *ḥakīm*; two of his contemporaries, for instance, who also had reputations as sages were Muḥammad ibn 'Umar Abū Bakr al-Warrāq al-Ḥakīm (d. 280/893) in Balkh and Abu'l-Qāsim Isḥāq ibn Muḥammad al-Ḥakīm al-Samarqandī (d. 342/953) in Samarqand. The former warned against one-sided training in *kalām*, *fiqh* and *zuhd* and advocated a synthesis of all three as the only safe approach. Reputed to be an outstanding spiritual guide (he was called 'trainer of friends of God', *mu'addib al-awliyā'*) and also a poet, he was the author of many works on training of novices, subduing the lower soul, proper behaviour, and renunciation, but his only extant work displays his expertise in non-spiritual areas of learning.[33] His disciple Abu'l-Qāsim Isḥāq al-Ḥakīm, who served as the qāḍī of Samarqand for a long time and composed the popular Ḥanafī creed *al-Sawād al-a'ẓam*, was learned in *kalām*, *fiqh*, *tafsīr* and in spiritual matters, and reportedly wrote on 'Sufi' conduct; mystical sayings (*ḥikam*) and sermons by him are recorded in later Sufi sources.[34] As a representative of the cultural type *ḥakīm*, Tirmidhī seems to have been from a socially prominent and respectable family; indeed, he was a wealthy man and owned a large piece of real estate in Tirmidh. In this connection, it is noteworthy that he stood firmly against the doctrine of prohibition of earning a living (*taḥrīm al-makāsib*), which was avidly propagated by the most prevalent renunciatory movement in Iran at the time, the Karrāmiyya.[35]

As a well-known sage, Tirmidhī was in contact with his counterparts in other towns in the region. He sent a copy of his work *Sīrat al-awliyā'* to Rayy (he was aware of the legacy of Yaḥyā ibn Mu'ādh, the major mystic of this town), and he held correspondence with Muḥammad ibn al-Faḍl (d. 319/931) of Balkh, Abū 'Uthmān al-Ḥīrī (d. 298/910) of Nishapur, and some unspecified inhabitants of Sarakhs. The subject of his letters to these last two figures was the proper handling of the lower self, which had emerged as a major fault line that separated Tirmidhī's approach (which he possibly shared with some other 'sages') from that of a mystical school that had taken shape, especially in Nishapur, known as the Malāmatiyya.

The Path of Blame in Nishapur

The Malāmatiyya, 'the Path of Blame', was a mystical tradition of piety that developed in Khurāsān, in particular in Nishapur, during the late third/ninth and early decades of the fourth/tenth century under the leadership of Ḥamdūn al-Qaṣṣār (d. 271/884–5), Abū Ḥafṣ al-Ḥaddād (d. c. 265/878–9) and this latter's disciple, Abū 'Uthmān al-Ḥīrī (d. 298/910).[36] Its distinguishing feature was constant and unrelenting suspicion against the lower self (*nafs*). The Malāmatīs thought that unless it was controlled, the lower self would inevitably waylay the pious believer through self-conceit (*'ujb*), pretence (*iddi'ā*), and hypocrisy (*riyā'*) and would thus prevent the believer from reaching his true goal, which was the achievement of sincere, selfless devotion to God (*ikhlāṣ*). They argued that the only effective methods of harnessing the appetitive self to the cause of *ikhlāṣ* were (1) to narrow the lower self's sphere of operation by shunning all public display of piety as well as omission of praiseworthy acts, and (2) better yet, to subject the *nafs* to constant blame, *malāma*, through self-censure.[37] Viewed from a different angle, the Malāmatī methods amounted to the complete concealment of one's inner spiritual states underneath a veil of anonymity (no ostentatious display of piety) and avoidance of praise (no conspicuous commission of praiseworthy acts). 'Spiritual states are valuable assets deposited in the hearts of their trustees; whoever externalises them forfeits the rank of a trustee.'[38] The concern for avoiding all public display of piety and the public praise attendant upon such display led them to a very mild interpretation of the religious dictum to 'command the right' (*amr bi'l-ma'rūf*), while this same concern prevented them from implementing the second part of the same dictum that required Muslims to 'forbid the wrong' (*nahy 'an al-munkar*), to the extent of letting this duty fall into abeyance. Such a mellowing of the duty of commanding the right and prohibiting the wrong also had clear social implications. In their effort to avert ostentation and pretentious conduct, the Malāmatīs laboured to weave a veil of anonymity around themselves and thus exhibited a strong conformist drive to blend into society:

> One of them was asked concerning the path of blame. He replied, 'it is to abandon being conspicuous (*shuhra*) in all matters which may distinguish one in the eyes of people, whether in one's manner of dressing, walking or sitting ... He should rather adopt the external behaviour of the people in whose company he is, while at the same time be isolated from them by way of contemplation, so that his exterior person conforms with society so as not to be distinquished in any way, while his interior reality is in utter distinction.'[39]

Accordingly, the 'People of Blame' refused to wear distinctive clothing, took care to earn their own living, and had no distinct public rituals; they performed *dhikr* silently and did not hold any *samāʿ* sessions.[40] Significantly, the overwhelming concern for social conformity rendered the Path of Blame into an ideal mode of religiosity for artisanal and merchant classes. If their names are accurate indicators of social origin, many teachers of *malāma* indeed belonged to these classes in Nishapur: al-Ḥaddād 'the ironsmith', al-Qaṣṣār 'the fuller', al-Ḥajjām 'the cupper', al-Khayyāṭ 'the tailor'.[41] The attraction that the Path of Blame must have had for craftsmen and traders might explain the presence in Malāmatī teachings of the ethical code of 'chivalry' known under the names *futuwwa* in Arabic and *javānmardī* in Persian (literally 'youngmanliness', signifying especially 'generosity') that was characteristic of artisanal professional circles and urban neighbourhood associations. Since the core value of *futuwwa* was altruism and self-sacrifice for one's social group, the veil that such corporate anonymity could provide as well as the opportunity to train the lower self through acts of self-sacrifice must have had a distinct appeal for the Malāmatīs.[42]

Ḥamdūn, who is reputed to have said 'blame is abandoning [any thought of] flawlessness' (*al-malāma tark al-salāma*), was the most uncompromising in the Path of Blame, to the extent of belittling the good works and ascetic exercises of his disciples for fear that their lower selves would be led to self-conceit by performing such praiseworthy acts.[43] Abū Ḥafṣ and, in particular, Abū ʿUthmān, whose disciples included women, were more moderate on this issue and aimed for the middle course; the latter said:

> At the beginning of his novitiate we train the disciple in the path of practices and we encourage him to follow it and establish himself in it. However, when he is established and consistent in this path he becomes attached to it and dependent on it. Then we show him the shortcomings of this path of actions [or efforts] and our disregard for it, until he becomes aware of his helplessness, and sees how remote his efforts are from completion. Thus we make sure that first he becomes grounded in practices, yet does not (later on) fall into self-delusion. Otherwise, how can we show him the shortcomings of his practices if he has no practices? … Between the two is the most balanced way.[44]

Behind this Malāmatī pedagogical method, whether extreme or moderate, based on criticism of the lower self and its delusions was the conviction that the *nafs* was simultaneously corrupt *and* indestructible. This conviction itself may have been rooted in a belief in the necessarily defective nature of all creation in comparison with the perfection of God.[45] Hopelessly caught in the trap of the lower self and the lower world, the aspirant to God's closeness had no choice but to remain vigilant at all times against the lower self and its guiles. For this reason, the People of Blame maintained a healthy suspicion against all claims of personal spiritual achievement and miracle-mongering by mystics; all talk of high spiritual states and miraculous feats reeked of the deceptions wrought by the lower self.

The relentless monitoring of the lower self cultivated as the only safe path of spiritual progress by the People of Blame came across to some other mystics in Khurāsān and Transoxania like Tirmidhī as a misguided preoccupation with the *nafs* that prevented the mystic from reaching higher. In the three-way correspondence that went on between Tirmidhī, Muḥammad ibn al-Faḍl and Abū 'Uthmān Ḥīrī, Tirmidhī made it clear that, in his opinion, the only way out of the trap laid by the lower self is to turn one's gaze away from the *nafs* directly to God. He wrote to Abū 'Uthmān:

> I have received your letter, my brother, one letter after another. You confirm repeatedly [how] the blemishes of the lower self (*nafs*) [are an obstacle] in the [attainment] of [spiritual] knowledge. My brother, if you can refrain from being occupied by this obstacle, since this is other than Allāh, do so. For Allāh has servants who indeed have knowledge of Him, and they ignore all things but Him. They are wary of being occupied with the lower self and instead they fear Him. Whenever anyone of them is afflicted by its memory, his stomach turns as if he were about to vomit. How can one who strolls through gardens of roses, jasmine and wild lilies graze in valleys of thorns? How can one who is nourished by the remembrance of the Majestic be aware of anything but Him?[46]

To judge by a letter that Abū 'Uthmān wrote to Muḥammad ibn al-Faḍl, he agreed with Tirmidhī that the goal of the mystic was to achieve release from slavery to the lower self:

> No action or state can become perfect unless God brings it about without any wish on the doer's part and without any awareness of the doing of the action, and without awareness of another's observation of the action.[47]

Whether Abū 'Uthmān concurred with Tirmidhī that such perfection of action was indeed possible is less clear, and, in general, it appears that the People of Blame refused to admit the possibility of transcending the lower self. If the mystic was, through divine intervention, released from bondage to the *nafs*, then he either kept the knowledge of this development to himself and never revealed it to others or, in a peculiar twist of Malāmatī logic, he himself remained unaware of his freedom from the lower self, as suggested in this passage by a later source:

> Among them [the people of divine realities] are those whom He hides from the eyes of creation, from their eyes, their hearts, and their inward secrets; they exist among people as one of them. They eat, drink, and mingle with others. God has allowed their exterior aspect to face creation while keeping their inner state exclusively to Himself. No one perceives their inner perfection, while He is completely aware of them. This is because of God's jealousy over them, for He is too jealous to allow other than Himself the knowledge of His elect.[48]

On the whole, however, the People of Blame, unlike Tirmidhī, had little to offer in the way of a theory of *walāya* and directed their energies predominantly to the pursuit of controlling the *nafs* through spiritual training. In this, their unwavering concentration on the lower self, they differed not only from Tirmidhī but also from the Sufis of Baghdad. Indeed, Abū Bakr Muḥammad ibn Mūsā al-Wāsiṭī (d. after 320/932), a disciple of Junayd and Nūrī who had recently arrived in Khurāsān, reportedly also criticised Abū ʿUthmān for directing his students to focus their attention on the acts of the lower soul, which he decried as dualism (self and God, as opposed to God alone).[49] Similarly, Junayd is known to have disagreed with Tustarī on the definition of turning to God through repentance (*tawba*): 'Asked about *tawba*, Sahl said '[it is] not to forget your sins.' They asked Junayd about *tawba*, and he said '[it is] forgetting your sins.'[50] Correct orientation toward the lower self was quite clearly one of the central issues tackled by mystics of all regions.

In conclusion, the sages of Transoxania as well as the People of Blame of Nishapur in Khurāsān, and possibly other mystics of the east addressed, in the late third/ninth and early fourth/tenth century, questions and topics similar to those that preoccupied their counterparts of the same time period in central and lower Iraq. While there was contact between the mystics of Iraq and those of eastern Iran and Central Asia at this stage (both Abū Ḥafṣ and Abū ʿUthmān visited Baghdad and met Junayd and Nūrī there; Tirmidhī, we have seen, had visited Basra; and Bāyazīd was well known to the Baghdad Sufis), the mystics of the two different regions evolved largely independently of one another. Yet there was a sense of generic affinity among the various regional mystical tendencies in spite of their real differences in approach, and the term Ṣūfiyya was already used by some at the beginning of the fourth/tenth century to express this shared commitment to the cultivation of the inner life if the following, admittedly formulaic, saying of Abū Bakr al-Ḥusayn ibn ʿAlī ibn Yazdānyār (d. 333/944–5) is authentic: 'Sufism of Khurāsān is practice and no talk; Sufism of Baghdad is talk and no practice; Sufism of Basra is talk as well as practice; and Sufism of Egypt is no talk and no practice!'[51]

Notes

1 Qushayrī, *Risāla*, 93; the English translation, with the exception of the actual prayer, is from Böwering, *Mystical Vision*, 45. Eventually, the uncle increases the number of repetitions of the formula from three to eleven.

2 The question that exercised Sahl for a while was: 'Does the heart prostrate?' The answer that he received was '[yes], forever', and the greatest name of God he saw was 'Allāh'; see Böwering, *Mystical Vision*, 48–9.

3 Böwering, *Mystical Vision*, 7–18.

4 Böwering, *Mystical Vision*, 69, citing from Tustarī's *Tafsīr al-Qurʾān al-ʿaẓīm* (Cairo, 1329/1911), 10. Tustarī's disciples did not have the slightest doubt that he himself was the man with the heavenly pomegranate who ate from it. For another 'pomegranate miracle' involving Tustarī, see Ibn al-Jawzī, *Talbīs*, 504.

5 See Sarrāj, *Luma'*, 181 / *Schlagrichter*, 280 (71.5) on how Sahl did not speak in public until the death of Dhu'l-Nūn, out of respect for him.

6 Böwering, *Mystical Vision*, 64, citing Sha'rānī's *al-Ṭabaqāt al-kubrā*, 2 vols. (Cairo, 1315/1897), 1: 67. Significantly, the term *ḥujja* had a special place in early Shī'ī thinking about the nature of the *imām*, as noted by Böwering, 63–5, but see also Mohammad Ali Amir Moezzi, *The Divine Guide in Early Shi'ism: The Sources of Esotericism in Islam* (Albany: State University of New York Press, 1994), 29–30 and *passim*, and Arzina Lalani, *Early Shī'ī Thought: The Teachings of Imam Muḥammad al-Bāqir* (London: I. B. Tauris in association with the Institute of Ismaili Studies, 2000), 83.

7 Böwering, *Mystical Vision*, 66 and 63, respectively.

8 Sarrāj, *Luma'*, 146 / *Schlagrichter*, 176 (50.4), as translated in Böwering, *Mystical Vision*, 72.

9 Sarrāj, *Luma'*, 292 / *Schlagrichter*, 420 (103.1), as translated by Böwering, *Mystical Vision*, 72.

10 Sarrāj, *Luma'*, 400 / *Schlagrichter*, 459–60 (116.2), as translated in Böwering, *Mystical Vision*, 84.

11 Qushayrī, *Risāla*, 703 / *Sendschreiben*, 514 (52.52), as reported in Böwering, *Mystical Vision*, 71.

12 Böwering, *Mystical Vision*, 70–1.

13 Böwering, *Mystical Vision*, 77–8. According to Sarrāj, *Luma'*, 417 / *Schlagrichter*, 581 (143.1), as noted by Böwering, Tustarī wanted his followers to be vegetarians but ordered them to eat meat on Fridays in order to have enough strength to worship.

14 Böwering, *Mystical Vision*, 241.

15 Kalābādhī, *Ta'arruf*, 69 / *Doctrine*, 46, also quoted by Böwering, *Mystical Vision*, 76.

16 For the report of Tustarī's favorable attitude to marriage, see Böwering, *Mystical Vision*, 91.

17 Qushayrī, *Risāla*, 416 / *Sendschreiben*, 237 (19.4); also cited in Böwering, *Mystical Vision*, 76.

18 Böwering, *Mystical Vision*, 149, translating from Tustarī's *Tafsīr al-Qur'ān al-'aẓīm* (Cairo, 1329/1911), 40f. Massignon, *Passion*, 1: 70 sees here a borrowing from extremist Shī'ī circles, but the idea of Muhammadan light appears to have been a feature of mainstream Shī'ī thought; see Moezzi, *Divine Guide*, 29–30, and Lalani, *Early Shī'ī Thought*, 80–3.

19 Böwering, *Mystical Vision*, 239, translating from Tustarī's *Tafsīr al-Qur'ān al-'aẓīm*, 48. Böwering rightly observes that this saying is also attributed to other Sufis.

20 Böwering, *Mystical Vision*, 237, translating from Tustarī's *Tafsīr al-Qur'ān al-'aẓīm*, 46.

21 On Tustarī's direct disciples and their variegated histories after his death, see Böwering, *Mystical Vision*, 75–99.

22 Meier, *Abū Sa'īd*, 4; his source is Abū Ṭālib Muḥammad ibn 'Alī Makkī, *Qūt al-qulūb fī mu'āmalat al-maḥbūb wa waṣf ṭarīq al-murīd ilā maqām al-tawḥīd*, ed. Sa'īd Nasīb Makārim (Beirut: Dār Ṣādir, 1995), 2: 324 (ch. 39) / *Die Nahrung der Herzen*, trans. Richard Gramlich (Stuttgart: F. Steiner, 1992), 3: 273 (39.9).

23 For Tustarī's stance on work, see, for instance, Qushayrī, *Risāla*, 421/ *Sendschreiben*, 240 (19.9) [with further references], where Sahl is credited with the saying 'Earning a living is prophetic example, and he who keeps to the Prophet's state does not abandon his example.'

24 On Abū Ḥātim al-ʿAṭṭār and his disciples, see Melchert, 'Baṣran origins', 234–40.
25 The autobiography is available in English, with annotations by the editors, in Muḥammad ibn ʿAlī al-Ḥakīm Tirmidhī, *The Concept of Sainthood in Early Islamic Mysticism: Two Works by al-Ḥakīm al-Tirmidhī*, trans. John O'Kane and Bernd Radtke (Richmond, Surrey: Curzon, 1996), 15–36; a facsimile publication of the original Arabic *unicum*, along with a German translation, was published earlier by Bernd Radtke, 'Tirmiḏiana Minora', *Oriens* 34 (1994): 242–98; Tirmidhī's known works, some with lingering questions of authenticity, are listed in Sezgin, *Geschichte*, 1: 654ff.
26 The phrase 'spiritual itinerary' is used by Yves Marquet in EI 'al-Tirmidhī', 10: 544a, but the substance of this article has been superseded by the numerous publications of Bernd Radtke on Tirmidhī after 1980; now also see Sara Sviri, *Perspectives on Early Islamic Mysticism: The World of al-Ḥakīm al-Tirmidhī and his Contemporaries* (London: Routledge, 2007); I have not seen this last work.
27 The book in question, which Tirmidhī tells us was by al-Anṭākī, may instead have been by al-Muḥāsibī, possibly his *Book on the Observance of God's Rights*, since this work is known to have circulated under the name of Aḥmad ibn ʿĀṣim al-Anṭākī (d. 220/853); see Bernd Radtke, *Al-Ḥakīm at-Tirmiḏī: Ein islamischer Theosoph des 3./9. Jahrhunderts* (Freiburg: Klaus Schwarz, 1980), 34; cf. Ess, *Theologie*, 1: 146; also noted by Knysh, *Short History*, 38.
28 Tirmidhī, *Concept of Sainthood*, 20.
29 The Arabic text of the *Sīrat al-awliyāʾ* can be found in Muḥammad ibn ʿAlī al-Ḥakīm Tirmidhī, *Thalātha muṣannafāt li'l-Ḥakīm al-Tirmidhī: Kitāb sīrat al-awliyāʾ, Jawāb masāʾil allati saʾalahu ahl Sarakhs ʿanhā, Jawāb kitāb min al-Rayy*, ed. Bernd Radtke (Stuttgart: F. Steiner, 1992), 1–134; an English translation with copious annotations is in Tirmidhī, *Concept of Sainthood*, 38–211. On the title of this work, see the review of *Thalātha muṣannafāt* by Hermann Landolt in *Journal of the American Oriental Society* 114 (1994): 303–4. The *Difference* is discussed in Bernd Radtke, 'Al-Ḥakīm al-Tirmidhī on Miracles', in *Miracle et karama: saints et leurs miracles à travers l'hagiographie chrétienne et islamique IVe–XVe siècles*, ed. Denise Aigle (Brepols: Turnhout, 2000), 287–99. The following exposé of Tirmidhī's views is largely based on the *Sīrat* and several articles of Radtke listed in the bibliography.
30 On this Islamic cosmology not yet influenced by Greek philosophical views of the universe, see Anton Heinen, *Islamic Cosmology: A Study of as-Suyūṭīs al-Hayʾa as-sanīya fī l-hayʾa as-sunnīya* (Beirut: In Kommission bei Franz Steiner Verlag, 1982) and Bernd Radtke, *Weltgeschichte und Weltbeschreibung im mittelalterlichen Islam* (Beirut: Orient-Institut der Deutschen Morgenländischen Gesellschaft, in Kommission bei F. Steiner Verlag, 1992), esp. chapters 3 and 4.
31 The seven stages, as found in Tirmidhī's *Manāzil al-ʿibād min al-ʿibāda* (*The Ranks of Worshippers According to Their Worship*), were 'repentance (*tawba*), abstention (*zuhd*), fighting the *nafs* (*ʿadāwat al-nafs*), love (*maḥabba*), cutting off the base inclination (*qaṭʿ al-hawā*), fear (*khashya*), and proximity [to God] (*qurba*)'; see Sviri, 'Self', 203.
32 On this subject, see especially Bernd Radtke, 'Theologien und Mystiker in Ḫurāsān und Transoxanien', *Zeitschrift der Deutschen Morgenländischen Gesellschaft* 136 (1986): 536–69, and Bernd Radtke, 'Theosophie (*ḥikma*) und Philosophie (*falsafa*): Ein Beitrag zur Frage der *ḥikmat al-mašriq/al-išrāq*', *Asiatische Studien* 42 (1988): 156–74.

33 See 'Abū Bakr al-Warrāq', Muḥammad ibn 'Umar al-Ḥakīm, EIr 1: 264–5 (B. Reinert); also Sezgin, *Geschichte*, 1: 646. The sobriquet *mu'addib al-awliyā'* is recorded in Hujwīrī, *Kashf*, 179 / *Revelation*, 142, noted by Fritz Meier, 'Khurāsān and the End of Classical Sufism', in *Essays on Islamic Piety and Mysticism*, trans. John O'Kane (Leiden: Brill, 1999), 211.

34 'Abu'l-Qāsem Esḥāq Samarqandī', EIr 1: 358–9 (W. Madelung); Sezgin, *Geschichte*, 1: 606.

35 See Radtke, 'Theosophie', 158–9, and Radtke, 'Theologien', 564–5. On *taḥrīm al-makāsib* among the Karrāmiyya, see, most recently, Michael Bonner, 'The *Kitāb al-Kasb* attributed to al-Shaybānī: poverty, surplus, and the circulation of wealth', *Journal of the American Oriental Society* 121 (2001): 423–5.

36 For detailed coverage of these figures, see Gramlich, *Alte Vorbilder*, 2: 113–241. A short account of one of them is in EIr: 'Abū Ḥafṣ Ḥaddād', EIr 1: 293–4 (J. Chabbi). For historical overviews of this tradition, see 'Malāmatiyya', EI 6: 223b–228b (Frederick de Jong, Hamid Algar, Colin Imber). Major sources for early Malāmatī history are discussed in Sarah Sviri, 'Ḥakīm Tirmidhī and the *Malāmatī* movement in early Sufism', in *Classical Persian Sufism from Its Origins to Rumi*, ed. Leonard Lewisohn (London: Khaniqahi Nimatullahi Publications, 1993), 587–92 and Naṣr Allāh Pūrjavādī, 'Manba'ī kuhan dar bāb-i malāmatiyān-i Nīshābūr', *Ma'ārif* 15, no. 1–2 (1998): 3–5.

37 The Qur'ānic locus for the concept of blame is verse 5 [al-Mā'ida]: 54 that refers to the Prophet and his companions, 'they struggle in the path of God and do not fear the blame of any blamer', though the Malāmatīs understood the word 'blame' to mean censure of lower self.

38 Abū 'Abd al-Raḥmān Muḥammad ibn al-Ḥusayn Sulamī, *Risālat al-malāmatiyya* [in *al-Malāmatiyya wa'l-ṣūfiyya wa ahl al-futuwwa*, pp. 86–120], ed. Abū al-'Alā al-'Afīfī (Cairo: Dār Iḥyā' al-Kutub al-'Arabiyya, 1364/1945), 93; the translation is from Sviri, 'Ḥakīm Tirmidhī', 608. Sulamī's work is our chief source of information on the Malāmatiyya.

39 Sulamī, *Malāmatiyya*, 103; translation from Sviri, 'Ḥakīm Tirmidhī', 608–9.

40 See especially the chapter on Malāmatiyya from Abū Sa'd al-Khargūshī's (d. 406/1015 or 407/1016), *Tahdhīb al-asrār*, which is possibly the earliest source on this form of piety, published in Pūrjavādī, 'Manba'ī kuhan', 32–6. This work has recently been published as a whole: 'Abd al-Malik ibn Muḥammad Kharkūshī, *Kitāb Tahdhīb al-Asrār*, ed. Bassām Muḥammad Bārūd (Abū Ẓabī, al-Imārāt al-'Arabiyya: Al-Majma' al-Thaqafī, 1999); I owe this reference to Carl Ernst.

41 Sviri, 'Ḥakīm Tirmidhī', 585–6 and 603–4.

42 The earliest exposition of *futuwwa* discourses is an independent treatise of Sulamī: Abū 'Abd al-Raḥmān Muḥammad ibn al-Ḥusayn Sulamī, *Tasavvufta Fütüvvet / Kitāb al-futuwwa*, ed. and trans. Süleyman Ateş (Ankara: Ankara Üniversitesi İlāhiyat Fakültesi Yayınları, 1977) / *The Book of Sufi Chivalry*, trans. Tosun Bayrak (New York: Inner Traditions, 1983).

43 For Ḥamdūn's saying, see Hujwīrī, *Kashf*, 74 / *Revelation*, 66; also quoted in Gramlich, *Alte Vorbilder*, 2: 156.

44 Sulamī, *Malāmatiyya*, 103; translation from Sviri, 'Ḥakīm Tirmidhī', 598. Cf. Meier, 'Khurāsān', 215–17, who argues that only Qaṣṣār was a Malāmatī, and that Sulamī erred in portraying Ḥaddād and Ḥīrī as members of the Path of Blame. It appears

quite likely that Ḥīrī was indeed a transitional figure, since he was in contact with Tirmidhī as well as with western Sufis like al-Wāsiṭī. For his female disciples, see Sulamī, *Early Sufi Women*, 32, note 52.

45 See Kenneth Honerkamp's translation of Sulamī's *Stations of the Righteous* in *Sulamī and al-Ḥakīm al-Tirmidhī, Three Early Sufi Texts*, 125 (section 13), and Honerkamp's comments, 108.

46 Sviri, 'Ḥakīm Tirmidhī', 610–11, translating from the Arabic original in Tirmidhī, *Thalātha Muṣannafāt*, 191.

47 Sulamī, *Malāmatiyya*, 106; translation from Sviri, 'Ḥakīm Tirmidhī', 599.

48 Kenneth Honerkamp's translation of Sulamī's *Stations of the Righteous* in *Three Early Sufi Texts*, 127 (section 17); see also Honerkamp's comments, 103–4. For a later discussion of the issue of self-recognition of one's status as a friend of God, see Qushayrī, *Risāla*, 520–1 / *Sendschreiben*, 359–60 (38.4).

49 Qushayrī, *Risāla*, 204–5 / *Sendschreiben*, 109 (2.2), as noted first in Meier, 'Khurāsān', 205, esp. note 64 [originally published 1971]. Also see Sulamī, *Ḥaqā'iq*, 1: 184 where Wāsiṭī, commenting on Qur'ān 5 [al-Mā'ida]: 92, is reported as saying 'Do not regard your acts of obedience', as noted in Florian Sobieroj, 'Ibn Khafīf's *Kitāb al-Iqtiṣād* and Abū al-Najīb al-Suhrawardī's *Ādāb al-Murīdīn*: a comparison between the two works on the training of novices', *Journal of Semitic Studies* (1998): 340, note 20.

50 Sarrāj, *Luma'*, 43 / *Schlaglichter*, 87 (21.1); translated in Sells, *Early Islamic Mysticism*, 199.

51 Pūrjavādī, 'Manba'ī kuhan', 13, quoting Ibn Mulaqqin's *Ṭabaqāt al-awliyā'*, ed. N. Shurayba (Beirut, 1406/1986), 2: 335.

3

The spread of Baghdad Sufism

The Sufi mode of piety that emerged as a distinctive synthesis in the largest and most cosmopolitan urban centre of the ʿAbbāsid empire during the second half of the third/ninth century proved to be both durable and adaptable. During the fourth/tenth century, this new approach to pious living spread to all major cultural centres of Islamdom and blended with indigenous interiorising trends where these existed. In the process, second-, third- and fourth-generation Sufis nurtured the legacy of their foundational figures and achieved a degree of self-consciousness and confidence that signalled the transformation of Sufism from a pioneering mode of piety to an established pietistic tradition.

Western Iran and Arabia

Already during the days of Junayd, Nūrī and Kharrāz, Baghdad Sufis acted as teachers to numerous students from different regions of the ʿAbbāsid empire. These students later spread the distinctive teachings and practices of their Sufi teachers especially to south-western Iran (Fārs), western Arabia (Ḥijāz), and north-eastern Iran (Khurāsān). Although they were interconnected and at times even united on certain issues, Baghdad Sufis were far from being in agreement with one another on all issues or homogenous in their approaches to Sufi thought and practice. Significant cleavages in temperament, lifestyles and teaching methods existed between, among others, Junayd and Nūrī, Junayd and Ruwaym, Junayd and Ibn ʿAṭāʾ, Shiblī and Junayd (even though the former was a student of the latter), and Ibn ʿAṭāʾ and Jurayrī.[1] Even when the students of these masters reproduced their teachers' preferences outside Baghdad, they ultimately served to extend and to strengthen the network of Baghdad Sufism in the different regions of the ʿAbbāsid empire. One such figure, Abū ʿAbdallāh Ibn Khafīf al-Shīrāzī (d. 371/982), is much better known than most of his counterparts because one of his own disciples, Abu'l-Ḥasan ʿAlī ibn Muḥammad al-Daylamī (fl. fourth/tenth century), wrote a biography of his teacher. Not counting the relatively short autobiography of Tirmidhī, this is the earliest biography we possess for any Muslim mystic. Ibn Khafīf was a 'traditionist' (*muḥaddith*) who studied and transmitted *ḥadīth*, and like many of his counterparts, he travelled widely in order to 'hear' prophetic reports from reputed *ḥadīth* authorities (and, in his case, also to meet Sufis). The list of major towns he visited is extensive: Isfahan and Rayy in central and western Iran, known as 'The Mountains'(*Jibāl*); Mecca and Medina in Ḥijāz; Basra, Kūfa, Qādisiyya, Baghdad and Wāsiṭ in Iraq; Jerusalem, Damascus, Tyre and Ramla in Syria; Shiraz, Fasā, Iṣṭakhr, Bayḍā and Fisinjān in Fārs. Since his biographer Daylamī took particular care in recording the conversations that Ibn Khafīf had with major Sufi figures in these towns (and these add up to forty-seven *shaykhs*, 'masters'), Ibn Khafīf's biography contains a fairly detailed portrayal of the state of mystical trends in these regions. When supplemented by other sources that include two recently published extant works of Ibn Khafīf himself, the biography not only enables us to reconstruct Ibn Khafīf's own views to a large extent but also opens for us a window into the lives of Sufis in Shiraz and beyond during the fourth/tenth century.[2]

A thorough examination of all the relevant evidence about Ibn Khafīf overturns many aspects of the received wisdom about this key figure. For instance, contrary to prevalent views in secondary literature, it emerges that Ibn Khafīf's true teaching master was not Ḥallāj but Ruwaym, though he was also influenced by Ibn 'Aṭā' and 'Amr ibn Uthmān. Apparently, Ibn Khafīf once had some loyalty to Ḥallāj, whom he visited while this latter was under house arrest in Baghdad, but later distanced himself from this controversial figure, whom he openly criticised, especially on account of the latter's provocative public statements.[3] To his own disciples, he recommended Muḥāsibī, Junayd, Ruwaym, Ibn 'Aṭā' and 'Amr ibn Uthmān as the five teachers 'worthy of emulation'. He rejected the most prominent figure of the Tustarī circle of his time, Aḥmad ibn Muḥammad ibn Sālim, because of this latter's rejection of Bāyazīd-i Basṭāmī and also because he thought Ibn Sālim taught the eternity of the world, but he was openly sympathetic to Tustarī.[4] His attitude to *samā'* was decidedly reserved, and it is likely that his approach to the thorny issue of 'witnessing' (detecting divine beauty in the creation) was equally cautious.[5] Even though he himself was a Shāfi'ī in legal matters, he had close affinities with the legal school of his teacher Ruwaym, the Ẓāhirī *madhhab*. Moreover, in spite of the fact that he had studied under Abu'l-Ḥasan al-Ash'arī in his youth, he had little sympathy for the emerging semi-rationalist Ash'arī theological approach, which gradually became the preferred *kalām* orientation of Shāfi'īs everywhere. He was, instead, a 'traditionalist' who mistrusted *kalām*, especially disliked the rationalist Mu'tazila, and eschewed speculative reasoning in favour of reliance on scriptuary sources, that is, the Qur'ān and the Sunna understood as the *ḥadīth*.[6] Politically, like his Baghdad teachers, Ibn Khafīf was a quietist, and earlier assertions that he must have offered protection in Shiraz to followers of Ḥallāj through his political influence are not supported by any evidence.[7]

When we use Ibn Khafīf's itinerary to peek into the Sufi communities of his time, Ibn Khafīf appears more representative than exceptional as a 'traditionalist' Sufi. In Shiraz and elsewhere, there were Ḥanbalī traditionists who were Sufis: two of them who narrated traditions on the authority of Ibn Khafīf were later teachers of the famous Ḥanbalī Sufi 'Abd Allāh-i Anṣārī. In Isfahan and Shiraz, most Sufis, some of whom must have been Shāfi'īs, seem to have been aligned with traditionalist Ḥanbalīs and Ẓāhirīs against rationalist Mu'tazilīs, who were hostile to Sufis and traditionalists alike. In Isfahan, the most prominent mystic at the beginning of the century was 'Alī ibn Sahl (d. 307/919–20). He was a student of Muḥammad ibn Yūsuf ibn Ma'dān al-Bannā' (d. 286/899), who was said to have been admired by Junayd and was the great grandfather of the well-known writer Abū Nu'aym (d. 430/1038). 'Alī ibn Sahl corresponded with Junayd and was close to 'Amr ibn 'Uthmān al-Makkī. In the town there were also students or companions of the famous renunciant Abū Turāb al-Nakhshabī (d. 245/859), who, as his name testifies (Nakhshab = Nasaf in Transoxania), was from the east but had spent his adult life in Iraq and the *Jibāl* and who, like Dhu'l-Nūn, was one of the central figures in the formative 'pre-Baghdad Sufism' era.[8] Isfahan's mystics seem to have been closely associated with traditionalist and pietist Ḥanbalīs and Ẓāhirīs, while the 'rationalist' Mu'tazilis were aligned with Zaydīs against traditionalists, Sufis and renunciants; the 'semi-rationalist' Ash'arīs were in a definite minority. Isfahan had close ties with Rayy, where the major mystic was Yūsuf ibn Ḥusayn al-Rāzī (d. 304/916–17), a disciple of Abū Turāb and Dhu'l-Nūn.[9]

In Shiraz, there were at least seven different Sufi centres, including Ibn Khafīf's own lodge (*ribāṭ*), and the number of Sufis – some of them women – was reportedly in the thousands. Many were disciples of Baghdad Sufis, especially Junayd and Ruwaym, but these were divided among themselves, most notably around the legacy of Shiblī. This latter had major opponents in Shiraz, including a certain disciple of Abū Ḥafṣ of Nishapur by the name Abū Muzāḥim (d. 345/956), whose debates with Shiblī over the issues of poverty and verbal expression of mystical experience were well known. Ibn Khafīf sided with Abū Muzāhim in this debate. The major figure in Shiraz in the generation before Ibn Khafīf's was Abū Muḥammad Ja'far-i Ḥadhdhā' (d. 341/952–3). He was connected both to Tustarī through this latter's disciple Abū 'Amr-i Iṣṭakhrī (d. 283/896–7), who headed the Tustarī circle in Basra, and to Junayd; indeed, Ḥadhdhā' was also a teacher of Shiblī, who had visited him in Shiraz. Nonetheless, the followers of Shiblī had a difficult time in the town, and one, Abū Bakr al-Ṭamastānī (d. 340/951–2), had to leave Shiraz and travel to Nishapur, where, it appears, he ended up as a Malāmatī![10]

In Mecca, the following seven students of Baghdad Sufis lived as metics (*mujāwir*) in the vicinity of the Holy Precincts (*al-Masjid al-Ḥarām*) at the beginning of the fourth/tenth century and all but one died there: Abu'l-Ḥasan ʿAlī ibn Muḥammad Muzayyin al-Ṣaghīr (d. 328/939–40), Abū Jaʿfar Muzayyin al-Kabīr (d. in Baghdad or Mecca), Abū Bakr Muḥammad ibn ʿAlī al-Kattānī (d. 322/934), Abū Yaʿqūb Isḥāq ibn Muḥammad al-Nahrajūrī (d. 330/941–2), Abū ʿAmr Muḥammad ibn Ibrāhīm al-Zajjājī, (d. 348/959–60), Abū Muḥammad ʿAbd Allāh ibn Muḥammad Murtaʿish (d. 328/939–40 in Baghdad), and Abū Saʿīd ibn al-Aʿrābī (d. 341/952–3). These figures, it appears, as well as others like Abu'l-Ḥusayn ʿAlī ibn Jaʿfar Sīrawānī the Younger (d. 396/1005–6 at an advanced age) and Abu'l-Ḥasan ʿAlī ibn ʿAbd Allāh Ibn Jahḍam al-Hamadhānī (d. 414/1023) initiated a Sufi tradition – in all likelihood adapted from renunciant circles – of living as metics in Mecca that has continued uninterrupted up until the present.[11]

Elsewhere, the picture was similar, with Sufi lodges (the term used is normally *ribāṭ*) reported in Tyre and Ramla in Syria, Baghdad and Basra in Iraq, Bayḍā in Fars, and Sūs in Khūzistān. The mystics of the regions Ibn Khafīf visited were all closely connected, keeping in touch with one another through travel and written correspondence.[12] The majority, it appears, were connected to the first generation of Baghdad Sufis as well as to Tustarī of Basra and honoured especially Junayd and Tustarī as the most important leaders. The legacy of more local figures, like Jaʿfar-i Ḥadhdhā' in Shīrāz and Abū ʿAbd Allāh Aḥmad ibn Muḥammad Ibn al-Jallā' (d. 306/918–19) in Syria, continued to exercise considerable influence but the impact of Baghdad and, to some extent, Basran networks was definitely on the rise.[13] While most mystics were thus interconnected through bonds of fellowship and discipleship, there were no doubt some solitary figures with no discernible ties to others, of whom Muḥammad ibn ʿAbd al-Jabbār al-Niffarī (d. 354/965 or around 366/977) appears to have been a spectacular example.

Niffarī is an enigmatic figure. Nothing is known about his biography, except, perhaps, his town of origin, Niffar in lower Iraq. He is known chiefly on account of two compilations of his writings, *Kitāb al-mawāqif* (*The Book of Standings*) and *Kitāb al-mukhāṭabāt* (*The Book of Addresses*), both of which were evidently compiled (posthumously?) by one of his descendants.[14] It is abundantly clear from his style and language that Niffarī was a truly original mystic. His stunningly vibrant verbal expressions, situated 'at the edge of the dissolution of the ego', betray the overwhelming presence of the Divine in Niffarī's mystical experiences, in which God stood or stayed Niffarī in a particular spiritual state and spoke through him in an act of 'ghostly ventriloquism'.[15] Indeed, Niffarī seems to have exemplified the highest stage of intimacy with God so ably described by Kharrāz, where the mystic's subjectivity is completely overwritten by the power of the sole real subject in existence. Significantly, the palpable presence of the Divine in Niffarī's writings infused his sayings with a distinctly apocalyptic tone, although it is impossible to know if his mystical vision was imbued with chiliastic expectations. While one can detect certain parallelisms between Niffarī's thought and the thinking of other mystics who were his predecessors or contemporaries (for instance, his saying 'If you cast off your fault, you will cast off your ignorance; if you recall your fault, you will forget your lord' coincides with the view of Junayd on the issue of repentance), such affinities do not come across as evidence of direct influence on Niffarī by other significant mystical figures.[16] In a very real sense, Niffarī was *sui generis*.[17]

Even though there may have been other solitary figures like Niffarī in this period, most mystics were embedded in relational and pedagogic networks that connected them with one another. On the whole, the ascendancy of Baghdad affiliations was everywhere in evidence, and this was increasingly the case also in Khurāsān and Transoxania, where Baghdad-style Sufism grew firm roots during the course of the fourth/tenth century.

Khurāsān and Transoxania

The spread of Sufism to Khurāsān, especially to its major urban centre Nishapur, its floresence there and its eventual absorption of this province's indigenous mystical movement, Malāmatiyya, have all attracted much scholarly attention. The relevant evidence has been assembled from both Sufi and non-Sufi sources.[18] On the one hand, the survey of onomastic practices in local Khurāsānian historiography suggests a sharp rise in the popularity of the term 'Sufi': previously unattested in the region, the term first appeared in Khurāsān at the beginning of the fourth/tenth century, when it was used to designate five pious individuals in Nishapur; by the end of the century, that number had leapt to forty-six, out of a total of about 100 renunciants and mystics noted in the sources for the same city. This rise certainly indicates the growing presence, if not domination, of Sufis among the mystics and pietists of Nishapur.[19] On the other hand, both Sufi and non-Sufi sources enable us to identify Abū Bakr al-Wāsiṭī (d. after 320/932) as the first unmistakably 'Baghdad-oriented' Sufi of Iraqi origin who migrated to Khurāsān and settled there in Marw, probably already before 298/910, though he may have been preceeded by Abū Hamza al-Khurāsānī (d. 293/903).[20] Wāsiṭī himself apparently did not have many students, but the only genuine student he had, Abu'l-'Abbās al-Qāsim ibn al-Qāsim al-Sayyārī (d. 342/953–4), succeeded in building a community on the basis of his master's teaching in and around Marw that survived for at least more than a century until the mid fifth/eleventh century when it was last attested.[21] There were others as well who, like Wāsiṭī, moved from the west, that is, Iraq and Syria, to the east: for instance, Abū Isḥāq Shāmī, a disciple of Abū 'Alī Mamshād Dīnawarī (d. 299/911–12), settled in Chisht near Herat and established a Sufi community there, which thrived through the efforts of his disciple Abdāl Chishtī (d. 355/966) and his descendants.[22] Nevertheless, it would be a mistake to characterise the growth of Sufism in Khurāsān as the result of an influx of Sufis into the region from its west.[23] Probably much more common was the example of several Khurāsānian students of the Malāmatī leaders Abū 'Uthmān al-Ḥīrī and Abū Ḥafṣ al-Ḥaddād, like Abū 'Alī al-Thaqafī (d. 328/940), Abū Muḥammad al-Murta'ish (d. 328/939 in Baghdad), Abū 'Amr al-Zajjājī (d. 348/959–60 in Mecca), Mu'ammil ibn Muḥammad al-Jaṣṣās (d. 322/933–4) and several others who also studied with Baghdad Sufis and who, therefore, represented a 'fusion' between Sufism of Iraq and Malāmatiyya of Khurāsān.[24] It is also possible that this fusion had also started to occur with the 'moderate' Malāmatīs Abū Ḥafṣ al-Ḥaddād and his disciple Abū 'Uthmān al-Ḥīrī, who may have moved away from the purely Malāmatī positions of Ḥamdūn Qaṣṣār because of their contact with the sages of Transoxania and Sufis of western Iran and Iraq.[25] In either case, these two mystical orientations that had evidently developed independently of one another shared some common ground, which must have facilitated their merger.[26] In addition to their intrinsic compatibility with each other, the two trends may have been similarly aligned against Karrāmiyya, which was, arguably, the most powerful renunciatory movement throughout Iran from the mid-third/ninth to the sixth/twelfth century. The extroverted piety of the Karrāmīs, built on ostentatious asceticism, prohibition of working for a living and activist preaching, was indeed diametrically opposed to the inward-looking religiosity of the Malāmatīs, who were socially conformist, economically productive and morally non-interventionist. Furthermore, the two movements had different legal affiliations: the Karrāmīs are most likely to have been affiliated with the Ḥanafī school, while the 'People of Blame' appear to have followed the school of Sufyān al-Thawrī.[27] While all this does not necessarily entail hostility towards the Karrāmīs on the part of the Malāmatīs of Nishapur, it certainly signals an oppositional stance. For their part, Sufi sources of Khurāsān most conspicuously fail to mention Karrāmiyya even once and maintain a complete silence about these renunciants. This silence is not easy to explain, but the Khurāsānian Sufis may have inherited their 'blindness' to Karrāmiyya from the Malāmatīs they merged with, and/or they may have been simply uninterested in Karrāmiyya as a form of piety that distinctly lacked any inner depth.[28] Whatever the reason, they appear to have shared the distrust of their Malāmatī counterparts towards the Karrāmīs.

Significantly, the fusion between Sufism and Malāmatiyya seems to have proceeded hand in hand with the increasing presence and popularity of the Shāfi'ī legal school in Nishapur. The reasons for the rise of the Shāfi'ī school are debated, but its outcome is clear: the fortunes of traditionalism in the town declined as Shāfi'īsm rose to prominence, and the latter largely absorbed the former.[29] Concomitant, and no doubt related, with this development was the ascendancy of Iraqi Sufism and its merger with the indigenous Path of Blame, a merger in which the dominant partner was increasingly Sufism, the new arrival in town. Since most Sufis in Nishapur were Shāfiʿīs, the changes in the matrix of the various legal and mystical schools in the town during the fourth/tenth century were clearly interlinked, though it is difficult to establish clear lines of causation in any direction.[30] Whatever the cause, the Sufis, now clearly aligned with the Shāfiʿī legal school, emerged as the more vocal and visible mystical movement in Nishapur and, it appears, also in many other locations in Khurāsān, while the Malāmatīs remained faithful to their principles of anonymity and disappeared into the woodwork. To judge by the unmistakable presence of Malāmatī features in later Sufi history, it would certainly be more accurate to understand the 'absorption' of the Path of Blame by Sufism as its continuation in the form of powerful subcurrents within the fabric of subsequent Sufi thought and practice (hence the terms 'merger' and 'fusion') rather than as its termination during the course of the fourth/tenth century. In this connection, it is tempting to speculate that in response to the growing popularity of Shāfiʿī Sufis, at least some Malāmatīs may have switched their legal allegiance to the Ḥanafī school and survived as a mystical orientation within this *madhhab*. This would explain the frequent re-emergence of distinctly Malāmatī phenomena in later Islamic history especially in Ḥanafī-dominated cultural environments, notably in the Ottoman Empire and Central Asia.[31]

Our understanding of the merger between Sufis and Malāmatīs in Nishapur is complicated by the complex legacy of a key figure whose many works form the principal source for the history of this phenomenon, Abū ʿAbd al-Raḥmān al-Sulamī (325 or 330–412/937 or 942–1021).[32] Both his parents were from socially-prominent Arab families of Nishapur, and in his youth Sulamī came into the care of his maternal grandfather Abū ʿAmr Ismāʿīl ibn Nujayd. According to Sulamī's own testimony, Ibn Nujayd was a disciple of Abū ʿUthmān Ḥīrī, and had also met Junayd at some point. Himself a *ḥadīth*-scholar of Shāfiʿī persuasion, he no doubt contributed to his grandson's study of *ḥadīth* and left his considerable wealth, including his house and his library, to Sulamī upon his death in 366/976–7. Sulamī converted this house into a small lodge (*duwayra*) and spent the rest of his long life there teaching and writing books.[33]

Curiously, Sulamī's initiatory credentials as a Sufi seem less than solid. He is said to have been formally inducted into Sufism by Abū Sahl al-Ṣuʿlūkī, a prominent Shāfiʿī jurist with Ashʿarī leanings (d. 369/980), who was himself a disciple of Abū ʿAlī al-Thaqafī, one of the 'first' Sufis in Khurāsān, but had also studied with Shiblī and Murtaʿish in Baghdad. But it is not clear that Ṣuʿlūkī trained disciples in Sufism, and Sulamī himself does not accord him any place in his *Generations of Sufis*.[34] Apart from Ṣuʿlūkī, Sulamī is also said to have received, sometime after 340/951, another *khirqa* from Abu'l-Qāsim al-Naṣrābādhī (d.

367/977–8), himself a direct disciple of Shiblī initiated by this latter in 330/942. Naṣrābādhī was a *bona fide* Sufi master, but even though Sulamī indeed includes him in his *Generations*, he does not give his readers any telltale signs of an initiatory connection between himself and Naṣrābādhī.[35] As a result, there is a question mark concerning the nature of Sulamī's initiatic affiliation with Sufism through Ṣuʿlūkī and Naṣrābādhī.

Nevertheless, in most of his treatises (and there are about thirty titles extant in manuscript, many now published, out of a total of over 100 attributed to him), Sulamī's voice is that of an authoritative representative of Sufism, and the care he took in recording the biographies, sayings and discourses of Sufis, male as well as female, is ample proof that he considered himself to be one of them. His biographical anthologies, *Ṭabaqāt al-ṣūfiyya* (*Generations of Sufis*) and *Dhikr al-niswa al-mutʿabbidāt al-ṣūfiyyāt* (*A Memorial of Female Sufi Devotees*), and his seminal compendium of Sufi Qur'ān interpretation, *Ḥaqā'iq al-tafsīr* (*Truths of Qur'ānic Exegesis*), are major sources for early Sufi history.[36] Whatever the nature of his initiatic relations with Ṣuʿlūkī and Naṣrābādhī, he definitely had close associations with Sufis, most notably with Ibn Khafīf and Abū ʿAbd Allāh Muḥammad 'Ibn Bākūya' of Shīrāz, popularly known as Bābā Kūhī (d. 428/1037), a member of Ibn Khafīf's outer circle of students who took over the direction of Sulamī's *khānaqāh* after his death.[37] There can be no doubt whatsoever about Sulamī's standing as a major Sufi figure.

Yet, Sulamī is also the author of *Risālat al-malāmatiyya* (*The Treatise on the People of Blame*) where he not only gives the most detailed account of these 'indigenous' mystics of Nishapur in most complimentary terms but even identifies them, in his introduction, as the highest spiritual achievers and explicitly ranks them, on the grounds that 'their inner [states] leave no traces on their exterior [behaviour]' (*lā yu'aththiru al-bāṭin 'alā'l-ẓāhir*), above the 'people of experiental knowledge', that is, the Sufis.[38] Was Sulamī disingenuous in making this last claim? Or did he simply harbour conflicting loyalties to Sufism and Malāmatiyya that he could not resolve? Neither reading seems realistic. Instead, it appears more plausible to think that Sulamī saw no contradiction between his allegiance to Sufism, whose authoritative figures were overwhelmingly products of the urban culture of Iraq, and his loyalty to the local People of Blame. On the contrary, he viewed the two mystical schools as being identical at their core and proceeded to present their histories in a unified fashion in his voluminous output. In effect, he forged a synthesis of the two in which the Malāmatīs, along with the trend in Baghdad Sufism that most resembled their socially conformist counterparts in Khurāsān, that is the circle of Junayd (as opposed, for instance, to Nūrī), emerged as the clear winners. This is evident in the *Generations of Sufis* where Sulamī manifestly privileges Junayd and his disciples Jurayrī, Shiblī, and Ibn al-Aʿrābī 'through a hierarchic pattern in the ordering of biographies' that are organised into five generations. However, he carefully interlaces his account of Iraq-based Ṣūfiyya with strategically-placed biographies of the Malāmatī masters Abū Ḥafṣ and Ḥamdūn in the first generation, Abū Uthmān in the second, Maḥfūẓ ibn Maḥmūd al-Naysābūrī in the third, Murta'ish, Thaqafī, and 'Abd Allāh ibn Munāzil in the fourth, and his grandfather Ibn Nujayd in the fifth.[39] *Generations of Sufis*, which contains biographies for a total of 103 figures, is, therefore, inclusive of 'generations of People of Blame'. Sulamī follows this same strategy in his work on eighty pious women, where he includes notices on thirty-four women from Iraq and twenty-five from Khurāsān.[40] The extent to which Sulamī fused Sufism and the Malāmatiyya is even more obvious in his short epistle entitled *Kitāb sulūk al-'ārifīn* (*On the Wayfaring of Mystic Knowers*), which also contains revealing information on how Sulamī himself viewed this fusion.

On the Wayfaring of Mystic Knowers opens with a commentary on the Qur'ānic phrase *ūlu'l-'ilm*, 'those who possess knowledge' (Sulamī is discussing Qur'ān 3 (āl 'Imrān): 18). Sulamī classifies these latter into four groups: the first two groups, the 'exotericists', are the people of *ḥadīth* and the jurists, while the other two, the 'esotericists', are the renunciants and the people of realities.[41] The last group, Sulamī writes, 'concentrate singlemindedly on the realities of God's unity, point to the way of singling out God without isolating themselves [from society] and discourse on the meaning of states – they are called the *ṣūfiyya*'. But then, in an interesting move, Sulamī proceeds to declare that there is yet another group of 'knowers':

> these are the knowers of affinity [between God and humanity]. These ... have become one with the One and the Everlasting. They know the meanings of the names of the Real as well as the truths of His attributes. They have seen the invisible realities and have been rendered safe from the concerns of the world of becoming. They have turned to the realities of the Real and have been realised in Him. They have sundered their connections to the creation, have united and joined with the Real and have completely authenticated their affinity with Him. They are the chiefs of the community. It is difficult for others to know their states just as their reports about themselves are not free of ambiguity. Their station has been fortified through authentication of their affinity to the Real and what enters and leaves them [that is, their minds] remains veiled from the people. They are the proof of God in the [different] countries and the shelter of God's servants.[42]

In this description of the highest group (*'ārifūn*) among those who possess knowledge, Sulamī clearly had both the People of Blame and the elite Sufis in mind. This is confirmed by the way he consistently differentiates between the views of the Khurāsānians and Iraqis in the rest of the treatise (which, it turns out, is devoted only to the path of the 'fifth' group of mystic knowers) and yet juxtaposes these views without any attempt to rank them vis-à-vis one another. The clear implication is that, while they have different approaches on many issues, the Khurāsānians and the elite Iraqis form a single group of mystic knowers. Sulamī's method of reconciling his loyalties to the Path of Blame and Sufism was to declare them to be in complete unison with one another, without, however, erasing out their differences. His synthesis proved to be powerful and assured a lasting imprint for the Malāmatī approach within the fabric of Sufi thought and practice in subsequent periods.

Not all of Sulamī's contemporaries shared his concern to synthesise the Path of Blame with Sufism. Abū Sa'd al-Khargūshī (d. 406/1015 or 407/1016), the author of one of the earliest surveys of Sufism entitled *Tahdhīb al-asrār* (*Refining the Secrets [of the Heart]*), devoted one chapter of his seventy-chapter work to the Malāmatīs, where he explicated the differences between them and the Sufis. Khargūshī had the same social background as Sulamī: he was a Shāfiʿī scholar of *ḥadīth* from Nishapur, whose teachers included Ibn Nujayd and Ṣuʿlūkī.[43] Unlike Sulamī who seems to have left his hometown only once to go on pilgrimage, Khargūshī spent possibly up to three decades after about 370 travelling in Iraq, Syria, Palestine, and Egypt and living in Mecca for some time. Once he returned to Nishapur, he founded a school (*madrasa*), a lodge (*khānaqāh*) and a hospital, and he ended his days as a celebrated preacher and teacher. *Refining the Secrets* is one of his three extant works (the other two are a compilation of *ḥadīth* on the topic of prophethood and especially Muḥammad, and a book of dream interpretation, which is one of the oldest extant dream manuals in Arabic), and its exact relationship with other early surveys of Sufism, especially with *Kitāb al-lumaʿ* of Sarrāj (see below), still awaits close scrutiny.[44] Having discussed *taṣawwuf* in his second chapter, which he squarely locates in Iraq, Khargūshī turns his attention to Khurāsān and the Malāmatīs in his third chapter and outlines the differences between Sufism and the Path of Blame in explicit and clear terms:

> One of the differences between the [Malāmatīs] and the Ṣūfiyya is that the principles of the Malāmatīs are built on knowledge while the principles of Sufis on [spiritual] states. The Malāmatīs insist on earning a living, which they prefer, while the Sufis insist on rejecting gainful employment, which they abandon. The Malāmatīs abhor fame through [distinctive] dress and display of patched cloaks, while the Sufis have a propensity for that. And the Malāmatīs reject dance (*raqṣ*), *samāʿ*, and crying out loud as well as feigning/mimicking ecstasy (*tawājud*) [during *samāʿ*] in the manner of the Sufis.[45]

This frank admission of disagreements between the mystics of Nishapur and the mystics of Baghdad suggests that the fusion of these two trends was not as smooth as Sulamī would have us believe, and that their differences likely continued to exist in and after the fourth/tenth century. The rift between the representatives of the two approaches is perhaps visible in their differing attitudes towards the culture of artisanal classes as well as the urban poor, as reflected in the tradition of *futuwwa*.

While the social referents of the concept of 'youngmanliness' that surfaced especially during the fourth/tenth and fifth/eleventh centuries remain elusive, there is little doubt that the concept of *futuwwa* reflected the unmistakably urban phenomenon of young men's corporate associations, whose membership came primarily from artisanal and wage-earning classes as well as the unemployed.[46] Seen in this light, it is telling that the pro-Malāmatī Sulamī who authored the first independent treatise on the Path of Blame also composed the first full-length separate epistle on *futuwwa*, entitled *Kitāb al-futuwwa*. Although Sulamī's account of *futuwwa* is highly spiritualised, it nevertheless bears clear traces of the corporate culture of young men's associations and urban neighbourhoods, and Sulamī's attention to this culture can be construed as evidence of close ties between the Malāmatīs and the urban working classes.[47] Indeed, since the Malāmatīs insisted on earning a living, their teaching contained a clear endorsement of the artisanal work ethic, and, as mentioned in the previous chapter, they probably recruited predominantly from among artisans and wage-earners. Sulamī's pairing of *malāma* and *futuwwa* was, therefore, neither accidental nor surprising.

Other, more 'purist' Sufis were less accommodating than Sulamī towards Malāmatīs and the culture of *futuwwa* associated with them. Al-Qushayrī (d. 465/1072), for instance, a younger but even more eminent representative of the Sufi tradition in Nishapur than Sulamī, who was the architect of a 'pure' Sufism aligned with legal and theological scholarship (discussed below in Chapter 4), did not include a separate treatment of *malāma* in his highly influential *Treatise on Sufism*, even though, following the example of Sulamī, he integrated major Malāmatī figures into the biographical section of his work. On the other hand, he did insert a separate chapter on *futuwwa* into the systematic section of the *Treatise*, where, however, he spiritualised the concept of *futuwwa* by reducing it only to its core, altruistic self-sacrifice.[48] Such an interiorising approach to this concept was not unprecedented in Nishapur: Abu'l-Ḥasan ʿAlī ibn Aḥmad al-Būshanjī (d. 348/959–60), disciple of Ibn ʿAṭā' and Jurayrī, had already interpreted *futuwwa* as altruism and established a Qur'ānic basis for it by linking it to verse 59 [al-Ḥashr]: 9, 'preferring others above themselves'.[49] Nevertheless, in Qushayrī's disregard for *malāma* and his abstract discussion of *futuwwa*, one can see an oblique sign of the rift that separated 'Iraq-oriented' Sufis, who generally maintained a thorough distrust of earning a living and criticised preoccupation with training the lower self as dualism, from the Malāmatīs, who embraced the work ethic of the urban manufacturing and wage-earning classes and viewed constant monitoring of the lower self as the only sure method of spiritual progress. The 'fusion' of these two mystical trends in Nishapur was therefore messier than the testimony of Sulamī alone would suggest.

The Path of Blame was mostly a Nishapur-based phenomenon. Elsewhere in

Khurāsān, the spread of Mesopotamian Sufism did not necessarily take the form of a blending of this latter trend with indigenous mystical approaches; rather it appears to have occurred through importation. It is likely that we owe one of the earliest surviving 'surveys' of Sufism, *Kitāb al-luma' fi'l-taṣawwuf* (*The Book of Light Flashes on Sufism*) of Abū Naṣr 'Abd Allāh ibn 'Alī al-Sarrāj (d. 378/988), to this process of the transplantation of a mystical school that had first taken shape in Iraq to the different cultural environment of Khurāsān. In his introduction, Sarrāj, who was from Ṭūs, observed that there was a clear need for the intelligent people of his time to know the principles of the authentic Sufis so that they could be distinguished from those who resembled them, who dressed like them and who were wrongly called Sufis. According to the author, there had been a surge in the number of those who took up the subject of Sufism, and many had begun to imitate the Sufis, to refer to them often, to answer questions about them, and even to write about them. However, their written work amounted to nothing more than exercises in ostentatious display of verbal ornamentation without any real experiential basis in genuine Sufism, and those who affected knowledge of Sufis in this manner were mostly social and cultural opportunists motivated by expectations of personal gain.[50] It was against this background of increased attention to Sufism, accompanied by widespread uncertainty and misinformation about its 'true' nature, Sarrāj informed his readers, that he set out to capture the authentic thinking and practice of the early Sufi masters in an authoritative documentary survey, which he appropriately titled *The Book of Light Flashes on Sufism.*

With hindsight, Sarrāj appears to have achieved his goal with singular success. He evidently travelled widely in Syria, Iraq and Egypt in order to meet Sufi shaykhs or their students and to collect accurate information about their lives and teachings. For instance, he went to Basṭām to check if ecstatic utterances attributed to Bāyazīd were really his. Even though he was of the opinion that any aspirant to Sufism needed to study with a teacher, Sarrāj himself apparently did not have a close relationship with any single Sufi master, but he struck up a working relationship with prominent representatives of the mystical groups in Baghdad (Ja'far al-Khuldī, the disciple of Junayd, Nūrī, Ruwaym, Jurayrī and the owner of an extensive library on Sufism), Damascus (Abū Bakr Muḥammad ibn Dāwūd al-Duqqī, d. c. 366/977) and Basra (Abu'l-Ḥasan Aḥmad ibn Muḥammad ibn Aḥmad ibn Sālim al-Baṣrī, d. 356/967, of the Tustarī-Sālimiyya school). He managed to gather first-hand information from thirty-nine Sufi authorities on a total of around 200 Sufis.[51] He poured his findings into 157 chapters and organised these chapters into an introduction on the place of Sufism within Islam and thirteen 'books' devoted, in order, to states and stations, adherence to the Qur'ān, following the model of the Prophet, Qur'ān interpretation, companions of the Prophet, Sufi conduct, differences of opinion among Sufis on certain matters, Sufi writings and poetry, audition, ecstasy, miracles, difficult Sufi terminology, ecstatic utterances, and errors associated with Sufism. As is evident from this list, Sarrāj did not shy away from addressing controversial and disputed subjects, nor did he hold back his own opinions. The result was a comprehensive compendium as solid in substance as it was rich in detail.

According to Sarrāj, the Sufis were the only Muslims who truly deserved to be called 'the heirs of the prophets'. He ranked them higher than the traditionalists (*ahl al-ḥadīth*) and the jurists (*fuqahā'*) on the grounds that while all three groups based themselves on the Qur'ān and the Sunna, the first two groups remained content with exoteric knowledge and the Sufis alone possessed applied knowledge of the esoteric realities of faith (significantly, Sarrāj clearly did not consider rationalising theologians or the philosophers as 'knowers', since he did not even refer to them in his discussion of knowledge). All the same, he conceded that some Sufis fell into error (*ghalaṭ*), both minor and major. Among those who committed minor errors, he listed those who thought that wealth was superior to poverty (here, he clearly had in mind the debate on this issue that had raged most forcefully between Ibn 'Aṭā', who was pro-wealth, and Jurayrī, who was against) and those who went to extremes in self-mortification and seclusion. Major errors, which Sarrāj thought amounted to heresy, were numerous, and these included: antinomianism (the belief that service to God was no longer needed after the Sufi attained to God), permissivism (roughly, the belief that all things were permitted unless explicitly prohibited), incarnationism, the belief that one can see God in this world, and belief in the eternity of the individual human spirit.[52]

Sarrāj's willingness to discuss openly the errors of the Sufis as well as heretical departures from Sufism, often seen as an attempt at apologetics, was instead a sure sign of his confidence in the security of the Islamic foundations of Sufism. *The Book of Light Flashes* was no 'apologia, in the strict sense of the term, or ... a purely defensive justification of Ṣūfism, but ... an argued and assured statement of the harmonious integration of mysticism within the bosom of Muslim religious life'.[53] Sarrāj's careful, and by and large remarkably accurate, portrayal of the core elements of Iraq-based Sufism shorn of its 'heretical' excesses was well in line with his goal of presenting a comprehensive overview of Sufi doctrines and practices to Khurāsānian readers largely unfamiliar with this relatively recent and exogenous mystical movement. Sarrāj was most probably not a major Sufi master himself: neither Sulamī, who was clearly highly indebted to *The Book of Light Flashes*, nor Qushayrī included him in their biographical compilations, and the only notice of any students of his, which comes in a source written fully two centuries after his own lifetime and in which Sarrāj himself is erroneously said to be a disciple of Murtaʿish, is not entirely credible.[54] It appears, therefore, that although Sarrāj most likely lived as a Sufi, he was in the first instance a scholar of Sufism rather than a Sufi master, and his masterful survey of *taṣawwuf* earned him an indelible reputation as one of the earliest reliable observers of Sufi history.

The spread of Sufism to Transoxania is difficult to trace, possibly because Sufis could not make much headway into this traditionally heavily Ḥanafī territory, at least not during the fourth/tenth century. Here, mystic thought and practice existed as an intrinsic part of the 'wisdom' (*ḥikma*) tradition, which continued to reign supreme in towns like Samarqand and Bukhārā in this period. In this region, as elsewhere, the Ḥanafī legal school was not theologically unified, but Māturīdiyya, the *kalām* orientation that later developed into the preferred theological affiliation of the majority of Ḥanafīs, was first formulated in Transoxania by Abū Manṣūr Muḥammad ibn Muḥammad al-Māturīdī (d. c. 333/944). Whether this rationalising school, which came to occupy the middle ground between the thoroughly rationalist Mu'tazilīs and the semi-rationalist Ash'arīs (and this latter was itself in its formative stages during the fourth/tenth century), was initially less receptive to Sufi approaches is not clear. However, we do know that Sufism was definitely 'introduced' to the Ḥanafīs in the region, since one of the earliest extant Sufi manuals, *at-Ta'arruf li-madhhab ahl al-taṣawwuf* (*Introducing the Way of the People of Sufism*) was written in Bukhārā by Abū Bakr Muḥammad ibn Ibrāhīm al-Kalābādhī (d. 380s/990s), who was a Ḥanafī traditionist.[55]

Unfortunately, Kalābādhī's biography is obscure, and his extant works (apart from the manual, he also wrote a *ḥadīth* commentary) do not contain significant pointers about the local context. Moreover, even though he quotes from over eighty Sufis, Kalābādhī displays a curiously 'academic' attitude toward his subject in that he does not mention any Sufi authorities who were his contemporaries except for Sarrāj, and he attests to having 'heard' Sufi reports directly from only one figure, Abu'l-Qāsim Fāris ibn 'Īsā Dīnawarī (d. after 340/951), a disciple of Junayd and Ibn 'Aṭā'.[56] Nowhere does he name his own Sufi teachers, nor does he mention by name any of the written sources he used to compile his own account, though his familiarity with Sarrāj's *Book of Flashes* is evident, for instance, in the similarity between the introductions of both works. It is difficult to avoid the impression that Kalābādhī himself had learned Sufism mostly from written sources and that he professed no particular allegiance to any specific living Sufi teacher. After all, representatives of Baghdad Sufism were probably still rare in Transoxania, though they were not completely absent: we know, for instance, that the father of the famous Ḥanbalī Sufi of Herat 'Abd Allāh-i Anṣārī (396/1006–481/1089) – his name was Abū Manṣūr – had spent several years of his youth in Balkh, before the birth of Anṣārī, as a disciple of a Sufi master called Sharīf Ḥamza 'Aqīlī, who also had other Sufi companions.[57] Not beyond the Oxus but still in Central Asia, to the east of Herat, a Sufi from Syria by the name of Abū Isḥāq (d. 329/940–1) who had been a disciple of Mamshād

Dīnawarī (d. 299/912) in Baghdad, had reportedly started what would become a steady Sufi presence in Chisht by converting Abū Aḥmad Abdāl (d. 355/966) to Sufism.[58] No doubt, at least some Sufis were to be found also in Transoxanian towns such as Bukhārā, Samarqand, Tirmidh and Nasaf. Nonetheless, even if they were present, Sufis were clearly not very well known. Indeed, the organisation of Kalābādhī's book, true to the somewhat prosaic and distanced ring of its title, also gives the impression that its author was engaged in an attempt to introduce his readers to a new and foreign subject. After a brief review of the possible meanings of the term Sufi and a listing of well-known Sufis by name in three categories – those who lived in the first two centuries of Islam, those who wrote books on Sufi sciences of symbolic expression (*'ulūm al-ishāra*), and those who wrote on Sufi conduct (*mu'āmalāt*) – Kalābādhī proceeds to a lengthy exposition of the theological views of the Sufis in twenty-nine chapters. In modern scholarship, this section has normally been perceived as an apologetic attempt to prove the mainstream credentials of Sufism brought about by an assumed controversy about the Islamic moorings of Sufi teachings and practices in the wake of the trial and execution of Ḥallāj.[59] Without denying the existence of debate and controversy about some aspects of Sufism from its very inception (after all, there were *no* approaches and orientations in this early phase of Islamic history whose credentials, authenticity, and truth were *not* debated or controversial), it seems more plausible to take Kalābādhī's remarks at their face value when he states in his introduction:

> I have sketched in my book their [that is, the Sufis'] sayings on [God's] unity and attributes as well as other related matters which have raised doubts for those who did not know their way and did not serve their masters. I have unveiled in discursive language what can be so unveiled and described in clear exposition what lent itself to such description so that these may be understood by those who have not understood their allusions and comprehended by those who have not comprehended their expressions. [In this way] accusations [against the Sufis] by slanderers and misinterpretations [of their beliefs] by the ignorant will be refuted, and [this book] will be a guide to those who desire to tread God's path.[60]

Judging by the historical record about Sufis in the fourth/tenth century presented so far, it would be erroneous to assume that Sufis were everywhere burdened by widespread suspicion of 'heresy' and suffered persecution at the hands of political authorities on account of their presumed association with Ḥallāj. On the contrary, in major towns of the 'Abbāsid empire, including Baghdad itself, most Sufis – indeed most mystics (also counting the 'People of Blame' and the 'Sages') – were affiliated with traditionalists and, increasingly as the century progressed, with the semi-rationalist legal schools, particularly Shāfi'iyya, and were thus perceived as 'mainstream', to the extent that it is possible to speak of a mainstream in any given locale. Accordingly, Kalābādhī's primary goal in writing his manual was, in all likelihood, not to exonerate Sufism from unspecified charges whose existence we postulate without any positive evidence but, instead, simply to introduce interested but largely uninformed, and quite possibly misinformed, Transoxanian readers and aspirants to 'genuine' Sufism, naturally 'cleansed' of what Kalābādhī considered misrepresentations and distortions. In an intellectual environment where fundamental theological issues formed the scales of social acceptability, it was entirely natural for a learned author to provide such crucial signposting to his readership at the outset. In brief, it is unjustified to reduce Kalābādhī's attempt to draw theological coordinates for Sufism to mere apologetics.

After the theological orientation, Kalābādhī switches, in the rest of his treatise, to an academic mode of presentation that is entirely composed of the enumeration of Sufi statements about states and stations, special Sufi terminology and Sufi conduct organised into an additional forty-five chapters. Interestingly, when Kalābādhī makes a transition in chapter 31 from his inital theological section to the discussion of 'states', he places Sufism squarely on the secure and familiar foundations first of acquired knowledge, by which he means legal and theological knowledge based on the Qur'ān and the Sunna, and then of *ḥikma*, which he explains as having 'knowledge of the soul and its evils, of the way to train the soul and to refine its traits, of the wiles of the enemy, of the trials of this world, and of the way to guard oneself against them'.[61] He thus builds his survey of Sufism on the familiar ground of the indigenous tradition of *ḥikma* for Transoxanian readers.

To judge by Kalābādhī's manual, therefore, the reading public in Bukhārā in particular and Transoxania in general was not very familiar with Sufism, though there was some interest in the subject, which may have grown out of the pre-existing *ḥikma* approach to the soul. In the absence of reliable and authentic Sufi teachers in the region, Kalābādhī set himself the goal of producing an 'authoritative written guide' to the path, and, in the light of the information available to us today about the early phase of Sufi history, he was remarkably successful in producing an accurate, comprehensive, yet concise manual. It appears that the *Ta'arruf* responded to a real need, since it was translated into Persian within a few decades of its completion by Ismā'īl ibn Muḥammad Mustamlī Bukhārī (d. 434/1043), who also provided a commentary. Later in the fifth/eleventh century the famous Ḥanbalī Sufi of Herat, 'Abd Allāh-i Anṣārī, also wrote a commentary on it. Clearly, Kalābādhī had achieved his goal.

Mystics in al-Andalus?

Although the beginnings of mystical trends in al-Andalus (the parts of Iberia controlled by Muslim rulers) are obscure, it seems safe to date them to 'the period from the final years of the third/ninth century to the second half of the fourth/tenth century'.[62] The figure whose name is inevitably evoked in this connection is Muḥammad ibn ʿAbd Allāh ibn Masarra al-Jabalī (269–319/883–931), who spent a good part of his life in a mountain retreat outside Córdoba engaged in ascetic practices with a group of disciples. There has been significant controversy about the true nature of Ibn Masarra's thought and practice even before the discovery of any of his written works, but close examination of two extant epistles by him suggests that he was primarily a Neoplatonist philosopher who was preoccupied with reconciling philosophy with the Qur'ān. It is true that in one of these two works, *Book of the Properties of Letters, Their True Natures and Their Principles* (*Kitāb khawāṣṣ al-ḥurūf wa-ḥaqā'iqihā wa-uṣūlihā*), on the unconnected letters that appear before certain chapters of the Qur'ān, Ibn Masarra cites from a similarly titled though no longer extant work, the *Kitāb al-ḥurūf*, of Sahl al-Tustarī, yet the text of Ibn Masarra's treatise is squarely philosophical in nature and bears no traces of the profile of Tustarī we know through his extant exegetical statements. The second work, entitled *Book of Reflection* (*Kitāb al-iʿtibār*), is even more clearly based on 'intellection' and far removed from mystical 'reflection' located in the heart by most mystics. Therefore, it is difficult to characterise Ibn Masarra as a mystic on the basis of his known works, and he is perhaps best viewed as an ascetic philosopher who refused to accept juristic knowledge as the only path to salvation and explored alternative ways of attaining knowledge of God that came perilously close to prophecy. It was probably for this last aspect of his practice that he was posthumously condemned by legal scholars in the mid-fourth/tenth century, his books were burned and his disciples were forced to recant his views.[63]

Though Ibn Masarra may not have been a mystic, it is nonetheless certain that there were mystics in al-Andalus during the fourth/tenth century. On the one hand, it appears that aspects of Sufism from Iraq and western Arabia, like many other cultural phenomena from the East, found their way into Iberia and were there adapted to local conditions. On the other hand, indigenous mystical tendencies became increasingly visible as the century progressed. As evidence, however tentative, of the former, one can point to the appearance in al-Andalus of terminology normally associated with Sufism in the east. The word 'Sufi' is used for the first time in the biography of a certain ʿAbd Allāh ibn Naṣr, who died in 315/927.[64] The term subsequently reappears in biographical notices for two eastern 'Sufis' who came to Iberia in the second half of the century (Ibrāhīm ibn ʿAlī ibn Muḥammad al-Daylamī, arrived in 358/968–9, and Aḥmad ibn Muḥammad ibn Ṣāliḥ al-Anṭākī, arrived in 372/982–3) as well as for two Andalusian figures – Saʿīd ibn Ḥamdūn ibn Muḥammad (d. 378/988) and Saʿīd ibn Khalaf (d. 387/997) – even though neither of these two Andalusians was important as a mystic. The expression *taṣawwafa* ('he practised Sufism') is used once, for ʿAlī ibn Mūsā ibn Ziyād al-Lakhmī (d. after 370/980) with no details supplied, and at least one figure trained in the east, ʿAṭiyya ibn Saʿīd (d. 403/1012–13 or 407/1016–17), is said to be of 'the Sufi school' (*madhhab al-ṣūfiyya*).[65] Other terms that could be Sufi-related, such as *abdāl* and *walī*, also occur, but they seem to be used in the generic traditionalist sense to describe people of great piety.[66]

This terminological evidence of eastern Sufism is highly ambigious, but it should be juxtaposed with the much more definite information we possess on the influx of ascetic-mystical ideas from the east, in the form of many Andalusians who studied with Sufi masters in the east. Most remarkable in this connection were the high numbers of Iberian Muslims, no less than sixty-seven, who flocked to the Sufi Abū Saʿīd Aḥmad ibn Muḥammad ibn Ziyād ibn al-Aʿrābī (246/860–341/952–3) in Mecca. This latter was a disciple of Junayd, Nūrī and ʿAmr ibn ʿUthmān. A traditionist who belonged to the Ẓāhirī legal school like the prominent Sufi Ruwaym, Ibn al-Aʿrābī spent his life mostly in Mecca and composed many treatises, only a few of which are extant. His lost works include possibly the very first biographical dictionary on renunciants (*Ṭabaqāt al-nussāk*), the first book on ecstasy (*Kitāb al-wajd*), a book on love (*Ikhtilāf al-nās fi'l-maḥabba*) and a book on 'poverty' (*Sharaf al-faqr*).[67] His better-known Andalusian disciples, at least some of whom no doubt only 'heard' *ḥadīth* from him and did not necessarily absorb his mystical ideas, included: (1) Abū Bakr Muḥammad ibn Saʿdūn al-Tamīmī al-Jazīrī; (2) ʿAṭiyya ibn Saʿīd, mentioned above as a follower of the *madhhab al-ṣūfiyya*; he left Iberia before 400/1009–10 to travel in the East, and he wrote a book defending *samāʿ*; (3) Maslama ibn Qāsim ibn Ibrāhīm ibn ʿAbd Allāh, in turn the teacher of ʿUmar ibn ʿUbādil, described as one of *awliyā' Allāh* in the only use of this phrase in the fourth/tenth century and of Muʿawwidh ibn Dā'ūd, both of whom likely 'belonged to a tendency that was more clearly mytical in nature'; and (4) Ibn ʿAwn Allāh (d. 378/988), who in turn was the teacher of a significant figure, al-Ṭalamankī.[68]

Abū ʿUmar Aḥmad ibn Muḥammad al-Ṭalamankī (d. 428/1036 or 429/1037) is a good example of how eastern Sufi ideas were adapted to local Iberian concerns.[69] He was a Mālikī legal scholar (*faqīh*) interested in jurisprudence (*uṣūl al-fiqh*), which was newly introduced to al-Andalus, as well as in non-rationalist theology (*uṣūl al-diyānāt*); at the same time, he was a *sharīʿa*-abiding mystic. Apart from Ibn ʿAwn Allāh, he had studied Sufism with the Mālikī Meccan Sufi Abū Ḥasan ʿAlī ibn ʿAbd Allāh ibn al-Ḥasan ibn al-Jahḍam al-Hamadhānī (d. 414/1023), himself a student of Khuldī and also linked through intermediaries with the Mālikī Shiblī as well as Tustarī.[70] Along with the prominent Mālikī jurisprudent and Ashʿarī theologian al-Bāqillānī (d. 403/1013), Ibn al-Jahḍam was a major participant in a debate about the miracles of the friends of God (*karāmāt al-awliyā'*) that raged among Mālikī scholars across the Middle East, North Africa and al-Andalus: al-Bāqillānī in Baghdad, Ibn al-Jahḍam in

Mecca, and Ibn ʿAwn Allāh in Iberia defended such miracles, while Ibn Abī Zayd (d. 386/996) of Qayrawān denied them. Following in the footsteps of his teachers Ibn al-Jahḍam and Ibn ʿAwn Allāh, al-Ṭalamankī also wrote a treatise in defence of miracles of friends against Ibn Abī Zayd, thereby clearly signalling the growing connectedness of al-Andalus with the theological and mystical concerns of North Africa and the East. The issue of *karāmāt* was, among other things, one clear testing ground for differing notions of authority that could be used to assign even political power to the friends of God as legitimate leaders (*imām*) of the Muslim community, and it is possible that al-Ṭalamankī held a 'dangerous' view of the imamate, that is, 'the imam should be the most excellent Muslim, thus freeing the caliphal insitution from the ties of genealogy'.[71] This would partially explain why he was accused of 'opposing the example of the Prophet Muḥammad' (*khilāf al-sunna*) and of Khārijism in Zaragoza in 425/1034, but since he was acquitted by the *qāḍī* after defending himself against the charges, the issue of the imamate must not have been on the surface. Al-Ṭalamankī died in Talamanca in a *ribāṭ*, but he may have set a precedent for the path of mystic thought taken by the later figures Ibn Barrajān and Ibn Qasī on the imamate issue.[72]

Concomitant with the increase in signs of familiarity with eastern mystical ideas during the fourth/tenth century, there may have been a turn towards markedly mystical ideas and practices among Andalusian renunciants. Renunciation (*zuhd*) as a mode of piety had roots going back to the earliest phase of Muslim presence in the peninsula, and it flourished in the fourth/tenth century. The chief characteristics of *zuhd* in this period were persistence in prayer, *dhikr*, and Qur'ān recitation; emphasis on giving of alms and extended fasting; service to others; cultivation of sermons and public readings; abstention from public manifestation of piety in the form of avoiding public authorities; and concealing one's virtues, which reminds one of the Malāmatiyya. Biographical notices, which form the principal sources for information of renunciants, do not contain references to miracles, but they often use the expression 'those whose petitions are answered'(*mujāb al-daʿwa*). Admittedly, however, our information on the renunciants is sketchy, and none of these features definitely points to the existence of mystical trends behind the facade of renunciation.[73] Back in the Islamic east, however, Sufism was developing into a literary and social tradition.

Notes

1 For instance, Gramlich, *Abu l-ʿAbbās b. ʿAṭā'*, Introduction, 4–8 on Ibn ʿAṭā' versus Junayd and Jurayrī. For further documentation of diverse views among early Sufis, see Meier, *Abū Saʿīd*, 1–18.

2 Ibn Khafīf's biography is extant only in a Persian translation of the Arabic original made by Ibn Junayd-i Shīrāzī in the early eighth/fourteenth century: Abu'l-Ḥasan

'Alī ibn Muḥammad Daylamī, *Sīrat al-Shaykh al-Kabīr Abū 'Abd Allāh ibn al-Khafīf al-Shīrāzī*, ed. Annemarie Schimmel (Tehran: Intishārāt-i Bābak, 1984) (including Ibn Khafīf's *al-Mu'taqad al-ṣaghīr* and his *Waṣiyya*); on Daylamī, see 'Deylamī, Abu'l-Ḥasan 'Alī', EIr 7: 338–9 (Gerhard Böwering). The following discussion on Ibn Khafīf is based mostly on Sobieroj, *Ibn Ḫafīf*; other than Ibn Khafīf's *vita*, and *Kitāb al-iqtiṣād*, Sobieroj uses his statements in Sulamī's *Ḥaqā'iq al-tafsīr* and excerpts from his large *'Aqīda* (not extant) found in Ibn Taymiyya's *Fatwā'l-Ḥamawiyya*. Two other works of Ibn Khafīf, extant only in later Persian translations of the original Arabic (these were apparently not available to Sobieroj) are edited in Fāṭima 'Alāqa, 'Risāla-i "Faḍl al-taṣawwuf 'alā'l-madhāhib" ta'līf-i Abū 'Abd Allāh Muḥammad ibn Khafīf', *Ma'ārif* 15, no.1–2 (1998): 51–80, and Fāṭima 'Alāqa, 'Risāla-i "Sharaf al-fuqarā" ta'līf-i Abū 'Abd Allāh Muḥammad ibn Khafīf', *Ma'ārif* 16, no. 1 (1999): 98–132 (these are nos 18 and 15, respectively, in the list of Ibn Khafīf's works given in Sobieroj, 305–12).

3 See Daylamī, *Sīrat*, 93–103. Earlier scholars who viewed Ibn Khafīf as a 'Ḥallājian' include Massignon, Vadet, and Schimmel.

4 Böwering, *Mystical Vision*, 93–4, and Sobieroj, *Ibn Ḫafīf*, 137.

5 Sobieroj, *Ibn Ḫafīf*, 173–5; Daylamī, *Treatise*, xxxvi–xl (translator's introduction).

6 Sobieroj, *Ibn Ḫafīf*, 243–8 (cf. 496 of summary in English), and Sobieroj, 'Mu'tazila and Sufism', 77–81. Even though Sobieroj appears more sanguine about Ibn Khafīf's attitude toward Ash'ariyya in the article, the evidence he assembled in his book on Ibn Khafīf's traditionalist stance is decisive; cf. Daylamī, *Treatise*, xxx–xxxiv.

7 For the earlier views, see for instance 'Ibn Khafīf', EI 3: 823–4 (Jean-Claude Vadet).

8 On al-Nakhshabī, see Gramlich, *Alte Vorbilder*, 1: 325–44.

9 Sobieroj, *Ibn Ḫafīf*, 111–26; sources on al-Bannā' and 'Alī ibn Sahl are listed in Naṣr Allāh Pūrjavādī, 'Abū Manṣūr-i Iṣfahānī: Ṣūfī-i Ḥanbalī', *Ma'ārif* 6, no. 1–2 (1989): 67–8, notes 110 and 117, respectively.

10 On Sufism in Shiraz during the fourth century, see Sobieroj, *Ibn Ḫafīf*, 152–84. The report about the number of Sufis, including women, in the town is from al-Tanūkhī's (329–84/941–94), *Nishwār al-muḥāḍara*, ed. 'Abbūd al-Shalijī (Cairo, 1392/1972) 3: 227ff; a passage from this section is translated in full in Sobieroj, 'Mu'tazila and Sufism', 79–80. Tanūkhī's report is corroborated by that of Abū 'Abd Allah Muḥammad ibn Aḥmad al-Maqdisī (less likely, al-Muqaddasī)'s in his *Aḥsan al-taqāsīm* (completed in Shiraz in 375/985), ed. de Goeje (Leiden, 1906), 439. He wrote that in Shiraz 'Sufis were numerous, performing the *dhikr* (*yukabbir*) in their mosques after the Friday prayer and reciting blessings on the Prophet from the pulpit', quoted in J. Spencer Trimingham, *The Sufi Orders in Islam* (Oxford: Oxford University Press, 1998), 6. A prominent female companion of Ibn Khafīf named al-Wahaṭiyya Umm al-Faḍl is included in Sulamī, *Early Sufi Women*, 226–9.

11 Sobieroj, *Ibn Ḫafīf*, 67–77 and 128–34. On metics in Mecca, see 'Mudjāwir', EI, 7: 293 (Werner Ende). Cf. the report from Kattānī in Sarrāj, *Luma'*, 185 / *Schlagrichter*, 285 (72.5) about some 300 *shaykhs* and *fuqarā'* living in the same place in Mecca (Gramlich inadvertently renders this number as 3,000); Laury Silvers-Alario, 'The teaching relationship in early Sufism: a reassessment of Fritz Meier's definition of the *shaykh al-tarbiya* and the *shaykh al-ta'līm*', *Muslim World* 93 (2003): 89 assumes that these were all Sufis, but many must have been renunciants with no intimate

connections to Iraqi Sufism.

12 The close relationship among the lodges in Fars (Bayḍā, Kāzarūn and Shīrāz) is documented in Florian Sobieroj, 'Mittelsleute zwischen Ibn Khafīf und Abū Isḥāq al-Kāzarūnī', *Asiatische Studien / Études Asiatiques* 51 (1997): 651–71.

13 Sobieroj, *Ibn Ḫafīf*, 111–210. For the report on Sufis in Sūs, from Maqdisī's *Aḥsan al-taqāsīm*, see Trimingham, *Sufi Orders*, 7.

14 Muḥammad ibn 'Abd al-Jabbār Niffarī, *The Mawāqif and Mukhāṭabāt of Muḥammad Ibn 'Abdi 'l-Jabbār al-Niffarī*, Arthur J. Arberry (London: Luzac & Co., 1935), in Arabic and English translation. Other writings by Niffarī are edited in Paul Nwyia, *Trois oeuvres inédites de mystiques musulmans/Nuṣūṣ ṣūfiyya ghayr manshūra* (Beirut: Dār al-Mashriq, 1973), 191–324.

15 The quotes are from Sells, *Early Islamic Mysticism*, 282 and 283, respectively; this book includes fresh translations of six 'standings', 284–301.

16 The quote, from Standing 67, is from Sells, *Early Islamic Mysticism*, 292.

17 For further consideration of Niffarī, see Arberry's introduction in Niffarī, *Mawāqif and Mukhāṭabāt*, 1–26; and Nwyia, *Exégèse coranique*, 348–407. Two 'standings' are analysed, respectively, in Michael A. Sells, 'Bewildered tongue: the semantics of mystical union in Islam', in *Mystical Union and Monotheistic Faith: An Ecumenical Dialogue*, ed. Moshe Idel and Bernard McGinn (New York: Macmillan, 1989), 108–15, and Renard, *Knowledge of God*, 27–8.

18 The Sufi sources include, most notably, the many works of the prominent Sufi historian of Khurāsān, Abū 'Abd al-Raḥmān al-Sulamī (d. 412/1021), in particular his biographical dictionary *Ṭabaqāt al-ṣūfiyya* and his account of the Path of Blame, *Risālat al-malāmatiyya*, as well as Abū Naṣr al-Sarrāj's *Kitāb al-luma'*. The most significant non-Sufi sources are *Ta'rīkh Naysābūr* of al-Ḥākim al-Naysābūrī (d. 405/1015) and its continuation *al-Siyāq li-ta'rīkh Naysābūr* by 'Abd al-Ghāfir al-Fārisī (d. 529/1135) – these last two form the basis for Richard Bulliet, *The Patricians of Nishapur: A Study in Medieval Islamic Social History* (Cambridge, MA: Harvard University Press, 1972).

19 The numbers are culled from *Ta'rīh Naysābūr* by Jacqueline Chabbi, 'Remarques sur le développement historique des mouvements ascétiques et mystiques au Khurāsān', *Studia Islamica* 46 (1977): 29–38 and 64; for a table that presents the same information in a slightly different manner, see Bulliet, *Patricians*, 41.

20 See Gramlich, *Alte Vorbilder*, 2: 267, who proffers Wāsiṭī's exchange of letters with his teacher Junayd (d. 298/910) as evidence of his move to Khurāsān already before Junayd's death. Chabbi, 'Remarques', 62–3, also 32–3, thinks that Wāsiṭī's arrival in Nishapur and hence to Khurāsān should be dated after the death of Ḥīrī, also in 298/910, on the basis of a conversation that Wāsiṭī had with this latter's disciples. Gramlich's reasoning seems preferable. It is worth mentioning here that Wāsiṭī had family connections in Transoxania: his father was from the town Farghānā, and Wāsiṭī was thus known as Ibn al-Farghānī. For a full discussion of this Sufi, see Gramlich, *Alte Vorbilder*, 2: 267–411, and Laury Silvers-Alario, 'Tawḥīd in early Sufism: the life and work of Abū Bakr al-Wāsiṭī (d. c. 320/932)' (PhD dissertation, SUNY Stony Brook, 2002); I have not seen this work. On Abū Hamza al-Khurāsānī, see 'Abū Ḥamza K̲orāsānī', EIr 1: 295 (B. Reinert).

21 On Sayyārī, see Gramlich, *Alte Vorbilder*, 2: 413–50; on the community around him, see Hujwīrī, *Kashf*, 323–33/ *Revelation*, 251–2.

22 'Abū Esḥāq Šāmī', EIr 1: 280 (Mutiul Imam), and 'Abdāl Češtī', EIr 1: 175 (Mutiul Imam).

23 Cf. Knysh, *Short History*, 100, who sceptically notes Massignon's view that Sufi émigrés to Khurāsān were most likely fleeing the 'persecution' of Sufis in the wake of Ḥallāj's execution. This view was apparently accepted by Chabbi (for instance, Jacqueline Chabbi, 'Réflexions sur le soufisme iranien primitif', *Journal Asiatique* 266 [1978]: 46 with reference to Wāsiṭī whom she, again following Massignon, erroneously makes into a 'Ḥallājian'), but Knysh's scepticism is justified, since there is no real evidence in favour of Massignon's speculation.

24 This confluence of Sufism and Malāmatiyya is documented by Christopher Melchert, 'Sufis and competing movements in Nishapur', *Iran* 39 (2001): 239–40, who lists known disciples of Ḥīrī; the term 'fusion' is Melchert's. Cf. Chabbi, 'Remarques', 41, note 1; Sviri, 'Ḥakīm Tirmidhī', 599; and Knysh, *Short History*, 96, who sees a 'rapprochement between the Sufi and Malāmatī traditions' already in Ḥīrī's teachings. On Mu'ammil, a student of Ḥīrī who corresponded with Junayd and 'Ali ibn Sahl in Isfahan, see Sobieroj, *Ibn Ḫafīf*, 158.

25 Meier, 'Khurāsān', 215–17.

26 Knysh, *Short History*, 97; Melchert, 'Competing movements', 239.

27 The case for rivalry between Malāmatiyya and Karrāmiyya is made most effectively by Chabbi, 'Remarques', 46–59 and is elaborated by Melchert, 'Competing movements', 240–1; also see Sviri, 'Ḥakīm Tirmidhī', 599–602. For legal affiliations, see Melchert, 'Competing movements', 242–3; the school of Sufyān al-Thawrī is attested only for Ḥamdūn al-Qaṣṣār.

28 On the Sufi 'silence' on Karrāmiyya, see Chabbi, 'Remarques', 67ff.

29 Bulliet, *Patricians*, 28–46, and Melchert, 'Competing movements', 243, with an evaluation of Bulliet's views on the subject. For a quick overview on the spread of Shāfi'īsm to Iran in general, see Wilferd Madelung, *Religious Trends in Early Islamic Iran* (Albany: Persian Heritage Foundation, 1988), 27, based on H. Halm, *Die Ausbreitung der šāfi'itischen Rechtsschule von den Anfängen bis zum 8./14. Jahrhundert* (Wiesbaden, 1974), 15–154.

30 Margaret Malamud, 'Sufi organizations and structures of authority in medieval Nishapur', *International Journal of Middle East Studies* 26 (1994): 427–42, argues 'that the spread of Sufism was linked to its connection with the Shāfi'ī *madhhab*', (429).

31 The 'afterlife' of Malāmatīs is discussed further in Chapter 6.

32 The dates are from Shams al-Dīn Muḥammad al-Dhahabī (d. 748/1374), *Siyar a'lām al-nubalā'*, ed. Shu'ayb al-Arna'ūt et al. (Beirut, 1996), 17: 247–55, as reported by Rkia Elaroui Cornell in Sulamī, *Early Sufi Women*, 31 (introduction); Dhahabī reproduces information supplied directly by Sulamī's personal secretary al-Khashshāb (d. 456/1054).

33 On Ibn Nujayd, see Sulamī, *Ṭabaqāt*, 454–7. The term *duwayra* is from al-Khaṭīb al-Baghdādī's *Ta'rīkh Baghdād* (Medina print, 2: 248), as quoted by Pūrjavādī in Abū 'Abd al-Raḥmān Muḥammad ibn al-Ḥusayn Sulamī, *Majmū'a-i āṯār-i Abū 'Abd al-Raḥmān Sulamī* (Tehran: Markaz-i Nashr-i Dānishgāhī, 1369–72), ix and in Massignon, *Passion*, 2: 210.

34 See Böwering, 'Qur'ān commentary', 44, note 6, who relies on Subkī, *Ṭabaqāt* (Cairo, 1324/1906–7, 3: 61 and Dhahabī, *Siyar* (Beirut, 1403/1983), 17: 251). Bulliet, *Patricians*, 115–17 does not give any information on this issue, except to note that

Sulamī was one of Ṣu'lūkī's students sometime between 337/949 and 369/980 when Ṣu'lūkī lived and taught in Nishapur. In the *Ṭabaqāt*, 344, Sulamī himself mentions Ṣu'lūkī by name only once – and in passing – in reporting on Shiblī, which seems odd treatment for one's master in Sufism! Contrary to Böwering (and Massignon, *Passion*, 2: 210), Ṣu'lūkī did not belong to the Ḥanafī legal school, but was called al-Ḥanafī because he was descended from Banū Ḥanīfa; see Bulliet, *Patricians*, 115. This point is also noted by Rkia Cornell in Sulamī, *Early Sufi Women*, 33, note 56. On Ṣu'lūkī's Sufi affiliations, see Melchert, 'Competing movements', 240 and 245, note 60, citing from Dhahabī's *Ta'rīkh al-islām*.

35 The earliest source for an alleged conferral of a robe by Naṣrābādhī to Sulamī appears to be Muḥammad ibn Munavvar, *Asrār al-tawḥīd fī maqāmāt al-Shaykh Abī Sa'īd*, ed. Muḥammad Rižā Shafī'ī-Kadkanī (Tehran: Mu'assasa-i Intishārāt-i Āgāh, 1366/1987), 1: 32 / *The Secrets of God's Mystical Oneness*, trans. John O'Kane (Costa Mesa, CA: Mazda Publishers, 1992), 100, who mentions this in connection with his claim that Sulamī supposedly bestowed a robe on Abū Sa'īd. But ibn Munavvar seems to have been too liberal about documenting Sufi lineages for Abū Sa'īd, and Sulamī himself does not appear to include the latter in any of his works (certainly not in his *Generations*); see Meier, *Abū Sa'īd*, 45 for doubts about this event. According to Bulliet, *Patricians*, 150, Naṣrābādhī resided in Nishapur from 340/951 to 365/976. Citing Bulliet, 115–16 and 150, as well as Gramlich, *Alte Vorbilder*, 1: 516 on Naṣrābādhī (and this latter is the best listing of primary sources on Naṣrābādhī), Knysh, *Short History*, 125 says this event occurred around 340/951, but this date would mean that Sulamī was ten or fifteen years old at the time. Sulamī himself is silent on this issue in his entry on Naṣrābādhī: Sulamī, *Ṭabaqāt*, 484–8, though various citations in the *Generations* make it clear that he certainly 'heard' from Naṣrābādhī, whom he is also supposed to have accompanied on pilgrimage to Mecca. Yet in his notices on women, he does not refrain from reporting that a woman by the name Umm al-Ḥusayn al-Qurayshiyya, who used to attend Naṣrābādhī's lectures, reproached this latter, saying 'How fine are your words and how ugly are your morals!' See Sulamī, *Early Sufi Women*, 224, also 34, where two other women are also named in this connection.

36 On Sulamī's works, see 'al-Sulamī, Abū 'Abd al-Raḥmān', EI 9: 811b (Gerhard Böwering). In the introduction to her edition and translation of *A Memorial of Female Sufis Devotees*, Rkia Cornell, relying on Dhahabī's *Siyar*, reports that 700 works were attributed to Sulamī by his secretary al-Khashshāb: Sulamī, *Early Sufi Women*, 38; these included a lost work entitled *Brothers and Sisters among the Sufis* (ibid., p. 39). The *Generations* was most recently studied by Mojaddedi, *Biographical Tradition*, 9–39. An up-to-date bibliography of studies on the *Truths of Qur'ānic Exegesis* (and on Sufi Qur'ān interpretation in general) appears in Mohammed Rustom, 'Forms of Gnosis in Sulamī's Sufi Exegesis of the *Fātiḥa*', *Islam and Christian-Muslim Relations* 16, no. 4 (2005): 327–44; I owe thanks to Mr Rustom for bringing this article to my attention by sending me an offprint of it. On Sufi Qur'ān exegesis, see also Sands, *Sufi Commentaries*, and 'Ṣūfism and the Qur'ān', *Encyclopaedia of the Qur'ān*, 5: 137–59 (Alexander D. Knysh).

37 On Ibn Bākūya, see 'Bābā Kūhī', EIr 2: 293–4 (M. Kasheff) and Sobieroj, *Ibn Ḫafīf*, 225–6; perhaps a Ḥanbalī, he was the author of a collection on Ḥallāj, which is extant, and another lost book entitled *Kitāb maqāmāt al-mashāyikh*, one of the main

sources used by Ibn al-Jawzī in his *Talbīs Iblīs*. Sulamī himself apparently also met Ibn Khafīf and received a written 'authorisation' (*ijāza*) to transmit reports from him; see Sobieroj, *Ibn Ḫafīf*, 214–15. He may have also taught Abū'l-Qāsim al-Qushayrī (465/1072), the author of one of the most celebrated Sufi manuals of all time, but this latter's primary Sufi teacher was Abū 'Alī al-Daqqāq (d. 405/1015), a disciple of Naṣrābādhī. Qushayrī possibly associated with Sulamī after the death of Daqqāq; see Bulliet, *Patricians*, 152, who relies on Subkī.

38 See Sulamī, *Malāmatiyya*, 87. Honerkamp, in Sulamī and al-Ḥakīm al-Tirmidhī, *Three Early Sufi Texts*, 104–5, sums up the discussion of Sulamī well: 'In this treatise, Sulamī places the Malāmatīya at the summit of the spiritual hierarchy. In his introduction he divides the spiritual aspirants into three basic groups: the exoterists (*ahl al-ẓāhir*) or scholars of the law (*'ulamā' al-sharī'a*), the Sufis or people of gnosis (*ahl al-ma'rifa*) and the Malāmatīya, in ascending order.'

39 On Sulamī's privileging of Baghdad Sufism, see also Mojaddedi, *Biographical Tradition*, 14–15; the quote is from p. 17. On 'Abd Allāh ibn Munāzil, who was the 'premier' disciple of Ḥamdūn, see Gramlich, *Alte Vorbilder*, 2: 169–74.

40 See Rkia Cornell's comments in Sulamī, *Early Sufi Women*, 48.

41 In making such classifications, Sulamī was no doubt drawing upon existing precedents supplied by earlier Sufis. Ibn Khafīf, for instance, divides those who follow the Sunna into *ḥadīth*-experts, legalists, and Sufis; see 'Alāqa, 'Faḍl al-Taṣawwuf', 54.

42 Abū 'Abd al-Raḥmān Muḥammad ibn al-Ḥusayn Sulamī, *Tasavvufun Ana İlkeleri: Sülemī'nin Risaleleri*, ed. and trans. Süleyman Ateş (Ankara: Ankara Üniversitesi Basımevi, 1981), Arabic, 155–69 (Turkish, 122–41); the quote is from Arabic, 156 (Turkish, 123).

43 On his biography and works, see Aḥmad Ṭāhirī-'Irāqī, 'Abū Sa'd-i Khargūshī', *Ma'ārif* 15, no 3 (1999): 5–33, which supersedes both 'al-Khargūshī', EI 4: 1074a (A. J. Arberry) and Arthur J. Arberry, 'Khargūshī's manual of Sufism', *Bulletin of the School of Oriental and African Studies* 19 (1938): 345–9.

44 For a discussion of Kharghūshī's dream book, which is noteworthy for its inclusion of the dreams of some Sufis, see John C. Lamoreaux, *The Early Muslim Tradition of Dream Interpretation* (Albany: State University of New York Press, 2002), 64–9, 76–7 and 170–1.

45 Pūrjavādī, 'Manba'ī kuhan', 34. As Pūrjavādī demonstrates in this article, Sulamī most likely used Khargūshī's work in composing his own treatise on the Malāmatīs. For an example of loud cries during *samā'* already at the time of Junayd, which he frowned upon, see Sarrāj, *Luma'*, 285 / *Schlaglichter*, 412 (101.1).

46 'Futuwwa', EI 2: 961a-965a (C. Cahen–F. Taeschner), 'pre-Mongol' section.

47 Sulamī, *Futuwwa*, 8–34 (Arabic), 22–36 (Turkish); these traces need to be fleshed out in a separate study.

48 Qushayrī, *Risāla*, 472–9 / *Sendschreiben*, 319–25 (33.1–14).

49 'Fūshanjī, 'Alī ibn Aḥmad Heravī', EIr 10: 230–1 (G. Böwering).

50 Sarrāj, *Luma'*, 1–4; *Schlaglichter*, 35–7 (0.1–6). The lacuna in the Arabic text edited by Nicholson (but included in Gramlich's German translation, chapters 132–7) was published by A. J. Arberry as *Pages from the Kitāb al-Luma' of Abū Naṣr al-Sarrāj* (London, 1947).

51 These figures are listed by Nicholson in Sarrāj, *Luma'*, xiii–xxii. For Sarrāj's opinion on studying with a teacher, see ibid., 410 and 417 / *Schlaglichter*, 573 (139.3) and

581 (143.1). As Gramlich observes in his introduction (p. 15), later reports that he may have studied with Murta'ish do not ring right; see, for instance, Muḥammad ibn Munavvar, *Asrār*, 1: 26 / *Secrets*, 91.

52 Sarrāj's catalogue of the errors of Sufis was later reproduced as a close but abbreviated paraphrase by Sulamī without acknowledgement: Abū 'Abd al-Raḥmān Muḥammad ibn al-Ḥusayn Sulamī, *Uṣūl al-malāmatiyya wa ghalaṭāt al-ṣūfiyya*, ed. 'Abd al-Fattāḥ Aḥmad al-Fāwī Maḥmūd (Cairo: Jāmi'a al-Qāhira, 1405/1980), 175–99. The characterisation of Sulamī's work as 'plagiarism' in Arthur J. Arberry, 'Did Sulamī plagiarize Sarrāj?', *Journal of the Royal Asiatic Society* (1937): 461–62 is rightly characterised as inappropriate by Jawad Qureshi in his masters thesis 'The book of errors: a critical edition and study of *Kitāb al-Aghālīṭ* by Abū 'Abd Al-Raḥmān Al-Sulamī' (University of Georgia, Athens, 2002); I have not seen the edition itself.

53 'Sarrāj, Abū Naṣr 'Abd Allāh b. Alī', EI 9: 95b (P. Lory). For an example of the interpretation of *The Book of Light Flashes* as apologetics, see, most recently, Knysh, *Short History*, 118–20.

54 Muḥammad ibn Munavvar, *Asrār*, 1: 26 / *Secrets*, 91, claims that Abu'l-Faḍl-i Sarakhsī (d. after 388/998), who was the first teacher of Abū Sa'īd-i Abū'l-Khayr, was a disciple of Sarrāj; on Abu'l-Faḍl, see Meier, *Abū Sa'īd*, 42–4. It is telling in this connection that even though the most important direct transmitter from Sarrāj was Sulamī and via this latter Qushayrī, Sulamī did not transmit Sarrāj's own views.

55 For a concise but up-to-date account on him, see 'Abū Bakr Kalābāḏī', EIr 1: 262–3 (W. Madelung). It is worth remembering here that Tirmidhī was a Ḥanafī.

56 On Faris, see Chabbi, 'Réflexions', 45, note 25, and 49, notes 45 and 46; also Massignon, *Passion*, 2: 198–202.

57 "Abdallāh al-Anṣārī al-Heravī', EIr 1: 187 (S. de Laugier de Beaurecueil); this figure is mentioned in Anṣārī's *Generations*, see English selection in Farhādī, *Anṣārī*, 54.

58 'Abū Esḥāq Šāmī', EIr 1: 280 (Mutiul Imam); 'Abdāl Češtī', EIr 1: 175 (Mutiul Imam); 'Češtīya', EIr 3: 333 (G. Böwering).

59 For instance, Arberry's introduction to his translation of the *Ta'arruf*, Kalābādhī, *Ta'arruf*, xiv–xv; Chabbi, 'Réflexions'; and Knysh, *Short History*, 123.

60 Kalābādhī, *Ta'arruf*, 7; cf. *Doctrine*, 3–4.

61 Kalābādhī, *Ta'arruf*, 99; cf. *Doctrine*, 75.

62 Manuela Marín, 'Muslim religious practices in al-Andalus', in *The Legacy of Muslim Spain*, ed. Salma Khadra Jayyusi (Leiden: Brill, 1994), 890.

63 The earliest full-length study of Ibn Masarra is Miguel Asín Palacios, *The Mystical Philosophy of Ibn Masarra and His Followers*, trans. Elmer H. Douglas (Leiden: Brill, 1978), originally published in Spanish in 1914. His two extant works are published in Muḥammad Kamāl Ibrāhīm Ja'far, *Min qaḍāyā al-fikr al-islāmī: dirāsah wa-nuṣūṣ* (Cairo: Maktaba Dār al-'Ulūm, 1978), 310–60, and are examined in Emilio Tornero, 'A report on the publication of previously unedited works of Ibn Masarra', in *The Formation of al-Andalus, Part 2: Language, Religion, Culture and the Sciences*, ed. Maribel Fierro and Julio Samso (Aldershot: Ashgate, 1998), 133–49. For a different reading of Ibn Masarra's philosophical views, see Lenn E. Goodman, 'Ibn Masarrah', in *History of Islamic Philosophy*, ed. Seyyed Hossein Nasr and Oliver Leaman (London: Routledge, 1996), 277–93. Addas makes an unpersuasive attempt to portray him as a Sufi; see Claude Addas, 'Andalusī mysticism and the rise of Ibn 'Arabī', in *The Legacy of Muslim Spain*, ed. Salma Khadra Jayyusi (Leiden: Brill, 1994), 912–18. Marín too,

in Marín, 'Religious practices', 390, sees 'a strong mystical component in the traces we have [of Ibn Masarra's thought]' but offers no details. On Tustarī's *Book of Letters*, see Böwering, *Mystical Vision*, 17–18. For the charges of heresy against Ibn Masarra and his followers who continued to be active well into the fifth/eleventh century, see María Isabel Fierro, 'Accusations of *zandaqa* in al-Andalus', *Quaderni di Studi Arabi* 5–6 (1987–8): 251–8, esp. 255–6, and Maribel Fierro, 'Opposition to Sufism in al-Andalus', in *Islamic Mysticism Contested: Thirteen Centuries of Controversies and Polemics*, ed. F. de Jong and Bernd Radtke (Leiden: Brill, 1999), 178–84. On Ibn Masarra's 'ascetic opposition to the clergy', see Dominique Urvoy, 'The *'Ulamā'* of al-Andalus', in *The Legacy of Muslim Spain*, ed. Salma Khadra Jayyusi (Leiden: Brill, 1994), 856.

64 Asín Palacios, *Mystical Philosophy*, 160, note 17; also noted by Manuela Marín, 'Zuhhād of al-Andalus (300/912–420/1029)', in *The Formation of al-Andalus, Part 2: Language, Religion, Culture and the Sciences*, ed. Maribel Fierro and Julio Samso (Aldershot: Ashgate, 1998), 105; also see Marín, 'Religious practices', 890.

65 Marín, 'Zuhhād', 105–6.

66 On *abdāl*, see Marín, 'Zuhhād', 106–7; the term *walī* was first used for Muḥammad ibn 'Isā ibn Hilāl al-Qurṭubi in the fourth/tenth century (*walī li'llāh min al-zuhhād*) but in an eastern source, see Maribel Fierro, 'The polemic about the *karāmāt al-awliyā'* and the development of Ṣūfism in al-Andalus (fourth/tenth-fifth/eleventh centuries)', *Bulletin of the School of Oriental and African Studies* 55 (1992): 237.

67 Sezgin, *Geschichte*, 1: 660–1; Manuela Marín, 'Abū Sa'īd Ibn al-A'rābī et le développement du ṣūfisme dans al-Andalus', *Revue du monde musulman et la Méditerranée* 63–4 (1992): 28–38; Sobieroj, *Ibn Ḫafīf*, 130. His book on ecstacy is quoted in Sarrāj, *Luma'*, 308, 5; 310, 1; 313, 6ff; 314, 17. His book on love was a major source for *Kitāb 'aṭf al-alif al-ma'lūf* of Daylamī, the disciple of Ibn Khafīf who wrote his master's biography; see Daylamī, *Treatise*, 77–83 (ch. 7). His biographical dictionary was used by later writers like Sulamī, Abū Nu'aym, and Dhahabī.

68 For these figures, see Marín, 'Ibn al-A'rābī', and Marín, 'Zuhhād', 127–9; and, for Ibn 'Awn Allāh, see Fierro, 'Polemic', 239, note 25. Marín, ibid., 129, thinks that 'Aṭiyya ibn Sa'īd clearly did not belong 'to an Andalusī tradition'. For 'Umar ibn 'Ubādil and Mu'awwidh ibn Dā'ūd, see Marín, 'Zuhhād', 116 and 128 (quote from this last page).

69 Sources on him are listed in Fierro, 'Polemic', 239, note 26, and in 'al-Ṭalamankī', EI 10: 158b (Maribel Fierro).

70 For Ibn al-Jahḍam, see Sobieroj, *Ibn Ḫafīf*, 133–4.

71 Fierro, 'Polemic', 248.

72 Fierro, 'Polemic', 249; 'al-Ṭalamankī', EI, 10: 158b (Maribel Fierro). Also Vincent J. Cornell, *Realm of the Saint: Power and Authority in Moroccan Sufism* (Austin: University of Texas Press, 1998), 15–16, where, on the basis of information found in Ibn Bashkuwāl (d. 578/1183), *Kitāb al-ṣila fī tārīkh a'immat al-andalus wa 'ulamā'ihim* ... (Cairo, 1955), 48–9, he is said to have studied with the Egyptian mystic Abū'l-Faḍl al-Jawharī, who evidently traced his lineage to Nūrī (I have not come across any information on this figure elsewhere). There may have been a link between Ṭalamankī's Sufism and his preference for the *uṣūlī* approach in scholarship, and he may have faced opposition from conservative scholars primarily on account of his jurisprudential views; see Cornell, *Realm*, 12–19.

73 Marín, 'Zuhhād'. On early *zuhd*, see Manuela Marín, 'The early development of *zuhd* in al-Andalus', in *Shia Islam, Sects, and Sufism: Historical Dimensions, Religious Practice and Methodological Considerations*, ed. Frederick de Jong (Utrecht: Houtsma, 1992), 83–94.

4

Specialised Sufi literature

The diffusion of Sufism to regions beyond Iraq during the course of the fourth/tenth century and its fusion with indigenous mystical trends went apace with the emergence of a self-conscious Sufi tradition. The situation in Syria, lower Iraq, Egypt and North Africa is less than clear, but in Iran, especially Khurāsān, and in Transoxania, the need to introduce Sufism to new audiences seems to have contributed to the construction of a coherent narrative about Sufism, as exemplified in the surveys of Sarrāj, Kalābādhī and Sulamī. But the 'foreign' nature of Sufism in regions other than Iraq was not the main reason for the appearance of somewhat academic overviews of *taṣawwuf* from the mid-fourth/tenth century onwards. More significant was the diachronic factor. Sufism, which had crystallised in Baghdad during the last quarter of the previous century, now literally had a history, and the Sufis of the Būyid period (after the mid fourth/tenth century), who were already a generation or two removed from the time of Junayd and his companions, felt the need to preserve, evaluate and analyse the complex legacy of the first masters. Their life examples, their sayings and their behaviour had to be recorded, their debates further scrutinised, their terminology dissected, and their vision perpetuated. Moreover, as was the case with all modes of piety, the boundaries of 'normative' Sufism needed to be ascertained in order to consolidate and fortify it and simultaneously to dissociate it from suspect approaches of all kinds. Such tradition-building was in keeping with general cultural trends in the Būyid period, when the major intellectual and pietist orientations that had taken shape in the period from the mid-third/ninth to the mid-fourth/tenth century – most notably, legal, theological, philosophical and scientific schools as well as Sunnī-Shīʿī sectarian identities – gradually developed into well-articulated and carefully-delineated traditions of learning and piety.

The emergence of a normative Sufi tradition during the fourth/tenth century can be traced most clearly in the appearance of a specialised literature that was self-consciously about Sufis and Sufism (as distinct from the written works of the first Sufis themselves on specific topics, which, as we have seen, began to appear roughly after the mid-third/ninth century). Very often, the fundamental building blocks of this body of writing were reports about individual Sufis, anectodal in nature and normally transmitting a saying or a statement of the Sufi in question. Two major genres grew out of these historical reports about the Sufis: the overview, or survey, and the biographical compilation. These two genres were sometimes combined in the form of discrete sections in a single work (notably by Qushayrī and Hujwīrī), and the material they conveyed was compiled and packaged in various ways to serve different but related functions: pedagogical guidance of aspirants, pious commemoration of past masters, building corporate solidarity among Sufis, and confident self-presentation and self-assertion vis-à-vis other groups competing for authority. Even though the surveys and the biographical compilations have normally been viewed as evidence of growing 'systematisation' and 'consolidation' of Sufism, the more focused treatises produced in the same period on such topics of Sufi thought and practice as pedagogy, *dhikr*, *samāʿ*, *khirqa*, and Qur'ān interpretation should also be viewed as unmistakable signs of the building of a Sufi tradition (see Tables 4.1–4.5).

Table 4.1 Major Sufi manuals and biographical compilations, fourth and fifth/tenth and eleventh centuries [in Arabic unless indicated otherwise] [a]

Extant

- Abū Naṣr al-Sarrāj (d. 378/988), *Kitāb al-lumaʿ fi'l-taṣawwuf* (*The Book of Light Flashes*)
- Abū Bakr al-Kalābādhī (d. 380s/990s), *al-Taʿarruf li-madhhab ahl al-taṣawwuf* (*Introduction to the Way of the People of Sufism*)
- Abū Ṭālib al-Makkī (d. 386/996), *Qūt al-qulūb* (*The Sustenance of Hearts*)
- Anonymous, *Adab al-mulūk* (*The Etiquette of Kings*, second half of fourth/tenth century)
- Abū Saʿd al-Khargūshī (d. 406/1015 or 407/1016), *Tahdhīb al-asrār* (*Refining the Secrets* [*of the Heart*])
- Abū ʿAbd al-Raḥmān al-Sulamī (d. 412/1021), *Ṭabaqāt al-ṣūfiyya* (*Generations of the Sufis*)
- Abū Nuʿaym al-Iṣfahānī (d. 430/1038), *Ḥilyat al-awliyā' wa ṭabaqāt al-aṣfiyā'* (*The Ornament of God's Friends and Generations of Pure Ones*)
- Abu'l-Qāsim al-Qushayrī (d. 465/1072), *Risala* (*Treatise*)
- ʿAlī ibn ʿUthmān al-Jullābī al-Hujwīrī (d. bet. 465/1073 and 469/1077), *Kashf al-maḥjūb* [in Persian] (*Uncovering the Veiled*).
- ʿAbd Allāh Anṣārī (d. 481/1089), *Ṭabaqāt al-ṣūfiyya* [in Persian] (*Generations of the Sufis*)

Lost[b]

- Abū Saʿīd Aḥmad ibn Muḥammad 'Ibn al-Aʿrābī' (246–341/860–952 or 3), *Ṭabaqāt al-nussāk* (*Generations of Renunciants*)

- Abū Bakr Muḥammad ibn Dāwūd 'Pārsā' (d. 342/953), *Akhbār al-ṣūfiyya* (*Reports of Sufis*)
- Abu'l-Faraj 'Abd al-Wāḥid ibn Bakr al-Warathānī (d. 372/982), *Ṭabaqāt al-ṣūfiyya* (*Generations of Sufis*)
- Ja'far al-Khuldī (d. 348/959), *Ḥikāyāt al-mashā'ikh* (*Stories of [Sufi] Masters*)
- Abū Bakr Shādhān al-Rāzī (d. 376/985), *Ḥikāyāt al-ṣūfiyya* (*Stories of Sufis*)
- Abū Sa'd al-Kharghūshī (d. 406/1015), *Siyar al-'ubbād wa'l-zuhhād* (*Lives of Devotees and Renunciants*)

Table 4.2 Earliest extant biographies/hagiographies of individual Sufis

- Abu'l-Ḥasan 'Alī ibn Muḥammad al-Daylamī (fl. fourth/tenth century), *Sīrat-i Ibn Khafīf*, on the life of Ibn Khafīf (d. 371/982), original Arabic lost, extant only in Persian translation by Ibn Junayd-i Shīrāzī (early fourteenth century).
- Abu'l-Faḍl Muḥammad ibn 'Alī Sahlagī (d. 477/1084), *Kitāb al-nūr min kalimāt Abī Ṭayfūr*[c]
- Abū Bakr Muḥammad ibn 'Abd al-Karīm ibn 'Alī ibn Sa'd (d. 502/1108), *Firdaws al-murshidiyya fī asrār al-ṣamadiyya*, on the life of Abū Isḥāq Ibrāhīm ibn Shahriyār Kāzarūnī (352–426/963–1033), original Arabic lost, extant only in Persian translation by Maḥmūd ibn 'Uthmān (fl. eighth/fourteenth centuries) completed in 728/1327
- Jamāl al-Dīn Abū Rawḥ Luṭf Allāh ibn Abī Sa'īd Sa'd ibn Abī Sa'īd As'ad (d. 541/1147), *Ḥālāt va sukhanān-i Shaykh Abū Sa'īd-i Abu'l-Khayr*, on the life of Abū Sa'īd-i Abu'l-Khayr (357–440/967–1049), in Persian
- Muḥammad ibn Nūr al-Dīn Munavvar ibn Abī Sa'īd As'ad, *Asrār al-tawḥīd fī maqāmāt Shaykh Abī Sa'īd* (compiled between 574/1179 and 588/1192), also on the life of Abū Sa'īd-i Abu'l-Khayr (357–440/967–1049), in Persian
- Sadīd al-Dīn Muḥammad-i Ghaznavī, *Maqāmāt-i Zhanda Pīl* (compiled c. 570/1175), on the life of Shihāb al-Dīn Abū Naṣr Aḥmad ibn Abi'l-Ḥasan Namaqī Jāmī, known as 'Zhanda Pīl' ('Colossal Elephant', 441/1049–50 to 536/1141), in Persian
- Anonymous, *Kitāb nūr al-'ulūm*, preserves the tradition of Abu'l-Ḥasan 'Alī ibn Aḥmad Kharaqānī (352–425/963–1033), extant in an abridgement made or copied in 698/1299, but clearly compiled much earlier, in Persian[d]
- Anonymous, *Dhikr-i quṭb al-sālikīn Abu'l-Ḥasan-i Kharaqānī*, also devoted to the tradition of Kharaqānī (352–425/963–1033), written sometime after 566/1170–1, in Persian[e]
- Aḥmad al-Azafī (d. 633/1236), *Di'āmat al-yaqīn fī zi'āmat al-muttaqīn*, on the life of the Berber Abū Yi'zzā (d. 572/1177), in Arabic[f]
- Abū Ya'qūb Yūsuf ibn al-Zayyāt al-Tādilī (d. 628/1230–1), *Akhbār Abi'l-'Abbās al-Sabtī* (d. 601/1204), in Arabic[g]

Table 4.3 Earliest extant Sufi pedagogical guidebooks[h]

- al-Ḥakīm al-Tirmidhī (probably d. between 295/905 and 300/910), *Adab al-nafs* and *Manāzil al-qāsidīn*[i]
- Abū 'Abd Allāh 'Ibn Khafīf' (d. 371/982), *Kitāb al-iqtiṣād*[j]
- Abū 'Abd al-Raḥmān al-Sulamī (d. 412/1021), *Manāhij al-'ārifīn*; *Kitāb jawāmi' ādāb al-ṣūfiyya*[k]
- Abū Manṣūr Ma'mar ibn Aḥmad al-Iṣfahānī (d. 418/1027), *Ādāb al-mutaṣawwifa wa-ḥaqā'iquhā wa-ishārātuhā*[l]
- Ṭāhir ibn Ḥusayn al-Jaṣṣāṣ (d. 418/1027), *Aḥkām al-murīdīn*[m]
- Abu'l-Qāsim al-Qushayrī (d. 465/1072), *al-Waṣiyya li'l-murīdīn* (*Advice to Aspirants*) and *Tartīb al-sulūk* (*The Structure of Wayfaring*) [attribution of this latter to Qushayrī not certain][n]
- 'Abd Allāh Anṣārī (d. 481/1089), *Manāzil al-sā'irīn*[o]
- Anonymous (probably a disciple of Anṣārī, evidently falsely attributed to Najm al-Dīn Kubrā'), *Ādāb al-murīdīn* or *Mukhtaṣar fī ādāb al-ṣūfiyya*[p]
- Abu'l-Najīb al-Suhrawardī (d. 563/1168), *Ādāb al-murīdīn*

Table 4.4 Works on dhikr and samā'

- Abū 'Abd Allāh 'Ibn Khafīf' (d. 371/982), *Kitāb al-faḍā'il wa-jamī' al-da'awāt wa'l-adhkār* [lost][q]
- Abū Manṣūr Ma'mar ibn Aḥmad al-Iṣfahānī (d. 418/1027), *Sharḥ al-adhkār* [extant][r]
- Abū 'Abd al-Raḥmān al-Sulamī (d. 412/1021), *Kitāb al-samā'*; *Mas'ala ṣifāt al-dhākirīn wa'l-mutafakkirīn* [both extant][t]
- Abu'l-Qāsim al-Qushayrī (d. 465/1072), *Kitāb al-samā'* [extant]
- Muḥammad ibn Ṭāhir al-Maqdisī 'Ibn al-Qaysarānī' (448–507/1058–1113), *Kitāb al-samā'* [extant][u]

Table 4.5 Works on dress (khirqa)

- Ibn Khafīf (d. 371/982), *Kitāb lubs al-muraqqa'āt* [lost][v]
- Abū Manṣūr Ma'mar ibn Aḥmad al-Iṣfahānī (d. 418/1027), untitled [lost]
- 'Alī ibn 'Uthmān al-Jullābī al-Hujwīrī (d. between 465–469/1073–1077), *Asrār al-khiraq wa'l-mulawwanāt* (*Mysteries of Patched and Coloured Cloaks*) [lost][w]

Notes to tables

a In these tables, only those works that do not appear separately in the bibliography are documented by short citations.

b All works under this heading, except the first by Ibn al-Aʿrābī, are listed and documented in Chabbi, *Réflexions*, 37–8; for Khuldī, mentioned by Chabbi only in note 3 without documentation, as well as for Ibn al-Aʿrābī, see Sezgin, *Geschichte*, 1: 661.
c Edited by A. R. Badawī (Cairo, 1949); new edition by Shafīʿī-Kadkanī to appear in Beirut soon.
d 'Abu'l-Ḥasan Ḵaraqānī', EIr 1: 306 (H. Landolt) under the bibliography.
e 'Abu'l-Ḥasan Ḵaraqānī', EIr 1: 306 (H. Landolt) under the bibliography.
f Cornell, *Realm*, 67–80.
g Cornell, *Realm*, 79–92.
h For a listing of works that are not extant, see Böwering, 'Ādāb literature', 68–9, note 31.
i Sezgin, *Geschichte*, 1: 656 (nos 21 and 17, respectively).
j Edited and translated in Sobieroj, *Ibn Ḫafīf*.
k Sulamī, *Tasavvufun Ana İkeleri*, 35–92 (Arabic), 34–76 (Turkish); also in Sulamī, *Majmūʿa-i āṯār*, 1: 341–408.
l Pūrjavādī, 'Ādāb al-mutaṣawwifa'.
m Trimingham, *Sufi Orders*, 29, note 1.
n These two works are discussed in Chapter 5 below.
o Farḥādī, *Anṣārī*, 73–89.
p Translated in Böwering, 'Ādāb literature,' 62–87.
q Sobieroj, *Ibn Ḫafīf*, 312, no. 30.
r Pūrjavādī, 'Sharḥ al-adhkār.'
s Both works appear in Sulamī, *Majmūʿa-i āṯār*, vol. 2.
t 'Abu 'l-Ḳāsim 'Abd al-Karīm b. Hawāzin', EI 5: 526a–527a, bibliography (H. Halm).
u Muḥammad ibn Ṭahir Ibn al-Qaysarānī, *Kitāb al-samāʿ* (Cairo: Lajnat Iḥyāʿ al-Turāth al-Islāmī, 1970). On him, see 'Ibn al-Ḳaysarānī,' EI 3: 821a (Joseph Schacht).
v Sobieroj, *Ibn Ḫafīf*, 311, no. 26.
w Hujwīrī, *Kashf*, 63 / *Revelation*, 56 (this latter with the variant reading *ma'ūnāt* instead of *mulawwanāt*).

Sufism among traditionalists

One of the persistent concerns of the authors of works on Sufism during the second half of the fourth/tenth as well as the fifth/eleventh century was to draw the boundaries of normative Sufism. This concern is readily visible in the work of Abū Ṭālib al-Makkī (d. 386/996). Makkī was a product of the traditionalist circles of his hometown Mecca, where one of his teachers in *ḥadīth* and Sufism was the influential Abū Saʿīd ibn al-Aʿrābī. Probably sometime after the death of this latter in 341/952–3, Makkī moved north, first to Basra where he became intimately associated with the followers of Tustarī known as the Sālimiyya, and then to Baghdad, where he ended his days. He is best remembered as the author of *Qūt al-qulūb* (*The Sustenance of Hearts*); another work under the title *ʿIlm al-qulūb* (*Knowledge of Hearts*) normally attributed to him is likely a mid-fifth/

eleventh-century composition that relies heavily on the *Sustenance* but is most certainly not by Makkī.[1] The *Sustenance* had a remarkable afterlife: one of the most celebrated Islamic works of all times, Abū Ḥāmid Muḥammad al-Ghazālī's (d. 505/1111) *Iḥyā' 'ulūm al-dīn* (*Bringing the Religious Sciences to Life*), was, in many ways, a brilliant reworking and expansion of this often dense and at times abstruse compendium on piety.[2]

In the *Sustenance* Makkī presented the central thesis that the only true knowledge was 'knowledge of hearts'. By 'knowledge of hearts', Makkī did not mean knowledge of spiritual states and stations, as one might expect, but divinely-inspired knowledge that is 'possessed by the hearts' of the pious devotees of God:

> God has said, 'When you do not know, then inquire of the people of recollection' (16 [al-Naḥl]: 43, 21[al-Anbiyā']: 7). They are the people ever-mindful of God and the people of the divine transcendent unity and of understanding from God. They have not acquired this knowledge throught the study of books, nor received it from one another by word of mouth. They were people of action and elegant deeds of devotion, so that when one of them was entirely dedicated to, and occupied with, God, he sought to labour in the service of the Master through deeds of the heart. They were with Him in seclusion before Him, remembering nothing but Him and occupying themselves with Him alone. And when they appeared in public and someone questioned them, God inspired them with right guidance and accommodated them with the perfectly apposite response ... He chose, in His exquisite providence, to inspire in them the spiritual reality of knowledge, and to disclose to them the hidden mystery, since they chose to serve Him and dedicated themselves to Him through worthy deeds of devotion. Thus, they would respond to any question put to them [and] would discourse of the knowledge of the divine power, bring to light the quality of wisdom, articulate the sciences of the faith, and reveal the inner meanings of the Qur'ān.[3]

In the *Sustenance*, Makkī tapped into this 'knowledge of hearts'. Since knowledge that is the province of hearts was the fruit of both outward and inward deeds of devotion, he carefully drew a veritable topography of the pious life, paying attention not only to such acts of piety as invocation, litany and the prescribed rituals of daily prayer, fasting, alms-giving and pilgrimage but also to questions of social life such as poverty, earning a living, marriage, visiting public baths, travelling, companionship and political leadership. Along the way, he took care to disparage in no uncertain terms 'outward knowledge', which he derisively called 'knowledge of tongues', and its practitioners. The exoterists, who clearly failed to attain 'knowledge of God' but nevertheless openly cherished the social and economic benefits of their prestigious professions, included not only rationalist and semi-rationalist jurists and theologians but also traditionalist 'professionals' who were transmitters of *ḥadīth* as well as Qur'ān reciters. In raising clear objections to the careerism of religious specialists of his time,

Makkī, himself a severe ascetic, was clearly reflecting the critical outlook of many renunciants, who, in the tradition of the early renunciant heroes Bishr al-Ḥāfī (d. 227/841) and Aḥmad ibn Abi'l-Ḥawārī (d. 230/844–5), looked askance at *ḥadīth* transmitters and their sense of self-importance.[4] In a posture reminiscent of the People of Blame, Makkī eschewed fame and social esteem and repeatedly extolled 'spiritual reticence'.

> The learned ones are … the heirs of the prophets; they are those who are spiritually reticent in the religion of God and who practise asceticism with respect to the vanities of this world … It is said that the Abdāl are dispersed over all parts of the earth and seek to be hidden from the eyes of the multitude, for they cannot bear to look at the religious scholars of this age, nor do they have the patience to listen to their discourse. The Abdāl regard these scholars as utterly ignorant of God, even though they themselves, and the ignorant, consider them endowed with genuine knowledge.[5]

In accordance with this inclination towards social anonymity, Makkī decried even 'itinerant Sufis who made ecstatic utterances', though he curiously exempted Ḥallāj and Bāyazīd from this category.[6] Also unacceptable was 'religious discourse based on diabolical insinuation and fleeting impulses without referring the associated inner experiences to the Book and the Sunna'.[7] Clearly, for all his insistence on the primacy of knowledge of hearts, Makkī remained a thorough traditionalist in orientation who refused to recognise any sources of knowledge other than the Qur'ān and the example of Muḥammad and who was willing to prefer weak *ḥadīth* that did not conflict with these two foundations over personal opinion based on rational judgment.[8]

Makkī's traditionalist outlook on Sufism, firmly rooted in Tustarī's renunciationist orientation, was shared by many of his *ḥadīth* specialist contemporaries. Among these latter, Abū Nuʿaym Aḥmad ibn ʿAbd Allāh al-Iṣfahānī (d. 430/1038) played a significant role in the preservation of the Sufi tradition. He belonged to a prominent Persian family with clear Sufi connections, but during his own lifetime he was known as a renowned traditionist.[9] After his death, he was remembered chiefly as the author of a voluminous biographical compendium entitled *Ḥilyat al-awliyā' wa ṭabaqāt al-aṣfiyā'* (*The Ornament of God's Friends and Generations of Pure Ones*), even though careful study of this work's composition indicates that Abū Nuʿaym was most likely not the only author, since this encyclopedic compilation appears to have been the product of a teaching milieu based on oral transmission from Abū Nuʿaym to his students, and these latter probably also contributed to the production of the work.[10] The *Ornament* is in ten volumes organised chronologically, and while Sufis (notably excluding Ḥallāj) dominate the last volume, the majority of the 649 biographies contained in it are overwhelmingly of pious individuals and renunciants of the first three centuries of Islam, with particular attention to those figures who were also *ḥadīth* transmitters. As was the case with Sulaymī in his *Generations of Sufis* (which was a major source for the *Ornament*), Abū Nu'aym's concern for *ḥadīth* transmission and training as a 'traditionist' are clearly in evidence in the organisation of each individual biographical entry into an introduction, main body and *ḥadīth* narration. Indeed, the work as a whole was manifestly written from the perspective of *ḥadīth* transmitters and reflected their perception of piety. In this vision, it was only natural for there to be a special place devoted to the articulation of the exemplary lives of the pious forefathers (the *salaf*, roughly the first three generations of Muslims, including most notably the 'rightly-guided' caliphs) as well as the *awliyā' Allāh*, the 'friends of God' (including all the foundational figures of *fiqh*, most notably Aḥmad ibn Ḥanbal and al-Shāfi'ī, but not the 'rationalising' Abū Ḥanīfa!) who were role models for early renunciants, *ḥadīth* transmitters and Sufis alike. It should not be forgotten that the notion of friendship with God, which later came to be associated primarily with Sufism, was cultivated in the first few centuries of Islam and beyond equally by renunciants and traditionalists in general.[11] Abū Nu'aym's introduction enunciates this perspective clearly. He starts with a discussion of the 'friends of God' and the 'pure ones' (pp. 4–17) and only then moves to consider the Sufis (17–28), before starting the main body of the work with the biography of Abū Bakr. In proceeding in this manner, Abū Nu'aym was not trying to justify Sufism by providing a pious genealogy for the Sufis; he was simply recording his perpective on the history of Islamic piety as a representative of the collectors and critics of *ḥadīth*. Admittedly, not all traditionalists would have completely shared his vision; for instance, the later Ḥanbalī Ibn al-Jawzī (d. 597/1200), though he admired Abū Nu'aym and even composed a work entitled *Ṣifat al-ṣafwa* (*The Way of the Elite*) as both a revision of and a supplement to the *Ornaments*, criticised his predecessor's association of pious forefathers with Sufism, his reliance – like Makkī – on weak *ḥadīth*, and his failure to include female renunciants in his work (Abū Nu'aym had given biographies of twenty-eight women, all from the Prophet's generation; Ibn al-Jawzī included 240 women in *The Way of the Elite*). Nor would all Sufis have been happy with being cast into the same mould with *ḥadīth* transmitters, since the study of *ḥadīth* could distract one from pursuing the only kind of knowledge that really mattered, namely 'experiential knowledge' (*ma'rifa*).[12] Nevertheless, the lines that separated Sufis, traditionists, and renunciants were simply not too rigid in Abū Nu'aym's day, and Abū Nu'aym was by no means being disingenuous by lumping them together. Instead, it is more plausible to view him as a *ḥadīth* transmitter who incorporated the Sufis into his traditionist vision of piety and therefore claimed them, so to speak, for himself, than to see him as a Sufi who craftily tried to justify and legitimate Sufism by constructing a nine-volume pious genealogy for the Sufis.[13]

Significantly, even when traditionists strongly disagreed among themselves, typically over the admissibility of *kalām*, they tended to be united in their esteem for 'traditionalist' Sufism. A clear illustration of the shared regard for Sufism among most traditionists is provided by a dispute that profoundly affected Abū Nu'aym himself: Muḥammad ibn Isḥāq Ibn Manda (d. 395/1005), the famous Ḥanbalī traditionist of Isfahan, denounced Abū Nu'aym on account of his supposed leanings towards *kalām* and banished him from the great mosque of the town. Yet this same Ibn Manda taught *ḥadīth* to, and had an extremely close teacher-pupil relationship with, Abū Manṣūr Ma'mar ibn Aḥmad al-Iṣfahānī (d. 418/1027), who was a prominent Ḥanbalī Sufi contemporary of Abū Nu'aym in Isfahan and who praised Ibn Manda as the model scholar of his age. Clearly, unlike the later Ibn al-Jawzī but very much like Abū Nu'aym himself, neither Ibn Manda nor his premier student the Sufi Abū Manṣūr excluded Sufism from their traditionalist vision of Islam.[14]

In fact, Abū Manṣūr Ma'mar comes across as more of a Sufi than Abū Nu'aym. He belonged to the local tradition of Sufism in Isfahan that had grown around the example of the prominent mystic 'Alī ibn Sahl (d. 307/919–20) and this latter's teacher al-Bannā' (d. 286/899, the great grandfather of Abū Nu'aym), both of whom were linked with Baghdad Sufism through Junayd and 'Amr ibn 'Uthmān al-Makkī. Among his authorities in Sufism, Abū Manṣūr himself listed Junayd, Kharrāz, and Nūrī of Baghdad, Abū 'Uthmān Ḥīrī and Abū Ḥafṣ Ḥaddād of Nishapur, and Tustarī (in addition to transitional figures like Dhu'l-Nūn and Dārānī).[15] Several of his works on Sufism are extant, including the earliest independent treatise on *dhikr* and a short work on Sufi conduct (*adab*). In these works, Abū Manṣūr developed a distinct voice of his own, refraining from frequent reliance on the sayings of past Sufi masters as proof texts for his views. Like his contemporaries Sarrāj, Sulamī and Kalābādhī, he paid attention both to Sufi teachings and to the question of Sufi conduct. In his *Nahj al-khāṣṣ* (*Way of the Elect*) and *Ādāb al-mutaṣawwifa* (*Good Manners of the Sufis*), he adopted a three-fold method of presentation (he divided each chapter into three sections), which gave his writing a formalistic flavour.[16] Moreover, his stipulations on Sufism had a distinctly idealising tone, suggesting that he may have viewed Sufi teaching more as ideals than practical recipes for the conduct of human life on earth.

Abū Manṣūr believed that the true meaning of God's unity could be attained only after the divine law (*sharī'a*) was realised through its scrupulous implementation. The correct application of the law, however, was not possible without an understanding of its inner meaning. All the same, one had to start at the outer level of the *sharī'a* with proper conduct (*ādāb*). If one maintained proper conduct with truthfulness (*ṣidq*), then one could work one's way towards the level of inner truths (*ḥaqā'iq*). If one observed these truths with righteousness (*ṣiddīqiyya*), one could finally reach the inner core of experiential knowledge of

God, at which point one became a Sufi.[17] The Sufis, who were rarer than red sulphur, ultimately achieved awareness of God as the only agent in existence, an inspired knowledge conveyed to them directly by God as a gift in the form of sublime 'indications' (*ishārāt*).

Abū Manṣūr applied this tripartite interiorising approach also in his treatise on *dhikr*. After he construed 'recollection of God' as the inner meaning that underlay the other duties of prayer, fasting, alms-giving, pilgrimage and charity in the first half of the treatise, he proceeded to elaborate on the different levels of recollection: recollection by the tongue (at the level of proper conduct and truthfulness), recollection by the heart (at the level of inner meanings and righteousness), and recollection by one's inner secret (*sirr* = at the level of indications and being a Sufi). Just as being a Sufi meant the eradication of any sense of self-agency and its replacement with complete God-consciousness, the recollection of Sufis, according to Abū Manṣūr, was stripped of all forms of speech and sound and could not be perceived by any being other than God.[18]

Abū Manṣūr thought that there were very few Sufis left in his day. Nevertheless, he commented, albeit briefly, on such aspects of Sufi conduct as dress, eating, companionship, service, charity, travel, solitude and poverty. He declared, for instance, that the Sufis behaved with courtesy towards all of God's creatures including animals, that they showed generosity to everyone without discrimination, and that they stayed aloof from people of power. This interest in Sufi conduct was clearly pedagogical in origin: Abū Manṣūr wanted to lead his readers to the path of becoming a Sufi. Indeed, Abū Manṣūr may have been the author of an anonymous work on Sufism entitled *Adab al-mulūk* (*Etiquette of Kings*) that stands testimony to the popularity of the issue of Sufi conduct at this time period.

Etiquette of Kings is a relatively short but comprehensive overview of Sufism, and in this respect it is comparable to Sarrāj's *Light Flashes* and Kalābādhī's *Introduction*.[19] Yet, its coverage is noticeably tilted towards the whole issue of right conduct and its inner meanings, and its author, who placed the highest premium on inspired knowledge that was located in the Sufi's innermost secret (*sirr*) and paid little attention to 'stations' and 'states' or to doctrinal teachings, had a distinctly different perspective from that of Sarrāj and Kalābādhī. The work opens with a long introduction, in which the author expresses his dismay over the shortcomings of the people of knowledge (he specifically discusses jurists, *ḥadīth* scholars, exegetes and philologists), who, with few exceptions, cultivate only the exterior of learning and fail to live by what they preach. The author contrasts these scholars with the Sufis: they alone live in conformity with both the exterior and the interior of the Qur'ān and the Sunna, and, therefore, they are the only true kings on earth. He then proceeds to discuss the 'royal manners' of the Sufis in separate chapters, which range in subject from clothing, eating and responding to invitations to banquets and travel, to questions of employment and shelter and issues such as generosity, humility, and ecstasy. On the question of 'profession' (*ḥirfa*, ch. 11), for instance, the author states that the Sufis avoid gainful employment of any kind in order to devote themselves solely to the recollection of God and that they rely on God for their sustenance, which may take the form of begging for bare necessities of living. Nor do Sufis maintain any steady residence (ch. 22), preferring to dwell in God's houses, that is, mosques. Not many Sufis are cited by name, but Junayd seems to be the most frequently-quoted Sufi authority.

On the whole, there is much in the *Etiquette of Kings* that overlaps with the writings of Abū Manṣūr, and the possibility that this latter was the unnamed author is very real. On the other hand, there are indications that the work may have been the product of the Sufi circle in Mecca, possibly connected with the venerable metic Sufis Sīrawānī the Younger (d. 396/1005–6 at an advanced age) and Ibn Jahḍam al-Hamadhānī (d. 414/1023).[20] In that case, the *Etiquette of Kings* would be a rare window into this little-known traditionalist Sufi circle around the Holy Precincts in Mecca. If so, the picture of the Sufi metics that emerges from the *Etiquette* bears a remarkable similarity to the Ḥanbalī Sufi milieu of Isfahan as represented by Abū Manṣūr, and this similarity should be seen as clear evidence of the existence of close links between the two Sufi circles. Indeed, we know that Abū Manṣūr definitely maintained contact with his counterparts in Mecca since he personally sent a copy of his *Way of the Elect* to Ibn Jahḍam. Whether Abū Manṣūr was its author or not, therefore, the *Etiquette of Kings* should be seen as proof that the respective Sufi milieu of Western Arabia and central Iran were closely interlinked and, further, that these Sufi circles were thoroughly traditionalist in orientation and, at least in Isfahan, predominantly Ḥanbalī.

Clearly, Makkī, Abū Nu'aym, Abū Manṣūr and, if different from this latter, the author of the *Etiquette of Kings* would not have seen eye to eye on all legal and theological matters, but their differences on this terrain should not hide from view their concurrence on the completely 'traditional' nature of Sufism. In the eyes of many traditionalists, irrespective of their pietistic orientation, Sufism was entirely mainstream, and according to its partisans, it actually defined the very core of traditionalism. This perspective on Sufism was defended vigorously by yet another key figure in the construction of Sufism as a tradition, 'Khwāja' 'Abd Allāh Abū Ismā'īl Anṣārī (396–481/1006–1089).

Anṣārī lived in the completely Persian-speaking environment of Herat in Khurāsān.[21] Unlike all other builders of the Sufi tradition from Khurāsān (Sarrāj, Kalabādhī, and Sulamī before him, and his contemporaries Qushayrī, and Hujwīrī), who had organic ties with the world of juristic-theological scholarship, Anṣārī cultivated the traditionalist orientation of Makkī, Abū Nu'aym and Abū Manṣūr Ma'mar. He knew and admired the works of this latter, with whom he shared his Ḥanbalī allegiance, and praised Abū Manṣūr as 'the doyen of exoteric knowledge as well as knowledge of inner realities, the singular master of his age'.[22] Also like Ma'mar, and unlike especially Kalabādhī, Sulamī and Qushayrī who were all more academic observers of Sufism than major Sufi shaykhs themselves, Anṣārī was first and foremost a Sufi master. Well-known as a Qur'ān commentator, traditionist and tireless polemicist and preacher on behalf of Ḥanbalī traditionalism, Anṣārī nevertheless directed his formidable talents and energy to the dissemination and popularisation of Sufi thought and practice by training disciples and preaching Sufi values to large audiences in his native Herat in Persian.

Born into a Sufi family, Anṣārī grew up under the care of Abū Ismā'īl Aḥmad ibn Muḥammad 'Shaykh 'Ammū' (d. 441/1049), a well-travelled master who was a disciple of Abu'l-'Abbās Aḥmad ibn Muḥammad al-Nihāwandī (d. 370/980–1, a pupil of Khuldī and companion of Shiblī).[23] Later, he continued his Sufi education with a Ḥanbalī Sufi named Muḥammad ibn Faḍl al-Ṭāqī al-Sijistānī (d. 416/1025–6, he had met Ibn Khafīf but was himself a disciple of Mūsā ibn 'Imrān, the shaykh of Jīruft in Fārs), whom he considered as one of the ten prominent Sufis of 'recent times'.[24] Yet, the precocious young Sufi was clearly eager to make more progress in his spiritual development as well as his Qur'ān and *ḥadīth* studies, and in 417/1026 he went to Nishapur to study *ḥadīth*, where, however, he refused to transmit from traditionists with Ash'arī leanings and did not meet the theologian-Sufi Qushayrī. But, in the process of travelling for his studies and attempting unsuccessfully to make the pilgrimage, he met some of the prominent Sufis of Khurāsān. In Dāmghān, he saw the illiterate Ḥanbalī shaykh of Āmul Abu'l-'Abbās Aḥmad ibn Muḥammad al-Qaṣṣāb. In Nishapur, he visited Ibn Bākūya (d. 428/1037), who had taken over the direction of Sulamī's *khānaqāh* after this latter's death, where he ran into the famous Abū Sa'īd-i Abu'l-Khayr (357–440/967–1049). This latter told him about another illiterate master, 'Alī ibn Aḥmad Abu'l-Ḥasan Kharaqānī (352–425/963–1033). When Anṣārī visited Kharaqānī in Kharaqān, the master made the deepest impact on him. He not only deterred Anṣārī from trying to go on the pilgrimage by making him realise 'that God was as likely to be in Khurāsān as in Hijāz' but also instructed him to start training his own disciples. About him, Anṣārī reportedly said, 'If I had not met Kharaqānī, I would never have known … reality (*ḥaqīqat*).'[25] Returning to Herat, he was admitted in 425/1034 to a meeting of sixty-two well-known Sufi masters in Nubādhān, south of Herat, where he tore his shirt in *samā'* and was given a grand reception for a twenty-eight year-old master.[26] Awakened to the dangers of public acclaim through this experience, he left the meeting precipitiously without taking the many gifts he was offered and decided not to participate in *samā'* any longer. He spent the rest of his life mostly in his home town, teaching *ḥadīth*, Qur'ān commentary and Sufism and engaging in polemics against theologians, who, in turn, lost no opportunity to denounce him as an anthropomorphist to the political authorities. His fame grew during the public persecution of Ashʿarīs by Saljūq political authorities between 445/1053 and 456/1064. He remained a staunch critic of rationalists of all types until the end of his life in 481/1089.

Anṣārī was 'not a writer but a teacher and orator'.[27] However, especially during the last decade of his life when he had gone blind, he dictated many works to his personal secretary and to several scribes from among his disciples. Among his many works, which include a manifesto against theology entitled *Kitāb dhamm al-kalām wa ahlihi* (*Condemnation of Kalām and its Practitioners*, dictated in Arabic in 474/1082), his Sufi compositions all stand testimony to his keen interest in pedagogy and training disciples. The earliest work that Anṣārī dictated in 448/1056–7, a spiritual itinerary in ten sections of ten stages called *Ṣad maydān* (*The Hundred Fields*), holds the distinction of being the first treatise on Sufism written in Persian. It was clearly inspired by Maʿmar's *Nahj*, and its tight decimal organisation may have been 'specifically intended to serve as a *mnemonic* manual for novices to help them remember [the master's] teaching'.[28] Anṣārī updated this spiritual itinerary twenty-five years later, this time in Arabic, with a treatise titled *Manāzil al-sā'irīn* (*The Stages of Wayfarers*, probably dictated in 474/1082). The order of spiritual stages in this later work is different than the *Hundred Fields*, and Anṣārī himself is careful to warn his audience not to reify this particular spiritual itinerary: 'Know that the wayfarers through these stages are very different from each other, not agreeing on a specific order, and not standing on a common goal.'[29] Towards the end of his life, Anṣārī dictated another work in Arabic on spiritual progress, probably also inspired by Abū Manṣūr Maʿmar, called *Kitāb 'ilal al-maqāmāt* (*The Diseases [that Afflict the] Stations*). Both these works, partly because they were in Arabic, proved to be popular and the *Stages of Wayfarers* especially attracted many commentaries. Remarkably, within less than half a century, both had made their way to al-Andalus, where they formed the basis of Abu'l-ʿAbbās Ibn al-ʿArīf's (d. 536/1141) *Maḥāsin al-majālis* (*The Beauties of Spiritual Sessions*).[30]

Anṣārī's concern for pedagogical guidance of his disciples, so conspicuous in the works mentioned so far, gave rise to another major work in Persian. It appears that Anṣārī used Sulamī's *Generations* as a basis for some of his lectures, and his students' notes of their master's commentary and expansion of Sulamī's work was later compiled to form another *Ṭabaqāt al-ṣūfiyya* (*Generations of Sufis*) (Anṣārī's *Generations*, in its turn, was the basis of ʿAbd al-Raḥmān Jāmī's (d. 898/1492) *Nafahāt al-uns min ḥaḍarāt al-quds*, which was also composed in Herat). Anṣārī was explicit about the pedagogical utility of the preservation and commemoration of the first Sufis: when asked, 'What is the benefit to novices of these stories (of the shaykhs)?', he replied that just as God had rendered the Prophet's heart firm by sending down stories of previous messengers,

> in the same way, to learn the sayings of the righteous and the stories of the shaykhs (pīrān) and the (spiritual) states (aḥwāl) helps the edification (tarbiyyat) of the novice and increases his strength and resolve. With all that, he gains firmness against the trials and His probations ... Also, knowing the shaykhs and their friends will make you (O novice) related to them ... The least benefit from learning about the shaykhs is to notice that one's own deeds, states and sayings is not like theirs ... [The novice] will then abandon selfishness from his behaviour and will view his own flaws ... There is a blessing in listening (and learning) the words of the shaykhs.'[31]

Clearly, Anṣārī was first and foremost a training master who narrated episodes from the lives of previous Sufis and repeated their statements to his disciples within the framework of a larger pedagogical agenda; he did not share the somewhat academic outlook of Sulamī and Qushayrī whose pedagogical concerns were leavened with scholarly motivations. The *Generations* is a work rich in detail, and apart from the information it holds on Sufi history, Anṣārī's frank commentary also gives us access to his original and highly independent views on many early Sufis. For instance, he declared Kharrāz to be the most eminent of the Baghdad Sufis, preferred Ruwaym to Junayd by a wide margin since he considered this latter to be too scholarly, and suspended judgment on Ḥallāj. In his list of ten prominent Sufis of recent times, including Ḥuṣrī, Sīrawānī the Younger, Nihāwandī, Naṣrābādhī, Kharaqānī, Qaṣṣāb and Ṭāqī, he seems to have given priority to traditionalists and notably excluded his contemporaries Abū Sa'īd or Qushayrī.[32]

Anṣārī lectured on the Qur'ān all his life, but he did not dictate a separate work on Qur'ān interpretation. Nevertheless, much of his Qur'ān commentary, no doubt in students' notes, is largely embedded in Rashīd al-Dīn Maybudī's (d. 520/1126) *Kashf al-asrār wa 'uddat al-abrār* (*Unveiling of Secrets and Equipment of the Devout*). This work also includes many short, pithy sayings of Anṣārī, which preserve something of the amazingly captivating rhetorical and oratory skills of the master in his native Persian.[33] Indeed, to this day, Anṣārī is best known among Persian-speaking audiences for a collection of such sayings that go under the name *Munājāt* (*Intimate Conversations*). The *Intimate Conversations* cannot be authenticated beyond doubt because its manuscript tradition is fairly late, but the sayings it contains, some very close in content and style to those reported by Maybudī, no doubt reflect the oral tradition that grew around Anṣārī's preaching.[34]

Sufism in the bosom of fiqh and kalām

For the traditionalists Makkī, Abū Nu'aym, Abū Manṣūr and Anṣārī as well as the circles of followers and students around them, Sufism was an integral part, even the very core, of 'true' Islam. In their writings on Sufi subjects, they spoke 'from within' with a confident and self-assured voice (with the partial exception of the author of the *Etiquette*, who adopted an outsider's perspective, perhaps for stylistic reasons) and they generally did not acknowledge the existence of contending views on Islam, such as semi-rationalist and rationalist legal and theological discourses, except when they denounced them. Their counterparts Sarrāj, Sulamī and Kalābādhī, however, struck a different note in their surveys on Sufism. Theirs was a slightly distanced approach, at times almost academic in tone, and motivated by a desire to introduce their audiences, the literate cultural elites of Khurāsān and Transoxania, to this new and largely foreign subject. To the extent that these elites were immersed in legal and theological discourses, the Sufi authors, themselves not necessarily hostile towards them, adopted a more accommodating stance than traditionalists vis-à-vis the prevalent Shāfiʿī and Ḥanafī legal schools as well as *kalām* and did not shirk away from using legal and theological yardsticks in parsing Sufism for their readers. Sarrāj's legal affiliation is not known, but Kalābādhī was a Ḥanafī and Sulamī a Shāfiʿī, and while the former had no reservations about interpreting Sufism in theological terms, the latter, who was a traditionist by formation, limited himself to faithful transmission of Sufi lore in the manner of *ḥadīth* study. However, theological discourses were on the rise (Ashʿarīsm for Shāfiʿīs, concentrated in Khurāsān, and Māturīdīsm for Ḥanafīs, mostly in Transoxania), and legal schools were consolidating themselves, so that the temptation to process Sufi thought with the new tools of *kalām* and *fiqh* in order to develop a theologically and legally savvy form of Sufism was too irresistible. A generation after Sulamī, two Sufi authors, Qushayrī and Hujwīrī, rose to this challenge with such skill that the surveys that they produced partly eclipsed all earlier attempts and came to assume almost canonical status for most later Sufis and observers of Sufism alike.

Abu'l-Qāsim ʿAbd al-Karīm ibn Hawāzin al-Qushayrī (d. 465/1072) was a product of the exceptionally-productive period for the combination of Shāfiʿī jurisprudence and Ashʿarī *kalām* in Nishapur.[35] Originally from outside the town, Qushayrī was introduced to this new and exciting intellectual cluster when he arrived in Nishapur in his youth and proceeded to excel in it with remarkable speed. He was especially precocious in *ḥadīth* and *kalām*; in this last area, he had two of the three real 'builders' of the Ashʿarī orientation as his teachers: Abū Bakr Muḥammad ibn al-Ḥasan ibn Fūrak (d. 406/1015) and Abū Isḥāq al-Isfarāyinī (d. 418/1027) (the third 'builder' was the Mālikī Abū Bakr al-Bāqillānī, d. 403/1013). Qushayrī soon achieved pre-eminence among the Shāfiʿī-Ashʿarī faction in town, and, along with the renowned theologian Abu'l-Maʿālī al-Juwaynī (d. 478/1085–6), he was one of the top four Ashʿarī scholars who were persecuted by the Saljūq political authorities between 445/1053 and 456/1064.

Thanks to the efforts of jurist-Sufis like Abū Sahl al-Ṣuʿlūkī and traditionist-Sufis like Sulamī, Shāfiʿīsm in Nishapur was already bundled with Sufism and had benefitted from the presence of training masters such as Abu'l-Qāsim al-Naṣrābādhī (d. 367/977–8), a disciple of Shiblī. From the very beginning of his academic studies, Qushayrī also frequented the popular preaching sessions of the Sufi Abū ʿAlī Ḥasan ibn ʿAlī al-Daqqāq (d. 405/1015), a disciple of Naṣrābādhī who preached first in a Shāfiʿī mosque and later in his own *madrasa* as well as in the marketplace in both Arabic and Persian, but Daqqāq, who had studied Shāfiʿī *fiqh* himself, is supposed to have encouraged Qushayrī to concentrate on scholarship instead of Sufism.[36] The relationship between Daqqāq and Qushayrī was particularly close: the disciple married his mentor's daughter and, after Daqqāq's death, inherited this latter's *madrasa* that came to be known under his own name, presumably because of his growing reputation. Along the way, he probably also studied with Sulamī, though theirs does not appear to have been a particularly close relationship, nor did Qushayrī share Sulamī's fascination with the Malāmatiyya. Nevertheless, he was definitely influenced by Sulamī's intellectual output, since after Daqqāq, Sulamī is the most frequently-quoted authority in Qushayrī's survey of Sufism, which is simply known as the *Treatise* (*Risāla*). Moreover, like Sulamī, Qushayrī composed a work on Sufi interpretation of the Qur'ān entitled *Laṭā'if al-ishārāt* (*Subtleties of [Mystical] Indications*). Unlike Sulamī's *Ḥaqā'iq al-tafsīr*, however, this was not a compilation of other Sufis' mystical 'plumbings' of select verses of the Qur'ān but an impressive attempt to discuss comprehensively the Qur'ān's inner meanings that lay hidden from the view of the common people but were perceptible to the spiritual elect.[37] Qushayrī was a prolific scholar, with no less than twenty-two titles to his name, yet his reputation as a Sufi author rests primarily on his *Treatise*.

While the *Treatise* is comparable in approach to *Introducing the Way of the People of Sufism* of Kalābādhī, in substance it can be viewed as a judicious combination and rewriting of Sulamī's *Generations* and Sarrāj's *Light Flashes*. In a short introduction, the author complains about the noticeable decline in the calibre of the 'so-called Sufis' of his time in comparison with masters of the past, and declares his intention to present a comprehensive picture of authentic Sufism in order to provide guidance to those who would like to become Sufis. There follows a relatively brief section on Sufi theology, where, right at the beginning, Qushayrī refers to Junayd as the 'leader' of the Sufis and quotes his definition of God's unity.[38] Qushayrī then proceeds to the first major section of the treatise, which is a biographical compendium of eighty-three Sufis condensed mostly from Sulamī's work, though not without some significant differences such as Qushayrī's omission of a separate entry on Ḥallāj.[39] The bulk of the treatise, however, is composed of the two sections that follow, one on Sufi terminology and the other on 'stations' and 'states' but also including several chapters on

Sufi conduct. In these sections, Qushayrī draws heavily upon Sarrāj, though he is more selective than this latter in his coverage, omitting, for instance, any separate discussion of 'ecstatic utterances' or 'errors of the Sufis'.[40] The work ends with a set of guidelines that should be followed by all who aspire to become Sufis.

Throughout the *Treatise*, Qushayrī's voice is authoritative and scholarly. However, while he clearly values scholarship highly, Qushayrī makes no bones about the superiority of Sufis to scholars in all respects:

> People cultivate either received knowledge or knowledge based on reason. The masters of this group [that is, the Sufis] have risen above both these options: what is hidden from people is manifest for them, and the knowledge that others aim at they already possess as a gift from God. They are the people of attainment, [while] everyone else is [still] seeking proof.[41]

There is, therefore, a complete correspondence between the goals of scholarship and Sufism, yet scholars should yield to the Sufi shaykhs and show humility towards them since these latter have reached the final destination; nevertheless, the shaykhs should not shirk away from using rational arguments in training their disciples when necessary.[42] This happy marriage between Sufism and legal-theological scholarship is the hallmark of the *Treatise*, and Qushayrī's harmonious packaging of the two modes of learning and piety, along with his overall reputation among scholars (that is due, at least in part, to the persecution he suffered) as well as the astute inclusion of biographical notices into his survey of Sufism, goes a long way to explaining the *Treatise*'s enduring popularity.

A similar blending of scholarly tendencies and Sufism, albeit in a different cultural milieu and a different language, can be seen in Abu'l-Ḥasan ʿAlī ibn ʿUthmān Jullābī Hujwīrī (d. between 465/1073 and 469/1077), the author of the first major survey of Sufism in Persian titled *Kashf al-maḥjūb* (*Uncovering the Veiled*).[43] Like Sarrāj before him, Hujwīrī travelled widely to meet the leading Sufis of his time, and lived for a time in Iraq, though he spent most of his life in his native town Ghazna and, in the latter part of his life, probably during the rule of the Ghaznavid ruler Masʿūd (r. 421–32/1030–40), in Lahore. After his death, his fame in Lahore increased to such an extent that he came to be regarded as the premier saint of the town and was given the honorific 'Data Ganjbakhsh' ('the giver who bestows treasure'). According to his own testimony, Hujwīrī authored nine works other than the *Unveiling*, but none of these has survived. However, the *Uncovering* itself is sufficient to prove its author's credentials as an astute observer of Sufism in his day as well as a shrewd commentator on its various aspects.

Hujwīrī opened the *Uncovering* with a complaint that had already been introduced by Sarrāj but that was fully developed a couple of generations after him by Qushayrī and, in short order, by Hujwīrī himself. These mid-fifth/eleventh-century observers ruefully remarked that there were no real Sufis left anymore, and that the few authentic figures who could still be found were 'veiled' over by a growing number of false pretenders.[44] Hujwīrī even had a name for these latter: he called them '*mustaṣwif*', that is, 'the would-be Sufi'.[45] He recognised that such pretenders had existed even during the earliest phase of Sufi history: already in the mid-third/ninth century, he reported, Yaḥyā bin Mu'ādh al-Rāzī had said, 'Avoid the society of three classes of men – heedless scholars, hypocritical renunciants, and ignorant pretenders to Sufism.'[46] Yet, the pretenders had multiplied to such an extent that even for genuine seekers it had become impossible to identify the real Sufis. It was as a response to this dire situation that Hujwīrī decided to write the *Uncovering*, to lift the veils that obscured the face of Sufism.

The theme of the disappearance of 'true' Sufism was, no doubt, a topos that served rhetorical and literary functions. It was sounded already by prominent second-generation Sufis: 'Alī ibn Aḥmad al-Būshanjī (d. 348/959–60), a disciple of Ibn 'Aṭā' and Jurayrī, famously replied, when asked about *taṣawwuf*, 'It is a name without a reality, but it used to be a reality without a name', and Ibn Khafīf observed, 'I still knew Sufis who mocked Satan; now Satan mocks them.'[47] Nevertheless, there is reason to think that in the case of Hujwīrī, as in that of Qushayrī, the use of this topos most probably pointed to a real social development. This was the gradual but unmistakable growth of a 'Sufi exoterism', a kind of formalism that paralleled the careerism rampant in the world of scholarship and religious devotion so ably criticised by Makkī. Sufism had become popular, and the number of aspirants to the Sufi way was on the rise, but it had also become notoriously difficult to differentiate between the authentic Sufis and those who thought they were Sufis or made themselves out to be Sufis. In this regard, the following report from Maqdisī's geographical work *Aḥsan al-taqāsīm* is very telling:

> When I entered Sūs [in Khūzistān] I sought out the main mosque ... It chanced that I was wearing a *jubba* [cloak] of Cypriot wool ..., and I was directed to a congregation of Sufis. As I approached they took it for granted that I was a Sufi and welcomed me with open arms. They settled me among them and began questioning me. Then they sent a man to bring food. I felt ill at ease about taking the food since I had not associated with such a group before this occasion. They showed surprise about my reluctance ... I felt drawn to associate myself with this congregation and find out about their method, and learn the true nature [of Sufism]. So I said within myself, 'This is your opportunity, here where you are unknown'. I therefore threw off all restraint with them, stripping the veil of bashfulness from off my face. On one occasion I might engage in antiphonal singing with them, on another I might yell with them, and at another recite poems to them. I would go out with them to visit *ribāṭ*s and to engage in religious recitals, with the result, by God, that I won a place both in their hearts and in the hearts of the people of that place to an extraordinary degree. I gained a great reputation, being visited [for my virtue] and

> being sent presents of garments and purses, which I would accept but immediately hand over intact to the Sufis, since I was well off, with ample means. Every day I used to spend engaged in devotions, and what devotions! and they used to suppose I did it out of piety. People began touching me [to obtain *baraka*, 'spiritual power'] and broadcasting my fame, saying that they had never seen a more excellent *faqīr* ['poor', 'renunciant']. So it went on until, when the time came that I had penetrated into their secrets and learnt all that I wished, I just ran away from them at dead of night and by morning had got well clear.[48]

Unlike Maqdisī, the majority of Sufi exotericists clearly must have been genuine seekers, and according to Qushayrī and Hujwīrī, they remained bogged down in supeficialities, misled into thinking that the adoption of Sufi habit and custom would be sufficient to make them into genuine Sufis.

In dress, for instance, Hujwīrī informed his readers in a special chapter in the first section of his work that Sufis seldom wore wool in his day, since wool had become scarce, and, more importantly, woollen habit had become associated with a heretical sect (Hujwīrī does not name this sect, though he probably had the Karrāmīs in mind). It had instead become customary for them to wear blue garments, blue being the colour of mourning. Yet the patched cloak (*muraqqa'a*), associated with Sufism from its beginnings, continued to be the Sufi apparel *par excellence*, and the Sufis shaykhs continued to invest their novices with it as a sign of spiritual maturity after they had subjected them to spiritual training for several years. But the formalists, complained Hujwīrī, tried to judge one's progress as a Sufi according to the way the patches on one's garment were sewn! Hujwīrī clearly respected the patched cloak as a 'traditional' Sufi habit, yet he decried the attempt to reduce Sufism to a set of concrete symbols. Patches were fine, but they needed to be put on one's garment only out of necessity, not for outward show, and in any manner possible, not sewn following any particular design. Similarly, Hujwīrī was critical of the tendency of formalist Sufis to exaggerate the significance of special Sufi paraphernalia such as staffs (*'aṣā*), ewers (*ibrīq*) and leather water-skins (*rakwa*), and he ridiculed their condescending attitude toward those who did not have this Sufi equipment.[49]

In order to drive home his point, that true Sufi practice could not be standardised or formalised, Hujwīrī quoted statements of Sufi masters to the effect that Sufism was not about 'formal practice' (*rusūm*) but about 'morals' (*akhlaq̄*). He also carefully pointed out that the master whom he considered to be his real teacher, a certain Abu'l-Faḍl Muḥammad ibn al-Ḥasan al-Khuttalī, did not wear the garb of the Sufis or adopt their external fashions. According to Hujwīrī, there could be no question about Khuttalī's Sufi credentials: connected to Junayd through Shiblī and this latter's disciple Abu'l-Ḥasan al-Ḥuṣrī (d. 371/982), he was 'well-versed in the science of Koranic exegesis and in traditions', and he had spent sixty years in retirement, mostly on Mount Lukkām overlooking Antioch, which was the premier site of retreat for renunciants in Syria.[50] Nonetheless, he was not one of those that Hujwīrī somewhat contemptuously called 'formalists' (*ahl-i rusūm*).[51] Clearly, Hujwīrī cared strongly about the issue of formalism, and most likely he focused on this subject in an independent work of his that did not survive, entitled *Asrār al-khiraq wa'l-mulawwanāt* (*Mysteries of Patched and Coloured Cloaks*).[52]

Hujwīrī was acutely aware, however, that a certain degree of desiccation was not the only 'veil' that obscured Sufism from those who took interest in it during his time. An even more intractable problem lay in the sheer multitude of different perspectives on various issues that prevailed among the Sufis. This was a difficulty that faced all those who set out to survey Sufism (not to mention those who aspired to become Sufis), and Hujwīrī's predecessors had normally dealt with it by emphasising forms of Sufism that they considered to be normative and authentic and excluding or downplaying the rest. Qushayrī, for instance, had most recently adopted such a normative approach as a natural outcome of his attempt to achieve a rapprochement between scholarship and Sufism. Hujwīrī, however, was the first to tackle the issue of diversity head on. In the long final chapter of the second section of the *Uncovering*, he took the innovative step, probably influenced by the theological genre of *al-milal wa'l-niḥal* (roughly, 'description of different doctrines', or 'doxography'), of discussing Sufi approaches by organising them into twelve different groupings (*gurūh*, *firqa*). He named each group after a major figure (Muḥāsibī, [Ḥamdūn] Qaṣṣār, Ṭayfūr [Bāyazīd], Junayd, Nūrī, Sahl [Tustarī], Ḥakīm [Tirmidhī], Kharrāz, Ibn Khafīf, Sayyārī, Abū Ḥulmān, and Ḥallāj), and pointed out that all were 'accepted' (*maqbūl*) except the last two, which were 'rejected' (*mardūd*).[53] Closer scrutiny of Hujwīrī's long discussion of these groupings suggests that he could have hardly meant them as actual social entities, since Hujwīrī explicitly identified and located only one of them, that is the Sayyārīs, the followers of Sayyārī in the towns Nasā and Marw, and he made no historical or social observations on any other group.[54] Indeed, it is obvious that he used this system of classification mainly to organise his presentation of diverse Sufi views on such key concepts as 'states and stations' (under Muḥāsibī), 'intoxication and sobriety' (under Bāyazīd and Junayd), 'altruism' (under Nūrī), 'lower soul and passion' (under Tustarī), 'friendship with God and miracles' (under Tirmidhī), 'subsistence and passing away' (under Kharrāz), 'union and separation' (under Sayyārī) and 'the nature of the human spirit' (under Ḥallāj). In this connection, it is telling that Hujwīrī adopted a similar system of pairing in the third and last section of the *Uncovering*, where he paired major rituals with key concepts: 'repentance' under ablution, 'love' under prayer, 'generosity' under alms-giving, 'hunger' under fasting, and 'witnessing' under pilgrimage. Here too 'pairing' functioned as an effective organising tool, which enabled the author to impose some order onto a complicated array of subjects.

In the light of information available from other sources, Hujwīrī's pairing of concepts with major Sufis is on the mark, and his discussion of the different views is at once detailed, well-informed and judicious. Overall, in this long section of the *Uncovering*, Hujwīrī succeeded in giving his readers an inclusive and panoramic survey of the different Sufi approaches to some key theoretical issues. In the process, he delineated the boundaries of normative Sufism without, however, homogenising or levelling significant differences of opinion current among Sufi masters, even while he took special care to identify and explain his own preferences among the different views he expounded.[55] In this manner, he managed to draw a broad portrait of Sufism and mystical movements that included the eastern Ḥanafī milieu (for instance, detailed presentation of Tirmidhī), and even provided more coverage on the 'Path of Blame' than did Qushayrī, who refrained from describing Malāmatīs in detail even though he was from Nishapur, the home of the Malāmatī orientation. It is possible to see this ecumenical approach of Hujwīrī as another permutation of the fusion of Sufism and legal-theological scholarship that Qushayrī had accomplished before him so effectively: like this latter, Hujwīrī used scholarly, specifically theological, tools to process Sufism for himself and for his readers. In so doing, he not only broadened the scope of Sufism to include indigenous mystical trends like the way of the *ḥakīm*s and the Path of Blame but also rendered this inclusive Sufism intelligible to cultural elites familiar with the approaches and idioms of the world of scholarship.

The rapprochement between Sufism and scholarship that took place largely in Khurāsān and Transoxania and is epitomised in the overviews of Sufism written by non-traditionalist, somewhat 'academic', surveyors of Sufism from Sarrāj to Hujwīrī threw into greater relief serious questions relating to the delineation of the boundaries of normative Sufism. For the traditionalist Sufis, this boundary was always defined in terms of 'departure from the Qur'ān and the Sunna' (*bid'a*). From Makkī to Anṣārī, however, traditionalist Sufis were self-confident in their Islamic credentials and more inward-looking in orientation; they claimed the moral high ground and did not feel the need to adopt a defensive attitude towards non-traditionalists, whether these were rationalists (the Mu'tazila) or semi-rationalists (especially Shāfi'ī and Ḥanafī *fiqh* and Ash'arī *kalām*). If anything, they were on the offensive, as is patently clear in the life story of Anṣārī, particularly against rationalising tendencies in scholarly circles. Nor did they have to worry about significant opposition from inside, that is from non-Sufi traditionalists. Such insider resistance to Sufism certainly existed, as illustrated by the inquisition against the Baghdad Sufis instigated by Ghulām Khalīl. Moreover, the memory of the criticism directed against some proto-Sufi figures, notably Muḥāsibī, by Aḥmad ibn Ḥanbal (164–241/780–855), the champion of traditionalists, was never forgotten.[56] But, it appears that during the period from the mid-third/ninth century to the mid-fifth/eleventh century, traditionalist views of Sufism were largely positive; the only borderline issues had to do with the legacy of Ḥallāj, who always had his defenders as well as detractors among the Ḥanbalīs (and this is why Anṣārī suspended judgment on him), and the supposedly heretical theological developments among the Sālimiyya, the movement that formed around the teachings of Tustarī and that had aligned itself with the Mālikī legal school.[57] Traditionalist opposition to Sufism seems to have surfaced forcefully only in the sixth/twelfth century, in the work of the Ḥanbalī Ibn al-Jawzī (d. 597/1200).

For Sufis like Qushayrī and Hujwīrī, who readily interacted with the Shāfiʿī-Ashʿarī and Ḥanafī-Māturīdī scholarly circles and who were the architects of a Sufism aligned with 'semi-rationalist' scholarship, the boundaries of Sufism also had to be ascertained in scholarly terms. There was already a basis for this project in the works of Sarrāj, Kalābādhī and Sulamī. Sarrāj, who had relied only on internal Sufi criteria in his discussion of the errors of the Sufis and had seen no need to cite any external authorities, had nevertheless quoted the key jurists Mālik ibn Anas (d. 179/796), Muḥammad ibn Idrīs al-Shāfiʿī (150–204/767–820) and Ibn Surayj (d. 306/918) on the permissibility of listening to music;[58] Kalābādhī had 'parsed' Sufism in theological terms; and Sulamī had most notably compiled the sayings of Shāfiʿī about Sufism.[59] Not surprisingly, Qushayrī went further in bringing major scholarly authorities into the Sufi fold. Indirectly, he incorporated Shāfiʿī into the saintly hierarchy by designating him, in the words of the hidden saint Khiḍr, as one of the 'tent-pegs' (*awtād*, sing. *watad*) that held the universe in place; he also attributed 'clairvoyance' (*firāsa*) to him and cited his support for listening to music. He portrayed Aḥmad ibn Ḥanbal as a righteous (*ṣiddīq*) and scrupulous scholar among the pious forefathers (*salaf*), who consulted the Sufi Abū Hamza al-Baghdādī and who, reportedly, ended up in heaven. Admittedly, the author of the *Treatise* was less complementary on Abū Ḥanīfa (d. 150/767): in a report where he was compared to the renunciant Dāwūd al-Ṭā'ī (d. 165/781–2), the leader of the Ḥanafī school appeared as a scholar who did not implement his knowledge; nevertheless, Qushayrī cited him elsewhere in passing as a legal authority. As for Mālik ibn Anas, he received a more neutral, if cursory, treatment, but Qushayrī was careful to include his approval of listening to music.[60] Even more telling is the readiness with which Qushayrī cited the leading Ashʿarī figures of the generation before him in his discussion of the issue of miracles: he invokes the authority of his Shāfiʿī teachers Ibn Fūrak (d. 406/1015) and Abū Isḥāq al-Isfarāyinī (d. 418/1027) as well as that of the Mālikī Abū Bakr al-Bāqillānī (d. 403/1013) in support of his view that the *awliyā'* can accomplish miraculous feats (*karāmāt*).[61] Clearly, on significant border issues between Sufism and legal-theological scholarship, such as the permissibility of music and the acceptability of saintly miracles, Qushayrī was more than prepared to utilise scholarly views as confirmation of Sufi positions.

Where such support was not easily available or when the topic was particularly contentious, as in the issue of nature of the human spirit, Qushayrī exercised caution and kept his coverage exteremely brief, or, as in the question of the legacy of Ḥallāj, he prudently charted a middle course by excluding Ḥallāj from his biographical section (thus going against his model Sulamī who had included him) but incorporating the 'Sufi' sayings of this controversial figure into the rest of his treatise.

In forging a rapprochement between Sufism and legal-theological discourse, the Ḥanafī Hujwīrī went even further than Qushayrī. Not only did he insert separate notices on Abū Ḥanīfa, Shāfiʿī and Aḥmad ibn Ḥanbal (but not Mālik) into his biographical section and thus claimed them as Sufis, but he also readily incorporated rational argumentation into his discussion of Sufi doctrine on a regular basis.[62] In other words, he not only evoked the authority of legal and theological scholars but adopted their style of exposition and argumentation over and above faithful reproduction of reports from and about the major Sufis of the past, which had been the method preferred by all previous surveyors of Sufism. Perhaps because of this overtly academic posture, Hujwīrī was also anxious to be inclusive in his coverage of borderline issues, as demonstrated by his rehabilitation of Ḥallāj in a relatively long biographical entry on him, where, however, he warned his readers not to take Ḥallāj as a model to follow on account of his idiosyncratic behaviour.[63] However, on certain questions Hujwīrī too drew the line sharply: incarnation, understood as inherence of the divine in humans (*ḥulūl*) or as mixing of the divine and the human in any form (*imtizāj*), and transmigration of souls (*naskh-i arwāḥ*) were not part of Sufism; nor was the belief in the eternity of the human spirit (*rūḥ*), which Hujwīrī thought was the root cause of the heretical views of the two 'rejected' groups, Ḥulmāniyya and Ḥallājiyya; and while *samāʿ* was certainly acceptable, dance (*raqṣ*) was off limits.

The Ḥulmāniyya (or the Ḥulūliyya) was named after Abū Ḥulmān al-Dimashqī (d. c. 340/951), a figure already mentioned by Sarrāj in his discussion of 'audition' (*samāʿ*), where he is noted for a kind of 'hearing' Nūrī was known for, that is, hearing a divine message through a human voice or a sound made by animals.[64] In time, Abū Ḥulmān and his followers came to be associated also with the visual counterpart of this auditory practice: seeing God in every beautiful being, especially in human beauty. These practices reeked of belief in the possibility of physical manifestation of God, which was roundly condemned under the name 'incarnation' by rationalists, semi-rationalists and traditionalists alike. Seeing or hearing God in this world while one was fully awake was therefore generally seen as a heretical practice in the post-prophetic era.[65] The Ḥulmānians were also accused of belief in transmigration of souls as well as permissivism in the sense of 'allowing practices that were forbidden' (*ibāḥa*), which was seen as a natural consequence of belief in incarnation.[66] In condemning the two rejected Sufi groups as believers in incarnation, Hujwīrī frankly acknowledged that some reprehensible elements had been associated with Sufis in the past even while he declared these elements beyond the pale and thus excised them from the body of 'accepted' Sufism. In a clever move, he also argued that Ḥallāj himself was free of such heretical thinking (and possibly Abū Ḥulmān as well), and that the 'Ḥallājians' had really been formed by a certain Fāris (Hujwīrī clearly meant Abu'l-Qāsim Fāris ibn 'Īsā Dīnawarī, the Sufi informant of Kalābādhī), who had departed from the true teachings of his master. He then proceeded to refute the belief in the eternity of the spirit by a theological discussion in order to sound the death knell to all of the heresies for which the two rejected groups were condemned.

In brief, Qushayrī and Hujwīrī succeeded in aligning Sufism with Shāfi'ī-Ash'arī and Ḥanafī-Māturīdī scholarship. Just as the Ash'arī and Māturīdī approaches in *kalām* that developed as compromises between the anti-rationalist traditionalists and the rationalist Mu'tazila came to occupy the centre in all subsequent Islamic history, the 'accredited' or 'well-tempered' Sufism that was forged in Khurāsān and Transoxania in the fifth/eleventh century as a compromise between inward looking – at times anti-social – traditionalist trends on the one hand and antinomian and libertinist tendencies on the other hand gradually but surely assumed authoritative status throughout Islamdom. In time, the bridge thus built between Sufis and scholars came to be crossed in both directions by an increasing number of Sufi-scholars and scholar-Sufis, leading to a cross-fertilisation that ushered a new phase in Islamic cultural history. Even though scholarly-minded Sufis such as Kalābādhī, Qushayrī and Hujwīrī were the principal architects of 'well-tempered' Sufism, in the eyes of many literate Muslims this new presentation of the Sufi approach came to be associated especially with a single work written by a singular intellectual, *Iḥyā' 'ulūm al-dīn* (*Bringing the Religious Sciences to Life*) of Abū Ḥāmid al-Ghazālī (450–505/1058–1111).

A product of the same scholarly milieu as that of Qushayrī in Nishapur just a generation after him, Ghazālī was first and foremost a theologian and a professor of law, though in his youth he had been exposed to Sufism at the hands of Abū 'Alī Faḍl ibn Muḥammad-i Fārmadhī (d. 477/1084–5).[67] This latter was originally a student of Qushayrī, first in scholarship and then in Sufism, but he had later placed himself under the care of Abu'l-Qāsim 'Alī ibn 'Abd Allāh-i Kurrakānī (d. 469/1076) of Ṭūs, whose spiritual legacy reached back to Junayd through Abū 'Alī Rūdhbārī (d. 322/934 in Egypt), Abū 'Alī ibn al-Kātib (d. after 340/951–2) and Abū 'Uthmān Maghribī (d. 373/983 in Nishapur).[68] Although Ghazālī truly excelled in theological and legal sciences, he was discontent with the prevailing scholarly ethos of his time, and, just like Qushayrī and Hujwīrī who complained of the loss of true Sufism and decried the formalism rampant in so-called Sufis of their time, he expressed sorrow at the disappearance of genuine religious knowledge, and criticised so-called scholars for their 'thoughtless imitation' or 'faith in authority' (*taqlīd*). In his judgment, this regrettable state of affairs was brought about by excessive this-worldliness among academics, who had grown enamoured with themselves and had increasingly directed their efforts solely to self-aggrandisement.[69] As a response to this intellectual malaise and the grave danger it represented for the Muslim community, Ghazālī adopted the ambitiously-expansive mission of developing a comprehensive 'academic articulation of Islam' aimed at a sweeping reform of the whole of the Islamic scholastic enterprise. Eager to utilise all the intellectual resources available to him, he reached out to philosophy (*falsafa*) and Ismāʿīlī teachings (*taʿlīm*), and harnessed philosophical tools and doctrines that he found in these arenas to his cause of reviving Islamic knowledge.[70] He envisaged the totality of reformed Islamic sciences as consisting of six disciplines. The first five were properly scholastic in nature: theology (*ʿilm al-kalām*), substantive law (*furūʿ al-fiqh*), principles of jurisprudence (*uṣūl al-fiqh*), study of *ḥadīth* (*ʿilm al-ḥadīth*), and Qur'ānic exegesis (*ʿilm al-tafsīr*). However, Ghazālī had realised, through a personal spiritual crisis that had caused him to interrupt his teaching career at the Niẓāmiyya *madrasa* in Baghdad, that his mission would be doomed to failure if his academic articulation of Islam was not supported, even upheld, by a genuine spiritual grounding. He thus added a sixth discipline to his reformulated curriculum of Islamic knowledge: 'inner science' (*ʿilm al-bāṭin*), that is, Sufism.[71]

The inclusion of Sufism in Ghazālī's sweeping vision was not merely indicative of the degree to which the 'Sufi science' deserved a place, in his eyes, alongside the other academic disciplines, though this alone would have provided clear evidence that the interiorising Sufi approach had become acceptable to legal and theological scholars. Ghazālī's incorporation of the 'science of the interior' into his programme of reform, however, signalled more than acceptance: Ghazālī positively embraced Sufism and assigned a pivotal role to it in his larger project of reviving Islamic knowledge. This is evident in the way in which he wove Sufi concerns into the fabric of his central work of reform, *Bringing the Religious Sciences to Life* (which Ghazālī also rendered into Persian in abbreviated form as *Kīmiyā-yi saʿādat* (*The Alchemy of Happiness*)). This compendium was conceived as a complete guidebook on piety addressed to the common people. Ghazālī organised it into four volumes of ten books each, devoted respectively to the topics of 'worship' (*ʿibādāt*), 'social behaviour' (*ʿādāt*), 'vices that lead to perdition' (*muhlikāt*), and 'virtues that lead to salvation' (*munjiyāt*). He hoped that his guidebook would serve a therapeutic function, and his goal was to infuse religious life with a new spirit, which he sought to develop through his consistent emphasis on the 'heart' (*qalb*). He viewed the heart as the hinge between the visible and invisible worlds and thus as the ultimate foundation of the pious life, but since his purpose was to revitalise everyday piety through spirited practice à la Sufism while simultaneously avoiding the potentially misleading, thus dangerous, territory of scholastic speculation, he focused on practical matters and refrained from going into theoretical details about the nature of this spiritual organ, just as he avoided any discussion of Sufi theories.[72] Given the centrality of the notion of purification (*taṭhīr, tazkīya*) of the heart to his project, it was not surprising that Ghazālī relied heavily on Makkī's *Sustenance* in writing his own compendium of piety, though he also made frequent use of the works of Sarrāj, Qushayrī and Abū Sa'd al-Khargūshī.[73] On the whole, he stayed faithful to Qushayrī's cautious middle course and endorsed a moderate, practical version of Sufism, locating the path of piety squarely between the solitary life and life in society. Ghazālī's appropriation of practical Sufi piety as 'the most efficient way of promoting individual participation in the divine realm' into his project of resuscitating true religiosity was to prove singularly influential.[74] *Bringing the Religious Sciences to Life* soon became, and remained, a best-seller, and the widespread circulation of both Ghazālī's 'therapeutic' guidebook and Qushayrī's 'definitive' summation of Sufi theory among Muslims everywhere who were literate in Arabic (Hujwīrī's *Uncovering* had a similarly wide readership among Persian speakers) stood testimony to the fact that Sufi piety was being ineradicably assimilated by scholastic circles.[75] Sufism was on its way to become a universally-known mode of piety.

Notes

1 This work has been published: Abū Ṭālib Muḥammad ibn 'Alī Makkī, *'Ilm al-qulūb*, ed. 'Abd al-Qādir Aḥmad 'Aṭā (Cairo: Maktaba al-Qāhira, 1384/1964); for the argument against its attribution to Makkī, see Naṣr Allāh Pūrjavādī, 'Bāzmāndahā-yi kitāb-i *al-ishāra wa'l-'ibāra*-i Abū Sa'd-i Khargūshī dar kitāb-i *'ilm al-qulūb*', *Ma'ārif* 15, no 3 (1999): 34–41.

2 Makkī, *Qūt al-qulūb*, 2 vols. On Makkī, see Makkī, *Nahrung*, 1: 11–21; Renard, *Knowledge of God*, 33–8 and 112–263 (selections from the *Sustenance* in translation); and Böwering, *Mystical Vision*, 25–7, where Böwering documents his relationship to Tustarī's legacy. For the relationship between Ghazālī's work and the *Sustenance*, see Makkī, *Nahrung*, 1: 19, and Mustapha Hogga, *Orthodoxie, subversion et réforme en Islam: Gazali et les seljuqides* (Paris: Librairie philosophique J. Vrin, 1993), 203; for in-depth demonstration of Ghazālī's reliance on Makkī, see Gramlich's translation of books 31–6: Abū Ḥāmid Muḥammad ibn Muḥammad Ghazālī, *Muḥammad al-Ġazzālīs Lehre von den Stufen zur Gottesliebe*, trans. Richard Gramlich (Wiesbaden: F. Steiner, 1984), passim.

3 Renard, *Knowledge of God*, 127–8.

4 About Makkī, 'it is reported that he ate nothing but grass and herbs for such a [long] time that his skin assumed a verdant hue'; see Renard, *Knowledge of God*, 35; sources for this report on his vegetarianism, which he probably picked up from the legacy of Tustarī as practised by the Sālimiyya, are given in Makkī, *Nahrung*, 1: 12. For the

reasons behind renunciant criticism of 'people of *ḥadīth*', see Christopher Melchert, 'Early renunciants as *ḥadīth* transmitters', *Muslim World* 92 (2002): 413–14. See Renard, *Knowledge of God*, 146–73 for Makkī's criticism of exoteric scholars.

5 Renard, *Knowledge of God*, 254; also esp. 190–6 on reticence. Meier, 'Khurāsān', 216, bases his assertion that 'Malāmatiyya also existed in Mesopotamia, only there they were known as "the wise madmen" (*'uqalā' al-majānīn*)' on Makkī, *Qūt* (Cairo: 1351), 3: 108, l. 3; this edition is unavailable to me, but he might have had in mind a passage like the one quoted here.

6 Renard, *Knowledge of God*, 165–6 and 36.

7 Renard, *Knowledge of God*, 222.

8 On the dangers of innovation, see Renard, *Knowledge of God*, 211–55; for reliance on weak *ḥadīth*, ibid., 256–63.

9 Muḥammad ibn Yūsuf ibn Ma'dān al-Bannā' (d. 286/899), the most prominent mystic of Isfahān at the end of the third/ninth century, was the maternal grandfather of Abū Nu'aym's father; see 'Abū No'aym el-Eṣfahānī', EIr 1: 354–5 (W. Madelung), which is a more perceptive treatment than 'Abū Nu'aym al-Iṣfahānī', EI 1: 142b (J. Pedersen).

10 Mojaddedi, *Biographical Tradition*, 64.

11 'Abdāl', EIr 1: 173–4 (Jacqueline Chabbi), and Chapter 5 below.

12 For Ibn al-Jawzī's criticism of Abū Nu'aym, see 'Abū No'aym el-Eṣfahānī', EIr 1: 355 (W. Madelung), and Melchert, 'Early renunciants', 409; Melchert, 413, gives examples of Sufi criticism of *ḥadīth* transmitters. The entries of both Abū Nu'aym and Ibn al-Jawzī on female figures are discussed in Ruth Roded, *Women in Islamic Biographical Collections: From Ibn Sa'd to Who's Who* (Boulder, CO: L. Rienner, 1994), 91–113, and in Laury Silvers-Alario, 'Women, gender, and early Sufi women', forthcoming in *Encyclopedia of Women in Islamic Cultures* (Leiden: Brill, 2003–7).

13 For a portrayal of Abū Nu'aym's *Ornament* as 'a recuperative reconstruction of a 'history' for Sufism', see Hamid Dabashi, *Truth and Narrative: The Untimely Thoughts of 'Ayn al-Quḍāt al-Hamadhānī* (Richmond, Surrey: Curzon, 1999), 113–14. On the relationship between *ahl al-ḥadīth* and Sufis in this early period, see further Silvers-Alario, 'Teaching Relationship', 72–7.

14 The details of the disagreement between Ibn Manda and Abū Nu'aym, which was on the thorny question of the 'uncreate Qur'ān', are not completely clear, though Ibn Manda seems to have accused Abū Nu'aym of being a *lafẓī*, that is one 'who held that the voicing (*lafẓ*) of the Qur'ān in recitation was something created and therefore distinct from God's eternal speaking', see Richard Frank, *Al-Ghazālī and the Ash'arite School* (Durham, NC: Duke University Press, 1994), 132–3, note 17. This incident and Ibn Manda's denunciation of Abū Nu'aym as a scholar with Ash'arī leanings, appears to have given the green light for later Shāfi'ī authors (like Subkī and Ibn 'Asākir) to claim Abū Nu'aym for their own legal school. Yet, the later Ḥanbalīs Ibn al-Jawzī and Ibn Taymiyya did not denounce him and in fact claimed him as one of their own, namely a Ḥanbalī. There is, therefore, a distinct probability that Abū Nu'aym too was a Ḥanbalī. For a detailed discussion of this issue that persuasively makes the case for an Ḥanbalī affiliation for Abū Nu'aym, see Pūrjavādī, 'Abū Manṣūr', esp. 32–9. This article of Pūrjavādī is also the most comprehensive study on Abū Manṣūr.

15 Naṣr Allāh Pūrjavādī, 'Du asar-i kūtāh az Abū Manṣūr-i Iṣfahānī', *Ma'ārif* 6 (1990): 41.

16 On the impact of the *Way of the Elect* on the development of Sufi terminology, see the important essay by Naṣr Allāh Pūrjavādī, 'Sayr-i iṣṭilāḥāt-i ṣūfiyān az "Nahj al-khāṣṣ"-i Abū Manṣūr-i Iṣfahānī tā "Futūḥāt"-i Ibn-i 'Arabī', *Ma'ārif* 16, no. 3 (2000): 3–55.

17 Naṣr Allāh Pūrjavādī, '*Ādāb al-mutaṣāawwifa wa-ḥaqā'iquhā wa-ishārātuhā* az Abū Manṣūr-i Iṣfahānī', *Ma'ārif* 9 (1993): 276 ('*Khātima*').

18 Naṣr Allāh Pūrjavādī, 'Kitāb sharḥ al-adhkār', *Ma'ārif* 19, no. 3 (2003): 3–30.

19 Bernd Radtke (ed.), *Adab al-mulūk: Ein Handbuch zur islamischen Mystik aus dem 4./10. Jahrhundert* (Beirut: Orient-Institut der Deutschen Morgenländischen Gesellschaft im Kommission bei F. Steiner Verlag Stuttgart, 1991), Arabic text; German translation: *Die Lebensweise der Könige: Adab al-mulūk, ein Handbuch zur islamischen Mystik*, trans. Richard Gramlich (Stuttgart: Deutsche Morgenländische Gesellschaft Kommissionsverlag Franz Steiner Stuttgart, 1993). The work was first introduced in Meier, 'Important manuscript', 159–68 (first published in 1967).

20 For a clear discussion on questions of authorship of the *Etiquette*, see the review of Radtke's edition by Hermann Landolt in *Journal of the American Oriental Society* 114 (1994): 457–9. Pūrjavādī has made the case for Abū Manṣūr's authorship of the *Etiquette* in various publications; see, for instance, his notes to his edition of *Ādāb al-mutaṣawwifa*, 277–82.

21 The following account of his biography is based mostly on "Abdallāh al-Anṣārī', EIr 1: 187–90 (S. L. de Beaureceuil), and Farhādī, *Anṣārī*.

22 Anṣārī al-Harawī, *Ṭabaqāt*, 624, my translation. An English translation of the whole entry on Abū Manṣūr is in Farhādī, *Anṣārī*, 53–4.

23 He was called 'Ammū because Nihāwandī had given him authority over his other disciples by designating him as their 'uncle', see Meier, *Abū Sa'īd*, 444.

24 On Ṭāqī, see Sobieroj, *Ibn Ḫafīf*, 85. Sobieroj also documents many other links that Anṣārī had with the circle of Ibn Khafīf, who maintained close connections with Ḥanbalīs.

25 Farhādī, *Anṣārī*, 13.

26 For some details of this forty-day affair, see Meier, *Abū Sa'īd*, 299.

27 "Abdallāh al-Anṣārī', EIr 1: 188 (S. L. de Beaureceuil).

28 Farhādī, *Anṣārī*, 59.

29 Farhādī, *Anṣārī*, 79.

30 Renard, *Knowledge of God*, 51–2; Meier, *Abū Sa'īd*, 289, note 8; Addas, 'Andalusī mysticism', 926. Meier, Renard and Addas all rely on B. Halff, 'Le *Maḥāsin al-majālis* d'Ibn al-'Arīf et l'oeuvre du soufi hanbalite al-Anṣārī', *Révue des études islamiques* 39 (1971): 321–33. The *Beauties* is available in a bilingual edition: Aḥmad ibn Muḥammad Ibn al-'Arīf, *Maḥāsin al-Majālis = The Attractions of Mystical Sessions*, trans. William Elliott and Adnan K. Abdulla (Amersham: Avebury, 1980).

31 Farhādī, *Anṣārī*, 45–7, translating from Anṣārī al-Harawī, *Ṭabaqāt*, 1–8.

32 "Abdallāh al-Anṣārī', EIr 1: 189 (S. L. de Beaureceuil). Cf. the translation of the entry on Kharrāz from the *Generations* in Farhādī, *Anṣārī*, 49.

33 Abu'l-Faḍl Rashīd al-Dīn Maybudī, *Kashf al-asrār va 'uddat al-abrār ma'rūf bi-tafsīr-i Khvājah 'Abd Allāh-i Anṣārī*, ed. 'Alī Aṣghar Ḥikmat, 10 vols (Tehran: Intishārāt-i Dānishgāh-i Tihrān, 1331–39/1952–60).

34 Bo Utas, 'The Munajat or Ilahi-Namah of 'Abdu'llah Ansari', *Manuscripts of the Middle East* 3 (1988): 83–7. This article is the best synopsis of what we know on the

Arabic and Persian works associated with Anṣārī's name.

35 On his biography, see Hamid Algar's introduction to 'Abd al-Karīm ibn Hawāzin Qushayrī, *Principles of Sufism*, trans. Barbara R. von Schlegell (Berkeley: Mizan Press, 1992), i–xvii; Richard Gramlich's introduction to Qushayrī, *Das Sendschreiben al-Qušayrīs über das Sufitum*, 11–19; Bulliet, *Patricians*, 150–3; and 'Abū 'l-Ḳāsim 'Abd al-Karīm b. Hawāzin', EI 5: 526a–527a (H. Halm), all with copious references.

36 'Abū 'Alī Daqqāq', EIr 1: 255–7 (J. Chabbi); Bulliet, *Patricians*, 150–3.

37 Qushayrī, *Principles of Sufism*, ix (H. Algar's introduction); see also 'Ṣūfism and the Qur'ān', *Encyclopedia of the Qur'ān*, 5: 143–6 (Alexander Knysh), and Sands, *Sufi Commentaries*, 71–2.

38 *Al-tawḥīd ifrād al-qidam 'an al-ḥadath*, 'God's unity is the isolation of the eternal from the created', Qushayrī, *Risāla*, 28–9 / *Sendschreiben*, 25 (0.8).

39 For a close comparative examination of Qushayrī's biographical section with that of Sulamī's, see Mojaddedi, *Biographical Tradition*, ch. 4. Curiously, although he wrote the *Treatise* in 437/1045, well after the deaths of Daqqāq in 405/1015 and of Sulamī in 412/1021, Qushayrī did not include separate entries on either of them in his biographical section. This raises the possibility that Daqqāq, like Sulamī, was not a major 'training' master, and that Qushayrī's frequent mention of him in the text of the *Treatise* was occasioned mostly by his intense loyalty to Daqqāq as his first (and probably only) spiritual director and as his father-in-law.

40 Similarly, see Mojaddedi, *Biographical Tradition*, 109–17 on how Qushayrī's portraits of Bāyazīd and Junayd, in his biographical section, are more conservative than Sulamī's portraits of them.

41 Qushayrī, *Risāla*, 731–2 / *Sendschreiben*, 536 (54.1).

42 Qushayrī, *Risāla*, 738 / *Sendschreiben*, 540 (54.8).

43 On his biography, see the introduction by Nicholson in Hujwīrī, *Revelation*, 13–20 (first published 1911), and the introduction by Qāsim Anṣārī in Hujwīrī, *Kashf*, 4–39 (first published 1926), as well as 'Hojvīrī', EIr 12: 429–30 (Gerhard Böwering).

44 Hujwīrī, *Kashf*, 7 / *Revelation*, 7.

45 Hujwīrī, *Kashf*, 40 / *Revelation*, 35.

46 Hujwīrī, *Kashf*, 19 / *Revelation*, 17 (Nicholson's translation slightly altered).

47 For al-Būshanjī's statement, see Sulamī, *Ṭabaqāt*, 459; Hujwīrī, *Kashf*, 49 / *Revelation*, 44 (with the alternative spelling of the name as 'Fūshanja'); also 'Fūshanjī, 'Alī ibn Aḥmad Heravī', EIr 10: 230–1 (G. Böwering). Ibn Khafīf's saying is reported in Fritz Meier, 'Soufisme et déclin culturel', in *Classicisme et déclin culturel dans l'histoire de l'Islam, actes du symposium international d'histoire de la civilisation musulmane, Bordeaux 25–29 juin 1956*, ed. Robert Brunschvig (Paris: Chantemerle, 1957), 217, and Sobieroj, 'Comparison', 344, note 25. For discussion and other examples of this topos, see Meier, 'Soufisme et déclin culturel', 217–19, and Richard Gramlich, *Die schiitischen Derwischorden Persiens* (Wiesbaden: Deutsche Morgenländische Gesellschaft Kommissionsverlag Steiner, 1965), 2: 154, note 853; cf. Naṣr Allāh Pūrjavādī, *Du mujaddid: pizhūhishhāyī dar bāra-'i Muḥammad-i Ghazzālī va Fakhr-i Rāzī* (Tehran: Markaz-i Nashr-i Dānishgāhī, 1381/2002), 124–5.

48 *Aḥsan al-taqāsīm* (completed in Shiraz in 375/985), ed. de Goeje (Leiden, 1906), 415, quoted in Trimingham, *Sufi Orders*, 7, with minor parenthetical additions. The author's name may have been al-Muqaddasī. For further discussion of these enigmatic Sufis who evidently called themselves 'Ḥubbiyya', see Ess, *Theologie*, 2: 622–3.

49 On Sufi dress, see Hujwīrī, *Kashf*, 49–65 / *Revelation*, 45–57. On the significance of Sufi paraphernalia, see the amusing anecdote in which Hujwīrī was pelted with melon skins by some formalist Sufis (Persian, 77–8 / English, 69). Other items mentioned in fifth/eleventh-century sources include prayer rugs, a pair of shoes/sandals, toothpicks, combs, needles, scissors and razors; see documentation in Fritz Meier, 'A book of etiquette for Sufis', in *Essays on Islamic Piety and Mysticism*, trans. John O'Kane (Leiden: Brill, 1999), 89, note 184.

50 Hujwīrī, *Kashf*, 208–9 / *Revelation*, 166–7. For statements on 'practice' versus 'morals', see Persian, 47–9 / English, 41–4.

51 Interestingly, Abū Ḥāmid al-Ghazālī (450–505/1058–1111) too uses the word '*rusūm*' to criticise theologians who practise 'thoughtless imitation' (*taqlīd*); see Frank, *Al-Ghazālī*, 108, note 16.

52 Hujwīrī, *Kashf*, 63 / *Revelation*, 56 (Nicholson opts for the variant reading *ma'ūnāt* instead of *mulawwanāt* in the title), where Hujwīrī also gives an early example of the interiorising interpretation of different aspects of Sufi dress as symbols of inner states; for another example of such 'symbolic reading' of dress that might have been contemporary with Hujwīrī, see Meier, 'Book of etiquette', 66–75; for the attribution of this latter work, not to Najm al-Dīn Kubrā (d. 617/1220) but possibly to the circle of Anṣārī, see Gramlich, *Derwischorden*, 1: 11, note 3.

53 The eleventh group is called *Ḥulūliyya* ('incarnationists') in the published edition and in Nicholson's translation, but at least one of the manuscripts has *Ḥulmāniyya* instead, which would match the pattern of naming that Hujwīrī follows in all the other groups. Abū Ḥulmān is discussed below in this chapter.

54 Cf. Meier, *Abū Sa'īd*, 10–1.

55 For more detailed discussion of the organisation of the *Uncovering*, see Mojaddedi, *Biographical Tradition*, 125–47 (ch. 4).

56 Melchert, 'Ḥanābila', 355–60.

57 For a brief recapitulation of what is known about Ḥallāj and the Ḥanbalīs during this period, see Ess, 'Sufism', 29–30; for details, see Massignon, *Passion*, 2: 101ff. On Sālimiyya and its Ḥanbalī critics, see the summary in Böwering, 'Early Sufism', 61–3.

58 Sarrāj, *Luma'*, 276–7/ *Schlaglichter*, 402–4 (97.9–10).

59 Meier, 'Important manuscript', 170–86.

60 See the *Treatise* (Arabic and German), index, under 'Shāfi'ī', 'Aḥmad ibn Ḥanbal', 'Abū Ḥanīfa', and 'Mālik ibn Anas'. On Khiḍr, see 'al-Khaḍir (al-Khiḍr)', EI 4: 902b (A. J. Wensinck).

61 Qushayrī, *Risāla*, 660–1/ *Sendschreiben*, 480–1 (52.2).

62 Hujwīrī, *Kashf*, 112–17 (Abū Ḥanīfa), 143–6 (Shāfi'ī and Aḥmad) / *Revelation*, 92–5 and 116–18.

63 Hujwīrī, *Kashf*, 189–93/ *Revelation*, 150–3.

64 Hearing a peddler selling 'wild thyme' (*yā sa'tarā barrī*), Abū Ḥulmān swoons, understanding the call as 'try and you will see my kindness' (*is'a tarā birrī*); see Sarrāj, *Luma'*, 289 / *Schlaglichter*, 417 (102.3). For other examples of this kind of *samā'*, see Fritz Meier, 'The dervish dance', in *Essays on Islamic Piety and Mysticism*, trans. John O'Kane (Leiden: Brill, 1999), 32–3. The death date for Abū Ḥulmān is according to Böwering, 'Early Sufism', 62, but he does not cite his source.

65 On the history of 'seeing God' as a theological and mystical concept, see Pūrjavādī, *Ru'yat-i māh*.

66 'Ḥulmāniyya', EI 3: 570 (J. Pedersen); 'Ḥulūl', EI 3: 570–1 (L. Massignon–G. C. Anawati); and 'Ibāḥa II', EI 3: 662a (W. Madelung, M. G. S. Hodgson). Also Ess, *Theologie*, 1: 144.

67 For a concise but comprehensive and up-to-date account on his biography, see 'Ḡazālī, Abū Ḥamed Moḥammad, i. Biography', EIr 10: 358–63 (G. Böwering).

68 On Kurrakānī, see Hujwīrī, *Kashf*, 211–12 / *Revelation*, 169–70; and on Fārmadhī, Muḥammad ibn Munavvar, *Asrār*, 1: 118–20 (and, Shafī'ī-Kadkanī's notes, 2: 228–9) / *Secrets*, 208–11; also Meier, *Abū Sa'īd*, esp. 56–7. Kurrakān or Kurragān was a village of Ṭūs, and the name Kurrakānī should not be corrupted to 'Gurgānī' (south of the Caspian), as it is often done (for instance, by Nicholson in his translation of Hujwīrī); see Meier, *Abū Sa'īd*, 56, note 99, and Muḥammad ibn Munavvar, *Asrār*, 2: 277–8.

69 See the introduction in Abū Ḥāmid Muḥammad ibn Muḥammad Ghazālī, *Iḥyā' 'ulūm al-dīn* (Beirut: Dār al-Kutub al-'Ilmiyya, 1996), 1: 9–12. The polemic against scholars does not appear in the preface of the Persian synopsis of this work: Abū Ḥāmid Muḥammad ibn Muḥammad Ghazālī, *Kīmiyā-yi sa'ādat*, ed. Ḥusayn Khidīvjam (Tehran: Shirkat-i Intishārāt-i 'Ilmī va Farhangī, 1364/1985), 1: 3–6.

70 There is a rich literature on Ghazālī's engagement with philosophy; two samples that evince recent trends in scholarship are Jules Janssens, 'Al-Ghazzālī's *Tahāfut*: Is it really a rejection of Ibn Sina's Philosophy?', *Journal of Islamic Studies* 12 (2001): 1–17, and Frank Griffel, 'Al-Ġazālī's concept of prophecy: the introduction of Avicennan psychology into Aš'arite theology', *Arabic Sciences and Philosophy* 14 (2004): 101–44. Ghazālī's indebtedness to Ismā'īlī thought is less well documented; for valuable leads in this direction, see Hermann Landolt, 'Ghazālī and "*Religionswissenschaft*": some notes on the *Mishkāt al-anwār*', *Asiatische Studien / Études Asiatiques* 45 (1991): 19–72, and Farouk Mitha, *Al-Ghazālī and the Ismailis: A Debate on Reason and Authority in Medieval Islam* (London: I. B. Tauris in association with the Institute of Ismaili Studies, 2001).

71 The listing of six disciplines is adopted from 'Uṣūl al-fiḳh', EI 10: 931b (N. Calder).

72 For a discussion of the *Iḥyā'* as an attempt at moral reform through Sufism, see Hogga, *Orthodoxie*, 179–203; for an attempt to discern the nature of the heart in the *Iḥyā'*, see Timothy J. Gianotti, *Al-Ghazālī's Unspeakable Doctrine of the Soul: Unveiling the Esoteric Psychology and Eschatology of the* Iḥyā' (Leiden: Brill, 2001).

73 On Ghazālī's Sufi sources, see Pūrjavādī, *Du mujaddid*, 213–78; on his reliance on Makkī, see also note 2 above in this chapter.

74 The quote is from Peter Heath, 'Reading al-Ghazālī: The case of psychology', in *Reason and Inspiration in Islam: Theology, Philosophy and Mysticism in Muslim Thought, in Honor of Hermann Landolt*, ed. Todd Lawson (London: I. B.Tauris in association with the Institute of Ismaili Studies, 2005), 196.

75 As an instance of the assimilation, albeit hotly contested, of Ghazālī's *Iḥyā'* in al-Andalus and Morocco especially during the fifth/eleventh century, see Maribel Fierro, 'Opposition', 185–97, and Cornell, *Realm*, 12–31.

5

Formation of communities

The development of a specialised Sufi literature was, naturally, only the literary manifestation of the emergence of the Sufi tradition as a major social and cultural phenomenon. The shaping of Sufism as a distinct tradition was evident equally in the formation of local communities around major Sufi masters. Such communities were of different kinds, reflecting the complex nature of Sufi shaykhs as social personalities.

At the most basic level was the community formed by pupils and disciples around individual shaykhs. This was a local community held together by the charisma of the master and the efficacy of his life example as perceived by his followers. Such local communities existed, of course, from the very first phase of Sufi history, and are exemplified by what appear to have been tightly-knit groups around Junayd in Baghdad and Tustarī in Basra. Both of these communities proved to have staying power for a few generations after the death of the first master around whose example they had formed: Junayd's community survived in Baghdad under the leadership of Jurayrī and later of Khuldī well into the mid-fourth/tenth century, while Tustarī's legacy also continued but gradually evolved into a theological orientation known as the Sālimiyya that could no longer be identified primarily as Sufi or mystical in nature.[1] Concomitantly with the formation of these first communities or in the next generation, similar locally-based groups came to exist in other locations, such as the ones around Ibn Khafīf in Shiraz and ʿAlī ibn Sahl in Isfahan. Practically nothing is known about the latter group, but the former may have numbered as many as a few hundred at any given time, since Ibn Khafīf claimed to have trained more than 1,000 disciples and his claim is confirmed in an independent source. The community of disciples possibly lived close to Ibn Khafīf's lodge (*ribāṭ*) in order to benefit from his guidance, and indeed, the master authored one of the earliest extant pedagogical guidebooks addressed to aspirants, entitled *Kitāb al-iqtiṣād* (*The Book of the Golden Mean*).[2] Ibn Khafīf's teachings in this book are not rich in social detail, but significantly, they suggest that the beginning-level aspirants were required to earn a living, though they were asked to avoid the company of 'the sons of this world' (*abnā' al-dunyā*) and political rulers.[3] They were to dress simply, refrain from eating meat, generally eat and sleep little and cultivate 'truthfulness' (*ṣidq*) and 'sincerity' (*ikhlāṣ*). Ibn Khafīf must have been an exceptionally-gifted trainer who cultivated close bonds with aspirants whom he took under his care, and, not surprisingly, he was one of the first Sufi masters whose life story was recorded in writing by one of his disciples, Abu'l-Ḥasan ʿAlī Daylamī.[4] Nothing is known about the fate of the lodge after Ibn Khafīf's death (one of his disciples, Abu'l Ḥusayn-i Sālbih, d. 415/1024, may have taken over), but an indirect disciple, Abū Isḥāq Ibrāhīm al-Kāzarūnī (352/963–426/1033), succeeded in building a widespread network of lodges centred in his hometown Kāzarūn that proved to be remarkably durable and lasted into the tenth/sixteenth century.

Kāzarūnī, who was probably initiated by a disciple of Ibn Khafīf, al-Ḥusayn ibn Muḥammad al-Akkār (d. 391/1000–1), was a lifelong celibate and vegetarian.[5] The son of a recent convert, he tirelessly preached and promoted Islam to the predominantly Zoroastrian peoples of his home town and its environs, though later legends of him making thousands of converts are surely exaggerated. He spearheaded the construction of a mosque in which he preached, but his singular mission in life was unconditional charity to the destitute and travellers, and the centre for the realisation of this goal was his own lodge. Charity and generosity to all living beings were the hallmarks of the Kāzarūnī way, which quickly spread throughout Fārs, in the form of sixty-five lodges all equipped with public kitchens. Since Kāzarūnī himself did not possess any wealth, these lodges depended on the generosity of wealthy patrons, whose donations the lodges channelled to the needy. This philanthropic enterprise survived the master and had an incredibly long and expansive after-life that extended to Anatolia in the west and South Asia and China in the east.[6] However, like Ibn Khafīf, Kāzarūnī was also an effective Sufi master who trained disciples and, like his spiritual master, he too became the subject of a biography composed within the circle of his disciples.[7] A chapter of this work, which contains the directions Kāzarūnī gave to a certain disciple, gives us a profile of the ideal disciple as envisioned by the master. The disciple was asked to acquire and apply knowledge of the *sharʿīa*; to avoid ostentatious dress and behaviour; to keep the company of the poor, the trustworthy (*ṣādiqān*) and the virtuous (*ṣāliḥān*), and to avoid the company of the powerful – these included kings, commanders, oppressors, judges and administrators – and 'those devoted to this world' (*ahl-i dunyā*); not to sit with women and beardless youths; to be kind, mild and modest, and to exercise nobility and generosity; not to go to the cemetery to recite the Qur'ān for a fee; not to overdo charity so as to avoid becoming needy oneself; not to accept gifts from commanders and high administrators; not to oppress anyone; to keep night prayers and to take an hour everyday for *dhikr*; and to serve companions, the poor and travellers.[8]

The training master and Sufi lineages

As a rule, the local communities that formed around particular masters did not survive beyond a few generations (in the case of Kāzarūnī, it seems to have been the charity operation and not his spiritual method that was kept alive). It was not long, however, before another kind of community came into existence that proved to have more staying power than the local circle of disciples. This was the 'spiritual lineage', the idea that those who studied under a particular master shared a common spiritual heritage in the form of the master's unique 'path' or 'method' (*ṭarīq* or *ṭarīqa*) and were thus connected with one another, even across time and space, into a far-flung spiritual family. Attaching 'chains of authorities' to sayings of particular figures – parallel to the *isnād*, the authenticating pedigree preceding an *ḥadīth* – was not unimportant to early Sufis, as evidenced by the occasional inclusion of such information in early Sufi literature. Soon, however, authentication of piecemeal Sufi statements and practices gave way to veritable spiritual genealogies, expressing the idea that one's whole Sufi outlook is authenticated by a pedigree. The earliest examples of such genealogies, known as *silsila* (literally, 'chain'), can be traced back to Khuldī (d. 348/959), who declared that Junayd had inherited his teachings ultimately from the 'Followers' (*tābiʿūn*, 'second-generation' Muslims) via a chain that included Ḥasan al-Baṣrī (d. 110/728), and, soon after Khuldī, to Abū ʿAlī al-Daqqāq (d. 405/1015), who also traced Junayd's teaching to the Followers, but via Dāwūd al-Ṭāʾī (d. 165/781–2).[9] From here it was but a short step to the idea that all those who shared the same pedigree made up a familial community. Such spiritual lineages took some time to develop, and the different stages of this development are difficult to document. It is, however, likely that the growing significance of the concept of *silsila* was bound up with an increasing emphasis, especially during the course of the fifth/eleventh century, on the role of the Sufi shaykh as 'master of training' (*shaykh al-tarbiya*) as opposed to his role as 'master of instruction' (*shaykh al-taʿlīm*), to borrow designations first used by Ibn ʿAbbād al-Rundī (d. 792/1390).[10]

In the first century of Sufi history, instruction took the form of a shaykh imparting Sufi wisdom in a conversation or in a lecture to a single aspirant (*murīd*) to Sufism or to a whole circle of aspirants and other interested listeners in random or regular meetings held in the shaykh's house, or more typically, in a mosque. Such instruction, as exemplified by the pedagogical instructions of Ibn Khafīf and Kāzarūnī, was considered a necessity and was valued highly by serious aspirants, who were expected to follow the example of their shaykhs. By contrast, training meant spiritual direction: the shaykh took interest in, and even assumed some responsibility for, the spiritual progress of the aspirants, and he directed, supervised and criticised their behaviour. It is clear that in this first phase of Sufi history, instruction and training were inextricably intertwined: Sufi masters taught by training and trained by teaching. From the mid-fourth/tenth century on, however, training gradually began to gain an added significance until in the following century, it even became a subject for detailed theoretical discussion. This is demonstrated by the growing trend to write independent treatises on pedagogy (see Table 4.3) and especially by two separate pieces on the subject from Qushayrī, *al-Waṣiyya li'l-murīdīn* (*Advice to Aspirants*, at the end of his *Treatise*) and *Tartīb al-sulūk* (*The Structure of Wayfaring*). This new emphasis on training manifested itself also in new expressions on the significance of obedience to one's shaykh. Perhaps the most striking example of this new rhetoric of obedience was the application of Tustarī's saying 'The first stage in trust is when the servant is in the hands of God like the corpse in the hands of the washer, turning him as he wishes while he has neither motion nor control', a statement that was patently about the lowest level of trust in God, to the aspirant's relationship to his master at the beginning of the sixth/twelfth century.[11] In this manner, the Sufi aspirant now appeared as the corpse in the hands of the Sufi master, who had unquestionable authority over his novices. In an analogy that became increasingly popular, the shaykh was compared to the physician; Hujwīrī declared, 'The shaykhs of this path [Sufism] are the physicians of hearts.' If there was any doubt about the status of the Sufi master, this was dispelled by establishing a clear correspondence between him and the Prophet: 'The shaykh in his congregation is like the Prophet in his community.'[12] The process of exalting the authority of the shaykh over the aspirant had clearly reached its culmination, so it was not surprising that at around the same time Muḥammad ibn Ṭāhir al-Maqdisī (d. 507/1113) formulated the saying, 'Service [to the shaykh] is better than worship' (*al-khidma afḍal min al-'ibāda*), and 'Ayn al-Quḍāt al-Hamadhānī (d. 526/1131) reported the maxim, 'One who does not have a shaykh does not have a religion' (*man lā shaykha lahu lā dīna lahu*).[13]

The master-disciple relationship at the core of this new emphasis on training is described in detail by Qushayrī in the final chapter of his *Treatise*, entitled *Advice to Aspirants*. This Sufi-scholar, who tempered Sufism in the crucible of scholarship, started his advice to aspirants by affirming unequivocably the superiority of Sufism to both received and rational scholarship. All the same, he proceeded to make the acquisition of knowledge of the *sharī'a* the very first condition that those who set out to become Sufis should meet. The aspirant needed this familiarity with the law, Qushayrī explained, in order to fulfil his/her legal obligations. The next condition that Qushayrī presented almost in the same breath as the first was training with a master: 'It is necessary for an aspirant to train with a shaykh; if he does not have a master, he will never be successful. As Bāyazīd [Basṭāmī] said: "The leader of one who does not have a master is Satan."'[14] Having found a master, the aspirant then needed to repent completely for all past sins and become reconciled with all opponents and enemies. The next stage was the severance of all ties with personal possessions and public image (*māl* and *jāh*). This was followed by submission to the authority of the master, both in deed and in inner disposition, and the necessity not to hide anything from the master, neither in behaviour nor in thought.[15] It was only when the aspirant had met these conditions that the master started the training process in earnest by 'infusing' a particular *dhikr* into him.[16] The aspirant was expected to maintain uttering this 'invocation' first with the tongue, then also with the heart, while he kept himself ritually pure on a continuous basis, slept and ate little, and avoided all company. He was asked to consult his master about the difficult obstacles he would inevitably encounter in this endeavour, all occasioned by the resistance of his lower self to this new discipline. Until he attained his goal, he was banned from interrupting this exercise in order to travel, even for making the pilgrimage, nor was he allowed to seek sustenance in any way, either by begging or through gainful employment, except for what came his way, but it was acceptable for him to serve other, more advanced aspirants in the meantime. He was also asked to refrain from all supererogotary worship and to remain content with performing only the obligatory observances. His participation in communal rituals (*samāʿ*) was to be strictly regulated, and particularly-detailed stipulations were given for any kind of bodily movement occasioned by ecstasy. Qushayrī also asked the aspirants to avoid the company of young boys, not to be friendly with women, and to stay away from all those who devote themselves to this world. Throughout, Qushayrī reminded the aspirants to respect the master and to cherish this latter's acceptance of them as his novices.[17]

Indeed, the matter of obedience to the master was so crucial to Qushayrī that he had earlier elaborated on this subject in a separate chapter of his *Treatise*. At the beginning of that chapter, he revealingly likened the relationship between disciple and master to that between Moses and his mysterious guide as these appear in a Qur'ānic story. In the Qur'ān (18 [Kahf]: 60–82), Moses meets an unidentified servant of God at a place designated as the confluence of the two seas. This nameless character, who was later identified as 'al-Khiḍr' by Qur'ān commentators, is a special figure: God had given him 'mercy from His own mercy' and had taught him 'knowledge of His core being' (*min ladunnī*).[18] Moses asks his permission to follow him so that he could teach Moses something of his special knowledge, and the guide accepts him as his follower only on the condition that Moses should not question him on anything he does. As the story unfolds, Moses cannot keep his promise, especially since the guide commits some apparently outrageous acts, and when Moses challenges the wisdom of his guide three times in a row, his defiance causes the guide to terminate their relationship before Moses can imbibe from the guide's special knowledge. Qushayrī's intention in establishing this analogy between 'master-disciple' and 'Khiḍr-Moses' must have been crystal clear to his readers: the Sufi shaykhs, like Khiḍr, are endowed with special mercy and knowledge directly from God that are denied even the prophet Moses. The aspirants, like Moses, should ask the permission of the masters to follow them and, if accepted by him, they should submit to their authority even if they are scandalised by the behaviour of their masters. By this analogy, Qushayrī also accurately described the difficulty of maintaining such unquestioning submission to the master: since even Moses failed to keep his promise, the disciple should exercise extra caution to respect his master and refrain from entertaining ill thoughts or harbouring suspicions about him. For Qusharī, the authority of the training master had virtually no bounds.[19]

In the *Tartīb al-sulūk* (*The Structure of Wayfaring*) attributed – with some degree of uncertainty – to Qushayrī, the level of attention given to the authority of the master and the training of the aspirants shifts to the experience of *dhikr* itself.[20] The author of this brief treatise that was clearly addressed to aspirants described in detail the deepening of the recollection (in this case, the recommended *dhikr* formula was the popular 'God, God, God') from the tongue to the heart and eventually to the 'secret' (the core of the heart), and the accompanying process of the passing away of the self as well as the subsequent return to one's senses. He also explained the phenomenon of 'ecstatic utterance' as God talking through the mystic, and gave instructions on how to differentiate between 'thoughts' (*khawāṭir*) that came from God and those that originated from Satan during recollection, and on how to navigate the turbulent mental states that occurred in *dhikr*. Significantly, the author carefully pointed out how the spiritual power (*himma*) of the master could propel the novice towards his goal; it was, therefore, crucial to have an experienced shaykh.

Another work, entitled *Mukhtaṣar fī ādāb al-ṣūfiyya* (*Summary of Sufi Etiquette*) or *ādāb al-murīdīn* (*The Etiquette of Aspirants*), that appears to have been the product of the tradition of Anṣārī as it was preserved by his followers demonstrates that the scope of the new emphasis on training was sufficiently extensive to cover outward behaviour and issues of communal living. The author of this treatise prescribed right conduct in dress (along with a discussion of its symbolism), sitting and rising in gatherings, entering lodges, eating, dinner invitations, *samāʿ*, and travel, all subjects that became increasingly more important in the era of training masters who were in charge of the communities of disciples around them. In the preface, this concern for exterior conduct is justified by recourse to a statement of Anṣārī that stands as elegant testimony to the intimacy of the master-disciple bond in the community for which this book of right conduct was produced: 'Smoke gives proof of fire, as the exterior gives proof of the interior and the student gives proof of the teacher.'[21] Clearly, the master and the disciple had almost become inseparable.

The new emphasis on pedagogy and the corresponding elevation of the master to the position of an awe-inspiring 'spiritual director' vis-à-vis novices must have formed the thread with which lasting spiritual lineages were woven around particularly efficacious masters of training. Increasingly, aspirants who were accepted as novices by a shaykh were 'initiated' not only into Sufism but also into a particular lineage held together by bonds of loyalty and devotion extending from the novices and experienced disciples to the master, and by bonds of guidance and protection running in the other direction from the master towards his novices and disciples. The aspirants submitted to the authority of the master with complete trust; in return, the master pledged to guide them to their goal and to protect them from the dangers on the road of spiritual development. This 'director-novice' relationship, often known as *ṣuḥba*, was increasingly solemnised through initiation and graduation ceremonies. These involved elements such as the oath of allegiance (*bay'a*) and the handclasp during the initial instruction of the *dhikr* formula, as well as the bestowal of a 'certificate of graduation' (*ijāza*) accompanied by special insignia, most notably a cloak (*khirqa*) when the novice attained his goal. Equally significantly, the training process and the pivotal role of the master's authority in this process were codified in the form of the so-called 'Eight Rules of Junayd'. Apparently first formulated by Najm al-Dīn Kubrā (d. 617/1220 or 618/1221) and attributed, questionably, to Junayd, these rules stipulate the following eight requirements for the novice: (1) ritual purity; (2) spiritual withdrawal; (3) fasting; (4) silence; (5) recollection of God; (6) rejecting stray thoughts; (7) binding the heart to the shaykh; (8) surrender to God and the master.[22] This efficacious combination of ceremonial markers and initiatic rules was the culmination of the rise of the training master to the position of undisputed authority over his disciples, and as such, it was to play a seminal role in the formation of tightly-knit master-disciple networks in all subsequent periods.[23]

Strongly personal ties of patron and client permeated the social fabric of Muslim communities of the fourth/tenth and fifth/eleventh centuries, and it was not surprising that they became increasingly more visible among Sufis as well.[24] It is also possible that in Khurāsān and Transoxania this development was linked with the blending of Sufis with the Malāmatīs and the *ḥakīms*, indigenous trends that had already developed strong traditions of disciplining and training the lower self.[25] In those same regions, especially in Khurāsān, the fusion of Sufism with scholarly culture, in which patron-client relationships were also on the rise with the proliferation of the institution of *madrasa* in the fifth/eleventh century, no doubt contributed to the reconfiguration of the shaykh-aspirant relationship into a master-apprentice mould. The conferral of robes was a practice of the Sufis from their first days, but the custom of issuing graduation certificates, already attested among *ḥadīth* scholars during the third/ninth century, must have been adapted from the scholarly professions.[26] Other components of Sufi initiation rituals may have been transplanted from artisanal culture and the urban associations that formed around the concept of *futuwwa* 'chivalrous qualities of manhood'. Whatever the exact causes of the ascendancy of the 'master of training', the rise to prominence of the director-novice relationship led to the gradual formation of spiritual lineages, some of which were powerful enough to spawn actual social communities held together through devotion to a particular master. Perhaps the most visible social manifestation of these new spiritual families and the main social locus for the formation of communities around them was the growing social visibility of the Sufi lodge.

The first Sufis of Baghdad met either in residences or in mosques (notably the Shūnīziyya mosque), but special places of shelter and assembly for the Sufis began to appear already around the mid-fourth/tenth century. Although details are sparse, the first lodges were likely residences of reputable training masters, like Ibn Khafīf and Kāzarūnī, that also served as multi-purpose gathering spaces and hostels for their novices and visiting Sufis. Others, however, appear to have been special buildings located at prominent places, like the Zawzanī (or Zūzanī) lodge across from the mosque of the caliph al-Manṣūr in Baghdad, which was originally built for Abu'l-Ḥasan al-Ḥuṣrī (d. 371/982), disciple of Junayd and Shiblī, but later came to be known under the name of Ḥuṣrī's student Abu'l-Ḥasan 'Alī ibn Maḥmūd al-Zawzanī (d. 451/1059), or the lodge of Muḥammad ibn al-Faḍl ibn Ja'far al-Qurashī close to the Friday mosque in Baṣra.[27] The terminology for these establishments was fluid and variable from region to region; in Arabic-speaking milieus and in south-western Iran the term *ribāṭ* was more common, while in Khurāsān, the Persian term *khānagāh* (Arabised as *khānqāh/khānaqāh*) was preferred, and in all regions other terms, such as *duwayra* ('little house or convent'), *buq'a* ('site'), *zāwiya* ('retreat', literally 'corner') and even *madrasa* ('school'), were also in use.[28] From its tentative beginnings during the first half of the fourth/tenth century, the Sufi lodge grew into a more durable institution, and by the time Qushayrī composed his *Treatise* in 437/1045 where, among other things, he recorded the growing emphasis on the 'master of training', the lodge too had emerged as a social site for the visible manifestation of the spiritual power of Sufi shaykhs as training masters.[29] Slowly but surely, Sufi spiritual lineages were being interwoven into the fabric of the greater society around them. Indeed, it was this very proliferation of Sufi enterprises and their increasingly predictable social markers – including special Sufi dress and paraphernalia, communal rituals such as the *dhikr* performed in assembly (*dhikr al-ḥaḍrā'*) along with 'formulaic' prescriptions for spiritual exercises issued by autocratic masters who resided in lodges – that led keen observers of the Sufi scene such as Qushayrī and Hujwīrī to decry the exoterism and formalism so rampant in the Sufi communities of their time.[30]

'Training masters' and the spiritual communities around them were in clear sight in Khurāsān during the first half of the fifth/eleventh century. Anṣārī (d.

481/1089), whose extant works are all expressive of his concern for guiding and training the circle of disciples that surrounded him, was clearly one of them. In this respect, it is telling that his legacy was preserved in works that were either his own dictations to disciples who acted as his scribes or later compilations of notes recorded by disciples during his teaching sessions. During his travels in his youth, Anṣārī had met several shaykhs renowned for the efficacy of their training, most notably the illiterate masters the Ḥanbalī Abu'l-'Abbās Aḥmad ibn Muḥammad al-Qaṣṣāb of Āmul, Abū 'Alī Siyāh of Marw (d. 424/1032–3) and Abu'l-Ḥasan-i Kharaqānī (352–425/963–1033).[31] The rise to prominence of these illiterate shaykhs, whose powers were universally acknowledged even by the most learned Sufis, can possibly be seen as an indication of the new emphasis on training. Qaṣṣāb was a skillful taskmaster, who was especially effective with beginners; Anṣārī sent some of his own students to him for training.[32] On the other hand, Kharaqānī, who had no formal learning and only poor knowledge of Arabic, seems to have had a deep impact mostly on adepts such as Abū Sa'īd-i Abu'l-Khayr, Qushayrī, and especially Anṣārī. His reputation was such that he is said to have been visited also by the Ghaznavid ruler Maḥmūd (r. 388–421/998–1030) as well as the famous philosopher Ibn Sīnā (370–429/980–1037).[33] He was from Kharaqān just north of Basṭām, the home town of Bāyazīd, and this latter appears to have been his spiritual model. Some of his sayings indeed reflect Bāyazīd's temperament: 'I am neither worshipper, nor scholar, nor Sufi: My God, You are One, and by that Oneness of Yours, I am One!' And, 'When my tongue was opened in the experience of God's Oneness (*tawḥīd*), I saw the earth and the skies perform ritual circumambulation around me, but the people were unaware of it.' Mirroring Bāyazīd's *mi'rāj* experience, he claimed to have undertaken an 'ecstatic journey beyond the worlds "to the place where no creature could follow"' and considered 'a moment of "joy (*shādī*, *nafas bā ḥaqq*) with God more precious than all divine worship"'. Interestingly, his assumption of Bāyazīd's mantle did not go undisputed, since the tradition of Bāyazīd evidently had been kept alive in Basṭām, and the chief representative of this tradition, the learned Abū 'Abd Allāh-i Dāstānī (d. 417/1026), reportedly had conflicts with Kharaqānī.

Another training master who had first set out to become a Shāfi'ī-Ash'arī scholar but became 'converted' to the Sufi path and achieved great fame, or rather notoriety, was Abū Sa'īd-i Abu'l-Khayr (357–440/967–1049).[34] Originally from the small town of Mīhana close to Sarakhs, he apparently spent many years of his youth in Marw and Sarakhs studying to become a scholar, but abandoned scholarship with the encouragement of a certain Shaykh Abu'l-Faḍl Ḥasan-i Sarakhsī – who may have been connected with Sarrāj – and returned to his home town, where he engaged in ascetic *dhikr* exercises for many years under the guidance, from Sarakhs, of Abu'l-Faḍl. Upon his mentor's death at the end of this period, he placed himself under the care of the well-known training master

Ḥanbalī Qaṣṣāb and received a *khirqa* from him after a year of training.[35] After this point, he became a training master himself as director of two *khānaqāhs*, one in Mīhana and the other, established probably after 415/1024, in Nishapur.

Judging by the reputation he had for his powers of spiritual insight (*firāsa*) that enabled him to read minds, Abū Saʿīd must have been a particularly effective spiritual director.[36] Yet, on account of his extravagant ways, which included the use of poetry in preaching and giving lavish banquets where young men participated in music and dance, he was also a controversial figure even in the eyes of his fellow Shāfiʿī Sufis of Nishapur like Qushayrī, let alone in scholarly circles that were not so sympathetic to Sufism.[37] Qushayrī, conspicuously, does not mention Abū Saʿīd by name in his works, since this flamboyant shaykh renowned for his unconventional, even iconoclastic, practices was a clear reminder of the unruly dimensions of Sufism that Qushayrī the scholar-Sufi attempted to temper in his written works. Anṣārī, in whose *Generations* Abū Saʿīd is not mentioned, seems to have refrained from criticising him openly, though, according to a much later source, he may have expressed his annoyance with Abū Saʿīd on account of their differences in matters of belief (alluding to Anṣārī's displeasure with Ashʿarī *kalām*) and the latter's departures from 'the way of previous masters'.[38] Abū ʿAbd Allāh-i Bākūya, who took over Sulamī's *khānaqāh* and most likely represented the tradition of Ibn Khafīf, may have also criticised Abū Saʿīd because of such 'departures from established practice' as allowing young disciples to sit with the elders and to dance during *samāʿ*.[39] In spite, or perhaps precisely because, of his borderline behaviour, Abū Saʿīd left a major imprint on the people of Khurāsān, especially in the form of a thriving community of followers headed by a series of his descendants in Mīhana.[40] Similar to the cases of Ibn Khafīf and Kāzarūnī, it was from within this circle that two hagiographies of the shaykh were produced by two of his fifth-generation descendants, one before the year 541/1147 and the other compiled between 574/1179 and 588/1192.[41]

Although these two sacred biographies naturally reflect more the conditions of sixth/twelfth century Sufism than those of the time of Abū Saʿīd, they nevertheless contain clear traces of the master's genuine practice. Among these, no doubt, were the ten rules that he is said to have imposed on those of his disciples who resided in his lodges. Abū Saʿīd expected the inhabitants of the lodge (1) to keep clean and ritually pure, (2) to reside only in a place or a lodge where they can engage in pious works, (3) to perform the ritual prayers in group at the beginning of the appointed time, (4) to pray during the night, (5) to pray for forgiveness at dawn, (6) to recite the Qur'ān and not to talk until sunrise, (7) to engage in *dhikr* and litany (*wird*) between the evening and night prayers, (8) to welcome the needy, the poor and whoever joins their company and to serve them, (9) to eat only in company, and (10) not to leave the company of others without their consent. In addition, the residents of the lodge were asked to spend whatever free time they have only for three purposes: to gain knowledge or to say litanies, to earn a living, and to bring benefit and comfort to others.[42] These rules that bear a close resemblance to Ibn Khafīf's and Kāzarūnī's recommendations to their aspirants, and like theirs, do not impose celibacy or avoidance of gainful employment on them, were not original with Abū Sa'īd, but this appears to be the first time that pedagogical directives were explicitly packaged by a training master as rules for communal living for his 'resident' disciples. Enumeration of such rules soon became a standard feature of works composed by Sufi authors, and the etiquette of companionship for lodge residents was reflected even in non-Sufi literature.[43] Abū Sa'īd apparently also gave two separate lists of ten qualifications that a 'true master' and a 'sincere disciple', respectively, should possess.[44] These too stand testimony to the intimate bond between the spiritual director and his novices as well as the possible abuse of such intimacy: the disciples were to trust the director fully and to submit to his authority, while the latter was to be generous and kind toward the novices and, significantly, to keep away from their possessions so that he would not be tempted to use them for himself. Clearly, communal living under the direction of a powerful master whose authority could not be so easily questioned could raise questions about abuse of power, which Abū Sa'īd predicted and attempted to pre-empt.

Another particularly powerful training master of Khurāsān whose spiritual progeny proved to be unusually prolific was Abu'l-Qāsim-i Kurrakānī (d. 469/1076) in Ṭūs.[45] His principal disciples were Abū 'Alī Fārmadhī (d. 477/1084–5) and Abū Bakr ibn 'Abd Allāh Nassāj-i Ṭūsī (d. 487/1094).[46] Between them, Nassāj and Fārmadhī trained two brothers who, each in his own unique way, were to play key roles in the unfolding history of Sufism: Abū Ḥāmid Muḥammad al-Ghazālī (450–505/1058–1111) and his younger brother Abu'l-Futūḥ Aḥmad ibn Muḥammad al-Ghazālī (b. c. 453/1061, d. 517/1123 or 520/1126). Even though he had a lodge in Ṭūs during the last phase of his life, Muḥammad, a towering figure in Islamic intellectual history, was not a training master, but Aḥmad, an eloquent preacher and itinerant spiritual director, was to leave a lasting imprint on subsequent Sufi history, not only as the premier theoretician of love (*'ishq*) and the foremost practitioner of the peculiar practice of contemplating God's beauty in the face of beardless boys known as the 'witness game' (*shāhid-bāzī*) but also as a powerful training shaykh who would appear as a key link in many later initiatic chains (of especially Suhrawardī and Kubrawī networks), primarily through his disciple Ḍīyā' al-Dīn Abu'l-Najīb 'Abd al-Qāhir ibn 'Abd Allāh al-Suhrawardī (d. 563/1168).[47] Other followers of Fārmadhī included Abu'l-Ḥasan-i Bustī (who was possibly also trained by Kurrakānī himself) as well as Ḥasan Sakkāk-i Samnānī and Abū 'Abd Allāh Muḥammad ibn Ḥamūya-i Juwaynī.[48] These two latter figures, who apparently pledged allegiance to Bustī after Fārmadhī's death, were in turn teachers of a contemporary of Aḥmad-i Ghazālī who, like him, came to enjoy a conspicuous place in later Sufi initiatic chains (especially in Yasawī and Naqshbandī networks): Abū Ya'qūb Yūsuf ibn Ayyūb-i Hamadhānī (440–535/1048 or 1049–1140).[49] It is through these and other spiritual directors that the figure of the powerful training master that was forged in Khurāsān during the late fifth/eleventh and early sixth/twelfth centuries was transmitted to later generations of Sufis and exercised an increasingly prominent role in all subsequent Sufi history.

The phenomenon of the awe-inspiring training master surrounded by a community of disciples who resided or received their training in a lodge may have first taken shape in Khurāsān (and to a lesser extent in Central Asia) during the fifth/eleventh century. But, just as in the case of the *madrasa* that also crystallised in north-eastern Iran within the same time frame yet soon spread to other regions, the Sufi institution of training too rapidly became visible elsewhere. This process is not easy to trace in its particulars, but it seems to have been largely confined to the territories of the Saljūq empire until the mid-sixth/twelfth century (most notably, western Iran, Iraq and Syria). After the disintegration of the empire after that point, it continued in Zangid and Ayyūbid Syria, and, during the seventh/thirteenth century, also in Egypt and northern India as well as Anatolia. Whether the westward spread of the institutional lodge extended as far as the Maghrib and al-Andalus during this period is difficult to discern, since the emergence of distinctively Sufi centres of training and practice in the far west of Islamdom is, like in most other regions, rather obscure.[50] The Arabisation of the Persian term *khānagāh* as *khānqāh/khānaqāh* can be seen as one sign of this generally westward spread of the new 'institutional' lodge, and the complex and multivalent term *ribāṭ*, which held its ground in Arabic-speaking environments, increasingly came to be associated mostly with Sufis.[51] By the time the celebrated Andalusian traveller Ibn Jubayr (d. 614/1217) undertook his first journey to the Near East in 578–580/1183–5, the Sufi lodge was an established feature of the Syrian landscape; of Damascus, Ibn Jubayr wrote:

> *Ribāṭs* for Sufis, which here go under the name of *khawāniq* [pl. of *khānqāh*], are numerous. They are ornamented palaces through all of which flow streams of water, presenting as delightful a picture as anyone could wish for. The members of this type of Sufi organisation are really kings in these parts, since God has provided for them over and above the material things of life, freeing their minds from concern with the need to earn a living so that they can devote themselves to His service. He has lodged them in palaces which provide them with a foretaste of those of Paradise. So these fortunates, the favoured ones among the Sufis, enjoy through God's favour the blessings of this world and the next. They follow an honourable calling and their life in common is admirably conducted. Their mode of conducting their forms of worship is peculiar. Their custom of assembling for impassioned musical recitals (*samā'*) is delightful. Sometimes, so enraptured do some of these absorbed ecstatics become when under the influence of a state that they can hardly be regarded as belonging to this world at all.[52]

Significantly, there are reports of lodges for women from the mid-sixth/twelfth century in Aleppo, Baghdad, Mecca and Cairo, but since detailed information on these early *ribāṭs/khānqāhs* is lacking, it is possible that these were charitable hospices for abandoned women, widows and divorcees rather than lodges specifically for female Sufis.[53]

Although the economic and legal dimensions of the intitutional lodge in its nascent phase remain largely obscure, two extant legal opinions (*fatwa*) of Abū Ḥāmid Ghazālī, one in Arabic and the other in Persian, throw some light into the various ways in which this new social institution was established. In the Arabic *fatwa*, Ghazālī was asked the following questions:

> What is his [Ghazālī's] opinion on one who endows a landed estate for the Sufis? Who can lawfully use [such an endowment]? What are the conditions for one to be considered a Sufi or not to be considered a Sufi? Are poverty and insolvency among these conditions or not? Is inability to earn a living one of them or not? Is a Sufi supposed to wear a particular kind of clothes or not? And if a jurist lives among Sufis who does not wear their clothes and is occupied with studying law or writing/copying books, can he make use of the endowment or not? Is a Sufi one who is bestowed a patched cloak by a shaykh and one who bestows it? Can a jurist who dresses as they [the Sufis] do and who performs their ceremonies yet teaches law [still] make use of the endowment or not? [Could the preceding questions be about Ghazālī himself?] Should one who uses the endowment be free of sin or not? For one who has a house and a family outside so that he comes and goes, is frequent attendance at the lodge (*khānqāh*) a condition for using the endowment or not? Is there a difference between setting up an endowment for a Sufi lodge (*ribāṭ*) and its residents and setting one up directly for the Sufis themselves?[54]

The questions that were directed to Ghazālī in the Persian *fatwa* are equally revealing: 'What does the Proof of Islam [Ghazālī] say about those who reside in the lodges (*khānqāh*) of Sufis and eat out of the endowment of these lodges? What are the conditions for eating out of the endowed [food] and bread of the Sufis? Is [this food] licit for them?'[55] Ghazālī started his answer to these questions by classifying food consumed in lodges into three categories: (1) legal alms (*zakāt*), (2) solicited and unsolicited donations, (3) endowed funds (*waqf*). He pointed out that use of legal alms was permissible only for those who were dervishes and who did not have the means to earn a living themselves. He then proceeded to elaborate upon the conditions for those who could receive legal alms, but also declared without equivocation that constant prayer and *dhikr* could never be an excuse for not earning a livelihood. All the conditions that applied to use of legal alms also applied to donations, but there were two additional stipulations: (1) donations needed to be solicited indirectly and privately, and (2) they needed to be 'licit' (*halāl*), which, Ghazālī acknowledged, was indeed very difficult to insure. Donations (but not *zakāt*!) that were given to the lodge indirectly but willingly, with the understanding that they would enable lodge dwellers to be engaged in constant prayer, were acceptable. As for endowments, if the endowment was directly for the lodge, this was a relatively simple set-up where only the stipulations of the endower needed to be observed. If, however, the endowment was specifically for Sufis, then it became obligatory to ascertain that those who made use of the endowed funds were indeed Sufis. In order to qualify for this status, one definitely needed to be free of all major sins (*kabā'ir*), but the evaluation of minor sins was more complicated. Ghazālī observed that some minor sins, like praising oneself or showing false humility in front of the powerful, were as bad as major sins if they became habitual behaviour. Other minor sins, however, nullified one's claims to being a Sufi even if they were committed only occasionally; these included, notably, sitting alone with women, wearing silk clothes and gold rings, accepting illicit wealth (*ḥarām*) from a sultan, sitting with beardless lads, having *samā'* with them, liking them, and talking about them often. Once these conditions were met, those who claimed to be Sufis also needed to be engaged in worship or service all day. Wearing Sufi garments and praying five times every day, Ghazālī declared, were simply not sufficient for one to be considered a Sufi.

These questions suggest that the economic and legal dimensions of residential Sufi life in lodges attracted considerable attention and that the legal and ethical status of the wealth that underwrote this lifestyle was carefully scrutinised, presumably not only by legal professionals but also by Sufis themselves. The construction and the maintainance of the physical premises that constituted a lodge as well as the provisioning of its residential Sufis needed, at least theoretically, to meet certain conditions, though it remains impossible to trace such details of any particular lodges in this early period. It is likely, however, that many were set up as foundations (*waqf*) by prosperous pious individuals who belonged to the cultural and political elites.

The master as patron and the cult of saints

> Know that God has servants who are neither prophets nor martyrs and who are envied by the prophets and martyrs for their position and their nearness to God … On the Day of Resurrection thrones of light will be placed at their disposal. Their faces will be of light … These are the *awliyā'* of God.'[56]

This prophetic report, known as the '*ḥadīth* of envy' (*ghibṭa*), was in circulation in Basra already in the early second/eighth century. It was first reported by the preacher and storyteller Yazīd ibn Abān al-Raqāshī (d. between 110/729 and 120/738) from the circle of Ḥasan al-Baṣrī (d. 110/728); Raqāshī evidently referred to this elect group as the *abdāl* ('substitutes') and numbered them at forty (twenty-two in Syria and eighteen in Iraq).[57] Several other *ḥadīth* on this same theme of God's elect that are found in later sources must have been cited in this same milieu.[58] Some of these prophetic reports were rather specific in detail:

> God has 300 [*awliyā'*] in his creation whose hearts are after the heart of Adam; forty whose hearts are after the heart of Moses; seven whose hearts are after the heart of Abraham; five whose hearts are after the heart of Gabriel; three whose hearts are after the heart of Michael; and one whose heart is after the heart of Seraphiel. When the one dies, God substitutes for him one from the three; when one of the three dies, God substitutes for him one from the five; when one of the five dies, God substitutes for him one from the seven; when one of the seven dies, God substitutes for him one from the forty; when one of the forty dies, God substitutes for him one from the 300; and when one of the 300 dies, God substitutes for him one from the common people. Life and death, rain and vegetation, and protection from distress are possible [only] because of them.[59]

The idea of a company of saints appointed directly by God gave rise to a number of difficult questions that included (1) the exact nature of the relationship between the *awliyā'* and God, (2) the role of the *awliyā'* in history and society, (3) the relationship between the *awliyā'* and the prophets (*nabī*, pl. *anbiyā'*). These questions were discussed and debated among proto-Sunnīs from the second/eighth century onward in the form of concrete issues, most notably the nature of 'proximity to God' (*walāya*), 'friendship with and love of God' (*khulla, maḥabba, ʿishq*), 'vision of God' (*ru'ya*), 'intercession' (*istighātha, shafāʿa*), comparative ranking of the prophets and the saints (*tafḍīl*), and prophetic versus saintly miracles (*muʿjiza* versus *karāma*).[60]

Although the Sufis of Iraq (especially Nūrī, Tustarī and Kharrāz) and mystics elsewhere of the third/ninth century (particularly Tirmidhī) took a special interest in these issues, and traditionalist Sufis of the following two centuries (notably Makkī, Abū Nuʿaym, Abū Manṣūr and Anṣārī) cultivated the idea of divine selection and documented its history, belief in the friends of God had a clear resonance well beyond mystical circles. Mirrored by nascent doctrines of divinely-sanctioned leadership (*imāma*) among the Shīʿīs, the idea of divine selection was especially deep-rooted among traditionalists, as evidenced, for instance, by Aḥmad ibn Ḥanbal's inclusion of many prophetic reports about the *abdāl* into his prestigious *ḥadīth* collection *Musnad* and Ibn Abi'l-Dunyā's (d. 281/894) separate treatment of this same topic in his *Book of God's Friends* (*Kitāb al-awliyā'*).[61] Accepted by the traditionalists and examined in detail by the Sufis, the *awliyā'* also began to attract the attention of theologians. The Egyptian Ḥanafī theologian Abū Jaʿfar Aḥmad ibn Salāma al-Ṭaḥāwī (239–321/853–933) affirmed the superiority of the prophets over the *awliyā'* but endorsed the *karāmāt* of the latter: 'We believe in what we know of *karāmāt*, the marvels of the *awliyā'* and in genuine stories about them from trustworthy sources.'[62] The rationalist Muʿtazila, however, rejected *karāmāt* and engaged in polemic against Sufi claims of working miracles, as exemplified clearly by Tanūkhī's (329–84/941–94) criticism of Ibn Khafīf, Shiblī, Ruwaym, and Hallāj.[63] During the fourth/tenth century, the question of prophetic versus saintly miracles became a serious issue of theological consideration and debate among Ash'arīs (discussed above in Chapter 2). It is noteworthy that Abū Muḥammad ibn Abī Zayd al-Qayrawānī (d. 386/996), the head of the Mālikīs of Qayrawān in Tunis who argued against *karāmāt*, nevertheless evidently praised the *awliyā'*; he wrote, 'God, may He be glorified, has created heaven as an eternal resting place for His *awliyā'*, whom he honours with the light of His noble countenance.'[64]

The intellectual scrutiny of the idea of divine selection no doubt occurred against a backdrop of popular perception of the *awliyā'* as saintly figures. If the belief in the existence of God's elect was not a common feature of popular religiosity already during the late second/eighth and early third/ninth century, it is likely that it became a widely-accepted notion through the activity of popular preachers (*wā'iẓ*, pl. *wu''āẓ*) and storytellers (*qāṣṣ*, pl. *quṣṣāṣ*) like Manṣūr ibn 'Ammār (d. 225/839–40), who was greatly admired by the people of Baghdad.[65] That the question of 'mass appeal' was never far from the minds of intellectuals of diverse persuasion who discussed the bundle of issues clustered around the notion of divine selection is illustrated by the sustained polemic that Tirmidhī directed against an unidentified group of 'false' mystics in his *The Life of the Friends of God*, where he wrote:

> They travel from land to land and defraud the weak, the ignorant and womenfolk, of their worldly goods. They eat their fill by making a display of their serenity and good behaviour, and by citing the words of men of spiritual distinction. Day in and day out you see them practicing deceit and pursuing their prey. They bring about benefits through magic charms ... They enjoy the lusts of the carnal soul such as banquets, the friendly reception of brethren, and the pleasure of silly chatter devoid of any meaning. And this continues until such a person acquires leadership in a village or a particular district over a group of incurables made up of the ignorant, adolescents and women. He is delighted that their eyes are turned towards him, that they honour him and behave towards him with piety ... When they take up some subject to do with the Friends of God, they say: 'The Friend of God is unperceived and the Friend of God does not know himself. He is kept uncertain about his situtation lest he be proud of himself and his situation. Moreover, the person who can walk on water and travel distances over the earth in a brief timespan, feeds himself by himself and he is granted this because of his weakness. The knower of God (*'ārif*), on the other hand, pays no attention to such things. Verily, his Lord is with him, and so he does not ask Him for these [powers].' And they deceive the people, saying: 'Since we do not have this power, you may know [for certain] that we are knowers of God and among those who pay no attention to these things.' And the fools accept this stupidity from them.[66]

Whoever these enigmatic figures were, Tirmidhī was extremely irritated by their attempts to curry the favour of the common people by manipulating their beliefs about saintly miracles. Even though the exact nature of these 'false mystics' remain obscure, it is clear that Tirmidhī's remarks carry the reflection of popular veneration of saintly figures in his lifetime.

In the next century, al-Muḥassin ibn 'Alī al-Tanūkhī (329–84/941–94) recounted with amusement the story of a married couple who successfully devised a strategem to defraud the people of the town of Ḥims in Syria by making them believe that the man, who started to pray at the mosque round the clock, was a true ascetic who never consumed any food. Soon people began to venerate him, and when the 'ascetic' rose from his place in the mosque to make his ablutions, 'they went to the place which he had been occupying and rubbed their hands thereon or carried away the dust from the places where he had walked, and they brought to him the sick that he might lay his hands on them.' After about a year, the couple disappeared from Ḥims with a huge sum of money and gifts. Public veneration of saintly figures, which for Tanūkhī merely illustrated the gullibility of the common people, was clearly an established feature of urban life during this period.[67]

The history of popular religiosity of this era is yet to be written, but all indications are that cults of saints began to take shape among Muslims during the third/ninth and fourth/tenth centuries. If, according to Sufi theorists of closeness to God, the *awliyā'* were friends and protégés of God due to their proximity to Him, by the common masses they were viewed simply as safe and direct pathways to God. Having excelled in devotion and service to God, they had become intermediaries as well as patrons who functioned as lynchpins in the relationship between God and human beings. In practical terms, the saint cults manifested themselves as an ideological and ritual complex organised around the basic concept of *baraka* 'spiritual power' and the ritualistic performance of *ziyāra*, 'visiting tombs and other holy places'. *Baraka* was the holy power inherent in a saintly figure that set him/her apart from everyone else; it was normally conceived as a fluid force that emanated from the saint, alive or dead, and permeated the places, persons and objects around him, and its ultimate proof was the saintly miracle, *karāma*.[68] *Ziyāra* was a complex of rituals that included prayer, supplication, votive offerings, sprinkling fragrances and water, lying on tombs, residing within funerary structures, circumambulation, touching and rubbing them, and taking soil and rocks from them.[69] Through *ziyāra*, devotees became beneficiaries of the saint's *baraka*; and in this sacred transaction, the saints were perceived as patrons who could intercede in the divine court on behalf of their devotees.

The seemingly meagre evidence for such cults in the third/ninth and fourth/tenth centuries still needs to be systematically assembled.[70] Not surprisingly, Shī'ī visitation literature appears much earlier than its Sunnī counterparts (the earliest Shī'ī guide dates back to the beginning of the third/ninth century), but saint cults among Sunnīs must have started to take shape also in early 'Abbāsid times.[71] In Egypt, for instance, 'sizable numbers of grave markers' that date back to the late eighth and early ninth century might be an indication of the practice of *ziyāra* during this early period.[72] At the beginning of the fourth/tenth century, the grave of the Qur'ānic figure Dhū'l-Qarnayn – normally identified with Alexander the Great – was 'discovered' in South Arabia; in the same century an old coffin said to have belonged to Joseph was venerated as a relic.[73] In any case, there is little doubt that saint cults were in full bloom by the fifth/eleventh century. In Bagdad, for instance, the grave of the famous renunciant Maʿrūf al-Karkhī (d. 200/815) was visited during Sulamī's lifetime for its healing qualities.[74] Somewhat later but still in the same town, the famous Ḥanbalī jurist, theologian and preacher Ibn ʿAqīl (431–513/1039–1119) strongly condemned the following practices associated with *ziyāra* as clear departures from the Sunna:

> kindling lights, kissing the tombs, covering them with fragrance, addressing the dead with needs, writing formulae on paper with the message: 'Oh my Lord, do such and such for me'; taking earth from the grave as a blessing, pouring sweet fragrances over graves, setting out on a journey for them, and casting rags on trees in imitation of those who worshipped the gods Lāt and ʿUzza.[75]

Such scholarly condemnations evidently had little impact on the populace, however. In an incident that took place in the year 535/1141, many in Baghdad who were duped by a charlatan ascetic to think that they had found the uncorrupted body of a young son of ʿAlī ibn Abī Ṭālib (d. 40/660) rushed to his burial site to receive blessings: 'Whoever was fortunate in obtaining a piece from his burial shroud, it was as if he ruled the world. They brought along incense, candles, and rosewater and took the earth of the tomb in order to obtain blessings.'[76] The impostor in Baghdad may have been inspired by an incident that had taken place just a few years earlier, in 530/1135–6, when the putative tomb and 'intact body' of ʿAlī was discovered in a village in the vicinity of the Central Asian town of Balkh through instructions given by the Prophet Muḥammad himself to hundreds of villagers in a recurrent dream.[77]

Incidents such as these and the veneration of dead saints in general raised a host of legal and theological questions for scholars. Few had problems with 'visiting tombs for the purpose of remembering the dead, reciting the Qur'ān, and remembering God, the Prophet Muḥammad, and the Day of Judgment', but practices such as seeking the intercession of the dead and building lavish structures on their tombs that suggested excessive veneration came dangerously too close to the sin of *shirk*, 'associating partners with God', and were rejected especially by traditionalists as reprehensible innovations (*bidʿa*), a trend that culminated much later in the extended polemics of the Ḥanbalī Ibn Taymiyya (661–728/1263–1328) and his student Ibn Qayyim al-Jawziyya (691–751/1292–1350) against *ziyāra*.[78] It appears, however, that scholars generally accepted, or at least condoned, the saint cults, and even the Ḥanbalīs, who vehemently denounced certain excessive practices associated with the cults, were united in their affirmation of sainthood and saintly miracles. The Ḥanbalī Ibn Qudāma

(541–620/1146–1223), for instance, criticised the 'rationalising' fellow Ḥanbalī Ibn 'Aqīl for his attack against saints and miracles and himself roundly endorsed the *awliyā'*:

> As for the people of the Sunna who follow the traditions and pursue the path of the righteous ancestors, no imperfection taints them, not does any disgrace occur to them. Among them are the learned who practise their knowledge, the friends of God and the righteous men, the God-fearing and pious, the pure and the good, those who have attained the state of sainthood and the performance of miracles, and those who worship in humility and exert themselves in the study of religious law. It is with their praise that books and registers are adorned. Their annals embellish the congregations and assemblies. Hearts become alive at the mention of their life histories, and happiness ensues from following their footsteps. They are supported by religion; and religion is by them endorsed. Of them the Koran speaks; and the Koran they themselves express. And they are a refuge to men when events afflict them: for kings, and others of lesser rank, seek their visits, regarding their supplications to God as a means of obtaining blessings, and asking them to intercede for them with God.[79]

Irrespective of what the intellectuals thought of them, the saint cults flourished from the sixth/twelfth century onwards. In the Near East, this was evidenced by the appearance of guidebooks for *ziyāra* as well as the proliferation of visitation sites and shrine complexes. The earliest guide to Cairo's cemeteries, *Maḥajjat al-nūr fī ziyārat al-qubūr* (*The Path of Light in Visiting Tombs*) of Abū 'Abd Allāh Muḥammad ibn Ḥāmid al-Māridīnī (d. 561/1166), though not extant, dates from the mid-sixth/twelfth century, while the oldest extant visitation guide, *Kitāb al-ishārāt ilā ma'rifat al-ziyārāt* (*The Book of Indications of the Knowledge of Places to Visit*), was written by 'Alī ibn Abī Bakr al-Harawī (d. 611/1215), 'who travelled throughout the Near East and the Mediterranean during the last quarter' of the same century, followed in short order by Abd al-Raḥmān ibn 'Uthmān's (d. 615/1218), *Murshid al-zuwwār ilā qubūr al-abrār* (*The Pilgrims' Guide to the Tombs of the Righteous*) about Egyptian sites.[80] The earliest guidebook about sacred sites in Central Asia, *Laṭā'if al-adhkār li'l-ḥuzzār va's-suffār* (*Pleasant Narratives for the Settled and the Travellers*) written in Persian by Burhān al-Dīn Muḥammad ibn 'Umar (d. 566/1170), also dates from the sixth/twelfth century.[81] In the Maghrib, hagiographical anthologies, the best-known of which is the *Kitāb at-tashawwuf ilā rijāl al-taṣawwuf* (*Book of Insight into the Tradition Bearers of Sufism*) by Abū Ya'qūb Yūsuf ibn al-Zayyāt al-Tādilī (d. 628/1230–1), along with several other hagiographical works from the same period, stand testimony to the increasing social prominence of the phenomenon of popular sainthood from the fifth/eleventh century onwards.[82]

To judge by visitation guidebooks written for Egypt between the seventh/thirteenth and tenth/sixteenth centuries, but which no doubt also reflect the situation immediately prior to that period, the 'main characteristics that defined the saints in the collective imagination' were mastery of personal desire, poverty, absence of material need, generosity, honesty, eccentricity, repentance, resistance to unbelief and hypocrisy, graciousness, and commitment to pious life.[83] These characteristics generally match the spiritual practices of popular saints that were most commonly recorded in three early hagiographical anthologies compiled in Morocco during the seventh/thirteenth and eighth/fourteenth centuries, which were, in order of importance: piety (*ʿibāda*), asceticism (*zuhd*), scrupulousness (*waraʿ*), seclusion (*ʿuzla*), poverty (*faqr*), humility (*tawaḍuʿ*), charity (*ṣadaqa*), and fasting (*ṣawm*).[84]

In both the Near East and the Maghrib, 'the most important criterion of whether a person merited the status of sainthood was the manifestation of evidentiary miracles', followed closely by mediation and intercession.[85] Saintly miracles covered a broad range of extraordinary phenomena, but it seems possible to divide them into two broad categories: (1) 'epistemological miracles' in the form of reading minds, clairvoyance, and spiritual vision, and (2) 'power miracles' such as 'subduing wild animals, food miracles, finding treasure, traversing great distances, healing, controlling spirits (*jinn*), and finding water'.[86] Miracles were often perceived as the realisation of the saint's intermediary and intercessory powers; it was through miracles that the saint functioned as a patron and intermediary for his devotees.

The reasons for the emergence of the cult of saints in the first few centuries of Islamic history and the sharp rise in their social visibility during the fifth/eleventh and sixth/twelfth centuries remain largely obscure, though it appears reasonable to link this phenomenon – along with the appearance of other components of popular religiosity such as celebrations of the Prophet's birthday (*mawlid* or *mawlūd*) – at least partly with larger social trends in Islamic societies such as increasing conversion to Islam and rapid urbanisation especially from the third/ninth century onwards.[87] Whatever the historical causes behind them, it is likely that 'the immediate reasons for the formation of saint cults were social and spiritual and in practical terms had little to do with the formulation of doctrines of sainthood …'[88] In other words, the cults were not simply the social realisation of theories of sainthood formulated by mystics; instead they developed separately from, though in conversation with, Sufi ideas on sainthood. In this regard, it is telling that the *awliyāʾ* venerated by the common masses were not necessarily identical with the *awliyāʾ* of the Sufis: popular saints were not, by any means, all mystics; conversely, those considered to be friends of God by the inner circle of mystics were not always accorded saintly status by the public. Analysis of relevant sources, most notably the *ziyāra* manuals devoted to sites in the Near East, indicates that the popular saints included (1) prophets, (2) family of the Prophet and his descendants, the Companions and Followers, martyrs of early battles and conquests, Shīʿī *imāms*, the first four caliphs, and

(3) Sufis, 'substitutes', rulers, scholars, theologians and judges.[89] In Morocco, for instance, it appears that religious learning was initially even more important than mystical expertise in the social construction of sainthood, since here the popular saint was normally an urban-educated intellectual, often an Arab or Arabised Berber. In terms of social origin, even though a significant minority of Moroccan saints 'belonged to the upper classes ... defined as urban and rural political elites', in general, sainthood was a 'middle-class phenomenon', with 'urban craftspeople, professional scholars, shopkeepers, or rural landowners' making up nearly half of all the saints recorded in three early hagiographical anthologies.[90] Overall, it is safe to state that while a high number of popular saints of the fifth/eleventh and sixth/twelfth centuries were learned, some acquainted with or actively practising Sufism, Sufis by no means had a monopoly over popular sainthood in this period.[91] In brief, the two spheres of sainthood, 'sainthood as a metaphysical "closeness" to God (*walāya*) and sainthood as the exercise of power and authority on earth (*wilāya*)' did not necessarily coincide.[92] Nevertheless, the overlap between the two spheres was remarkable even in this period, and Sufis, along with those learned and proficient in religious matters, easily formed the majority of the saints.

When viewed against this backdrop of the formative history of the saint cults, the ascendancy of the training master and the elevation of the authority of the Sufi shaykh to new heights from the fifth/eleventh century onwards gain new meaning. Indeed, it is likely that the rise of the authoritative spiritual director (*murshid*) who presided over the community of disciples under his rule occured in tandem with the rise of the popular saint who acted as a patron and an intermediary for the broad community of his devotees. In this way, many a training master came to exercise authority not only over his immediate disciples on the Sufi path but also over a much larger community of devotees who relied on him for intercession and intermediation with both divine and mundane powers. Through this conjunction of the Sufi and the popular spheres of sainthood, Sufism gradually ceased to be a form of piety that appealed almost exclusively to the urban middle and upper-middle classes and began to spread through the whole social canvas of pre-modern Islamic societies, from political elites to wage-earners in urban centres to peasants and nomads in the countryside.

Notes

1 On the Sālimiyya, see Böwering, *Mystical Vision*, 89–99.

2 On the lodge and the number of disciples, see Sobieroj, *Ibn Ḫafīf*, 176. Sobieroj's work includes an edition and translation of *Kitāb al-iqtiṣād*. For an extensive summary, see Sobieroj, 'Comparison', 329–35.

3 On earning a living, see Sobieroj, *Ibn Ḫafīf*, 474, 482–3 (Arabic), 366, 378–81 (German), and Sobieroj's own discussion, 300–3; also Sobieroj, 'Comparison', 332

and 343. On avoiding rulers, see Sobieroj, *Ibn Ḫafīf*, 485 (Arabic), 383 (German), and Sobieroj, 'Comparison', 341.

4 Daylamī, *Sīrat*, extant only in this eighth/fourteenth-century Persian translation. On Daylamī, see 'Deylamī, Abu'l-Ḥasan 'Alī', EIr 7: 338–9 (G. Böwering); also the English translation of his treatise on love: *A Treatise on Mystical Love*.

5 See the detailed coverage in Meier's introduction to Maḥmūd ibn 'Uthmān, *Firdaws al-murshidiyya fī asrār al-ṣamadiyya. Die Vita des Scheich Abū Isḥāq al-Kāzarūnī*, ed. Fritz Meier (Leipzig: Bibliotheca Islamica, 1948), 17–71; for more recents accounts, see Sobieroj, 'Mittelsleute' and Denise Aigle, 'Un fondateur d'ordre en milieu rural: le cheikh Abū Ishāq de Kāzarūn', in *Saints Orientaux*, ed. Denise Aigle (Paris: De Boccard, 1995), 181–209.

6 For a summary account, see 'Kāzarūnī', EI 4: 851a–b (H. Algar).

7 Like the biography of Ibn Khafīf, this work is extant only in an eighth/fourteenth-century Persian translation; the details of the text's history are discussed in Maḥmūd ibn 'Uthmān, *Firdaws*, 1–16.

8 Maḥmūd ibn 'Uthmān, *Firdaws*, 369–90 (ch. 30).

9 See Massignon, *Essay*, 89–91; and Gramlich, *Derwischorden*, 2: 171–2. Khuldī's chain is cited from Ibn al-Nadīm's *Fihrist*; Daqqāq's is given in Qushayrī, *Risāla*, 578–9 / *Sendschreiben*, 408 (44.8).

10 As noted and discussed in Fritz Meier, 'Qushayrī's *Tartīb al-sulūk*', in *Essays on Islamic Piety and Mysticism*, trans. John O'Kane (Leiden: Brill, 1999), 94–5 (first published in 1963); see also Meier, 'Khurāsān', 190–2. These should now be read in conjunction with Silvers-Alario, 'Teaching relationship'.

11 The first ones to transpose Tustarī's saying in this fashion were 'Ayn al-Quḍāt al-Hamadhānī (d. 526/1131) and a certain 'Abd al-Karīm al-Rāzī, a student of Abū Ḥāmid al-Ghazālī; see Meier, 'Khurāsān', 202.

12 Both quotes are from Hujwīrī, *Kashf*, 62; cf. *Revelation*, 55.

13 Massignon, *Essay*, 81, quoting al-Maqdisī 's saying from his *Ṣafwa al-taṣawwuf*; I follow the English translation in Meier, 'Khurāsān', 197, and 'Abd Allāh ibn Muḥammad 'Ayn al-Quḍāt al-Hamadhānī, *Tamhīdāt*, ed. 'Afīf 'Usayrān (Tehran: Dānishgāh-i Tihrān, 1341/1962), 11 and 28.

14 Qushayrī, *Risāla*, 735 / *Sendschreiben*, 538 (54.5).

15 Earlier, such intimacy was viewed as the condition for companionship; see, for instance, the report found in Sarrāj, *Luma'*, 178 / *Schlaglichter*, 276 (70.4): 'Yūsuf ibn al-Ḥusayn [al-Rāzī, d. 304/916–17] said, 'I asked Dhu'l-Nūn, With whom should I associate? He replied, One from whom you do not hide anything that God knows about you'.'

16 The term normally used for this crucial first step of the training process is *talqīn*, which, tellingly, is the same term used to refer to the 'instructions' given to the newly deceased at the funeral ceremony over their graves about how they should answer the questions of the two questioning angels Munkar and Nakīr (see EI 7: 576b) in order to avoid punishment in the tomb; the use of this term for the infusion of the *dhikr* is, therefore, clearly another reference to the completely submissive state of the aspirant vis-a-vis the master.

17 Qushayrī, *Risāla*, 731–52 (this edition drastically abbreviates the section on young boys) / *Sendschreiben*, 536–48 (54.1–30).

18 Translation of *min ladunnī*, lit. 'of my core being', is from Sells, *Early Islamic Mysticism*, 370, note 14.

19 Qushayrī, *Risāla*, 633–6 / *Sendschreiben*, 458–60 (50.1–5), chapter on 'guarding the hearts of the shaykhs and abandoning opposition to them'; also see chapter on *walāya*, Arabic, 520–5 / German, 358–63 (38.1–9).
20 Meier, 'Qushayrī's *Tartīb al-sulūk*', Arabic text 108–21, translation 122–32. For the question of attribution, see Meier, 'Khurāsān', 190–1, note 1.
21 This work is paraphrased in Meier, 'Book of etiquette', 65–90; the quote is on p. 66. A full English translation appears in Gerhard Böwering, 'The ādāb literature of classical Sufism: Anṣārī's code of conduct', in *Moral Conduct and Authority: The Place of Adab in South Asian Islam*, ed. Barbara D. Metcalf (Berkeley: University of California Press, 1984), 71–87. The Persian text was published in S. de Laugier de Beaurecueil, 'Un opuscule de Khwādja 'Abdallāh Anṣārī concernant les bienséances des Soufis', *Bulletin de l'Institut Français d'Archéologie Orientale* 59 (1960): 203–39. For the attribution of this work, not to Najm al-Dīn Kubrā (d. 617/1220) as Meier initially assumed on the basis of the evidence available to him when he published the above article but most probably to the circle of Anṣārī, see Gramlich, *Derwischorden*, 1: 11, note 3, and Böwering, 'Ādāb literature', 70.
22 Bernd Radtke, 'The Eight Rules of Junayd: a general overview of the genesis and development of Islamic dervish orders', in *Reason and Inspiration in Islam: Theology, Philosophy and Mysticism in Muslim Thought, in Honor of Hermann Landolt*, ed. Todd Lawson (London: I. B. Tauris in association with the Institute of Ismaili Studies, 2005), 495; Radtke cites Arabic phrases for the rules on p. 492.
23 For rich leads on how to approach the complex social phenomenon of Sufi social formations, see Meier, *Abū Sa'īd*, 438–67, and Bernd Radtke, 'Eight Rules of Junayd'.
24 Roy P. Mottahedeh, *Loyalty and Leadership in an Early Islamic Society* (Princeton: Princeton University Press, 1980).
25 Meier, 'Khurāsān', 215–16 discards the Malāmatī factor on the grounds that Abū Ḥafṣ Ḥaddād and Abū 'Uthmān Ḥīrī were not really Malāmatīs. But even if this point were to be granted to him, it is not clear why one should downplay the influence that the Malāmatī insistence on training might have had on Sufis.
26 'Idjāza', EI 3: 1020b–1022a (G. Vajda, I. Goldziher [S. A. Bonebakker]). For further observations on the parallelism between the evolution of legal schools and the development of 'Sufi structures of authority', see Malamud, 'Sufi organisations'.
27 Wilferd Madelung, 'Yūsuf al-Hamadānī and the Naqšbandiyya', *Quaderni di Studi Arabi* 5–6 (1987–8): 500, note 9 documents the Zawzanī lodge, and the lodge in Basra is noted in Meier, *Abū Sa'īd*, 306, and Sobieroj, 'Mittelsleute', 654–5.
28 'Khānḳāh', EI 4: 1025a–1027a (J. Chabbi); 'Ribāṭ', EI 8: 493b–506b, especially 503bff (J. Chabbi); 'Zāwiya', EI 11: 466b–470a (S. Blair, J. Katz, C. Hamīs).
29 For this early phase of the Sufi lodge, see evidence assembled in Meier, *Abū Sa'īd*, 302–11; cf. 'Ribāṭ', EI 8: 493b–506b, especially 505a–b (J. Chabbi).
30 Ironically, it is quite possible that the attempts of Qushayrī and Hujwīrī to temper Sufism through scholarly accreditation may have exacerbated the problem of formalism rather than alleviating it by encouraging a certain degree of standardisation within Sufism in the light of legal and theological criteria. The dating of the 'assembly-*dhikr*' to this period is only conjectural; cf. Meier, 'Dervish dance', 28.
31 Qaṣṣāb's death date is not known, but see Meier, *Abū Sa'īd*, 45, note 29. For references on Abū 'Alī Siyāh, see Naṣr Allāh Pūrjavādī, *'Ayn al-Quẓāt va ustādān-i ū* (Tehran: Asāṭīr, 1995), 98, note 1.

32 Meier, 'Khurāsān', 199. According to Muḥammad ibn Munavvar, *Asrār*, 1: 49 / *Secrets*, 112, Qaṣṣāb's pedigree reached back to Jurayrī through a certain Muḥammad ibn ʿAbd Allāh-i Ṭabarī.

33 On him, see 'Abu'l-Ḥasan K̲araqānī', EIr 1: 305–6 (H. Landolt), and Muḥammad Riżа Shafīʿī-Kadkanī, *Nivishta bar daryā: az mīrās̱-i ʿirfānī-i Abu'l-Ḥasan-i Kharaqānī* (Tehran: Intishārāt-i Sukhan, 1384/2005), which supersedes the convenient collection of materials on him in Mujtabā Mīnūvī, *Aḥvāl va aqvāl-i Shaykh Abu'l-Ḥasan-i Kharaqānī* (Tehran: Kitābkhāna-i Ṭahūrī, 1359/1980). His impact on Abū Saʿīd and Anṣārī is amply documented, but Qushayrī mentions him only once in his *Treatise*: Qushayrī, *Risāla*, 518 / *Sendschreiben*, 357 (37.11), reading 'Kharaqānī' for 'Khazafānī.' The Ismāʿīlī poet and philosopher Nāṣir-i Khusraw (394/1004–c. 470/1077) was also reported, most likely falsely, to have visited Kharaqānī; see Alice C. Hunsberger, *Nasir Khusraw, the Ruby of Badakhshan: A Portrait of the Persian Poet, Traveler and Philosopher* (London: I. B. Tauris in association with The Institute of Ismaili Studies, 2000), 22–4.

34 The most detailed and comprehensive study on him is Meier, *Abū Saʿīd*. Meier's findings are incorporated into the concise account 'Abū Saʿīd Fażlallāh b. Abi'l-K̲ayr Aḥmad Mēhanī (or Mayhanī)', EIr 1: 377–80 (G. Böwering). Shafīʿī-Kadkanī's long introduction to his edition of Muḥammad ibn Munavvar, *Asrār*, vol. 1, and his much more recent study, *Chashīdan-i ṭaʿam-i vaqt: az mīrās̱-i ʿirfānī-i Abū Saʿīd-i Abu'l-Khayr* (Tehran: Intishārāt-i Sukhan, 1385/2006) are indispensable. Also see John O'Kane's introduction to Muḥammad ibn Munavvar, *Secrets*, 7–59, and Terry Graham, 'Abū Saʿīd ibn Abi'l-Khayr and the School of Khurasan', in *Classical Persian Sufism from Its Origins to Rumi*, ed. Leonard Lewisohn (London: Khaniqahi Nimatullahi Publications, 1993), 583–613.

35 For a somewhat questionable report that he also received a robe from Sulamī, see Chapter 3, note 35.

36 On his well-attested thought-reading abilities, see for instance the testimony of Hujwīrī, *Kashf*, 206–8 / *Revelation*, 164–6.

37 See the amusing story, no doubt containing traces of the conflict between the Ḥanafīs and Shāfiʿīs, of a Ḥanafī-Karrāmī attempt to turn the Ghaznavid ruler against the Sufis, which is foiled by the clairvoyance of Abū Saʿīd, in Muḥammad ibn Munavvar, *Asrār*, 1: 68–73 / *Secrets*, 146–51. On poems attributed to Abū Saʿīd, see Shafīʿī-Kadkanī, *Chashīdan-i ṭaʿam-i vaqt*, 41–3.

38 Muḥammad ibn Munavvar, *Asrār*, editor's introduction, forty-one; the later source is ʿAbd al-Raḥmān-i Jāmī (d. 898/1492).

39 Muḥammad ibn Munavvar, *Asrār*, 1: 207–8 / *Secrets*, 318–19. According to his hagiographer, Abū Saʿīd had answers to these criticisms: all disciples deserved equal respect, and it was better for young men to disperse their sensual passion through innocuous dance than falling into major sin. For more information on Abū Saʿīd's estimation by his contemporaries, see Meier, *Abū Saʿīd*, 288–95.

40 As in the case of Kharaqānī, Abū Saʿīd's popularity led to the emergence of various accounts of his meetings with other famous figures, most notably Ibn Sīnā. Indeed, stories about the encounter between Abū Saʿīd and Ibn Sīnā may have been modelled after reports of a meeting between Kharaqānī and Ibn Sīnā; see Shafīʿī-Kadkanī, *Chashīdan-i ṭaʿam-i vaqt*, 31–5. There were also accounts of a correspondence between Abū Saʿīd and Ibn Sīnā that involved ten texts, but these texts

appear to have been adopted from the broader Avicennan tradition and do not reflect any actual correspondence between the two figures; for details, see David C. Reisman, *The Making of the Avicennan Tradition: The Transmission, Contents, and Structure of Ibn Sīnā's al-Mubāḥaṯāt* (Leiden: Brill, 2002), 138–62.

41 Jamāl al-Dīn Abū Rawḥ Luṭf Allāh ibn Abī Sa'īd ibn Abī Sa'd, *Ḥālāt va sukhanān-i Abū Sa'īd-i Abu'l-Khayr*, Muḥammad Riżā Shafī'ī Kadkanī (Tehran: Mu'assasa-i Intishārāt-i Āgāh, 1366/1987); and Muḥammad ibn Munavvar, *Asrār / Secrets*. That there were other hagiographic accounts in circulation during this same time period is now documented by the publication of a new version of *Maqāmāt-i Abū Sa'īd* by Shafī'ī-Kadkanī in *Chashīdan-i ṭa'am-i vaqt*, 125–220, with a detailed introductory discussion of the text, 76–123.

42 Muḥammad ibn Munavvar, *Asrār*, 316–17 / *Secrets*, 493–5. Rules 2 and 3 of the translation of these rules as found in Reynold A. Nicholson, *Studies in Islamic Mysticism* (Cambridge: Cambridge University Press, 1967), 46, and then also included in Trimingham, *Sufi Orders*, 167, as well as Annemarie Schimmel, *Mystical Dimensions of Islam* (Chapel Hill: University of North Carolina Press, 1975), 243, need to be corrected in the light of the text as established by Shafī'ī-Kadkanī.

43 Qushayrī did not list rules for resident Sufis, but Hujvīri, who made a clear distinction between resident and travelling Sufis, included such rules in his survey: Hujwīrī, *Kashf*, 445–9 / *Revelation*, 341–5; for an example from non-Sufi literature, see Kaykāvūs ibn Iskandar ibn Qābūs 'Unṣur al-Ma'ālī, *Qābūsnāma*, ed. Ghulām Ḥusayn Yūsufī (Tehran: Shirkat-i Intishārāt-i 'Ilmī va Farhangī, 1375/1996 [1345/1966]), 254–6 (in ch. 44); the *Qābūsnāma*, a book of counsel, was written in 475/1082–3.

44 Muḥammad ibn Munavvar, *Asrār*, 1: 315–16 / *Secrets*, 491–3.

45 He is briefly discussed above in Chapter 4.

46 Not much is known about him; see Muḥammad ibn Munavvar, *Asrār*, 2: 247.

47 On Aḥmad, see 'Ġazālī, Aḥmad', EIr 10: 377–80 (Naṣr Allāh Pūrjavādī); and Omid Safi, 'The Sufi path of love in Iran and India', in *A Pearl in Wine*, Zia Inayat Khan (New Lebanon, NY: Omega Press, 2001), 228–38. The witness game and related issues are discussed in Hellmut Ritter, *The Ocean of the Soul: Man, the World, and God in the Stories of Farīd al-Dīn 'Aṭṭār*, ed. Bernd Radtke, trans. John O'Kane (Leiden: Brill, 2003), 448–519, and Safi, 'Sufi path of love', 247–51. For Abū Najīb, see 'al-Suhrawardī, Abū Najīb 'Abd al-Ḳāhir ibn 'Abd Allāh', EI 9: 778a–b (F. Sobieroj). Other disciples of Aḥmad are listed in Aḥmad ibn Muḥammad Ghazālī, *Majmū'a-i āsār-i fārsī-i Aḥmad-i Ghazzālī 'ārif-i mutavaffā-yi* 520 H.Q., ed. Aḥmad Mujāhid (Tehran: Dānishgāh-i Tihrān, 1370/1991), 28–9.

48 On these, see Naṣr Allāh Pūrjavādī, *Zindagī va āsār-i Shaykh Abu'l-Ḥasan-i Bustī* (Tehran: Mu'assasa-'i Muṭāla'āt va Taḥqiqāt-i Farhangī, 1364/1985).

49 'Abū Ya'qūb Yūsof b. Ayyūb Hamadānī', EIr 1: 395–6 (Hamid Algar), which should be read in conjunction with Madelung, 'Yūsuf al-Hamadānī'; see also Paul Ballanfat, 'Théorie des organes spirituels chez Yūsuf Hamadānī', *Studia Islamica* 87 (1998): 35–66, which is a study of Hamadhānī's Persian work *Rutbat al-ḥayāt*. Two other short works on him have also been made available recently: 'Abd al-Jalīl Misgarnizhād, 'Khwāja Abū Ya'qūb-i Hamadānī va risāla-i *dar bayān-i tawḥīd*', *Ma'ārif* 17, no. 2 (2000): 90–6, and 'Abd al-Jalīl Misgarnizhād, '*Ṣafāwa al-tawḥīd li-taṣfiya al-murīd*, dar bayān-i 'al-ṣūfī ghayru makhlūqin", *Ma'ārif* 18, no. 2 (2001): 153–68. Also relevant is Naṣr Allāh Pūrjavādī, 'Majālis-i Aḥmad-i Ghazzālī bā ḥuẓūr-i Yūsuf-i

Ṣūfī', *Ma'ārif* 19, no. 1 (2002): 3–20.

50 The earliest Sufi lodge in Morocco would appear to be the *rābiṭa*, 'Sufi hermitage', of Abū Muḥammad Ṣāliḥ ibn Ḥirzihim (d. after 505/1111–2)'; see Cornell, *Realm*, 24–8.

51 The most detailed documentation of this spread is 'Ribāṭ', EI 8: 493b–506b, especially 503bff (J. Chabbi); also see Omid Safi, *The Politics of Knowledge in Premodern Islam: Negotiating Ideology and Religious Inquiry* (Chapel Hill: University of North Carolina Press, 2006), 97–100. For broader contextualisation of the spread of the *madrasa* and the *khānaqāh*, see Richard Bulliet, *Islam: The View from the Edge* (New York: Columbia University Press, 1994), esp. 145–68.

52 Muḥammad ibn Aḥmad Ibn Jubayr, *The Travels of Ibn Jubayr*, ed. William Wright and M. J. de Goeje (Leiden: Brill, 1907), 284, as translated in Trimingham, *Sufi Orders*, 9–10.

53 For details of these reports, see Trimingham, *Sufi Orders*, 18, and Meier, *Abū Sa'īd*, 355–6 (and 350–4 on the vexed question of female participation in Sufi rituals). Trimingham's statement that 'There were seven convents for women in Aleppo alone, all founded between AD 1150 and 1250', for instance, is based on the much later report of Ibn al-Shihna (d. 890/1485), *al-Durr al-muntakhab fī ta'rīkh mamlakat Ḥalab*, as found in the partial translation of this work by J. Sauvaget, *Les Perles choisies* (Beirut, 1933), 105–6.

54 The text of this document is reproduced in Pūrjavādī, *Du mujaddid*, 96–100; the quote is from 96.

55 Pūrjavādī, *Du mujaddid*, 87–91; the quote is from 87.

56 Chodkiewicz, *Seal*, 25, translating from the *ḥadīth* collections of Tirmidhī (*zuhd*, 53) and Aḥmad ibn Ḥanbal (5: 229, 239, 341–3).

57 Ess, *Theologie*, 2: 89–91. A slightly different version of this *ḥadīth* is reported in Makkī, *Qūt al-qulūb*, 1: 448 (1: 222 of 1310 Cairo edition) / *Nahrung*, 2: 141 (32: 217), and translated in Massignon, *Passion*, 3: 206.

58 Many of these are conveniently collected in Abū Nu'aym al-Iṣfahānī, *Ḥilyat al-awliyā'*, 1: 4–17, as noted in 'Walāyah', *Encyclopedia of Religion*, 2nd edn, ed. Lindsay Jones (Detroit: Macmillan Reference USA, 2005), 14: 9660 (Hermann Landolt), with partial translations of some; a few are given in English translation in Elmore, *Islamic Sainthood*, 128–30. See also Massignon, *Essay*, 88–9, and Tirmidhī, *Concept of Sainthood*, 109, note 1.

59 Abū Nu'aym al-Iṣfahānī, *Ḥilyat al-awliyā'*: 8–9; as noted by Landolt, 'Walāyah', *Encyclopedia of Religion*, 2nd edn, ed. Lindsay Jones (Detroit: Macmillan Reference USA, 2005), 14: 9660, this *ḥadīth* was normally known as the '*ḥadīth* of 'Abd Allāh ibn Mas'ūd'. See Hujwīrī, *Kashf*, 269 / *Revelation*, 214, where the 300 are called *akhyār* ('the excellent'), the forty *abdāl* ('the substitutes'), the seven *abrār* ('the pious'), the four *awtād* ('the anchors' – literally 'tent-pegs'), the three *naqībs* ('the chiefs'), and the one *quṭb* ('pole') and *ghawth* ('rescue').

60 Cf. Massignon, *Passion*, 3: 205–10. *Walāya* and *maḥabba*/*'ishq* were discussed above in Chapter 1. On *ru'ya*, see Pūrjavādī, *Ru'yat-i māh*, and Ess, *Theologie*, 4: 411–15. A brief overview on *shafā'a*, though with no reference to Sufism, is 'Shafā'a', EI 9: 177b–179b (A. J. Wensinck [D. Gimaret] and A. Schimmel). The issue of *tafḍīl* is discussed in Elmore, *Islamic Sainthood*, 131–62. The question of prophetic miracles versus saintly *charismata*, a topic of intense interest for the earliest mystics such as

Kharrāz and Tirmidhī as noted in Chapters 1 and 2 above, was discussed by Sarrāj, *Luma'*, 324–8 / *Schlaglichter*, 459–62 (116.1–8); for broad surveys, see Richard Gramlich, *Die Wunder der Freunde Gottes: Theologien und Erscheinungsformen des islamischen Heiligenwunders* (Wiesbaden: F. Steiner, 1987), esp. 41–58; Ess, *Theologie*, 4: 630–44; Denis Gril, 'Le miracle en islam, critère de la sainteté?', in *Saints orientaux*, ed. Denise Aigle (Paris: De Boccard, 1995), 69–81; and Éric Geoffroy, 'Attitudes contrastées des mystiques musulmans face au miracle', in *Miracle et karama: saints et leurs miracles à travers l'hagiographie chrétienne et islamique IVe-XVe siècles*, ed. Denise Aigle (Brepols: Turnhout, 2000), 301–16.

61 Melchert, 'Ḥanābila', 356, and 'Ibn Abi'l-Dunyā', EI 3: 684a–b (A. Dietrich). For the early history of the belief in *awliyā'*, see Ess, *Theologie*, 2: 88ff. For concise discussions of Shī'ī views on *walāya/wilāya*, see 'Walāyah', *Encyclopedia of Religion*, 14: 9656–62 (Hermann Landolt), and 'Wilāya, 2. In Shī'ism', EI 11: 208b–209b (P. Walker).

62 Josef W. Meri, *The Cult of Saints Among Muslims and Jews in Medieval Syria* (Oxford: Oxford University Press, 2002), 68, quoting from Ṭaḥāwī, *Uṣūl al-'aqīda al-islāmiyya*, ed. 'A. al-'Izzī (Beirut, 1987), 198.

63 Sobieroj, 'Mu'tazila and Sufism', 82–6.

64 Cornell, *Realm*, 7, quoting from his *Matn al-risāla* (Rabat, 1984), 12. On him, see 'Ibn Abī Zayd al-Ḳayrawānī', EI 3: 695a–b (H. R. Idris).

65 Ess, *Theologie*, 3: 102–4. Sulamī, and following him Qushayrī, included Manṣūr ibn 'Ammār in their biographical notices: Sulamī, *Ṭabaqāt*, 130–6, and Qushayrī, *Risāla*, 112–13 / *Sendschreiben*, 64 (1.21). On preachers and storytellers, see 'Ḳāṣṣ', EI 4: 733b–735a (Ch. Pellat) and 'Wā'iẓ, 1. In Classical Islam', EI 11: 56a–b (B. Radtke).

66 Tirmidhī, *Concept of Sainthood*, 54 (paragraph 12), 59 (paragraph 19), and 196 (paragraph 147).

67 al-Muḥassin ibn 'Alī Tanūkhī, *The Table-Talk of a Mesopotamian Judge*, trans. D. S. Margoliouth (London: Royal Asiatic Society, 1922), 289–92. 'Swindler ascetics and mystics' have attracted commentary from cultural elites like Tanūkhī, but an unusually-detailed account of fraudulent Sufis came much later during the seventh/thirteenth century from a writer who may have been a professional juggler: 'Abd al-Raḥīm ibn 'Umar Jawbarī, *Mukhtār fī kashf al-asrār wa-hatk al-astār*, ed. 'Iṣām Muḥammad Shibārū (Beirut: Dār al-Taḍāmun, 1992), 35–45 / *Le voile arraché: l'autre visage de l'Islam*, René Khawam (Paris: Phébus, 1979–80), 1: 55–90; see also Stefan Wild, 'Jugglers and fraudulent Sufis', in *Proceedings of the VIth Congress of Arabic and Islamic Studies, Visby 13–16 August, Stockholm 17–19 August, 1972*, ed. Frithiof Rundgren (Stockholm: Almqvist & Wiksell International, 1975), 58–63.

68 On *baraka*, see Meri, *Cult of Saints*, esp. 101–8.

69 Meri, *Cult of Saints*, 25. The most detailed discussion of the different aspects of *ziyāra* is Niels Henrik Olesen, *Culte des saints et pèlerinages chez Ibn Taymiyya (661/1263–728/1328)* (Paris: P. Geuthner, 1991).

70 Still indispensable on the background for the emergence of the saint cults are Ignác Goldziher, 'On the veneration of the dead in paganism and Islam', in *Muslim Studies*, ed. S. M. Stern, trans. C. R. Barber and S. M. Stern (London: Allen & Unwin, 1967), 1: 209–38; and Ignác Goldziher, 'Veneration of saints in Islam', in *Muslim Studies*, ed. S. M. Stern, trans. C. R. Barber and S. M. Stern (London: Allen & Unwin, 1967), 2: 255–341. A promising new source is the ongoing publication

Thesaurus d'Epigraphie Islamique, which is to bring together all of the inscriptions in Arabic, Persian and Turkish (as well as in other relevant languages) from the Muslim world up to the year 1000 of the Islamic calendar.

71 On Shīʿī *ziyāra* literature, see Meri, *Cult of Saints*, 157–61.

72 Christopher Schurman Taylor, *In the Vicinity of the Righteous:* Ziyāra *and the Veneration of Muslim Saints in Late Medieval Egypt* (Leiden: Brill, 1999), 41.

73 Goldziher, 'Veneration of saints', 321 and 322, respectively, relying on *Jazīrat al-ʿarab* and al-Muṭahhar ibn Ṭāhir al-Maqdisī, who composed an historical work called *Kitāb al-badʾ waʾl-taʾrīkh* around 355/966.

74 Sulamī, *Ṭabaqāt*, 85.

75 Meri, *Cult of Saints*, 129, translating from Ibn Qayyim al-Jawziyya, *Ighāthat al-lahfān min maṣāyid al-shayṭān*, ed. M. H. al-Fiqī, 2 vols. (Beirut, 1986), 1: 221. I have left out the Arabic phrases that Meri includes. This same passage is also quoted in Ibn al-Jawzī, *Talbīs*, 528.

76 Meri, *Cult of Saints*, 78, quoting from Ṣibt Ibn al-Jawzī, *Mirʾāt al-zamān fī taʾrīkh al-aʿyān* (Hyderabad, 1951–2), 8 (1): 176.

77 R. D. McChesney, *Waqf in Central Asia: Four Hundred Years in the History of a Muslim Shrine, 1480–1889* (Princeton: Princeton University Press, 1991), 27–28, where the relevant passage from the Andalusian traveller Abū Ḥāmid al-Gharnāṭī's *Tuḥfat al-albāb* (pp. 145–8) is given in translation, as edited by G. Ferrand, *Journal Asiatique* 207 (1925): 1–148, 195–303. Gharnāṭī traveled through Central Asia in the mid-sixth/twelfth century.

78 Meri, *Cult of Saints*, 126. The arguments for and against *ziyāra* are reviewed by Meri, 126–40, and in Taylor, *Ziyāra*, 168–218.

79 Muwaffaq al-Dīn ʿAbd Allāh ibn Aḥmad Ibn Qudāma, *Ibn Qudāma's Censure of Speculative Theology*, ed. and trans. George Makdisi (London: Luzac, 1962), 10 (Arabic, 14); I have changed Makdisi's phrase 'active learned men' to 'the learned who practise their knowledge'. Also quoted in full in Meri, *Cult of Saints*, 71–2. For a later Ḥanbalī endorsement of sainthood 'shorn of its excesses', see Aḥmad ibn ʿAbd al-Ḥalīm Ibn Taymiyya, *al-Furqān bayna awliyāʾ al-raḥmān wa-awliyāʾ al-shayṭān*, ed. Aḥmad Ḥamdī Imām (Cairo: Maṭbaʿat al-Madanī, 1401/1981).

80 Taylor, *Ziyāra*, 5–6, and Meri, *Cult of Saints*, 7 and 44, respectively.

81 'Central Asia, Islam in', *Encyclopedia of Islam and the Muslim World*, ed. Richard C. Martin (New York: Macmillan, 2005), 1: 141 (D. DeWeese), and Devin DeWeese, 'From Bukhārā to Madīna: a twelfth-century pilgrim's progress', unpublished paper delivered at the 2004 annual meeting of the Middle East Studies Association; I owe thanks to DeWeese for making a copy of this paper available to me.

82 A convenient listing of these works is given in Fritz Meier, 'Ṭāhir al-Ṣafadī's forgotten work on western saints of the sixth/twelfth century', in *Essays on Islamic Piety and Mysticism*, trans. John O'Kane (Leiden: Brill, 1999), 423–5. Three hundred and sixteen biographies found in three such works – *Kitāb at-tashawwuf* by Tādilī, *Kitāb al-mustafād* by Muḥammad ibn Qāsim al-Tamīmī (d. 604/1207–8), and *al-Maqṣad al-sharīf* by ʿAbd al-Ḥaqq al-Bādisī (d. after 722/1322) (titles cited partially) – are subjected to a quantitative analysis in Cornell, *Realm*, 93–120; the translation of the title of Tādilī's book is Cornell's.

83 Taylor, *Ziyāra*, 80–126; the quote is on 87, and I reproduce the list of characteristics using the subtitles of ch. 3 of this study.

84 Cornell, *Realm*, 110–1.
85 Cornell, *Realm*, 112.
86 Cornell, *Realm*, 116. Taylor, *Ziyāra*, 129, adopts a three-fold classification of miracles: 'relationships between humanity and the natural world; interactions among human beings; relationships between the human and metaphysical realms'. For a more extensive treatment, see Gramlich, *Wunder*, 139–47; also Gramlich, *Derwischorden*, 2: 198–210.
87 Bulliet, *View from the Edge*, 37–79 Clearly, there were multiple factors at work in this process; for instance, as noted in Meri, *Cult of Saints*, 122–3, 'pilgrimage sites were also centres of social and economic activity', and 'visitation to saints' tombs often coincided with agricultural festivals or seasonal celebrations of pre-Islamic or Christian origin'. On the *mawlid*, first attested by the Andalusian Ibn Jubayr, who travelled through the Near East between 578–81/1183–5), see 'Mawlid or Mawlūd, 1. Typology of the Mawlid and its diffusion through the Islamic world', EI 6: 895a–897a (H. Fuchs [F. de Jong]).
88 Meri, *Cult of Saints*, 71.
89 Meri, *Cult of Saints*, 80–1; cf. Taylor, *Ziyāra*, 87.
90 For a detailed and highly informative quantitative analysis, see Cornell, *Realm*, 93–120; the quotes are from p. 107.
91 Cf. Meri, *Cult of Saints*, 117, bottom, and Taylor, *Ziyāra*, 83–4.
92 Cornell, *Realm*, xxxv. On the alternate vocalisations *walāya*, associated more with 'friendship, alliance, assistance', and *wilāya*, connoting 'authority, power, control'; see ibid, xvii-xxi; Chodkiewicz, *Seal*, 22; and Elmore, *Islamic Sainthood*, 113–14.

6

Sainthood triumphant

The history of Sufism during its formative period is in many ways the story of how Sufis gradually moved to the centre of Islamic societies and became part of the mainstream in both urban and rural environments. From its original habitat in Iraq, Sufis travelled in all directions, blended with indigenous mystics wherever these existed, and developed a self-conscious and confident form of piety complete with its distinctive set of theories and practices. Along the way, socially-responsible and scholarly-minded Sufis like Sarrāj, Kalābādhī, Qushayrī and Hujwīrī took successful steps to 'temper' Sufism by containing, and sometimes condemning, the socially and legally-explosive aspects of the highly-variegated cluster of Sufi teachings and customs. The theoretical interventions of these figures were paralleled by the pedagogical and organisational skills of the 'masters of practice', the great training shaykhs who guided the communities of disciples around them with a firm and steady hand and kept them within socially and legally-respectable bounds. While these attempts established a solid and durable bridge between the Sufis and the *'ulamā'* in particular and rendered Sufi piety not only palatable but attractive to scholarly circles, the spread of Sufism among both urban and rural masses no doubt only came about as a direct consequence of the increasing conjunction of Sufi sainthood with popular cults of saints during the fifth/eleventh and sixth/twelfth centuries.

Social spread and political influence

The process by which certain powerful training masters also came to be venerated as popular saints is most clearly visible in cases where the master's example was perpetuated in local shrine communities. Such social groups became prominent during the sixth/twelfth century particularly in small provincial towns, as illustrated in Khurāsān by the case of Abū Sa'īd (357–440/967–1049) in Mīhana. Aspects of life in his shrine community are reflected in the two sacred biographies that were composed by two of his descendants. According to the *Asrār al-tawḥīd fī maqāmāt al-Shaykh Abī Sa'īd* (*The Secrets of [God's] Unity in the Spiritual Stations of Shaykh Abū Sa'īd*), 'the cult practice at the shrine' included:

> five ritual prayers in congregation, food served mornings and at night, every morning a recital of the whole Qur'ān at his sanctified tomb, candles every evening until bedtime and every dawn until daylight, providing Qur'ān reciters mornings and evenings, and a group of Sufis resident at his sanctified tomb amounting to more than 100 persons from among his offspring and devotees.[1]

The hagiographies of Abū Sa'īd were in a real sense the products of the cultic life of this shrine community, and as such, these two sacred biographies arguably convey less information about the historical life of Abū Sa'īd than about his image in the community that constructed him as a popular saint. Consequently, they can be decoded to reveal the social imaginary that produced the phenomenon of popular sainthood around Abū Sa'īd. The *Secrets* in particular lends itself to such treatment. Here, Abū Sa'īd's public persona took different faces depending on whether he was presented '(a) as the rival of other spiritual celebrities of his age, (b) as a *walī* [that is, protector and intercessor], (c) as a *pīr* or spiritual director in the *khanaqāh*, and (d) as God's representative who appoints great men of the world to power'.[2]

With respect to other religious authorities of his time, Abū Sa'īd was consistently portrayed as the superior figure. He was categorically more powerful than scholars, and his rank as a saint was higher than that of other Sufis, with only a couple of noteworthy exceptions: Kurrakānī, another powerful training master with whom he was placed on an equal footing, and Kharaqānī, who, as an elder figure of undisputed spiritual authority, was depicted as endorsing Abū Sa'īd's superior status vis-à-vis his contemporary 'rivals'. This presumption of rivalry with other authority figures was maintained relentlessly throughout the narrative, and evidently, saintly one-upmanship was the natural mode in which popular sainthood was conceived in local communities. Such competition was also transposed into the spiritual domain so that, just as political powers ruled over particular earthly territories, saints had authority over their spiritual territories. Conveniently, the term *wilāya* that also carried the meaning of 'administrative domain' could be used for this purpose: the spiritual authority of the saint was co-terminous with his spiritual domain. In the *Secrets*, Abū Sa'īd was naturally depicted as having unrivalled authority in Mīhana as well as in Nishapur, where he 'outpowered' the town's other famous Sufis, notably Qushayrī and Abū 'Abd Allāh Ibn Bākūya. However, his jurisdiction had limits, since saints in other locations such as Marw jealously guarded their own territories; nevertheless, his hagiographer had no doubt that Abū Sa'īd was the greatest saint of all times.[3]

As the *walī* par excellence, Abū Sa'īd appeared to the members of his shrine community as the ultimate protector and intercessor as well as the most formidable master of training for his circle of disciples. The real measure of the saint's powers for his followers and devotees, however, may well have been his authority over political and military elites. The author of the *Secrets* attributed the worldly power of the major political figures of his time such as the Saljūq rulers Ṭuğrıl (r. 429–55/1038–63) and Çağrı (d. 452/1060) to Abū Saʿīd; he even detected Abū Saʿīd's endorsement behind the success of the famous vizier Abū ʿAlī Ḥasan ibn ʿAlī 'Niẓām al-Mulk' (d. 485/1092) whose long political career actually post-dated Abū Saʿīd's death in 440/1049.[4] In his eyes, and therefore possibly in the eyes of the 'hagiographical community', the spiritual clearly undergirded the political; in the final analysis, true sovereignty belonged not to the sultans but to the saints. Thus, the members of the shrine community that had formed around Abū Saʿīd's spiritual and biological lineage in Mīhana were convinced that their patron saint stood at the zenith of the cosmic saintly hierarchy. Not surprisingly, such precious spiritual capital was transformed into social power at the hands of the shaykh's family, who exercised a quasi-aristocratic function in the area through their supervision of *ziyāra* to the shrine as well as through their control of agricultural fields that generated income for the tomb-complex, though how the family came into possession of these land holdings remains obscure. The exact nature of the relationship, if any, between Abū Saʿīd's descendants and Saljūq political authorities is also difficult to establish, but claims made by his fifth-generation hagiographers about Saljūq patronage of the shrine may well have had some basis in reality.[5]

Another shrine community in Khurāsān that proved to be much more durable than Abū Saʿīd's was the one organised around the long-lived Abū Naṣr Aḥmad ibn Abi'l-Ḥasan Nāmaqī (440–536/1049 or 1050–1141) in Jām, who came to be popularly known as 'Zhanda-Pīl' ('the Colossal Elephant').[6] Born into a farmer family that claimed Arab descent, Aḥmad-i Jām spent his youth engrossed in the earthly pleasures of love, wine-drinking and raising partridges, but after a conversion experience in his early twenties, he reportedly opted for a life of solitude, mostly in the mountains, until about age forty. At that point, he established himself in a village to the north of Jām, where he built a Friday mosque as well as a *khānaqāh* and devoted himself to preaching, training disciples, writing books and travelling in Khurāsān. Eight of the thirteen works attributed to him, including one collection of letters and one collection of poems, are extant (though one of the prose works is preserved only in part, and there are serious problems of attribution about the collection of poems), and these treatises, all written in eloquent Persian, stand testimony to the forceful spiritual presence of their author.

It appears that Aḥmad-i Jām was a Ḥanafī, like Hujwīrī.[7] There are no reports of him having received a formal education, though his works, replete with Qur'ān and *ḥadīth* citations along with their complete Persian translations, demonstrate his firm grasp of basic Islamic learning. In his own writings, there are no indications that he was initiated into Sufism at the hands of a Sufi master, and the claim made by his earliest hagiographer – Sadīd al-Dīn Muḥammad ibn Mūsā of Ghazna, a follower of the master who wrote an account titled *Maqāmāt-i Zhanda-Pīl* (*The Spiritual Stations of the Colossal Elephant*) sometime towards the end of the sixth/twelfth century – that he inherited the mantle of Abū Sa'īd of Mīhana through this latter's son Abū Ṭāhir is no doubt spurious.[8] Aḥmad-i Jām's works were directed to a broad audience; accordingly, he avoided theoretical questions and returned often to his basic theme of urging his readers to reorient their lives towards God (*tawba*). In the *Miftāḥ al-najāt* (*The Key to Salvation*), one of his later treatises that he started composing in 522/1128 on the occasion of the repentance of one of his sons, he gave instructions to his son in seven chapters on (1) knowing God and experiential knowledge of His unity, (2) the meaning of prophetic tradition (*sunnat*) and community (*jamā'at*), (3) repentance (*tawba*), (4) commanding right, forbidding wrong and observing God's decrees, (5) permissible acts, earning a living, renunciation and piety, (6) continence (*qanā'at*), submission, being content with one's lot, and (7) the path of the righteous (*ṣiddīqān*), substitutes (*abdāl*) and the 'people of truth' (*arbāb-i ḥaqīqat*). In chapter 1, he emphasised the importance of God's direct guidance and asserted that there could be no true affirmation of unity (*tawḥīd*), faith or knowledge of God without it, while in chapter 4 he passionately made the case for the necessity of having accurate knowledge of the divine law. In a tone that served as an unmistakable sign of his frustration with the rising popularity of saints cults, he warned against 'supposed saints' who claimed to work miracles even while they could not recite the opening chapter of the Qur'ān (*Fātiḥa*) or perform the prayers:

> I have seen several of those who claimed to work miracles. When I looked closer, [I saw that] they could not recite [the *sūra*] al-Ḥamd properly, nor could they talk knowledgeably about ablution and prayer, fasting, major ablution or about any duty and prophetic custom. When I offered to teach them, they displayed no serious interest. I was truly unable to decide who was the more dim-witted: the one who claimed to be the miracle-worker *par excellence*, or the ignorant who upheld his claim, or the liar who claimed to have witnessed his miracles![9]

In the following chapter, he pointed out that in and of themselves this-worldly things were not forbidden; they were all permissible and could indeed be beneficial if they were used for the right reason. It was, however, positively harmful to love this world, and he urged his readers to be ready to divorce the lower world at will. In the rest of the treatise, Aḥmad-i Jām presented a clear theory of sainthood, defended the practice of *samā'* for true Sufis even while he denounced its excesses, and provided further practical information concerning the Sufi life. In many ways, the *Key* was a synopsis of his earlier works like *Uns* (or *Anīs*) *al-tā'ibīn va ṣirāṭ Allāh al-mubīn* (*Intimacy of the Repentant* [or] *Companion to the Repentant and God's Clear Path*), in which he gave more detailed instructions on topics such as the conditions of being a training master and a novice, the meaning of the 'path', the terms 'love and lover', the nature of *samā'*, and sainthood.[10]

Aḥmad-i Jām's preaching proved to be highly effective, and the shrine community he left behind, dominated by an ever-growing number of his descendants down to this day, eventually turned into a major settlement in the area, Turbat-i Jām. Not surprisingly, the hagiographical literature produced within this community, most notably the *Spiritual Stations*, portrayed Aḥmad-i Jām as a confident, miracle-mongering saint who routinely bested all his rivals and enemies, wielded power over politicians, and worked indefatigably to impose the divine law and to defeat the heretics.[11] As in the *Secrets* about Abū Sa'īd, Aḥmad-i Jām's public persona was drawn with all the different faces of the paradigmatic popular saint: he was the supreme friend of God, the best spiritual director, the most efficacious intercessor with both divine and worldly powers. Saintly one-upmanship was much in evidence, with Aḥmad-i Jām asserting his authority over other major shrines in the region, notably the Anṣārī community of Herat and the Chishtī community of Chisht, the latter headed by Quṭb al-Dīn Mawdūd Chishtī (d. 527/1133).[12] The saint's jurisdiction extended also to the political sphere: just as Abū Sa'īd was portrayed by his descendants as the facilitator of the vizier Niẓām al-Mulk's worldly success, Aḥmad-i Jām was described by the author of his *Spiritual Stations* as the spiritual patron and protector of Sanjar, the Saljūq ruler of his time (r. 511–52/1118–57).[13]

The distance between the popular image of the shaykh and Aḥmad-i Jām's personality as evidenced in his own writings, at times quite jarring, suggests that the overlap between the two spheres of sainthood, popular sainthood of intercession and protection and Sufi friendship with God, was still less than complete soon after Aḥmad-i Jām's death. In any event, the social construction of popular sainthood within local shrine communities in Khurāsān and Central Asia, especially in the form of hagiographies devoted to individual saints written in Persian, was well underway in the second half of the sixth/twelfth century.[14] The shrine communities of Herat, Mīhana and Turbat-i Jām, which no doubt preserved and cultivated living oral hagiographic traditions about their revered saints, produced written accounts of their sacred heroes (the *Spiritual Stations* of Abū Sa'īd and Aḥmad-i Jām, the latter possibly modelled on the former) or committed the tradition of the saint into writing (Anṣārī). It is likely that a similar process was under way among those who were devoted to Kharaqānī, who may well have produced the two different extant written compilations of the master's tradition, *Nūr al-'ulūm* (*The Light of Knowledge*) and *Dhikr quṭb al-sālikīn Abu'l-Ḥasan Kharaqānī* (*The Memorial of the Axis of Wayfarers Abu'l-Ḥasan Kharaqānī*) at around the same time.[15] This hagiographical enterprise should be seen as a clear indication of the spread of popular sainthood among Persian speakers.[16]

Outside local shrine communities such as the ones of Anṣārī, Abū Saʿīd and Aḥmad-i Jām, the presence of Sufi ideas and practices in new social identities formed around 'popular saints' could be somewhat thin during the fifth/eleventh century and even the sixth/twelfth century. At the extreme west of Islamdom in Morocco, for instance, this period witnessed the formation of new Islamic identities among pastoralist Berber tribal communities around rural mosques and centres of instruction generally known under the name *ribāṭ* or *rābiṭa*.[17] It appears that in some instances, such as Ribāṭ Tīṭ-n-Fiṭr among the Ṣanhāja Berbers and Ribāṭ Shākir among the Maṣmūda Berbers, the pious figures who founded these centres and their descendants and followers first came to be venerated as popular saints; only later some of these gradually assumed unmistakable Sufi identities as Sufi ideas and practices began to circulate more widely in the far Maghrib from roughly the end of the fifth/eleventh century. Abū ʿAbd Allāh Amghār of the Banū Amghār (Berber, 'chieftain') who became head of Ribāṭ Tīṭ-n-Fiṭr after 470/1083, for instance, was 'noted for his love of spiritual retreat and bodily mortification' and he

> required his disciples to follow ten Rules of Companionship (*shurūṭ al-ṣuḥba*): (1) the avoidance of disputes, (2) the pursuit of justice, (3) generosity, (4) contentment with whatever God provides, (5) forbearance, (6) upholding the existence of divine secrets (*ḥifẓ al-ghuyūb*), (7) concealment of the sins of others, (8) conceding the final word in an argument, (9) satisfaction with one's lot in life, and (10) refusing to exert oneself for worldly goods.[18]

There is nothing particularly mystical or Sufi about these rules, and it would be premature to characterise Abū ʿAbd Allāh as a Sufi on the basis of this evidence alone. Similarly, Abū ʿAbd Allāh al-Ragrāgī (fl. c. 480/1087–8) of Ribāṭ Shākir appears to have been 'more a miracle worker than an actual Sufi mystic', and the first clearly Sufi figure associated with this establishment was apparently the vegetarian scholar Abū Ibrāhīm Ismāʿīl u-Gmāten (d. 595/1198–9), who had spent years in the east and was known to have studied Makkī's *Sustenance*.[19] Admittedly, the information on these figures is sparse, yet it seems reasonable to assume that the cult of saints preceded Sufi sainthood in these instances as it must have done in many other Muslim communities. Nevertheless, there can be little doubt that once Sufi sainthood began to be imbricated with popular cults of saints in such rural tribal contexts, Sufi figures, like other popular saints, began to play increasingly visible social roles in the formation of new Islamic identities along ethnic lines.

Apart from hereditary shrine communities (located mostly in provincial towns) and pastoralist tribes, Sufi sainthood found new social arenas in major urban centres as a result of its confluence with the cult of saints. As noted in earlier, mystical movements in Islam – Sufis in Iraq, People of Blame in Nishapur, Sages in Transoxania – had started out among urban, largely literate, middle and upper-middle classes, and it is plausible to think that during the course of the fourth century when these movements began to coalesce into an interconnected trend under the name Sufism, this original urban base was not only preserved but expanded. During the fifth/eleventh and sixth/twelfth centuries, however, when Sufism made major inroads into rural communities, it also spread among all urban classes. Much later, after the seventh/thirteenth century, the growing popularity of Sufi figures as urban saints would manifest itself in the form of close associations between particular urban districts, professional associations, ethnic and linguistic factions on the one hand and particular saints on the other hand. However, during the period under consideration, the social ascendancy of Sufi saints became visible especially in their emergence, in some instances, as unofficial 'patron-saints' of whole towns.

The belief that pious figures could protect towns from danger likely manifested itself primarily around popular saints who were not Sufis. Muḥriz ibn Khalaf (d. 413/1022) of Tunis, today known as Sīdī Maḥrez, is a case in point.[20] A jurist and teacher who was renowned more for his piety than for his learning, he achieved fame as a saint early on: according to his hagiography written by his grandson Abū Ṭāhir Muḥammad ibn al-Ḥusayn al-Fārisī (d. around 450/1058), the townspeople attempted to obtain his blessings by grabbing his hand, touching his clothes and throwing their turbans or their pilgrimage garments towards him which they then rubbed to their eyes and faces.[21] A century later, it had become customary for sailors to throw soil taken from Muḥriz's tomb into the sea in order to calm its rough waters.[22]

Increasingly, however, Sufi saints began to enjoy the same kind of veneration from urban populations. In Damascus, an ancient town that was rich in sacred sites, the rise to fame of Sufi saints is exemplified by the case of Arslān (a Turkish name meaning 'lion', often Arabised as 'Raslān') ibn Yaʿqūb al-Dimashqī (d. 540/1145–6). Arslān was born in Qalʿat Jaʿbar in north-eastern Syria but moved to Damascus, where he worked for twenty years as a sawyer in Bāb Tūmā.[23] After receiving several signs that called him to the Sufi way of life, he became a disciple of Shaykh Abū ʿĀmir al-Mu'addib, whose spiritual lineage reportedly reached back to Junayd's uncle Sarī Saqaṭī (d. 253/867) via Kharrāz. Having established himself at the mosque of the early military commander Khālid ibn al-Walīd (d. 21/642), he soon attracted his own disciples, and, perhaps partly because of his association with this mosque that was symbolic of *jihād* during a period of continuous Crusader presence in the region, there arose a remarkably durable popular belief in his sacred power to protect Damascus from external danger. There is no doubt that he was an accomplished Sufi master, and although he left behind only a brief treatise on the meaning of *tawḥīd*, this dense piece on the perennial Sufi theme of the necessity of self-annihilation in order to realise the unity of God attracted many commentators in later times.[24]

If Arslān's case is illustrative of the growing popularity of Sufi saints among all urban classes, the case of the Ḥanbalī saint Abū 'Umar Muḥammad ibn Aḥmad (d. 607/1210) demonstrates that even at the end of the sixth/twelfth century, popular sainthood had by no means come to be monopolised by Sufis. A member of the Maqdisī family that had established the Ṣāliḥiyya neighbourhood on Mount Qāsiyūn, Abū 'Umar was a preacher-scholar who was venerated for his healing miracles and powers of intercession.[25] There is no sign of Sufi ideas or practices (apart from a generic ascetic piety) in his hagiography, and his life example is a reminder that pious figures with non-Sufi backgrounds continued to be viable candidates for popular sainthood at this time. However, the number of Sufi saints was definitely on the rise, and during the seventh/thirteenth century they dominated the scene in Damascus.[26]

It was probably another consequence of the increasing overlap between saint cults and Sufi sainthood that a prominent social type of medieval urban culture, the 'wise fool' (collectively referred to as *'uqalā al-majānīn* in Arabic), was assimilated into Sufi thought and practice as 'the one captivated by God' (*majdhūb*) from the fifth/eleventh century onwards. The wise fools lived beyond the pale, violating all social conventions, yet they were tolerated, even admired, especially on account of their total disregard for this world and their readiness to admonish their fellow citizens, particularly the wealthy and the powerful, against negligence of the hereafter.[27] As Sufism made greater inroads into urban society, the wise fool came to be identified with the mystic who lost all self-consciousness in the encounter with God and became totally bewildered. The overpowering effect of divine intimacy had been described by the earliest Sufis such as Kharrāz (especially his discussion of 'those who are rendered close to God' in the *Book of Serenity*, summarised above in Chapter 1) and Nūrī (note his statement, 'the chosen ones God pulls to Himself and effaces them from themselves', quoted in Chapter 1 above), and the bewilderment that resulted from such intimacy had been, at least to a certain extent, exemplified in the lives of Nūrī and Shiblī. About two or three generations after Shiblī, as Sufism became established in Khurāsān during the second half of the fourth/century, certain wise fools now appeared in Sufi garb as 'holy fools'. Most notable were Muḥammad Ma'shūq of Ṭūs and Luqmān of Sarakhs. These figures were widely considered to have been freed of all constraints including 'reason' and, as madmen, they were not expected to abide by the law. Abū Sa'īd reportedly venerated Muḥammad Ma'shūq, and about Luqmān he observed, 'No one is more unconnected and unattached and more pure than Luqmān. He has no ties whatsoever with anything, not with this world or the hereafter, and not with the self'. Luqmān himself is supposed to have said, 'Thirty years ago the True Sultan conquered my heart and since then no one else has dared exercise dominion over it and dwell therein'.[28] The holy fools were not particular to Khurāsān;

in Syria, where they were better known under the name *muwallah*, 'one madly enamoured of God', Qaḍīb al-Bān of Mosul (471–573/1078–1177) was an early representative of this type. However, this figure, who reportedly 'was heedless of urine on his garments and legs and used to be immersed in mud', does not appear to have been clearly associated with Sufism.[29] In time, the incorporation of the ones captivated by God into the Sufi sphere gave rise to theoretical discussions about the comparison between 'divine attraction' (*jadhba*) versus 'wayfaring' (*sulūk*); by common consensus, the holy fools were not deemed suitable candidates for spiritual directorship, but they were accorded a high degree of respect and veneration.[30]

Another phenomenon that reflected the increasing visibility of Sufis in the urban public sphere was the rise to prominence of preacher-masters. Shunned by some eminent early authorities such as Junayd, public preaching gradually became an acceptable activity for many Sufis by the fifth/eleventh century, and, from this point on, it is possible to talk of a growing confluence between Sufism and popular preaching as well as storytelling.[31] Indeed, eloquent orator-Sufis such as Aḥmad Ghazālī and, even more spectacularly, the Ḥanbalī 'Abd al-Qādir al-Jīlānī (d. 561/1166) no doubt owed their fame partly to their widely popular sermons.[32] Clearly, at least some Sufis were prepared to assume the role of public intellectuals for their communities.

The broadening in the social basis of the Sufi mode of piety was explicitly acknowledged and, to an extent, sanctioned by a major Sufi figure for the first time in the *Kitāb ādāb al-murīdīn* (*The Book of Conduct for Aspirants*) by Abu'l-Najīb al-Suhrawardī (d. 563/1168).[33] Although Abu'l-Najīb, a prominent disciple of Aḥmad Ghazālī who taught *ḥadīth* and Shāfi'ī *fiqh* in Baghdad, relied heavily in this work on earlier Sufi manuals of this same genre (especially on Ibn Khafīf's *Book of the Golden Mean*), he departed from them slightly in a final section that he devoted to the issue of 'dispensations' (*rukhṣa*, pl. *rukhaṣ*).[34] A dispensation was understood as a relaxing or suspension of primary legal injunctions (*'azīma*) under certain conditions, and, as a rule, earlier Sufi authors like Makkī, Sarrāj, and Qushayrī considered the use of dispensations to be off limits for Sufis.[35] Abu'l-Najīb agreed with his predecessors on this crucial point, but, in a move that reflects the growing appeal of Sufism to the social mainstream, he argued that resort to certain dispensations was perfectly permissible for a category of people whom he identified as 'truthful simulators' (*al-mutashabbihūn al-ṣādiqūn*). He carefully differentiated these simulators, whose chief characteristic was that they genuinely desired to be like Sufis, from novices or beginner-level aspirants to Sufism (*murīd*); the latter, as with all genuine Sufis, were to avoid dispensations altogether, while the former could allow themselves dispensations like the possession of an estate or reliance on a regular income, owning a business, carrying food during travel, dance during *samā'*, wearing 'custom-made' patched robes, visiting political rulers and old women, and keeping the company of young men.[36] The special attention that Abu'l-Najīb paid to 'truthful simulators' was no doubt a direct measure of their increasing importance during his lifetime: many urbanites of all walks of life genuinely aspired to participate in the Sufi mode of piety, even though full participation, which would have compelled them to abandon the social mainstream, was not an option that they were able or willing to consider. With his positive interpretation of the category of simulators – unlike, for instance, Hujwīrī who had rejected them with the pejorative term *mustaṣwif* 'pretender Sufis' – the pragmatic Abu'l-Najīb embraced these new 'affiliates' to Sufism, albeit without admitting them to the ranks of genuine Sufis.[37] It was, most likely, on account of the accommodationist stance of Sufis like Abu'l-Najīb that new Sufi customs such as bestowing a 'robe of blessing' (*khirqat al-tabarruk*) to sympathetic but uninitiated affiliates came into being, as distinct from the 'robe of aspiration' (*khirqat al-irāda*) conferred to genuine Sufi aspirants upon initiation.[38] Furthermore, it can be speculated that such a broadening in the social base of Sufism might have led to a tightening of ranks and possibly to a greater degree of hierarchical organisation within inner Sufi circles. Indeed, Abu'l-Najīb himself makes a tripartite distinction between beginner/aspirant (*murīd*), initiate/adept (*mutawassiṭ*), and consummate/achiever (*muntahin*). More generally, it is likely that the distinctions between master (*shaykh*), accomplished disciple (*khalīfa*), and novice (*murīd*), and the elevation of particular masters to the rank of 'pole/axis' (*quṭb*) gelled in this era.[39]

Increasingly popular in provincial and major urban centres among all social classes including legal and theological scholars, it was not long before the Sufis began to attract the attention of political circles. One unmistakable marker of such attention was the appearance, in historical literature produced in the ambit of royal courts, of legitimisation narratives in which the reign of particular rulers were 'blessed' by saintly figures. An early paradigmatic example is the story of the meeting between the Saljūq ruler Ṭughrıl and the enigmatic saintly poet Bābā Ṭāhir, nicknamed ''Uryān', (the 'Naked'), as reported by Muḥammad ibn 'Alī Rāvandī, who wrote at the very end of the sixth/twelfth century:

> When Ṭughril Beg came to Hamadān, there were three saints there: Bābā Ṭāhir, Bābā Ja'far, and Shaykh Ḥamshā. They were standing on a small mountain called Khiḍr close to the gate of Hamadān. The Sultan saw them. He stopped the army and went to see them on foot along with the vizier Abū Naṣr al-Kundurī. He kissed their hands. Bābā Ṭāhir, the enthralled soul, said to the Sultan: 'O Turk! What will you do with God's people?' The Sultan relied: 'Whatever you state.' Bābā said: '[Rather], do that which God orders: "*Verily God commands justice and spiritual excellence*"' [Qur'ān 16 (al-Naḥl): 90]. The Sultan wept, and said: 'I will do so'. Bābā held his hand and said: 'Do you accept this from me?' The Sultan said: 'Yes!' Bābā had a broken ewer, which for years he had used for ablutions, and kept the tip of it [as a ring] on his finger. He took it out and put it in the finger of the Sultan and

> said: 'Thus, I have handed to you dominion of the world. Stand firm on justice.' The Sultan kept the ring among his charms. Whenever he would go on battle, he would put on this ring.[40]

Bābā Ṭāhir's historical personality is obscure, and the story of his meeting with Sultan Ṭughrıl may well be apocryphal. As in the case of hagiographical literature, however, historical writing produced for courtly consumption tends to reflect values and assumptions prevalent at the cultural circles of high politics, and, seen from this angle, the legitimisation narrative of Bābā Ṭāhir and Ṭughrıl demonstrates that by the end of the sixth/twelfth century, the view that political rulers needed to bolster their legitimacy through saintly benediction was ensconced in political culture.[41]

Actual contacts between Sufis and important political figures during the fifth/eleventh century and the first half of the following century are not easy to document or to contextualise. The famous Saljūq vizier Niẓām al-Mulk, whose close association with *'ulamā'* including Abū Ḥāmid Ghazālī has attracted much attention, is said to have also cultivated ties with Sufis, yet, apart from the fact that in his youth he had studied *ḥadīth* with Qushayrī, particular instances of his association with Sufis remain elusive.[42] While it is certainly possible that he met Abū Sa'īd in his youth, details of their meetings provided in the *Secrets* are not verified in any other source, and they are best viewed as legitimisation narratives.[43] One exception in this regard, however, is that Niẓām al-Mulk is known to have written to some well-known scholars and Sufis, probably in the 460s/1067–77 or early 470s/1077–87, asking for advice and 'testimonials' (*maḥḍar, ishtihādnāma*). Anṣārī and Abu'l-Ḥasan-i Bustī were among those who responded with letters of advice; a third respondent, the great Shāfi'ī legal scholar Abū Isḥāq Ibrāhīm ibn 'Alī al-Shīrāzī (d. 476/1083) who, not without some compunction, taught at the prestigious Niẓāmiyya *madrasa* that the vizier had established in Baghdad, is said to have written the terse testimonial 'Ḥasan [that is, Niẓām al-Mulk] is the best of oppressors'.[44] Whatever the vizier's real intentions, it is clear that neither Anṣārī nor Bustī saw any harm in responding to the solicitation of advice issued by this most powerful politician.

The correspondence between Niẓām al-Mulk on the one hand and Anṣārī and Bustī on the other may be seen as the beginning of a type of relationship between Sufis and politicians in which the latter gave advice to, and interceded with, the former instead of ignoring the world of politics. It should not be imagined, however, that the existence of contacts between Sufis and political leaders automatically translated into patronage of the former by the latter through financial donations and the bestowal of political privileges such as tax exemption. Nor would it be justified to think that those Sufis who tolerated or even cultivated such contacts with political powers necessarily expected concrete 'returns' in the form of material or political benefits from the politicians. Rather, it appears that in choosing to have contact with rulers they were motivated by an 'inner mission' to convert people (through 'repentance', *tawba*) from a purely exoteric understanding of Islam to a holistic Islam properly grounded on 'inner knowledge', just as, in the same spirit, they invited the general public to repent in their public and private preaching and teaching.[45] Apart from the involvement of Anṣārī and Bustī with Niẓām al-Mulk, this stance is clearly illustrated in the case of Aḥmad-i Jām and Sultan Sanjar.

In a letter he wrote in response to a question that Sanjar had directed to him about the characteristics of saints, Aḥmad-i Jām made it immediately clear that the friends of God served only God, not mortals, and that they had no interest in this world and its riches. He then narrowed his focus to the question of the relationship of the saints to the 'people of the world', in particular the military, and stated: 'The friends of the Almighty God shy away even from the company of divine angels; how could they descend and mingle in the camps of oppression and the tents of lust?' Since his tone was clearly derogatory, he proceeded to explain:

> The Lord of Creation knows that these words are but words of kindly counsel, not of censure ... Not every preacher or admonisher can preach to the king of the age; a preacher knowledgeable about mystical states and the requirements of religious law is needed, one with insight into the Sufi path, aware of the frailties of the material world, informed of the excellences and virtues of creation and human nature.

It appears quite likely that here Aḥmad-i Jām was engaged in polemics directed at unidentified saintly figures (or perhaps these were astrologers and practitioners of occult sciences?) in Sanjar's entourage: he was anxious to distance himself and the true saints from such 'treasure hunters' who hovered about the Sultan under the false pretence of helping the army capture fortresses and uncover hidden treasure through their sacred powers, as mentioned elsewhere in the letter. He elaborated further:

> May the Sultan of the day and the leader of the age – God confirm him with perfect assistance – not receive these words with a hostile and judgmental ear, but rather consider them a kindly counsel. Just as he would look for perfection in a tailor, a cupper and a physician, let him look for perfection in the way of religion and if he should see one who is perfect, let that one be chosen. If he chooses to forget the present author, no harm will come to me, for my object is that he should attain to God the Almighty through this perfect guidance. This author is saying that he has no enmity or quarrel with anyone, but there is no neglecting [the duty to give] correct advice.

Clearly, by this letter Aḥmad-i Jām attempted to direct Sanjar's attention away from certain false advisors who surrounded the Sultan to the Sufis, who, in his opinion, were the true guides in religious matters. It is impossible to know whether Sanjar had indeed solicited his counsel or not, but, to judge by this one letter, Aḥmad-i Jām appears to have been motivated by a true desire to provide guidance to Sanjar and to have expected only a fair hearing from the ruler of his time in giving forthright advice to him.[46]

Another kind of contact between political rulers and Sufis came about when the former felt threatened by the growing popular influence of the latter and sought to contain or eliminate this perceived threat. Perhaps the earliest and best-known instance of this kind of political supervision and/or persecution of popular Sufi masters took place in the Maghrib when the Almoravid sultan ʿAlī bin Yūsuf ibn Tāshfīn (r. 500–37/1107–43) summoned Abu'l-ʿAbbās Aḥmad ibn Muḥammad of Almería, known as Ibn al-ʿArīf (d. 536/1141) and Abu'l-Ḥakam ibn Barrajān of Seville (d. 536/1141) to Marrakesh. Although the details of this incident remain obscure, the summons proved to be fatal for these figures: the latter died in prison while the former, though set free by the sultan, is generally thought to have been poisoned while still in Marrakesh. Since nothing in the extant historical record of either man suggests that they would have advocated rebellion or disobedience to the political ruler, this instance of political intervention into the lives of two prominent Sufis seems to have been occasioned by the fear that they may have been tempted to use to their popularity against the Almoravid regime. That ʿAlī bin Yūsuf's fears concerning popular religious figures was not always baseless was demonstrated a year later, in 537/1142, when the self-styled messiah (*mahdī*) Abu'l-Qāsim Aḥmad ibn Ḥusayn, known as ibn al-Qasī, initiated a rebellion in the Algarve (in present-day southern Portugal) which ended with his assasination only a decade later in 546/1151, but this messianic leader's association with Sufism appears to be tenuous.[47] In any event, close scrutiny of popular Sufi saints by political authorities is incontrovertible evidence of the rising appeal of the Sufi mode of piety to both urban and rural populations.

Antinomians and nonconformists

The early Sufis of the third/ninth century occupied a peculiar place in the social and mental world of Islamic Iraq. Unlike many itinerant renunciants who roamed the countryside, the Sufis firmly implanted themselves into the major urban centres of Baghdad and Basra, yet they were not altogether 'mainstream' and harboured anti-social and antinomian tendencies side by side with socially and legally-conformist ones. Socially, their nonconformist strains included distinct strands of celibacy, vegetarianism, avoidance of gainful employment, withdrawal and seclusion, as well as a certain proclivity for outlandish even outrageous behaviour (Nūrī and Shiblī stand out in this regard), though these were not universally accepted or practised by all or even most Sufis. Other characteristic Sufi practices and beliefs, notably *samāʿ* – which tended to be a peculiar blend of music, poetry and dance – and discourses of closeness to God, did not necessarily deviate from the social mainstream and may have even been popular, yet they could be legally and theologically suspect. In this sense, the Sufis of Iraq, who can be said to have harboured anarchist tendencies, were among the social and intellectual avant-garde of early Islam.

As an inward-orientated form of piety, Sufism contained an intensely self-critical strain from its very beginnings, and astute Sufi observers who surveyed the Sufi scene tackled the task of disentangling the 'questionable and undesirable' elements of their heritage from its 'genuine' solid core. On this front, Sarrāj and Hujwīrī stand out as forthright and honest surveyors of the whole canvas of Sufism who documented and discussed critically the contentious aspects of their tradition without making any undue compromises from what they considered to be its core (which, for them, definitely included *samā'* – but not dance – and discourses of proximity and special access to God). The *oeuvre* of Anṣārī and Sulamī, both inclusive and expansive, are also revealing in this regard. Kalābādhī and Qushayrī, however, were more circumspect; they had a somewhat less inclusive and 'sanitised' picture of Sufism, one that was so closely aligned with their scholarly predilections that there was little room left for unruly elements.

Naturally, Sufis were not the only ones to write critically on Sufi subjects. As Sufism became socially more prominent, it caught the attention of 'outsiders' who recorded their reactions to this form of pious living in their works, mostly in the form of brief incidental comments. Since Sufism of Iraq first emerged as a synthesis of pre-existing strands of piety, it is not surprising that some of the themes sounded by its outsider critics had precedents in earlier 'heresiographical' literature. A revealing example is the following passage on heretics called 'pneumatics' (*rūḥāniyya*) from Abū 'Āṣim Khushaysh ibn Aṣram al-Nasā'ī's (d. 253/867) *Kitāb al-istiqāma fi'l-sunna wa al-radd 'alā ahl al-ahwā* (*The Book of Sound Tradition and Refutation of Dissenters*):

> They are so called because they believe that their spirits see the *malakūt* ['the divine dominion'] of the heavens, that they see the pasture of paradise, and further, that they have sexual intercourse with the houris. Furthermore, they believe that they wander with their spirits in paradise. They are also called *fikriyya* ['meditationists'] because they meditate and believe that in their meditation they can reach God in reality. Thus they make their meditation the object of their devotions and of their striving towards God. In their meditation they see this goal by means of their spirit, through God speaking to them directly, passing his hand gently over them, and – as they believe – looking upon them directly, while they have intercourse with the houris and dally with them as they lay upon their couches, and while eternally young boys bring them food and drink and exquisite fruit.[48]

Khushaysh prodeeded to report on other groups of mystics.

> Other mystics teach that when love of God has supplanted all other attachments in the heart (*khulla*), legal bans are no longer valid (*rukhaṣ*). And some teach a

> method of ascetic training (especially of the diet) that so mortifies yearnings for the flesh that when the training is finished the 'ascetic' gains licence to everything (*ibāḥa*). Another group maintains that the heart is distracted when mortification becomes too vigorous; it is better to yield immediately to one's inclinations; the heart, having experienced vanity, can then detach itself from vain things without regret. One last group affirms that renunciation (*zuhd*) is applicable only to things forbidden by religious law, that enjoying permitted wealth is good and riches are superior to poverty.[49]

Such criticisms, when directed against mystics, normally gravitated toward the major generic accusations of *ibāḥa*, 'permissivism and antinomianism', and *ḥulūl*, 'incarnationism or inherence of the Divine in the material world, especially in human form'. To these was added, especially by the Muʿtazila and Shīʿa, the charges of obscurantist anti-rationalism, making 'false claims' to work miracles as well as rash dismissal of discursive learning. It was against the backdrop of these general accusations that specific Sufi practices such as *samāʿ*, tearing the cloak in ecstasy, and searching for manifestations of God in the creation – most notoriously in the form of 'gazing at beardless youths' – came under fire from critics of Sufism. Such frontal attacks against Sufism began to appear from very early on, with the Muʿtazila and the Twelver Shiʿa explicitly attacking Sufis already during the fourth/tenth century, but they crescendoed only in the sixth/twelfth century with two critical chapters in the *Tabṣirat al-ʿawāmm fī maʿrifat maqālāt al-anām* (*Instructions for the Common People concerning the Knowledge of Human Discourses*) of the Twelver Shīʿī Jamāl al-Dīn al-Murtaḍā al-Rāzī (lived first half of sixth/twelfth century) and a long chapter contained in the famous Ḥanbalī preacher and writer ʿAbd al-Raḥmān ibn ʿAlī Ibn al-Jawzī's (510–97/1126–1200) polemical work *Talbīs Iblīs* (*The Devil's Delusion*).

Jamāl al-Dīn al-Murtaḍā divided the Sufis into six sects: (1) those who believed in unification with God (*ittiḥād*); here, he specifically named Ḥallāj, Basṭāmī and Shiblī; (2) lovers (*ʿushshāq*); these thought that only God was worthy of love; (3) *Nūriyya* (the 'Light Sect') who believed that two kinds of veils existed between humanity and God, one of light, and the other of fire; those who were veiled by light were to be condemned because they falsely belittled Paradise and Hell, while those who were veiled by fire were positively followers of Satan, who was himself made of fire; (4) *Wāṣiliyya* (the 'Attainers'), who attained union with God and thus saw no need to observe religious duties; (5) those who were against books and learning; and (6) those who cared only for sensual pleasures such as eating, dancing, and wearing nice clothes. In a separate chapter, al-Rāzī scrutinised the work of Qushayrī'and took the Sufis to task for sanctioning *samāʿ*, believing in incarnation, misunderstanding *walāya* (which he thought was reserved only for the Shīʿī *imāms*), and falsely claiming to perform miracles, while they only engaged in sorcery (*siḥr*).[50]

Compared to al-Rāzī's criticism of the Sufis, Ibn al-Jawzī's denunciation of

Sufism was at once more substantive and better informed. In *The Devil's Delusion*, Ibn al-Jawzī set out to document and expose the delusions that the Devil worked on different social groups, including philosophers, theologians, jurists, *ḥadīth* experts and rulers, but he reserved his longest chapter to cataloguing the errors of the Sufis.[51] The beginning of this chapter is revealing about how Ibn al-Jawzī classified Sufis:

> The Sufis belong to the renunciants. We already described the delusions the devil works on the renunciants [in the chapter that precedes this one], but the Sufis are distinguished from them by certain qualities and states and are marked by [special] characteristics, and we need to discuss them separately. Sufism started out as a path of renunciation, but later its adherents allowed themselves *samāʿ* and dance. Those who seek the next world from among the common people began to view them favourably on account of their renunciation, and those who seek after this world looked upon them with favour when they saw how they [the Sufis] enjoyed comfort and amusement.[52]

Clearly, in Ibn al-Jawzī's eyes the Sufis were a special branch of renunciants. They were distinguished from the renunciants by their distinctive practices and beliefs. These, which Ibn al-Jawzī proceeded to discuss in separate sections, included the following practices: *samāʿ*; ecstasy; dance and hand-clapping; gazing at beardless youths; an excessive concern for cleanliness and ritual purity; dwelling in lodges; celibacy; giving up property; wearing *fuwaṭ*, 'aprons', and *muraqqaʿa*, 'patched cloak'; investiture with the cloak; refraining from eating meat; rejection of trade and employment; withdrawal from society through solitude and seclusion; abandoning marriage and desire of children; travelling without provisions with no particular destination, sometimes in solitude and walking at night; avoiding medical treatment; refusal to mourn the death of close companions; abandoning scholarship.They also included the following beliefs: distinction between *ʿilm al-bāṭin* 'inner knowledge', and *ʿilm al-ẓāhir*, 'outer knowledge', this latter equated with *ʿilm al-sharīʿa* 'knowledge of the *sharīʿa*; 'loving God passionately' (*ʿishq*); visions of angels, jinns, demons, and even God in this world.

These practices and beliefs were indeed associated with Sufism, even though no single Sufi necessarily accepted all of them. Ibn al-Jawzī, for his part, rejected them as reprehensible innovations (*bidʿa*, pl. *bidaʿ*) and attempted to prove his case with the help of reliable *ḥadīth*.[53] He was most unhappy with how the Sufis, in his eyes, undermined the supremacy of the *sharīʿa* by their claim to possess an 'inner knowledge'. The distinction that the Sufis drew between *sharīʿa* and *ḥaqīqa*, 'reality', he argued, was patently wrong since the two were completely identical, and, contrary to Sufi views, inspiration (*ilhām*) was not a separate means of communication with God but was simply the result of genuine knowledge (*ʿilm*). It was clear to Ibn al-Jawzī that the Devil had succeeded in deluding the Sufis mainly by diverting them from discursive knowledge.

Interestingly, Ibn al-Jawzī's criticism of the Sufis sounded like the self-critical remarks of Sarrāj, Hujwīrī and Abū Ḥāmid Ghazālī. In his discussion of dress, for instance, Ibn al-Jawzī lashed out against formalism and, criticising the Sufi fascination with patched cloaks, he was moved to state, 'Sufism is a concept not a form!'[54] Particularly telling in this regard is his account of 'libertines' who discredited the Sufis.[55] According to Ibn al-Jawzī, certain antinomians and libertines had infiltrated Sufism and assumed Sufi identities in order to protect themselves by masking their true identities. These fell into three classes: (1) outright infidels; (2) those who professed Islam but followed their shaykhs without asking for any evidence or even 'specious arguments' (*shubha*) about the legal-theological status of the acts they were asked to perform [this is clearly a reflection of the elevation of the training master's authority to new heights during the lifetime of Ibn al-Jawzī]; and (3) those who did produce 'specious arguments' for their actions but were deluded by the devil into thinking that their false arguments were sound. Ibn al-Jawzī reviewed and rejected six such 'specious arguments', all quasi-theological props for libertinism and abolition of the *sharīʿa*, some of which recall the heresiographical observations by Khushaysh quoted above. According to him, some justified their hedonism through predestinarian arguments; some argued that God did not need our worship; some took refuge in God's infinite mercy; others gave up the effort to discipline the lower self as an unattainable goal; and still others claimed to have transcended the law by having successfully tamed their lower selves or by having experienced clear signs of God's approval of their behaviour in the form of miraculous occurrences or visions and dreams.

In his decision to exclude libertines from the body of Sufism, Ibn al-Jawzī was in agreement with most Sufi observers of the Sufi landscape, who also sought to domesticate or eliminate the antinomian trends interwoven into their tradition of piety. It is noteworthy that the scope of Sufism as it was viewed by its most powerful critic largely coincided with its scope as it was understood by its most astute 'insider' observers from Sarrāj to Hujwīrī. Ibn al-Jawzī rejected the practices and beliefs that he associated with Sufism, while the Sufi authorities evaluated them critically, endorsing many and ruling out others, but outsider critics and insider 'experts' alike agreed on the boundaries of the form of piety that they picked out for review. Ibn al-Jawzī's assault, in other words, was certainly directed at the right target. The frontal nature of this attack was most obvious in Ibn al-Jawzī's account of various reprehensible actions of Sufis, where the author focused on the more notorious aspects of the lives of especially Shiblī and Nūrī and related flagrantly-unconventional and shocking anecdotes about them, with extreme disapproval.[56] In brief, Ibn al-Jawzī found practically nothing to approve in Sufism, even though he did not refrain from using statements of Sufis with approval if these neatly fit into his arguments.

Remarkably, in his attempt to refute the whole of Sufism as antinomianism plain and simple, Ibn al-Jawzī relied directly on the views of the eminent scholar-Sufi Abū Ḥāmid Ghazālī. In his discussion of libertines in particular, Ibn al-Jawzī reproduced materials that can be traced back to the works of the 'Proof of Islam'. Indeed, since all six of the specious arguments and their correct answers given by Ibn al-Jawzī in his *Delusions* appear in a Persian treatise of Ghazālī entitled *The Idiocy of Antinomians* (*Ḥamāqat-i ahl-i ibāḥat*), it is certain that Ibn al-Jawzī had access to an Arabic version of Ghazālī's treatise or to another Arabic text that reproduced this latter's content.[57] For his part, Ghazālī naturally did not write the *Idiocy of Antinomians* as a refutation of Sufism, but he meant it instead as an attack against antinomians who masqueraded as Sufis. While Ghazālī debunked such 'false' Sufis and expostulated in several of his other works the necessity of obeying the *sharī'a*, the *Idiocy* was his most extensive and vehement criticism of 'permissivists' (*ibāḥīs*).[58] In this treatise, Ghazālī decried antinomians as the worst of all people. Misled by lust and laziness, they had dropped all prescribed ritual observances and embraced total sexual promiscuity. In so doing, they had allowed themselves to become mere toys in the hands of Satan, who used them to misguide others. Deprived of any critical faculty, they had accepted Satan's insinuation that scholarship was but a veil for true seers such as themselves and had turned into venomous critics of scholars. While admittedly not all such antinomians were 'Sufi-pretenders' (*ṣūfī-numā*), Ghazālī focused on these latter, for whom he reserved his most ascerbic tone. Like the Sufis, these impostors dressed in blue gowns or wore the patched cloak, shaved their moustaches, and carried prayer-rugs and tooth-brushes but, unlike the Sufis, they freely consumed wine, used illicit funds without shame and availed themselves of all bodily pleasures. Ghazālī discussed in some detail eight 'specious arguments' (*shubhāt*) that the Sufi-pretenders produced, and he refuted them one by one (the two that were not directly reproduced by Ibn al-Jawzī were the denial of after-life and the argument that the true poverty meant the absence of all knowledge, including knowledge of good and bad deeds or of paradise and hell!). Irked beyond measure by these would-be Sufi libertines and their hostile attitude towards scholarship, Ghazālī the scholar-Sufi declared them beyond the pale of Islam in no uncertain terms and advised political rulers to exterminate ruthlessly these incorrigible sinners.

Who exactly were the libertines and antinomians associated with Sufism that were universally rejected by Sufis and non-Sufi observers? It is difficult to trace these shady characters, but Sarrāj gave a full listing of them in the 'Book of Errors' of his *Light Flashes*, under the heading 'On those who erred in fundamentals and were led to misbelief'.[59] These included the following: (1) those who thought that once mystics reached God they should be called 'free' instead of 'Godservants'; (2) a group of Iraqis who thought that the Godservant could not achieve true sincerity unless he ceased to pay attention to how others viewed him and who thus proceeded to ignore social norms in his actions, whether these were right or wrong; (3) those who placed sainthood above prophecy on account of their baseless interpretation of the Qur'ānic story of Moses and Khiḍr (Qur'ān, 18 [Kahf]: 60–82, summarised in Chapter 4 above); (4) those who argued that all things were permitted and that prohibition applied only to excessive licence taken with others' property; (5) those who believed in divine inherence in a person; (6) those who understood discourse of 'passing away' (*fanā'*) as the passing away of human nature; (7) a group in Syria and a group in Basra ('Abd al-Wāḥid ibn Zayd is named) who believed in vision of God with the heart in this world; (8) those who believed that they were permanently and perfectly pure; (9) those who believed that their hearts contained divine lights that were uncreated; (10) those who sought to avert blame from themselves when they incurred the punishments laid down by the Qur'ān and violated the custom of the Prophet by arguing that they were compelled by God in all their actions; (11) those who surmised that their closeness to God exempted them from observing the same etiquette that they followed prior to achieving proximity to the Divine; (12) a group in Baghdad who thought that in passing away from their own qualities they had entered God's qualities; (13) a group in Iraq who claimed to lose all their senses in ecstasy and thus to transcend sensory phenomena; (14) those who erred in their beliefs concerning the spirit (*rūḥ*), with many versions of this error listed, most notably the belief in the uncreatedness of the spirit and the belief in transmigration of spirits.

Sarrāj did not claim to have personally seen all these groups, but there is little doubt that they existed (although their detractors no doubt exercised their imagination in their descriptions of them) and that they were generally linked with Sufism. A contemporary of Sarrāj, al-Muṭahhar ibn Ṭāhir al-Maqdisī, who composed an historical work called *Kitāb al-bad' wa'l-ta'rīkh* around 355/966, gave the names of four Sufi groups he came across as Ḥusniyya (*ḥusn* means 'beauty'), Malāmatiyya, Sūqiyya/Sawqiyya – which should most likely be amended to Shawqiyya (*shawq* 'longing') – and Ma'dhūriyya (*ma'dhūr* 'excused'). He made the following observation about them:

> These are characterised by the lack of any consistent system or clear principles of faith. They make judgments according to their speculations and imagination, and they constantly change their opinions. Some of them believe in incarnationism (*ḥulūl*), as I have heard one of them claim that His habitation is in the cheeks of the beardless youth (*murd*). Some of them believe in permissiveness (*ibāḥa*) and neglect the religious law, and they do not heed those who blame them.[60]

Although it is possible to match these groups with those discussed by Sarrāj (for instance, Ma'dhūriyya possibly to be associated with numbers 4, 10, or 11; Ḥusniyya with 7; Malāmatiyya with 2 and 10; and Shawqiyya with 13), it would be hazardous to attempt a one-to-one correspondence on the basis of such meagre evidence. Noteworthy, however, is Maqdisī's use of the name 'Malāmatī' for those who neglected the law and were not concerned with public blame. This is a different reading of the term Malāmatī than in the case of the 'Path of Blame' in Nishapur. The followers of this latter movement understood 'blame' primarily to mean 'self-censure', not 'public censure', and certainly did not neglect the law. Nor is there strong evidence that they sought to discipline the lower self by subjecting it to public blame through commission of deliberate and conspicuous acts that violated social norms.[61] After all, attracting public blame would have been contrary to their goal of attaining complete public anonymity in an effort to conceal their true spiritual state from all others and thus deny the *nafs* the opportunity to gloat in public attention of any kind. It appears, however, that sometime during the ascendancy of Iraq-orientated Sufism in Khurāsān during the fourth/tenth century, the term Malāmatī came to be applied increasingly to real or imaginary libertines, who justified their social and legal transgressions, genuinely or in dissimulation, either as 'indifference to public blame occasioned by true sincerity' (number 2 in Sarrāj's list of errors above) or as 'disciplining the lower self by abasing it through public blame'. Maqdisī's usage certainly reflects this different use of the term outside Nishapur, and other independent evidence corroborates his observation. In a work written by the Caspian Zaydī Imam Aḥmad ibn al-Ḥusayn al-Mu'ayyad bi'llāh (d. 411/1021) that apparently is 'the earliest extant Zaydī literary reaction to Sufism', the author referred to some Sufis who called themselves 'the people of blame' (*ahl al-malāma*) and stated, 'They claim that by involving themselves in evil situations and committing reprehensible acts they abase their ego, yet in reality they fall from the state of repentance and may well revert to being offenders (*fussāq*)'.[62]

Sulamī, who was a contemporary of al-Mu'ayyad bi'llāh, seems oblivious to this use of the term Malāmatī to designate libertines and portrays the members of the Path of Blame as law-abiding mystics, but in spite of his attempts at preserving the good name of his spiritual ancestors, the name Malāmatī continues to be used during the fifth/eleventh century to refer to antinomians who are indifferent to the *sharīʿa*. Not surprisingly, Qushayrī, whose conception of Sufism was carefully circumscribed, mentioned the Malāmatīs of Nishapur only in passing in three entries in the biographical section of his *Treatise*, possibly because the term Malāmatī was already tainted with antinomianism in his eyes, but Hujwīrī devoted a whole chapter to the question of 'blame', which is packed with interesting information.[63] Referring to the Qur'ānic locus of the concept of blame – Qur'ān 5 [al-Mā'ida]: 54 that refers to the Prophet and his companions, 'they struggle in the path of God and do not fear the blame of any blamer' – Hujwīrī reminded his readers that 'God's elect [that is, prophets and saints] are distinguished from the rest by public blame' and that 'public blame is the sustenance of God's friends'.[64] He then proceeded to differentiate the different meanings of the concept with admirable clarity:

> Blame is of three kinds: (1) [blame attached] to following the right path, (2) blame [incurred] intentionally, (3) [blame attached] to abandoning [the law]. Blame is attached to following the right path when one who minds his own business, practises religion and abides by the rules of social interaction, is blamed by the people; this is the way people behave towards him but he is indifferent to all that. Intentional blame is when one attracts great public esteem and becomes a centre of attention, and his heart inclines towards that esteem and grows attached to it, yet he wants to rid himself of the people and devote himself to God, he incurs public blame by dissimulating a [blameworthy] act that is not against the law so that people would turn away from him. Blame is attached to abandoning the law when one is gripped in his nature by infidelity and misbelief so that people say that he abandoned the law and prophetic custom, while he thinks that he is walking the path of blame.[65]

Hujwīrī explained and endorsed the first two kinds, citing examples for them, and rejected the third, decrying it as a ploy to win fame and popularity. The proponents of this last kind often justified their actions as a deliberate attempt on their part to abase the lower self, and while Hujwīrī thought that public blame could certainly have that therapeutic effect – he proffered an example from his personal experience about how being pelted with melon skins by formalist Sufis saved him from a spiritual snare that had seized him – he could not countenance such flagrant violation of the religious law.[66]

Hujwīrī's attitude toward blame was shared by other fifth/eleventh century- and, later, sixth/twelfth-century figures who discussed the concept. Both Anṣarī and Abū Ḥāmid Ghazālī, like Hujwīrī, objected to those who contravened the law in the name of *malāma*, but accepted shocking though licit acts in order to repel public attention and along with it the desire for fame or good name (*jāh*); Ghazālī cited an unnamed renunciant who began to eat voraciously when he was visited by the political ruler in order to avert this latter's attention from himself.[67] The Ẓāhirī traditionist and Sufi Muḥammad ibn Ṭāhir al-Maqdisī 'Ibn al-Qaysarānī' (448–507/1058–1113) criticised Malāmatīs of his time as antinomians.[68] Muḥammad ibn Munavvar, the biographer of Abū Sa'īd-i Abu'l-Khayr who wrote towards the end of the sixth/twelfth century, quoted Abū Sa'īd as having said, 'The Malāmatī is he who, out of love of God, does not fear whatever happens to him and does not care about blame'.[69] At around the same time as Ibn Munavvar, Ibn al-Jawzī decried Malāmatīs in much the same way as Hujwīrī and Ghazālī, though in more caustic terms:

> Certain Sufis, who are called the Malāmatiyya, plunged into sins and then said, 'Our goal was to demote ourselves in the public eye in order to be safe from the disaster of good name and hypocrisy.' They are like a man who fornicated with a woman and impregnated her, and when he was asked, 'Why didn't you practise *coitus interruptus* ('*azl*?)' he replied, 'I had heard that '*azl* is reprehensible.' Then they told him, 'And

> you had not heard that fornication is prohibited?' These ignorant people have lost their standing with God and have forgotten that Muslims are the witnesses of God on earth.[70]

Ibn al-Jawzī was in principle against intentional blame, and he stated unequivocably, 'it is no religious act for a man to humiliate himself in public'.[71] He narrated with disapproval what he considered clear examples of outrageous behaviour about, especially, Nūrī and Shiblī, though he was mostly silent about similar behaviour of Sufis closer to his own time. Like Hujwīrī and Ghazālī, however, he had no qualms about pious exemplars repelling public attention for the right reasons, and he repeated with approbation the anedote about the renunciant who pretended to be a glutton in front of the political ruler.[72]

Were there really many libertines around who claimed to be Malāmatīs during the fourth/tenth and fifth/eleventh centuries? This question is rendered more complex by the emergence, at this period, of other terms that in time came to represent libertinism, notably *darvīsh* (Persian 'pauper, beggar') and *qalandar* (Persian, 'uncouth'). Although the linguistic origins of these terms, as well as the history of the social types they designate, are obscure, it is likely that they were originally used equally for regular beggars as well as for itinerant renunciants who practised extreme *tawakkul* ('trust in God'). Some of these latter accepted charitable offerings without, however, actively seeking charity, while others no doubt survived through active begging or, at least, were commonly perceived as beggars. It is, therefore, reasonable to see a confluence of voluntary and involuntary poverty, of wandering renunciants and the destitute, in the origin of *darvīsh*s and *qalandar*s, even though the etymologies of the two terms remain uncertain.[73]

During the fifth/eleventh and sixth/twelfth centuries, *darvīsh* seems to have mostly retained its primary meaning of 'poor, beggar', but the term must have already started to assume the added connotation of a particular kind of piety characterised by itinerant mendicancy in this period, since the use of the term in this sense and the image of a wandering dervish – complete with his hallmark accoutrements of a begging bowl (*kashkūl*), a trumpet made from the horn of a ram or deer (*nafīr* or *būq*), a hat of felt (*tāj*), a short axe or hatchet (*tabarzīn*), a patched bag (*chanta*), a gnarled staff (*'aṣā*), an animal skin (*pūst*), and a rosary (*tasbīḥ*) – is well attested from the late fifth/eleventh century onwards.[74] The term *qalandar* may have had similar origins, but unlike *darvīsh*, it came to be associated very early on with libertinism, primarily because of the emergence of the *qalandar* as a peculiar literary type in Persian poetry during the late fifth/eleventh and early sixth/twelfth centuries, significantly, at the same time as the appearance of the *ghazal* as a new poetic form. More properly, one should talk of the emergence of a cluster of images organised around the central character *qalandar*. This cluster, which finds its first full-fledged expression in the poetry of

Majdūd ibn Ādam Sanā'ī (d. 525/1131), sometimes gelled into a separate genre called *qalandariyyāt*, but more commonly it existed as a free-floating bundle of imagery found most conspicuously in lyric poetry but also in other poetic genres. It was composed of several sets of images connected, most notably, to the central themes of wine-drinking, sexual promiscuity, gambling and playing games of backgammon and chess, and entering into non-Islamic, especially Zoroastrian and Christian, cults, all located at the *kharābāt*, meaning literally 'ruins' but with the very real connotation of 'tavern' and 'brothel'. Through the use of this provocative cluster woven around the figure of an unruly libertine, a highly-positive spin was given to the *qalandar*'s way of life as the epitome of true piety cleansed of all dissimulation and hypocrisy, and the *qalandar* (along with his 'look-alikes', *rind* ('heavy drinker') and *qallāsh* ('rascal')) was portrayed as the truly sincere devotee of God unconcerned with 'the blame of blamers', in other words, as the real Malāmatī.[75] In this way, the term *qalandar* was brought within the orbit of the term Malāmatī.

Did this intriguing poetic development reflect an actual social phenomenon? In the absence of non-literary evidence about the *qalandar*s as social types before the seventh/thirteenth century when they are attested as mendicant renunciants, it is impossible to answer this question. As in the case of the *darvīsh*, the literary figure probably did have some real counterpart already during the sixth/twelfth century, possibly as a continuation of the earlier antinomians discussed above, but this cannot be ascertained.[76] Apart from the issue of whether the literary *qalandar* corresponded to some real libertines in Persian-speaking Muslim communities, however, the flowering of the *kharābāt* cluster gives rise to another significant question: could this new and potent poetic imagery be read as a literary commentary on the state of Sufism during the time period under consideration? More specifically, did the web of images spun around the figure of the *qalandar* consitute a criticism of the new Sufi communities that had taken shape under the leadership of powerful training masters? Indeed, the emergence of the *kharābāt* imagery in Persian poetry was most likely the literary counterpart of Qushayrī and Hujwīrī's theoretical critique of the formalism that was so evident in the new Sufi social enterprises built around increasingly more authoritarian training shaykhs resident in their lodges. Whether it had an actual social base or not, the *kharābāt* complex was the poetic response to the *khānaqāh*, and the *qalandar*s emerged as the authentic Sufis who were willing to sacrifice absolutely everything for the sake of God, while those *khānaqāh*-residents actually called 'Sufis' were transformed in poetry to mere 'exoterists' who had abandoned the search for God in their greed for this world and thus had turned Sufism into a profitable social profession. In this sense, the so-called Sufis of the lodge comunities were indistinguishable from all the other social types, such as the *ḥadīth*-experts or the jurists of the *madrasas*, that for most mystics exemplified compromise, even corruption, of true piety because of their willingness to translate their expertise in religion to social, economic and political power. It was for this reason that in the 'strange looking glass' of the *kharābāt* complex, 'the norms and values of Sufi piety [were] all reversed', and the *qalandar* was elevated to the role of the genuine mystic.[77] This complete role-reversal suggests that whether real or imaginary, the antinomian, nonconformist edge of Sufism always functioned as an indispensable mirror in which Sufis could look to see a critical reflection of their true place in society and on the spiritual path.

Notes

1 Muḥammad ibn Munavvar, *Asrār*, 341/ *Secrets*, 527–8; also reproduced in O'Kane's introduction, 46.
2 Muḥammad ibn Munavvar, *Secrets*, 18 (translator's introduction).
3 See John O'Kane's discussion in Muḥammad ibn Munavvar, *Secrets*, 18–36. On the idea of 'spiritual domain', see Meier, *Abū Sa'īd*, 410–18.
4 The 'patterns of interaction' between Abū Sa'īd and politicians in the *Secrets* are discussed in detail by Safi, *Politics of Knowledge*, 137–44.
5 Muḥammad ibn Munavvar, *Secrets*, 47–8 (O'Kane's comments).
6 For a concise account on him, see 'Aḥmad-e Jām', EIr 1: 648–9 (H. Moayyad); longer treatments are: 'Alī Fāżil, *Sharḥ-i aḥvāl va naqd va taḥlīl-i āṣār-i Aḥmad-i Jām* (Tehran: Intishārāt-i Tūs, 1374/1995); and, more recently, Sadid al-Dīn Muḥammad ibn Mūsā Ghaznavī, *The Colossal Elephant and His Spiritual Feats, Shaykh Ahmad-e Jām: The Life and Legend of a Popular Sufi Saint of Twelfth Century Iran*, trans. Heshmat Moayyad and Franklin Lewis (Costa Mesa, CA: Mazda Publishers, 2004), 1–67 (introduction by the translators).
7 Fāżil, *Sharḥ-i aḥvāl*, 99–112.
8 Ghaznavī, *Colossal Elephant*, 268–9 (story 166); cf. the translators' comments on 15–16.
9 Aḥmad-i Jām [Abū Naṣr Aḥmad ibn Abu'l-Ḥasan], *Miftāḥ al-Najāt*, ed. 'Alī Fāżil (Tehran: Intishārāt-i Bunyād-i Farhang-i Īrān, 1347/1968), 141.
10 Aḥmad-i Jām [Abū Naṣr Aḥmad ibn Abu'l-Ḥasan], *Uns al-Tā'ibīn*, ed. 'Alī Fāżil (Tehran: Intishārāt-i Tūs, 1368/1989), in forty-five chapters.
11 For a summary account, see Ghaznavī, *Colossal Elephant*, 21–8.
12 Ghaznavī, *Colossal Elephant*, 147–8 (story 24) and 154–60 (story 27); also 15–17 (translators' introduction). For later versions of the meeting of Aḥmad-i Jām with Quṭb al-Dīn, see Lawrence Potter, 'Sufis and sultans in post-Mongol Iran', *Iranian Studies* 27 (1994): 87, note 56.
13 Relevant anectodes are summarised by Moayyad and Lewis in their introduction to Ghaznavī, *Colossal Elephant*, 18–21.
14 As noted earlier, hagiographies of individual Sufis were written in Arabic already in the fourth/tenth century, namely the accounts of Ibn Khafīf and Kāzarūnī, but these have survived only in later Persian translations. In this connection, one can also mention Abu'l-Faḍl Sahlajī's (d. 474/1084) *Kitāb al-nūr min kalimāt Abī Ṭayfūr* (*The Book of Light [Issuing forth] from the Words of Bāyazīd*), a work of the fifth/eleventh century.

15 See 'Abu'l-Ḥasan Karaqānī', EIr 1: 306 (H. Landolt) under the bibliography; according to Landolt, the *Memorial* was writtten sometime after 566/1170–71, and while the date of the *Light* remains obscure, it was certainly in existence well before 698/1299, which was the date when the extant extract from it was made or copied. The Chishtī community is not known to have produced any literature at this stage.

16 For general treatment of Persian hagiographies, see 'Hagiographical literature', EIr 11: 536–9 (J. Paul); and Jürgen Paul, 'Au début du genre hagiographique dans le Khurassan', in *Saints orientaux*, ed. Denise Aigle (Paris: De Boccard, 1995), 15–38.

17 The following discussion on Morocco is based on my reading of Cornell, *Realm*, 32–62.

18 Cornell, *Realm*, 45; I have modified Cornell's translation of *ḥifẓ al-ghuyūb*, which is 'concealment of esoteric teachings from the uninitiated.'

19 Cornell, *Realm*, 53.

20 'Muḥriz ibn Khalaf', EI 7: 473b–474b (Ch. Pellat).

21 As reported in Giovanna Calasso, 'Les ramparts et la loi, les talismans et les saints: la protection de la ville dans les sources musulmanes médiévales', *Bulletin d'Études Orientales* 44 (1992): 99.

22 'Muḥriz ibn Khalaf', EI 7: 474a (Ch. Pellat), reporting from the mid-sixth/twelfth century Andalusian traveller Abū Ḥāmid al-Gharnāṭī's *Tuḥfat al-albāb*, 138, as edited by G. Ferrand, *Journal Asiatique* 207 (1925): 1–148, 195–303.

23 On him, see Éric Geoffroy, *Djihad et contemplation: Vie et enseignement d'un soufi au temps des croisades* (Paris: Dervy, 1997), who relies mostly on his hagiography by Muḥammad ibn 'Alī Ibn Ṭūlūn (d. 953/1546), entitled *Ghāyat al-bayān fī tarjamat al-Shaykh Arslān al-Dimashqī* (Damascus, 1984), and the modern works of 'Izzat Ḥuṣriyya; also G. W. J. Drewes, *Directions for Travellers on the Mystic Path* (The Hague: Martinus Nijhoff, 1977), 6–25 (ch. 1) (I owe this last reference to John Renard). Geoffroy dates Arslān's death to between 555/1160 and 560/1165, it seems in an effort to link him with the ruler Nūr al-Dīn Maḥmūd ibn Zangī, but I follow Louis Pouzet, *Damas au VIIe/XIIIe siècle: vie structures religieuses d'une métropole islamique* (Beirut: Dar el-Machreq, 1988), 209, and Drewes, *Directions*, 6–8.

24 The Arabic text of this treatise is reproduced in Geoffroy, *Djihad et contemplation*, 59–61; Geoffroy provides a French translation of the piece along with three of the commentaries, 65–123; on the commentary tradition around this work, also see Drewes, *Directions*, chs 3–6.

25 Meri, *Cult of Saints*, 85–90.

26 Pouzet, *Damas*, 207–43.

27 Michael W. Dols, *Majnūn: The Madman in Medieval Islamic Society* (Oxford: Oxford University Press, 1992), 349–65; ''Uqala' al-majānīn', EI Supplement: 816b–817a (U. Marzolph).

28 Muḥammad ibn Munavvar, *Asrār*, 199 and 264 / *Secrets*, 306 and 400. Muḥammad Ma'shūq is discussed in detail in Pūrjavādī, *'Ayn al-Quẓāt*, 55–94; on Luqmān, other than *The Secrets*, see Hujwīrī, *Kashf*, 234 / *Revelation*, 189.

29 For discussions of the *muwallahs* in Syria during the seventh/thirteenth century and after, see Meri, *Cult of Saints*, 91–100 (the discussion and the quote on Qaḍīb al-Bān are on 97–8); Pouzet, *Damas*, 222–6; and Michael Chamberlain, *Knowledge and Social Practice in Medieval Damascus, 1190–1350* (Cambridge: Cambridge University Press, 1994), 130–3.

30 See Gramlich, *Derwischorden*, 2: 189–94 for discussion with references.

31 Cf. Jonathan P. Berkey, *Popular Preaching and Religious Authority in the Medieval Islamic Near East* (Seattle: University of Washington Press, 2001), 20.

32 On Jīlānī, see "Abd al-Qādir al-Jīlānī', EIr 1: 132–3 (B. Lawrence); Knysh, *Short History*, 179–83; and more substantively, André Demeerseman, *Nouveau regard sur la voie spirituelle d''Abd al-Qādir al-Jilānī et sa tradition* (Paris: Librairie Philosophique J. Vrin, 1988).

33 'Abd al-Qāhir ibn 'Abd Allāh Suhrawardī, *Kitāb ādāb al-murīdīn*, ed. Menahem Milson (Jerusalem: Hebrew University, Institute of Asian and African Studies, distributed by Magnes Press, 1977); abridged translation: *A Sufi Rule for Novices:* Kitāb ādāb al-Murīdīn *of Abū al-Najīb al-Suhrawardī*, trans. Menahem Milson (Cambridge, Mass.: Harvard University Press, 1975).

34 For Abu'l-Najīb's reliance on Ibn Khafīf, see Sobieroj, 'Comparison'.

35 'Rukhṣa, 1. In law', EI 8: 595b–596a (R. Peters), and 'Rukhṣa, 2. In Sufism', EI 8: 596a–b (J. G. J. ter Haar).

36 'Abd al-Qāhir ibn 'Abd Allāh Suhrawardī, *Ādāb*, 80–99 / *Sufi Rule*, 72–82; this section is discussed in detail in Ian R. Netton, 'The breath of felicity: *adab, aḥwāl, maqāmāt* and Abū Najīb al-Suhrawardī', in *Classical Persian Sufism from Its Origins to Rumi*, ed. Leonard Lewisohn (London: Khaniqahi Nimatullahi Publications, 1993), 464–7.

37 Netton, 'Breath of felicity', 480–1, and Sobeiroj ('al-Suhrawardī, Abū Najīb 'Abd al-Ḳāhir ibn 'Abd Allāh', EI 9: 778b; and 'Comparison') interpret Abu'l-Najīb's accommodating attitude towards simulators as incorporation of an 'element of instability' into rules of Sufi conduct, even as a 'decline from the high ground' of Sufi spirituality prior to Abu'l-Najīb, but there is no compelling reason to adopt this interpretation.

38 The locus classicus of this distinction is in the famous work of Abu'l-Najīb's nephew: 'Umar ibn Muḥammad Suhrawardī, *'Awārif al-ma'ārif*, ed. Adīb al-Kamdānī and Muḥammad Maḥmūd al-Muṣṭafā (Mecca: Al-Maktaba al-Makkiya, 2001), 1: 162, passage translated in Trimingham, *Sufi Orders*, 185.

39 Rich leads with ample documentation on these and related issues are given in Gramlich, *Derwischorden*, 2: 139–252. For Abu'l-Najīb's tripartite distinction, see 'Abd al-Qāhir ibn 'Abd Allāh Suhrawardī, *Ādāb*, 16 / *Sufi Rule*, 35–6.

40 Safi, *Politics of Knowledge*, 133–4, translating from Rāvandī, *Rāḥat al-ṣudūr wa āyat al-surūr*, ed. Muḥammad Iqbāl (London: Luzac, 1921), 98–9; Rāvandī's work is discussed in Julie Scott Meisami, *Persian Historiography to the End of the Twelfth Century* (Edinburgh: Edinburgh University Press, 1999), 237–56, where the same passage is translated (p. 243).

41 The narrative is analysed by Safi, *Politics of Knowledge*, 131–6, who also introduces Bābā Ṭāhir. For a brief discussion of his poetry, see J. T. P. de Bruijn, *Persian Sufi Poetry: An Introduction to the Mystical Use of Classical Persian Poems* (Richmond, Surrey: Curzon, 1997), 13–16.

42 Details are provided in Safi, *Politics of Knowledge*, 47–50.

43 These are summarised by O'Kane in the introduction to Muḥammad ibn Munavvar, *Secrets*, 42–3; also see Meier, *Abū Sa'īd*, 331–3.

44 Pūrjavādī, *Zindagī*, 12–20. On Niẓām al-Mulk's relationship with the *'ulamā'* in general, and Ghazālī's involvement with the Saljūq state, see the comprehensive discussion of Safi, *Politics of Knowledge*, 43–81 and 105–24, respectively.

45 On the 'inner mission', see Meier, 'Soufisme et déclin culturel', 232.

46 The English translation of this letter is in *Epistle to the Samarqandians* included in Ghaznavī, *Colossal Elephant*, 430–2. For a different assessment of the relationship between Aḥmad-i Jām and Sanjar as one in which the saint blesses and supports the king in exchange for royal patronage and protection of Sufis, see Safi, *Politics of Knowledge*, 144–53; Safi builds his case on the premise that the dedication of Aḥmad-i Jām's *Rawẓat al-muẕnibīn*, which is addressed to Sanjar, was indeed written by Aḥmad-i Jām himself. The introduction of this work, however, appears to have been 'revised' by a later editor, and the absence of any mention, let alone praise, of Sanjar or any other political figure later in the book or in any of Aḥmad-i Jām's other works makes it highly likely that the dedication was added to the work later; see Aḥmad-i Jām [Abū Naṣr Aḥmad ibn Abu'l-Ḥasan], *Rawẓat al-muẕnibīn va jannat al-mushtāqīn*, ed. 'Alī Faẓil (Tehran: Intishārāt-i Bunyād-i Farhang-i Īrān, 1355/1976), 3–14.

47 For detailed discussion of Ibn Barrajān, Ibn al-'Arīf and Ibn Qasī, see Addas, 'Andalusī mysticism', 919–27; Cornell, *Realm*, 19–23; and Maribel Fierro, 'Opposition', 184–97. For Ibn Qasī's connection to Sufism in particular, see Josef Dreher, *Das Imamat des islamischen Mystikers Abūlqāsim Aḥmad ibn al-Ḥusain ibn Qasī (gest. 1151): eine Studie zum Selbstverständnis des Autors des 'Buchs vom Ausziehen der beiden Sandalen' (Kitāb ḫal' an-na'lain)* (Bonn, 1985), 52–4.

48 Bernd Radtke, 'Mystical union', 189, translating from Abu'l-Ḥusayn al-Malaṭī, *al-Tanbīh wa al-radd 'alā ahl al-ahwā' wa al-bida'*, ed. Sven Dedering (Leipzig: Biblioteca Islamica, 1936), 73ff (the passage from Khushaysh is on the margins).

49 Massignon, *Essay*, 80, paraphrasing from Abu'l-Ḥusayn al-Malaṭī, *al-Tanbīh wa al-radd 'alā ahl al-ahwā' wa al-bida'*, fols 160–7 (I omitted personal names); German translation of relevant passages are given in Bernd Radtke, *Kritische Gänge*, 261–2. On Khushaysh, see Sezgin, *Geschichte*, 1: 600.

50 Al-Rāzī's attack against Sufis is summarised in Naṣr Allāh Pūrjavādī, 'Opposition to Sufism in Twelver Shiism', in *Islamic Mysticism Contested: Thirteen Centuries of Controversies and Polemics*, ed. F. de Jong and Bernd Radtke (Leiden: Brill, 1999), 615–19, on the basis of chs 16 and 17 of his *Tabṣirat*, ed. 'Abbās Iqbāl (Tehran, 1313/1934).

51 Ibn al-Jawzī, *Talbīs*, 211–487 (ch. 10); the last pages of this chapter, 487–96, contain passages from an unidentified work of Ibn 'Aqīl (431/1040–513/1119). Chapters 9 and 11 also contain material relevant to Sufis. An English translation by D. S. Margoliouth appeared serially in *Islamic Culture* 9 (1935) to 12 (1938) and 19 (1945) to 22 (1948); I have used this in making my own translations. On Ibn al-Jawzī, see 'Ibn al-Djawzī, 'Abd al-Raḥmān ibn 'Alī' EI 3: 751a–752a (H. Laoust); his attitude toward Sufism is discussed in Makdisi, 'Hanbali school', 69–71.

52 Ibn al-Jawzī, *Talbīs*, 211.

53 The standard Sufi responses to the charge of *bid'a* was (1) to deny the accusation and to prove that the practice in question was instead 'recommended' (*sunna*); this, for instance, was the strategy adopted by most Sufi authors who discussed the question of *sama'* though they carefully circumscribed the practice with qualifications; for brief overviews, see 'Samā', 1. In Music and Mysticism', EI 8: 1018a–1019b (J. During) as well as Arthur Gribetz, 'The *Samā'* controversy: Sufi vs. legalist', *Studia Islamica* 74 (1991): 43–62; and (2) to accept that the practice under discussion was an innovation but to cast it as an 'acceptable innovation' and not a reprehensible one;

this option was adopted especially in the cases of wearing patched frocks, building *khānaqāhs*, and extended seclusion; see Meier, 'Book of etiquette', 52–3.

54 Ibn al-Jawzī, *Talbīs*, 244.

55 Ibn al-Jawzī, *Talbīs*, 479ff.

56 Ibn al-Jawzī, *Talbīs*, 460ff. Among other authories, Ibn al-Jawzī relied on Sarrāj in this section.

57 An excellent recent edition of the *Ḥamāqat* is in Pūrjavādī, *Du mujaddid*, 153–209; this now replaces the earlier published edition in Otto Pretzl, *Die Streitschrift des Ġazālī gegen die Ibāḥīja* (Munich: Bayerischen Akademie der Wissenschaften, 1933), 63–118. The overlap between this work and Ibn al-Jawzi's *Delusions* is also pointed out by Hamid Algar in 'Ebāhīya', EIr 7: 653–4.

58 See, for instance, his Persian letter on the same subject in Pūrjavādī, *Du mujaddid*, 139–45; Pūrjavādī discussess the contents of the letter on pp. 126–38.

59 Sarrāj, *Luma'*, 410–35 / *Schlaglichter*, 584–602 (144–57).

60 Sviri, 'Ḥakīm Tirmidhī', 591, translating from *Kitāb al-bad' wa'l-ta'rīkh* (Paris 1899), 5: 147. Sviri gives the reading 'Ḥasaniyya' and translates *ibāḥa* as 'promiscuity'.

61 In Sulamī's treatise on them, the following statement of Abū Ḥafṣ Ḥaddād is one of the rare statements that addresses the issue of public blame: 'They [the Malāmatīs] show to people their shameful deeds and conceal from them their good qualities. And the people blame them for their outer [behaviour] while they blame themselves for they know about their inner [state]', Sulamī, *Malāmatiyya*, 89. This is best understood not as active commission of blameworthy acts but as non-concealment of such acts that naturally occur. The Malāmatīs of Nishapur were more concerned with avoiding praiseworthy acts than seeking to attract public blame, cf. Sviri, 'Ḥakīm Tirmidhī', 607.

62 W. Madelung, 'Zaydī attitudes to Sufism', in *Islamic Mysticism Contested: Thirteen Centuries of Controversies and Polemics*, ed. F. de Jong and Bernd Radtke (Leiden: Brill, 1999), 126.

63 Hujwīrī, *Kashf*, 68–78 / *Revelation*, 62–9.

64 Hujwīrī, *Kashf*, 69–70 / *Revelation*, 62–3.

65 Hujwīrī, *Kashf*, 70–1 / cf. *Revelation*, 63–4.

66 Hujwīrī, *Kashf*, 77–8 / *Revelation*, 69.

67 Ghazālī, *Kīmiyā*, 2: 199; Ghazālī, *Iḥyā'*, 3: 304–5; Meier, *Abū Sa'īd*, 497.

68 Pūrjavādī, *Du mujaddid*, 147, reporting from Ibn al-Qaysarānī's *Ṣafwat al-taṣawwuf* (Beirut, 1416/1995), 473. On this figure, see 'Ibn al-Ḳaysarānī', EI 3: 821a (Joseph Schacht).

69 Muḥammad ibn Munavvar, *Asrār*, 1: 288 / *Secrets*, 436; I have corrected O'Kane's 'does not think of it as reproach' to 'does not care about blame'. Graham, 'Abū Sa'īd', 128 gives the right translation.

70 Ibn al-Jawzī, *Talbīs*, 468; see also 478.

71 Ibn al-Jawzī, *Talbīs*, 468.

72 Ibn al-Jawzī, *Talbīs*, 201–2.

73 Cf. 'Begging, ii. In Sufi Literature and Practice', EIr 3: 81–2 (Algar).

74 'Darvīš, ii. In the Islamic Period', EIr 7: 73–6 (H. Algar); 'Darvīsh', s.v. *Lughātnāma*. Two early attestations of mendicant dervishes are Hujwīrī, *Kashf*, 432–79, esp. 449–53 / *Revelation*, 334–66, esp. 345–7; and 'Unṣur al-Ma'ālī, *Qābūsnāma*, 253; this book of counsel was written in 475/1082–3.

75 J. T. P. de Bruijn, 'The *Qalandariyyāt* in Persian mystical poetry, from Sanā'ī onwards', in *The Legacy of Medieval Persian Sufism*, ed. Leonard Lewisohn (London: Khaniqahi Nimatullahi Publications, 1992), 75–86; Bruijn, *Persian Sufi Poetry*, 71–6.

76 See Meier, *Abū Sa'īd*, 494–516, and Ahmet T. Karamustafa, *God's Unruly Friends: Dervish Groups in the Islamic Later Middle Period, 1200–1550* (Salt Lake City: The University of Utah Press, 1994), 31–8 for more extended discussions.

77 The quotes are from Bruijn, *Persian Sufi Poetry*, 76.

Conclusion

Accounting for the emergence of mystical trends in early Islam has been a thorny problem for historians of Islamic mysticism. On the one hand, there is the issue of 'external influence'. Whether or not earlier religious traditions played a clearly formative role on Muslim mystics, and if they did, through what social channels they did so, remain open questions that call for detailed research. Although the assumption that such external influence must have occurred appears to be fairly unproblematic, in practice it proves to be difficult to trace actual instances in which particular patterns of mystical thought and practice in one religious community 'travelled' to another community in a different religious tradition. In this study, the issue of influence has not been addressed, primarily because scholarship on the subject is not high in volume or quality. On the other hand, since at least some mystical ideas and practices must have evolved from within particular religious traditions in the absence of any ostensible external influence, it is warranted to ask where, under what social conditions, and from which modes of piety, mystical trends emerged in early Islam. The preceding historical overview has produced some answers to this set of questions.

First, it became clear that a number of different mystical currents ran through early Muslim communities. Although we know more about the mystical milieu in Iraq, the historical record about the People of Blame in Khurāsān and the Sages in Transoxania is not inconsiderable. These different communities of mystics were not completely disconnected from one another, yet they appear to have originated independently in geographically and culturally-separate, albeit not completely unconnected, environments.

Second, the name Sufism was initially associated only with particular groups in Iraq, where mystical circles formed primarily within communities of renunciants. Originally quite radical in both thought and practice, these circles gelled into distinct mystical movements in Basra and especially in Baghdad when, during the second half of the third/ninth century, they repositioned themselves closer to the social mainstream by taming their radical approach to issues such as experiencing paradise on earth. The mystical currents in north-eastern Iran and Central Asia, on the other hand, likely did not originate from within movements of renunciation, though admittedly our knowledge of the prehistory of the People of Blame and the Sages is rather thin. Nevertheless, the former appears to have taken shape among gainfully-employed artisanal and merchant classes, and the latter, to judge by the example of Tirmidhī himself who was a well-to-do landowner, might have been equally removed from the ideal of renunciation. Mysticism, in other words, did not everywhere emerge from within the bosom of renunciation, though the later ascendancy of Iraq-based Sufism over its counterparts elsewhere ensured a cherished place for the ideals of renunciation within the later Sufi tradition.

Third, early mystics were not necessarily located in the periphery of urban social life. While Sufis of Iraq had to contend with a radical past which they never completely relinquished (recall, for instance, the tension between Junayd on the one hand and Nūrī and Shiblī on the other), the People of Blame were perfectly mainstream, and their name acquired pejorative connotations only after the indigenous mystical trend of Khurāsān was taken over by Iraq Sufism. For their part, the Sages of Central Asia hardly appear to have been social iconoclasts. Mystics in early Islam, therefore, generally assumed an 'inner-worldy', albeit critical, orientation towards social life, and it would be erroneous to characterise their piety as anti-social.[1]

Finally, mystical modes of piety were prevalent primarily among educated members of the urban middle classes. Although the actual number of people involved in mystical groups must have been fairly limited, they attracted the attention of some cultural elites on account of the strong claims to religious authority that they advanced. In particular, the mystics tended to come into conflict with at least some scholars who saw themselves as the only rightful bearers of cultural authority. Naturally, such conflicts played themselves out in the form of debates on whether or not particular articles of faith or particular practices were divinely sanctioned. At times, as in the cases of Tustarī and Tirmidhī, as well as Nūrī and company in the inquisition of Ghulām Khalīl, this kind of friction was brought to the attention of politicians, but early mystics generally remained outside the vision of political rulers, since they rarely commanded a sizeable social following to form a political threat or possessed skills coveted by rulers. For their part, the mystics themselves generally preferred to remain aloof from politics.

Moving beyond the stage of emergence, the present study traced the spread of originally Iraq-based Sufism to other regions of Islamdom and, at least in the case of Khurāsān, documented its fusion with the Malāmatī movement of Nishapur. The encounter of Iraq Sufism with Malāmatiyya led to a merger of the two in which Sufism, now affiliated with the Shāfi'ī legal school, emerged as the dominant party, yet it is more than likely that the People of Blame contributed some of their distinctive traits to the new synthesis. The Malāmatī emphasis on vigilant training of the lower soul, for instance, may be reflected in the new emphasis on the training master, who emerged as a trademark of the reconstituted Sufism of Khurāsān. Similarly, the Malāmatī concern for social conformity may have facilitated the ascendancy, in the 'Sufism of Khurāsān', of the socially-conformist, 'sober' aspect of Iraq Sufism associated with Junayd (characterised by an inner-worldly, though politically-quiescent orientation) over its socially-unconventional, 'intoxicated' dimensions represented in part by Kharrāz, Nūrī and Shiblī (including a preference for celibacy or at least neglect of family, cultivation of poetry, and a developed discourse of love). Finally, the Malāmatī predilection for the concealment of inner spiritual states may well have informed the growing critique, by figures such as Hujwīrī, of Sufi 'formalism' that was exhibited in the concern with 'ritualistic' patterns of behaviour and appearance among many Sufi circles.

The new Sufism of Khurāsān was relatively friendly towards legal and theological scholarship, and this characteristic secured for it an enduring appeal among scholarly classes everywhere. Poured into academically attractive moulds by scholar-Sufis like Qushayrī and Hujwīrī and popularised by Sufis adept in scholarly discourses like Fārmadhī and Aḥmad Ghazālī, the Sufism of Khurāsān proved to be a potent mode of piety for cultural elites of Muslim communities. When, in his *Bringing the Religious Sciences to Life*, Abū Hāmid Ghazālī presented practical aspects of Sufism as the therapeutic cure for the ills that plagued the scholastic ethos of his time, he was merely endorsing in new terms this marriage between scholarly and mystical modes of piety.

Yet, for all its success among educated elites, the Sufism of Khurāsān was but one, albeit the most powerful, outcome of the fusion of Iraq-based Sufism with its 'provincial' counterparts. If figures such as Sarrāj, Kalābādhī and Sulamī paved the way towards the academically 'well-tempered' Sufism of Khurāsān, others like Makkī, Abū Manṣūr and Anṣārī resisted the pull of new scholastic approaches and adamantly presented their version of Sufism as the crown-piece of a traditionalist vision of Islam. It is highly likely that such a vision of the mystical life that stayed faithful to the renunciatory origins of Iraq-based Sufism was prevalent not only in towns such as Basra, Isfahan and Herat, but also among the mystical circles in Mecca. It is most probably from Iraq and western Arabia, via Egypt, that this traditionalist Sufism found its way into the the Maghrib and al-Andalus, much before the Sufism of Khurāsān arrived there with Abū Ḥāmid Ghazālī's works. Traditionalist Sufism found fertile ground especially among adherents of the Ḥanbalī and Mālikī legal schools and never totally lost its vigour in these circles. In addition to the Sufism of Khurāsān and traditionalist Sufism, there may well have been other alternative Sufi visions, though they are obscured in the historical record of Islamic mysticism. In particular, it would not be surprising if there existed in the Ḥanafī milieu of Central Asia yet another vision of Sufism that built upon the strong foundation laid by Tirmidhī and the other Sages of the area. Indeed, it is entirely possible that such a peculiarly Central Asian and eastern Khurāsānian vision informed the mysticism of a seminal figure like Aḥmad-i Jām, whose formation as a Sufi otherwise assumes an inexplicably *sui generis* appearance.

If the spread of Iraq-based Sufism to other regions and its fusion with other mystical trends led to the formation of new syntheses which harboured alternative visions of mystical Islam, it was inevitable that these visions would find literary expression in written works. The appearance of a specialised Sufi literature was the literary reflection of tradition-building efforts of third-fourth-fifth generation Sufis that responded to multiple needs. Foremost among these was the need to demonstrate the primacy of the Sufi mode of piety to all other ways of pious living that were current in early Islam. A close second was the need to draw normative boundaries around 'true Sufism' in order to differentiate it from 'fake', 'false', or simply 'misguided' mystical movements. Other practical needs also weighed in: the preservation of the legacy inherited from the early masters and its transmission to subsequent generations; the necessity of building solidarity within emerging Sufi communities through shared discourses of theoretical and practical guidance; introducing Sufism to new audiences previously unfamiliar with it; and confident self-assertion over competing modes of piety, these were all significant factors that contributed to the appearance of Sufi surveys and biographical compilations. It would be an error to assume that such self-conscious efforts at tradition-building were undertaken primarily for 'apologetic' purposes in order to defend Sufism against its detractors, especially since there is no real evidence that mystics suffered exceptional or even serious cultural or political persecution at this stage. The shadow of Ḥallāj's fate, itself only indirectly related to Sufism, did not loom that far.

The production of a specialised Sufi literature went in tandem with the formation of communities of disciples around increasingly authoritative masters who took a special interest in spiritual pedagogy and training. Tightly-knit master-disciple relationships formed the backbone of these communities, whose interconnectness expressed itself in highly-ritualised patterns of human interaction articulated in manuals of 'right conduct'. Eventually, such behavioural recipes were condensed into popular codes authenticated by reference to the earliest masters, most notably the 'Eight Rules of Junayd'. Increasingly, Sufi groups began to congregate, and even reside, in lodges specifically set aside for Sufi activities. Such communal living needed regulation, and all aspects of residential life, including financial, legal and ethical dimensions, began to attract scrutiny by Sufis and non-Sufis alike. The delineation of a communal Sufi identity, demarcated by public appearance, place of residence, distinct daily routines and specific rituals, was a complicated social process.

The emergence of sizeable Sufi communities was a sign of the increasing popularity of the Sufi way of life. This growing social visibility was, in part, the outcome of forces that were internal to Sufism. Although, as inward-oriented mystics, Sufis lived as though they were not 'of this world', Sufism was a mystical mode of piety that was squarely grounded 'in this world', and it harboured powerful internal tendencies to transform the world in its own image. Sufis, in other words, could become activists in their keenly-felt 'inner mission' to work towards the realisation of a holistic Islam, and this inner-worldly stance must have informed their increasing social and cultural popularity.[2] Yet, there were also broader cultural forces at work, and the spread of Sufi piety in all aspects of social life was no doubt due, in large measure, to its imbrication with the cult of saints that was becoming increasingly prevalent in Muslim communities. Indeed, the rise to prominence of communally-cherished, authoritative training masters with their communities of disciples around them occurred against the formation of the cults of saints in popular religiosity. The saint cults, built on notions of popular sainthood and the intercessory powers of divinely-chosen saints, came into their own especially during the fifth/eleventh and sixth/twelfth centuries. The growing confluence between Sufi and popular sainthood opened up new social arenas for the dissemination of the Sufi mode of piety, and Sufi masters increasingly found greater social purchase as popular saints. Hitherto confined to the urban middle classes, Sufism gradually spread to all social strata, and made major inroads into all aspects of popular religiosity.

It was at this stage that 'inner' Sufi circles built around bonds of master and disciple came to be broadened to include larger 'outer' circles of adherents or sympathisers connected to the inner circles through ties of loyalty and patronage, and Sufi piety came to inform the formation of larger social identities in Islamic societies. Predictably, it was also at this juncture that Sufis began to come within the purview of politicians, who began to take notice of their increasing social popularity. Both as individuals and as representatives of political regimes, politicians too stood to benefit from the saintly powers of major Sufi figures, and it was not long before narratives of contact between Sufis and rulers began to circulate within Muslim communities to serve multiple needs. Alternatively, politicians as well as other cultural elites with claims to authority viewed powerful Sufis with apprehension for fear that such popular appeal might be directed against them, and these fears at times led to increased scrutiny and even persecution of certain Sufi masters.

The phenomenal rise in the popular appeal of the Sufi mode of piety and its transformation into a social 'profession' did not occur uncontested. Alongside their powerful inner-worldly orientations, most strands of early Islamic mysticism also harboured potentially 'anarchist' tendencies that were critical of mainstream social life, although these normally did not translate into total renunciation. Such tendencies, most clearly documented in the case of early Iraq-based Sufism, continued to be present in and around all communities of mystics and at times percolated into libertine and iconoclastic social behaviour. It appears that as Sufism became socially more mainstream and acquired widespread popularity, its socially subversive potential rose to the surface in the form of antinomian and nonconformist beliefs and practices as an inner critique of 'Sufi exoterism' and Sufi accommodation with mainstream social institutions. It is in this sense that the appearance of *qalandars* and latter-day, socially unconventional 'Malāmatīs' should be understood. Even when it did not take the form of explicit departure from social norms, this internal, self-reflexive Sufi criticism of 'formalism' remained a prominent feature of Sufi discourse and behaviour in all subsequent periods.

Mainstream or iconoclastic, conformist or antinomian, Sufi saints of all types had clearly become major social players by the sixth/twelfth century, and the time was ripe for the gradual emergence of trans-generational, and in certain cases, trans-regional Sufi communal identities around their examples. A mystical mode of piety that had started among a limited number of middle-class urbanites had become a way of pious living that attracted followers, devotees and enthusiasts from all social strata in Muslim communities. Sufism had arrived.

Notes

1 For a detailed presentation of this perspective, see the fourth essay in Bernd Radtke, *Kritische Gänge*, 251–91.

2 In this respect, see the characteristically incisive remarks of Meier in 'Sufisme et déclin culturel', 227–38 (fourth question).

Bibliography

Abdel-Kader, Ali Hassan, *The Life, Personality and Writings of al-Junayd*, London: Luzac, 1962.

Abrahamov, Binyamin, *Islamic Theology: Traditionalism and Rationalism*, Edinburgh: Edinburgh University Press, 1998.

Abū Nuʿaym al-Iṣfahānī, Aḥmad ibn ʿAbd Allāh, *Ḥilyat al-awliyāʾ wa-ṭabaqāt al-aṣfiyāʾ*, Cairo: Maktaba al-Khānjī, 1932–8, 10 vols.

Addas, Claude, 'Andalusī mysticism and the rise of Ibn ʿArabī', in *The Legacy of Muslim Spain*, ed. Salma Khadra Jayyusi, Leiden: Brill, 1994, 909–33.

Aḥmad-i Jām [Abū Naṣr Aḥmad ibn Abu'l-Ḥasan], *Miftāḥ al-najāt*, ed. ʿAlī Fāẓil, Tehran: Intishārāt-i Bunyād-i Farhang-i Īrān, 1347/1968.

Aḥmad-i Jām [Abū Naṣr Aḥmad ibn Abu'l-Ḥasan], *Rawẓat al-muẕnibīn va jannat al-mushtāqīn*, ed. ʿAlī Faẓil, Tehran: Intishārāt-i Bunyād-i Farhang-i Īrān, 1355/1976.

Aḥmad-i Jām [Abū Naṣr Aḥmad ibn Abu'l-Ḥasan], *Uns al-tāʾibīn*, ed. ʿAlī Fāẓil, Tehran: Intishārāt-i Tūs, 1368/1989.

Aigle, Denise, 'Un fondateur d'ordre en milieu rural: le cheikh Abū Ishāq de Kāzarūn', in *Saints orientaux*, ed. Denise Aigle, Paris: De Boccard, 1995, 181–209.

ʿAlāqa, Fāṭima, 'Risāla-i 'Faḏil al-taṣawwuf ʿalāʾl-madhāhib' ta'līf-i Abū ʿAbd Allāh Muḥammad ibn Khafīf', *Maʿārif* 15, nos 1–2 (1998): 51–80.

ʿAlāqa, Fāṭima, 'Risāla-i 'Sharaf al-fuqarā'' ta'līf-i Abū ʿAbd Allāh Muḥammad ibn Khafīf', *Maʿārif* 16, no. 1 (1999): 98–132.

Andrae, Tor, *In the Garden of Myrtles: Studies in Early Islamic Mysticism*, Albany: State University of New York Press, 1987.

Anṣārī al-Harawī, ʿAbd Allāh ibn Muḥammad, *Ṭabaqāt al-ṣūfiyya*, ed. ʿAbd al-Ḥayy Ḥabībī, Tehran: Intishārāt-i Furūghī, 1942/1963.

Arberry, Arthur J., 'Did Sulamī plagiarize Sarrāj?', *Journal of the Royal Asiatic Society* (1937): 461–2.

Arberry, Arthur J., 'Khargūshī's manual of Sufism', *Bulletin of the School of Oriental and African Studies* 19 (1938): 345–9.

Asín Palacios, Miguel, *The Mystical Philosophy of Ibn Masarra and His Followers*,

trans. Elmer H. Douglas, Leiden: Brill, 1978.
Ateş, Süleyman, *Cüneyd-i Bağdâdî: Hayatı, Eserleri ve Mektupları*, Istanbul: Sönmez Neşriyat, 1969.
Avery, Kenneth S., *A Psychology of Early Sufi Samāʿ: Listening and Altered States*, London: Routledge Curzon, 2004.
ʿAyn al-Quḍāt al-Hamadhānī, ʿAbd Allāh ibn Muḥammad, *Tamhīdāt*, ed. ʿAfīf ʿUsayrān, Tehran: Dānishgāh-i Tihrān, 1341/1962.
Badawī, ʿAbd al-Raḥmān, *Shahīda al-ʿishq al-ilāhī Rābiʿa al-ʿAdawiyya*, Cairo: Maktaba al-Nahḍa al-Miṣriyya, 1962.
Baldick, Julian, 'The legend of Rābiʿa of Baṣra: Christian antecedents, Muslim counterparts', *Religion* 19 (1990): 233–47.
Baldick, Julian, *Mystical Islam: An Introduction to Sufism*, New York: New York University Press, 1989.
Ballanfat, Paul, 'Théorie des organes spirituels chez Yūsuf Hamadānī', *Studia Islamica* 87 (1998): 35–66.
Beaurecueil, S. de Laugier de, 'Un opuscule de Khwādja ʿAbdallāh Anṣārī concernant les bienséances des Soufis', *Bulletin de l'Institut Français d'Archéologie Orientale* 59 (1960): 203–39.
Berg, Herbert (ed.), *Method and Theory in the Study of Islamic Origins*, Leiden: Brill, 2003.
Berkey, Jonathan P., *Popular Preaching and Religious Authority in the Medieval Islamic Near East*, Seattle: University of Washington Press, 2001.
Bonner, Michael D., *Aristocratic Violence and Holy War: Studies in the Jihad and the Arab-Byzantine Frontier*, New Haven, CT: American Oriental Society, 1996.
Bonner, Michael D., 'The *Kitāb al-kasb* attributed to al-Shaybānī: poverty, surplus, and the circulation of wealth', *Journal of the American Oriental Society* 121 (2001): 410–27.
Bonner, Michael D., 'Poverty and charity in the rise of Islam', in *Poverty and Charity in Middle Eastern Contexts*, ed. Michael Bonner, Mine Ener and Amy Singer, Albany: State University of New York Press, 2003, 13–30.
Böwering, Gerhard, 'The Ādāb literature of classical Sufism: Anṣārī's code of conduct', in *Moral Conduct and Authority: The Place of Adab in South Asian Islam*, ed. Barbara D. Metcalf, Berkeley: University of California Press, 1984, 62–87.
Böwering, Gerhard, 'Early Sufism between persecution and heresy', in *Islamic Mysticism Contested: Thirteen Centuries of Controversies and Polemics*, ed. Frederick de Jong and Bernd Radtke, Leiden: Brill, 1999, 45–67.
Böwering, Gerhard, 'The major sources of Sulamī's Minor Qur'ān commentary', *Oriens* 35 (1996): 35–56.
Böwering, Gerhard, *The Mystical Vision of Existence in Classical Islam: The*

Qur'ānic Hermeneutics of the Ṣūfī Sahl at-Tustarī (d, 283/896), Berlin: De Gruyter, 1980.

Böwering, Gerhard, 'The Qur'ān commentary of al-Sulamī', in *Islamic Studies Presented to Charles J. Adam*, ed. Wael B, Hallaq and Donald P, Little, Leiden: Brill, 1991, 41–56.

Bruijn, J. T. P. de, *Persian Sufi Poetry: An Introduction to the Mystical Use of Classical Persian Poems*, Richmond, Surrey: Curzon, 1997.

Bruijn, J. T. P. de, 'The *Qalandariyyāt* in Persian mystical poetry, from Sanā'ī onwards', in *The Legacy of Medieval Persian Sufism*, ed. Leonard Lewisohn, London: Khaniqahi Nimatullahi Publications, 1992, 75–86.

Bulliet, Richard, *Islam: The View from the Edge*, New York: Columbia University Press, 1994.

Bulliet, Richard, *The Patricians of Nishapur: A Study in Medieval Islamic Social History*, Cambridge, MA: Harvard University Press, 1972.

Calasso, Giovanna, 'Les ramparts et la loi, les talismans et les saints: la protection de la ville dans les sources musulmanes médiévales', *Bulletin d'études orientales* 44 (1992): 83–104.

Carrette, Jeremy R., and Richard King, *Selling Spirituality: The Silent Takeover of Religion*, London: Routledge, 2005.

Chabbi, Jacqueline, 'Fuḍayl b. 'Iyāḍ, un précurseur du ḥanbalisme', *Bulletin d'études orientales* 30 (1978): 331–45.

Chabbi, Jacqueline, 'Remarques sur le développement historique des mouvements ascétiques et mystiques au Khurāsān', *Studia Islamica* 46 (1977): 5–72.

Chabbi, Jacqueline, 'Réflexions sur le soufisme iranien primitif', *Journal Asiatique* 266 (1978): 37–55.

Chamberlain, Michael, *Knowledge and Social Practice in Medieval Damascus, 1190–1350*, Cambridge: Cambridge University Press, 1994.

Chittick, William C., *Sufism: A Short Introduction*, Oxford: Oneworld, 2000.

Chodkiewicz, Michel, 'La sainteté et les saints en Islam', in *Le culte des saints dans le monde musulman*, ed. Henri Chambert-Loir and C. Guillot, Paris: École Française d'Extrême Orient, 1995, 13–22.

Chodkiewicz, Michel, *Seal of the Saints: Prophethood and Sainthood in the Doctrine of Ibn Arabi*, Cambridge: Islamic Texts Society, 1993.

Cooperson, Michael, *Classical Arabic Biography: The Heirs of the Prophets in the Age of al-Ma'mūn*, Cambridge: Cambridge University Press, 2000.

Cornell, Vincent J. *Realm of the Saint: Power and Authority in Moroccan Sufism*, Austin: University of Texas Press, 1998.

Crussol, Yolande de, *Le rôle de la raison dans la réflexion éthique d'al-Muḥāsibī:* 'aql *et conversion chez al-Muḥāsibī, 165/243–782/857*, Paris: Concep, 2002.

Dabashi, Hamid, *Truth and Narrative: The Untimely Thoughts of 'Ayn al-Quḍāt al-Hamadhānī*, Richmond, Surrey: Curzon, 1999.

Daylamī, Abu'l-Ḥasan 'Alī ibn Muḥammad, *Sīrat al-Shaykh al-Kabīr Abū 'Abd Allāh ibn al-Khafīf al-Shīrāzī*, ed. Annemarie Schimmel, Tehran: Intishārāt-i Bābak, 1984.

Daylamī, Abu'l-Ḥasan 'Alī ibn Muḥammad, *A Treatise on Mystical Love*, Joseph Norment Bell and Hassan Mahmood Abdul Latif Al Shafie, Edinburgh: Edinburgh University Press, 2005.

Demeerseman, André, *Nouveau regard sur la voie spirituelle d''Abd al-Qādir al-Jilānī et sa tradition*, Paris: Librairie Philosophique J. Vrin, 1988.

Dols, Michael W, *Majnūn: The Madman in Medieval Islamic Society*, Oxford: Oxford University Press, 1992.

Dreher, Josef, *Das Imamat des islamischen Mystikers Abūlqāsim Aḥmad ibn al-Ḥusain ibn Qasī (gest. 1151): eine Studie zum Selbstverständnis des Autors des 'Buchs vom Ausziehen der beiden Sandalen' (Kitāb ḫal' an-na'lain)*, Bonn, 1985.

Drewes, G. W. J., *Directions for Travellers on the Mystic Path*, The Hague: Martinus Nijhoff, 1977.

Elmore, Gerald, *Islamic Sainthood in the Fullness of Time: Ibn al-'Arabī's Book of the Fabulous Gryphon*, Leiden: Brill, 1999.

Ernst, Carl W., *The Shambhala Guide to Sufism*, Boston, MA: Shambhala, 1997.

Ernst, Carl, *Words of Ecstasy in Sufism*, Albany: State University of New York Press, 1985.

Ess, Josef van, *Die Gedankenwelt des Ḥāriṯ al-Muḥāsibī*, Bonn: Selbstverlag des Orientalischen Seminars der Universität Bonn, 1961.

Ess, Josef van, 'Der Kreis des Dhu'l-Nūn', *Die Welt des Orients* 12 (1981): 99–105.

Ess, Josef van, 'Sufism and its opponents: reflections on topoi, tribulations, and transformations', in *Islamic Mysticism Contested: Thirteen Centuries of Controversies and Polemics*, ed. F. de Jong and Bernd Radtke, Leiden: Brill, 1999, 22–44.

Ess, Josef van, *Theologie und Gesellschaft im 2. und 3. Jahrhundert Hidschra: Eine Geschichte des religösen Denkens im frühen Islam*, Berlin: De Gruyter, 1991–97, 6 vols.

Farhādī, A. G. Ravān, *'Abdullāh Anṣārī of Herāt (1006–1089 CE): An Early Ṣūfī Master*, Richmond, Surrey: Curzon, 1996.

Fāẓil, 'Alī, *Sharḥ-i aḥvāl va naqd va taḥlīl-i āsār-i Aḥmad-i Jām*, Tehran: Intishārāt-i Tūs, 1374/1995.

Fierro, María Isabel, 'Accusations of *zandaqa* in al-Andalus', *Quaderni di Studi Arabi* 5–6 (1987–88): 251–58.

Fierro, Maribel, 'Opposition to Sufism in al-Andalus', in *Islamic Mysticism Contested: Thirteen Centuries of Controversies and Polemics*, ed. F. de Jong and Bernd Radtke, Leiden: Brill, 1999, 174–206.

Fierro, Maribel, 'The polemic about the *karāmāt al-awliyā'* and the development of Ṣūfism in al-Andalus (fourth/tenth-fifth/eleventh Centuries)', *Bulletin of the School of Oriental and African Studies* 55 (1992): 236–49.

Frank, Richard, *Al-Ghazālī and the Ash'arite School*, Durham, NC: Duke University Press, 1994.

Furūzānfar, Badī' al-Zamān, *Aḥādīs̱-i Mas̱navī*, Tehran: Amīr Kabīr, 1361/1982.

Geoffroy, Éric, 'Attitudes contrastées des mystiques musulmans face au miracle', in *Miracle et karama: saints et leurs miracles à travers l'hagiographie chrétienne et islamique IVe–XVe siècles*, ed. Denise Aigle, Brepols: Turnhout, 2000, 301–16.

Geoffroy, Éric, *Djihad et contemplation: Vie et enseignement d'un soufi au temps des croisades*, Paris: Dervy, 1997.

Ghazālī, Abū Ḥāmid Muḥammad ibn Muḥammad, *Iḥyā' 'ulūm al-dīn*, Beirut: Dār al-Kutub al-'Ilmiyya, 1996, 5 vols.

Ghazālī, Abū Ḥāmid Muḥammad ibn Muḥammad, *Kīmiyā-yi sa'ādat*, ed. Ḥusayn Khidīvjam, Tehran: Shirkat-i Intishārāt-i 'Ilmī va Farhangī, 1364/1985, 2 vols.

Ghazālī, Abū Ḥāmid Muḥammad ibn Muḥammad, *Muḥammad al-Ġazzālīs Lehre von den Stufen zur Gottesliebe*, trans. Richard Gramlich, Wiesbaden: F. Steiner, 1984.

Ghazālī, Aḥmad ibn Muḥammad, *Majmū'a-i ās̱ār-i fārsī-i Aḥmad-i Ghazzālī 'ārif-i mutavaffā-yi* 520 H.Q, ed. Aḥmad Mujāhid, Tehran: Dānishgāh-i Tihrān, 1370/1991.

Ghaznavī, Sadīd al-Dīn Muḥammad ibn Mūsā, *The Colossal Elephant and His Spiritual Feats, Shaykh Ahmad-e Jām: The Life and Legend of a Popular Sufi Saint of Twelfth Century Iran*, trans. Heshmat Moayyad and Franklin Lewis, Costa Mesa, CA: Mazda Publishers, 2004.

Gianotti, Timothy J., *Al-Ghazālī's Unspeakable Doctrine of the Soul: Unveiling the Esoteric Psychology and Eschatology of the* Iḥyā', Leiden: Brill, 2001.

Goldziher, Ignác, *Introduction to Islamic Theology and Law*, trans. Andras Hamori and Ruth Hamori, Princeton: Princeton University Press, 1981.

Goldziher, Ignác, 'On the veneration of the dead in paganism and Islam', in *Muslim Studies*, ed. S. M. Stern, trans. C. R. Barber and S. M. Stern, London: Allen & Unwin, 1967, 1: 209–38.

Goldziher, Ignác, 'Veneration of saints in Islam', in *Muslim Studies*, ed. S. M. Stern, trans. C. R. Barber and S. M. Stern, London: Allen & Unwin, 1967, 2: 255–341.

Goodman, Lenn E., 'Ibn Masarrah', in *History of Islamic Philosophy*, ed. Seyyed Hossein Nasr and Oliver Leaman, London: Routledge, 1996, 277–93.

Göran Ogén, 'Did the term "ṣūfī" exist before the Sufis?' *Acta Orientalia* 43 (1982): 33–48.

Graham, Terry, 'Abū Sa'īd ibn Abi'l-Khayr and the School of Khurasan', in *Classical Persian Sufism from Its Origins to Rumi*, ed. Leonard Lewisohn, London: Khaniqahi Nimatullahi Publications, 1993, 583–613.

Graham, William A, *Divine Word and Prophetic Word in Early Islam: A Reconsideration of the Sources, with Special Reference to the Divine Saying or Hadîth Qudsî*, The Hague: Mouton, 1977.

Gramlich, Richard, *Abu l-'Abbās b. 'Aṭā': Sufi und Koranausleger*, Stuttgart: Deutsche Morgenländische Gesellschaft Kommissionsverlag, F. Steiner, 1995.

Gramlich, Richard, 'Abū Sulaymān ad-Dārānī', *Oriens* 33 (1992): 22–85.

Gramlich, Richard, *Alte Vorbilder des Sufitums*, Wiesbaden: Harrassowitz, 1997, 2 vols.

Gramlich, Richard, *Die schiitischen Derwischorden Persiens*, Wiesbaden: Deutsche Morgenländische Gesellschaft Kommissionsverlag Steiner, 1965–81, 3 vols.

Gramlich, Richard, *Weltverzicht: Grundlagen und Weisen Islamischer Askese*, Wiesbaden: Harrassowitz, 1997.

Gramlich, Richard, *Die Wunder der Freunde Gottes: Theologien und Erscheinungsformen des islamischen Heiligenwunders*, Wiesbaden: F. Steiner, 1987.

Gribetz, Arthur, 'The *Samā'* controversy: Sufi vs. legalist', *Studia Islamica* 74 (1991): 43–62.

Griffel, Frank, 'Al-Ġazālī's concept of prophecy: the introduction of Avicennan psychology into Aš'arite theology', *Arabic Sciences and Philosophy* 14 (2004): 101–44.

Gril, Denis, 'Le miracle en islam, critère de la sainteté?', in *Saints orientaux*, ed. Denise Aigle, Paris: De Boccard, 1995, 69–81.

Ḥaqīqat, 'Abd al-Rafī', *Sulṭān al-'ārifīn Bāyazīd-i Basṭāmī*, Tehran: Intishārāt-i Āftāb, 1361/1982.

Heath, Peter, 'Reading al-Ghazālī: the case of psychology', in *Reason and Inspiration in Islam: Theology, Philosophy and Mysticism in Muslim Thought, in Honor of Hermann Landolt*, ed. Todd Lawson, London: I. B. Tauris in association with the Institute of Ismaili Studies, 2005, 185–99.

Heinen, Anton, *Islamic Cosmology: A Study of as-Suyūṭī's al-Hay'a as-sanīya fī l-hay'a as-sunnīya*, Beirut: Franz Steiner, 1982.

Hogga, Mustapha, *Orthodoxie, subversion et réforme en Islam: Gazali et les seljuqides*, Paris: Librairie philosophique J. Vrin, 1993.

Hujwīrī, 'Alī ibn 'Uthmān, *Kashf al-maḥjūb*, ed. Valentin Zhukovsky, Tehran: Kitābkhāna-i Ṭahūrī, 1378/1999.

Hujwīrī, 'Alī ibn 'Uthmān, *Revelation of the Mystery (Kashf al-Mahjub)*, trans. Reynold A Nicholson, Accord, NY: Pir Press, 1999 [1911].

Hunsberger, Alice C, *Nasir Khusraw, the Ruby of Badakhshan: A Portrait of the Persian Poet, Traveller and Philosopher*, London: I. B. Tauris in association

with The Institute of Ismaili Studies, 2000.
Ibn al-ʿArīf, Aḥmad ibn Muḥammad, *Maḥāsin al-Majālis = The Attractions of Mystical Sessions*, trans. William Elliott and Adnan K. Abdulla, Amersham: Avebury, 1980.
Ibn al-Jawzī, Abū al-Faraj ʿAbd al-Raḥmān ibn ʿAli, *Talbīs Iblīs*, ed. ʿIṣām Ḥarastānī and Muḥammad Ibrāhīm Zaghlī, Beirut: Al-Maktab al-Islāmī, 1994.
Ibn Jubayr, Muḥammad ibn Aḥmad, *The Travels of Ibn Jubayr*, ed. William Wright and M. J. de Goeje, Leiden: Brill, 1907.
Ibn Qudāma, Muwaffaq al-Dīn ʿAbd Allāh ibn Aḥmad, *Ibn Qudāma's Censure of Speculative Theology*, ed. and trans. George Makdisi, London: Luzac, 1962.
Ibn Taymiyya, Aḥmad ibn ʿAbd al-Ḥalīm, *al-Furqān bayna awliyā' al-raḥmān wa-awliyā' al-shayṭān*, ed. Aḥmad Ḥamdī Imām, Cairo: Maṭbaʿat al-Madanī, 1401/1981.
Jaʿfar, Muḥammad Kamāl Ibrāhīm, *Min qaḍāyā al-fikr al-islāmī: dirāsa wa-nuṣūṣ*, Cairo: Maktaba Dār al-ʿUlūm, 1978.
Jamāl al-Dīn Abū Rawḥ Luṭf Allāh ibn Abī Saʿīd ibn Abī Saʿd, *Ḥālāt va sukhanān-i Abū Saʿīd-i Abu'l-Khayr*, Muḥammad Riżā Shafīʿī Kadkanī, Tehran: Mu'assasa-i Intishārāt-i Āgāh, 1366/1987.
Janssens, Jules, 'Al-Ghazzālī's *Tahāfut*: Is it really a rejection of Ibn Sīnā's philosophy?' *Journal of Islamic Studies* 12 (2001): 1–17.
Jarrar, Maher, and Sebastian Günther, 'Ġulām Ḫalīl und das *Kitāb Šarḥ as-sunna*: Erste Ergebnisse einer Studie zum Konservatismus hanbalitischer Färbung im Islam des 3./9. Jahrhunderts', *Zeitschrift der Deutschen Morgenländischen Gesellschaft* 153 (2003): 6–36.
Jawbarī, ʿAbd al-Raḥīm ibn ʿUmar, *Mukhtār fī kashf al-asrār wa-hatk al-astār*, ed. ʿIṣām Muḥammad Shibārū, Beirut: Dār al-Taḍāmun, 1992.
Jawbarī, ʿAbd al-Raḥīm ibn ʿUmar, *Le voile arraché: l'autre visage de l'Islam*, René Khawam, Paris: Phébus, 1979–80, 2 vols.
Kalābādhī, Abū Bakr Muḥammad ibn Ibrāhīm, *al-Taʿarruf li-madhhab ahl al-taṣawwuf*, ed. Aḥmad Shams al-Dīn, Beirut: Dār al-Kutub al-ʿIlmiyya, 1993.
Kalābādhī, Abū Bakr Muḥammad ibn Ibrāhīm, *The Doctrine of the Sufis*, trans. Arthur J. Arberry, Cambridge: Cambridge University Press, 1993 [1935].
Karamustafa, Ahmet T., *God's Unruly Friends: Dervish Groups in the Islamic Later Middle Period, 1200–1550*, Salt Lake City: The University of Utah Press, 1994.
Karamustafa, Ahmet T., 'Walāyah according to al-Junayd', in *Reason and Inspiration in Islam: Theology, Philosophy and Mysticism in Muslim Thought, in Honor of Hermann Landolt*, ed. Todd Lawson, London: I. B. Tauris in association with the Institute of Ismaili Studies, 2005, 64–70.

Kharkūshī, 'Abd al-Malik ibn Muḥammad, *Kitāb tahdhīb al-asrār*, ed. Bassām Muḥammad Bārūd, Abū Ẓabī, al-Imārāt al-'Arabiyya: Al-Majma' al-Thaqafī, 1999.

Kharrāz, Abū Sa'īd, *The Book of Truthfulness (Kitāb al-Ṣidq)*, Arthur J. Arberry, London: Oxford University Press, 1937.

Kinberg, Leah, 'Compromise of commerce: a study of early traditions concerning poverty and wealth', *Der Islam* 66 (1989): 193–212.

Kinberg, Leah, 'What is meant by *zuhd*?' *Studia Islamica* 61 (1985): 27–44.

Knysh, Alexander, *Islamic Mysticism: A Short History*, Leiden: Brill, 2000.

Kohlberg, Etan (ed.), *Shi'ism*, Burlington, VT: Ashgate, 2003.

Lalani, Arzina, *Early Shī'ī Thought: The Teachings of Imam Muḥammad al-Bāqir*, London: I. B. Tauris in association with the Institute of Ismaili Studies, 2000.

Lamoreaux, John C., *The Early Muslim Tradition of Dream Interpretation*, Albany: State University of New York Press, 2002.

Landolt, Hermann, 'Gedanken zum islamischen Gebetsteppich', in *Festschrift Alfred Bühler*, ed. Carl August Schmitz, Basel: Pharos Verlag, 1965, 243–56.

Landolt, Hermann, 'Ghazālī and "*Religionswissenschaft*": some notes on the *Mishkāt al-anwār*', *Asiatische Studien / Études Asiatiques* 45 (1991): 19–72.

Die Lebensweise der Könige: Adab al-mulūk, ein Handbuch zur islamischen Mystik, trans. Richard Gramlich, Stuttgart: Deutsche Morgenländische Gesellschaft Kommissionsverlag Franz Steiner, 1993.

Madelung, Wilferd, *Religious Trends in Early Islamic Iran*, Albany: Persian Heritage Foundation, 1988.

Madelung, Wilferd, 'Yūsuf al-Hamaḏānī and the Naqšbandiyya', *Quaderni di Studi Arabi* 5–6 (1987–88): 499–509.

Madelung, Wilferd, 'Zaydī attitudes to Sufism', in *Islamic Mysticism Contested: Thirteen Centuries of Controversies and Polemics*, ed. F. de Jong and Bernd Radtke, Leiden: Brill, 1999, 124–44.

Maḥmūd ibn 'Uthmān, *Firdaws al-murshidiyya fī asrār al-ṣamadiyya, Die Vita des Scheich Abū Isḥāq al-Kāzarūnī*, ed. Fritz Meier, Leipzig: Bibliotheca Islamica, 1948.

Makdisi, George, 'The Hanbali school and Sufism', *Humaniora Islamica* 2 (1974): 61–72.

Makkī, Abū Ṭālib Muḥammad ibn 'Alī, *'Ilm al-qulūb*, ed. 'Abd al-Qādir Aḥmad 'Aṭā, Cairo: Maktaba al-Qāhira, 1384/1964.

Makkī, Abū Ṭālib Muḥammad ibn 'Alī, *Die Nahrung der Herzen*, trans. Richard Gramlich, Stuttgart: F. Steiner, 1992, 4 vols.

Makkī, Abū Ṭālib Muḥammad ibn 'Alī, *Qūt al-qulūb fī mu'āmalat al-maḥbūb wa waṣf ṭarīq al-murīd ilā maqām al-tawḥīd*, ed. Sa'īd Nasīb Makārim, Beirut: Dār Ṣādir, 1995, 2 vols.

Malamud, Margaret, 'Sufi organizations and structures of authority in medieval Nishapur', *International Journal of Middle East Studies* 26 (1994): 427–42.

Marín, Manuela, 'The early development of *zuhd* in al-Andalus', in *Shi'a Islam, Sects, and Sufism: Historical Dimensions, Religious Practice and Methodological Considerations*, ed. Frederick de Jong, Utrecht: Houtsma, 1992, 83–94.

Marín, Manuela, 'Muslim religious practices in al-Andalus', in *The Legacy of Muslim Spain*, ed. Salma Khadra Jayyusi, Leiden: Brill, 1994, 878–94.

Marín, Manuela, 'Zuhhād of al-Andalus (300/912–420/1029)', in *The Formation of al-Andalus, Part 2: Language, Religion, Culture and the Sciences*, ed. Maribel Fierro and Julio Samso, Aldershot: Ashgate, 1998, 103–31.

Marín, Manuela, 'Abū Sa'īd Ibn al-A'rābī et le développement du ṣūfisme dans al-Andalus', *Revue du monde musulman et la Méditerranée* 63–64 (1992): 28–38.

Mason, Herbert, *Al-Hallaj*, Richmond, Surrey: Curzon, 1995.

Massignon, Louis, *Essay on the Origins of the Technical Language of Islamic Mysticism*, trans. Benjamin Clark, Notre Dame, IN: University of Notre Dame Press, 1997.

Massignon, Louis, *The Passion of al-Hallāj, Mystic and Martyr of Islam*, trans. Herbert Mason, Princeton: Princeton University Press, 1982, 4 vols.

Maybudī, Abu'l-Faḍl Rashīd al-Dīn, *Kashf al-asrār va 'uddat al-abrār ma'rūf bi-tafsīr-i Khvājah 'Abd Allāh-i Anṣārī*, ed. 'Alī Aṣghar Ḥikmat, Tehran: Intishārāt-i Dānishgāh-i Tihrān, 1331–9/1952–60, 10 vols.

McChesney, R. D., *Waqf in Central Asia: Four Hundred Years in the History of a Muslim Shrine, 1480–1889*, Princeton: Princeton University Press, 1991.

McGregor, Richard J. A., *Sanctity and Mysticism in Medieval Egypt: The Wafā' Sufi Order and the Legacy of Ibn 'Arabī*, Albany: State University of New York Press, 2004.

Meier, Fritz, *Abū Sa'īd-i Abū l-Ḫayr (357–440/967–1049): Wirklichkeit und Legende*, Tehran: Bibliothèque Pahlavi, 1976.

Meier, Fritz, 'A book of etiquette for Sufis', in *Essays on Islamic Piety and Mysticism*, trans. John O'Kane, Leiden: Brill, 1999, 49–92.

Meier, Fritz, 'The Dervish Dance', in *Essays on Islamic Piety and Mysticism*, trans. John O'Kane, Leiden: Brill, 1999, 23–48.

Meier, Fritz, 'An important manuscript find for Sufism', in *Essays on Islamic Piety and Mysticism*, trans. John O'Kane, Leiden: Brill, 1999, 135–88.

Meier, Fritz, 'Khurāsān and the end of classical Sufism', in *Essays on Islamic Piety and Mysticism*, trans. John O'Kane, Leiden: Brill, 1999, 189–219.

Meier, Fritz, 'Qushayrī's *Tartīb al-sulūk*', in *Essays on Islamic Piety and Mysticism*, trans. John O'Kane, Leiden: Brill, 1999, 93–133.

Meier, Fritz, 'Soufisme et déclin culturel', in *Classicisme et déclin culturel dans l'histoire de l'Islam, actes du symposium international d'histoire de la civili-*

sation musulmane, Bordeaux 25–29 juin 1956, ed. Robert Brunschvig, Paris: Chantemerle, 1957, 217–41.
Meier, Fritz, 'Ṭāhir al-Ṣafadī's forgotten work on western saints of the 6th/12th century', in *Essays on Islamic Piety and Mysticism*, trans. John O'Kane, Leiden: Brill, 1999, 423–504.
Meisami, Julie Scott, *Persian Historiography to the End of the Twelfth Century*, Edinburgh: Edinburgh University Press, 1999.
Melchert, Christopher, 'The adversaries of Aḥmad Ibn Ḥanbal', *Arabica* 44 (1997): 234–53.
Melchert, Christopher, 'Baṣran origins of classical Sufism', *Der Islam* 82 (2005): 221–40.
Melchert, Christopher, 'Early renunciants as *ḥadīth* transmitters', *Muslim World* 92 (2002): 407–18.
Melchert, Christopher, 'The Ḥanābila and the early Sufis', *Arabica* 58 (2001): 352–67.
Melchert, Christopher, 'Sufis and competing movements in Nishapur', *Iran* 39 (2001): 237–47.
Meri, Josef W, *The Cult of Saints Among Muslims and Jews in Medieval Syria*, Oxford: Oxford University Press, 2002.
Mīnūvī, Mujtabā, *Aḥvāl va aqvāl-i Shaykh Abū al-Ḥasan-i Kharaqānī*, Tehran: Kitābkhāna-i Ṭahūrī, 1359/1980.
Misgarnizhād, 'Abd al-Jalīl, 'Khwāja Abū Ya'qūb-i Hamadānī va risāla-i *dar bayān-i tawḥīd*', *Ma'ārif* 17, no. 2 (2000): 90–6.
Misgarnizhād, 'Abd al-Jalīl, '*Ṣafāwa al-tawḥīd li-taṣfiya al-murīd*, dar bayān-i "al-ṣūfī ghayru makhlūqin"', *Ma'ārif* 18, no. 2 (2001): 153–68.
Mitha, Farouk, *Al-Ghazālī and the Ismailis: A Debate on Reason and Authority in Medieval Islam*, London: I. B. Tauris in association with the Institute of Ismaili Studies, 2001.
Moezzi, Mohammad Ali Amir, *The Divine Guide in Early Shi'ism: The Sources of Esotericism in Islam*, Albany: State University of New York Press, 1994.
Mojaddedi, Jawid A, *The Biographical Tradition in Sufism: The Ṭabaqāt Genre from al-Sulamī to Jāmī*, Richmond, Surrey: Curzon, 2001.
Mottahedeh, Roy P, *Loyalty and Leadership in an Early Islamic Society*, Princeton: Princeton University Press, 1980.
Muḥammad ibn Munavvar, *Asrār al-tawḥīd fī maqāmāt al-Shaykh Abī Sa'īd*, ed. Muḥammad Riżā Shafī'ī-Kadkanī, Tehran: Mu'assasa-i Intishārāt-i Āgāh, 1366/1987, 2 vols.
Muḥammad ibn Munavvar, *The Secrets of God's Mystical Oneness*, trans. John O'Kane, Costa Mesa, CA: Mazda Publishers, 1992.
Netton, Ian R., 'The breath of felicity: *adab, aḥwāl, maqāmāt* and Abū Najīb al-Suhrawardī', in *Classical Persian Sufism from Its Origins to Rumi*, ed. Leonard

Lewisohn, London: Khaniqahi Nimatullahi Publications, 1993, 457–82.
Nicholson, Reynold A., 'An early Arabic version of the mi'raj of Abu Yazid al-Bistami', *Islamica* 2 (1926): 403–8.
Nicholson, Reynold A., 'An historical enquiry concerning the origin and development of Sufism', *Journal of the Royal Asiatic Society* 38 (1906): 303–48.
Nicholson, Reynold A., *Studies in Islamic Mysticism*, Cambridge: Cambridge University Press, 1967.
Niffarī, Muḥammad ibn 'Abd al-Jabbār, *The Mawāqif and Mukhāṭabāt of Muḥammad Ibn 'Abdi 'l-Jabbār al-Niffarī*, ed. and trans. Arthur J. Arberry, London: Luzac & Co., 1935.
Nwyia, Paul, *Exégèse coranique et langage mystique: nouvel essai sur le lexique technique des mystiques musulmans*, Beirut: Dar el-Machreq, 1970.
Nwyia, Paul, 'Le tafsīr mystique attribué à Ǧa'far Ṣādiq: éditions critique', *Mélanges de l'Université Saint-Joseph* 43 (1968): 181–230.
Nwyia, Paul, 'Textes mystiques inédits d'Abū-l-Ḥasan al-Nūrī (m. 295/907)', *Mélanges de l'Université Saint-Joseph* 44 (1968): 117–43.
Nwyia, Paul, *Trois oeuvres inédites de mystiques musulmans / Nuṣūṣ ṣūfiyya ghayr manshūra*, Beirut: Dār al-Mashriq, 1973.
Ogén, Gören, 'Religious ecstasy in classical Sufism', in *Religious Ecstasy Based on Papers Read at the Symposium on Religious Ecstasy Held at Åbo, Finland, on the 26th–28th of August 1981*, Stockholm: Distributed by Almqvist & Wiksell International, 1982, 226–40.
Olesen, Niels Henrik, *Culte des saints et pèlerinages chez Ibn Taymiyya (661/1263–728/1328)*, Paris: P. Geuthner, 1991.
Paul, Jürgen, 'Au début du genre hagiographique dans le Khurassan', in *Saints orientaux*, ed. Denise Aigle, Paris: De Boccard, 1995, 15–38.
Potter, Lawrence, 'Sufis and sultans in post-Mongol Iran', *Iranian Studies* 27 (1994): 77–102.
Pouzet, Louis, *Damas au VIIe/XIIIe siècle: vie structures religieuses d'une métropole islamique*, Beirut: Dar el-Machreq, 1988.
Pretzl, Otto, *Die Streitschrift des Ġazālī gegen die Ibāḥīja*, Munich: Bayerischen Akademie der Wissenschaften, 1933.
Pūrjavādī, Naṣr Allāh, 'Abū Manṣūr-i Iṣfahānī: Ṣūfī-i Ḥanbalī', *Ma'ārif* 6, no. 1–2 (1989): 3–80.
Pūrjavādī, Naṣr Allāh, 'Ādāb al-mutaṣawwifa wa-ḥaqā'iquhā wa-ishārātuhā az Abū Manṣūr-i Iṣfahānī', *Ma'ārif* 9 (1993): 249–82.
Pūrjavādī, Naṣr Allāh, *'Ayn al-Qużāt va ustādān-i ū*, Tehran: Asāṭīr, 1374/ 1995.
Pūrjavādī, Naṣr Allāh, 'Bāzmāndahā-yi kitāb-i *al-ishāra wa'l-'ibāra*-i Abū Sa'd-i Khargūshī dar kitāb-i *'ilm al-qulūb*', *Ma'ārif* 15, no. 3 (1999): 34–41.
Pūrjavādī, Naṣr Allāh, 'Du a̱sar-i kūtāh az Abū Manṣūr-i Iṣfahānī', *Ma'ārif* 6 (1990): 235–83.

Pūrjavādī, Naṣr Allāh, *Du mujaddid: pizhūhishhāyī dar bāra-'i Muḥammad-i Ghazzālī va Fakhr-i Rāzī*, Tehran: Markaz-i Nashr-i Dānishgāhī, 1381/2002.

Pūrjavādī, Naṣr Allāh, 'Kitāb sharḥ al-adhkār', *Ma'ārif* 19, no. 3 (2003): 3–30.

Pūrjavādī, Naṣr Allāh, 'Majālis-i Aḥmad-i Ghazzālī bā ḥużūr-i Yūsuf-i Ṣūfī', *Ma'ārif* 19, no. 1 (2002): 3–20.

Pūrjavādī, Naṣr Allāh, 'Manba'ī kuhan dar bāb-i malāmatiyān-i Nīshābūr', *Ma'ārif* 15, no. 1–2 (1998): 3–50.

Pūrjavādī, Naṣr Allāh, 'Opposition to Sufism in Twelver Shiism', in *Islamic Mysticism Contested: Thirteen Centuries of Controversies and Polemics*, ed. F. de Jong and Bernd Radtke, Leiden: Brill, 1999, 614–23.

Pūrjavādī, Naṣr Allāh, *Ru'yat-i māh dar āsumān: barrasī-yi tārīkhī-yi mas'ala-i liqā' Allāh dar kalām va taṣavvuf*, Tehran: Markaz-i Nashr-i Dānishgāhī, 1375/1996.

Pūrjavādī, Naṣr Allāh, 'Sayr-i iṣṭilāḥāt-i ṣūfiyān az "Nahj al-khāṣṣ"-i Abū Manṣūr-i Iṣfahānī tā "Futūḥāt"-i Ibn-i 'Arabī', *Ma'ārif* 16, no. 3 (2000): 3–55.

Pūrjavādī, Naṣr Allāh, *Zindagī va āṯār-i Shaykh Abu'l-Ḥasan-i Bustī*, Tehran: Mu'assasa-'i Muṭāla'āt va Taḥqiqāt-i Farhangī, 1364/1985.

Qushayrī, 'Abd al-Karīm ibn Hawāzin, *Principles of Sufism*, trans. Barbara R. von Schlegell, Berkeley: Mizan Press, 1992.

Qushayrī, 'Abd al-Karīm ibn Hawāzin, *al-Risāla al-Qushayriyya*, ed. 'Abd al-Ḥalīm Maḥmūd and Maḥmūd ibn al-Sharīf, Cairo: Dār al-Kutub al-Ḥadītha, 1375/1956.

Qushayrī, 'Abd al-Karīm ibn Hawāzin, *Das Sendschreiben al-Qušayrīs über das Sufitum*, trans. Richard Gramlich, Wiesbaden: F. Steiner, 1989.

Radtke, Bernd (ed.), *Adab al-mulūk: Ein Handbuch zur islamischen Mystik aus dem 4./10. Jahrhundert*, Beirut: Orient-Institut der Deutschen Morgenländischen Gesellschaft im Kommission bei F. Steiner Verlag Stuttgart, 1991.

Radtke, Bernd, 'The concept of *wilāya* in early Sufism', in *Classical Persian Sufism from Its Origins to Rumi*, ed. Leonard Lewisohn, London: Khaniqahi Nimatullahi Publications, 1993, 483–96.

Radtke, Bernd, 'The eight rules of Junayd: a general overview of the genesis and development of Islamic dervish orders', in *Reason and Inspiration in Islam: Theology, Philosophy and Mysticism in Muslim Thought, in Honor of Hermann Landolt*, ed. Todd Lawson, London: I. B. Tauris in association with the Institute of Ismaili Studies, 2005, 490–502.

Radtke, Bernd, 'Al-Ḥakīm al-Tirmidhī on miracles', in *Miracle et karama: saints et leurs miracles à travers l'hagiographie chrétienne et islamique IVe–XVe siècles*, ed. Denise Aigle, Brepols: Turnhout, 2000, 287–99.

Radtke, Bernd, *Al-Ḥakīm at-Tirmiḏī: Ein islamischer Theosoph des 3./9. Jahrhunderts*, Freiburg: Klaus Schwarz, 1980.

Radtke, Bernd, 'How can man reach the mystical union: Ibn Ṭufayl and the

divine spark', in *The World of Ibn Ṭufayl*, ed. Lawrence I. Conrad, Leiden: Brill, 1996, 165–94.
Radtke, Bernd, 'Iranian and gnostic elements in early *taṣawwuf*: observations concerning the *Umm al-kitāb*', in *Proceedings of the First European Conference of Iranian Studies Held in Turin, September 7th–11th, 1987 by the Societas Iranologica Europaea*, ed. Gherardo Gnoli and Antonio Panaino, Rome: Istituto italiano per il Medio ed Estremo Oriente, 1990, 2 vols, 2: 519–30.
Radtke, Bernd, *Neue kritische Gänge: Zu Stand und Aufgaben der Sufikforschung*, Utrecht: Houtsma, 2005.
Radtke, Bernd, 'Theologien und Mystiker in Ḫurāsān und Transoxanien', *Zeitschrift der Deutschen Morgenländischen Gesellschaft* 136 (1986): 536–69.
Radtke, Bernd, 'Theosophie (*ḥikma*) und Philosophie (*falsafa*): Ein Beitrag zur Frage der *ḥikmat al-mašriq/al-išrāq*', *Asiatische Studien* 42 (1988): 156–74.
Radtke, Bernd, 'Tirmiḏiana Minora', *Oriens* 34 (1994): 242–98.
Radtke, Bernd, 'Warum ist der Sufi orthodox?' *Der Islam* 71 (1994): 302–7.
Radtke, Bernd, *Weltgeschichte und Weltbeschreibung im mittelalterlichen Islam*, Beirut: F. Steiner, 1992.
Reinert, Benedikt, *Die Lehre vom* tawakkul *in der klassischen Sufik*, Berlin: De Gruyter, 1968.
Reisman, David C., *The Making of the Avicennan Tradition: The Transmission, Contents, and Structure of Ibn Sīnā's al-Mubāḥaṯāt*, Leiden: Brill, 2002.
Renard, John, *Historical Dictionary of Sufism*, Lanham, MD: Scarecrow Press, 2005.
Renard, John, *Knowledge of God in Classical Sufism: Foundations of Islamic Mystical Theology*, trans. John Renard, New York: Paulist Press, 2004.
Renard, John, *Seven Doors to Islam: Spirituality and the Religious Life of Muslims*, Berkeley: University of California Press, 1996.
Ritter, Hellmut, *The Ocean of the Soul: Man, the World, and God in the Stories of Farīd al-Dīn 'Aṭṭār*, ed. Bernd Radtke, trans. John, O'Kane, Leiden: Brill, 2003.
Roded, Ruth, *Women in Islamic Biographical Collections: From Ibn Sa'd to Who's Who*, Boulder, CO: L. Rienner, 1994.
Rustom, Mohammed, 'Forms of gnosis in Sulamī's Sufi exegesis of the *Fātiḥa*', *Islam and Christian-Muslim Relations* 16 (2005): 327–44.
Safi, Omid, *The Politics of Knowledge in Premodern Islam: Negotiating Ideology and Religious Inquiry*, Chapel Hill: University of North Carolina Press, 2006.
Safi, Omid, 'The Sufi path of love in Iran and India', in *A Pearl in Wine*, ed. Zia Inayat Khan, New Lebanon, NY: Omega Press, 2001, 221–66.
Sands, Kristin, *Sufi Commentaries on the Qur'an in Classical Islam*, London: Routledge, 2005.
Sarrāj, Abū Naṣr 'Abd Allāh ibn 'Alī, *Kitāb al-luma' fi'l-taṣawwuf*, ed. Reynold

A. Nicholson, London: Luzac & Co., 1914.

Sarrāj, Abū Naṣr 'Abd Allāh ibn 'Alī, *Schlagrichter über das Sufitum*, trans. Richard Gramlich, Stuttgart: F. Steiner, 1990.

Schimmel, Annemarie, 'Abu'l-Ḥusayn al-Nūrī: "Qibla of the Lights"', in *Classical Persian Sufism from Its Origins to Rumi*, ed. Leonard Lewisohn, London: Khaniqahi Nimatullahi Publications, 1993, 59–64.

Schimmel, Annemarie, *Mystical Dimensions of Islam*, Chapel Hill: University of North Carolina Press, 1975.

Schmidt, Leigh Eric, 'The making of modern "mysticism"', *Journal of the American Academy of Religion* 71 (2003): 273–302.

Sedgwick, Mark J., *Sufism: The Essentials*, Cairo: American University in Cairo Press, 2000.

Sells, Michael A., 'Bewildered tongue: the semantics of mystical union in Islam', in *Mystical Union and Monotheistic Faith: An Ecumenical Dialogue*, ed. Moshe Idel and Bernard McGinn, New York: Macmillan, 1989, 108–15.

Sells, Michael A., *Early Islamic Mysticism: Sufi, Qur'an, Mi'raj, Poetic and Theological Writings*, New York: Paulist Press, 1996.

Sezgin, Fuat, *Geschichte des arabischen Schrifttums*, Leiden: Brill, 1967–2000.

Sha'bānzāda, Maryam, 'Abū Sa'īd-ī Kharrāz', *Ma'ārif* 19, no. 1 (2002): 131–44.

Shafī'ī-Kadkanī, Muḥammad Riżā, *Chashīdan-i ṭa'am-i vaqt: az mīrāṣ-i 'irfānī-i Abū Sa'īd-i Abu'l-Khayr*, Tehran: Intishārāt-i Sukhan, 1385/2006.

Shafī'ī-Kadkanī, Muḥammad Riżā, *Daftar-i rawshanāyī: az mīrāṣ-i 'irfānī-i Bāyazīd-i Basṭāmī*, Tehran: Intishārāt-i Sukhan, 1384/2005.

Shafī'ī-Kadkanī, Muḥammad Riżā, *Nivishta bar daryā: az mīrāṣ-i 'irfānī-i Abu'l-Ḥasan-i Kharaqānī*, Tehran: Intishārāt-i Sukhan, 1384/2005.

Al-Shaibi, Kamil M, *Sufism and Shiism*, Surbiton: LAAM, 1991.

Silvers-Alario, Laury, 'The teaching relationship in early Sufism: a reassessment of Fritz Meier's definition of the *shaykh al-tarbiya* and the *shaykh al-ta'līm*', *Muslim World* 93 (2003): 69–97.

Smith, Margaret, *Al-Muḥāsibī: An Early Mystic of Baghdad*, London: The Sheldon Press, 1935.

Smith, Margaret, *Rabi'a: The Life and Work of Rabi'a and Other Women Mystics in Islam*, Oxford: Oneworld, 1994.

Sobieroj, Florian, *Ibn Ḫafīf aš-Šīrāzī und seine Schrift zur Novizenerziehung (Kitāb al-Iqtiṣād)*, Beirut: Orient-Institut der Deutschen Morgenländischen Gesellschaft im Kommission bei F. Steiner Verlag Stuttgart, 1998.

Sobieroj, Florian, 'Ibn Khafīf's *Kitāb al-iqtiṣād* and Abū al-Najīb al-Suhrawardī's *Ādāb al-murīdīn*: a comparison between the two works on the training of novices', *Journal of Semitic Studies* (1998), 327–45.

Sobieroj, Florian, 'Mittelsleute zwischen Ibn Khafīf und Abū Isḥāq al-Kāzarūnī', *Asiatische Studien / Études Asiatiques* 51 (1997): 651–71.

Sobieroj, Florian, 'The Mu'tazila and Sufism', in *Islamic Mysticism Contested: Thirteen Centuries of Controversies and Polemics*, ed. Frederick de Jong and Bernd Radtke, Leiden: Brill, 1999, 68–92.

Suhrawardī, 'Abd al-Qāhir ibn 'Abd Allāh, *Kitāb ādāb al-murīdīn*, ed. Menahem Milson, Jerusalem: Hebrew University, Institute of Asian and African Studies, distributed by Magnes Press, 1977.

Suhrawardī, 'Umar ibn Muḥammad, *'Awārif al-ma'ārif*, ed. Adīb al-Kamdānī and Muḥammad Maḥmūd al-Muṣṭafā, Mecca: Al-Maktaba al-Makkiya, 2001, 2 vols.

Sulamī, Abū 'Abd al-Raḥmān Muḥammad ibn al-Ḥusayn, *The Book of Sufi Chivalry*, trans. Tosun Bayrak, New York: Inner Traditions, 1983.

Sulamī, Abū 'Abd al-Raḥmān Muḥammad ibn al-Ḥusayn, *Early Sufi women:* Dhikr an-niswa al-muta'abbidāt aṣ-ṣūfiyyāt, Edited and trans. Rkia Elaroui Cornell, Louisville, KY: Fons Vitae, 1999.

Sulamī, Abū 'Abd al-Raḥmān Muḥammad ibn al-Ḥusayn, *Ḥaqā'iq al-tafsīr*, ed. Sayyid 'Imrān, Beirut: Dār al-Kutub al-'Ilmiyya, 1421/2001.

Sulamī, Abū 'Abd al-Raḥmān Muḥammad ibn al-Ḥusayn, *Majmū'a-i āsār-i Abū 'Abd al-Raḥmān Sulamī*, ed. Naṣr Allāh Pūrjavādī, Tehran: Markaz-i Nashr-i Dānishgāhī, 1369–72/1980–3, 2 vols.

Sulamī, Abū 'Abd al-Raḥmān Muḥammad ibn al-Ḥusayn, *Risālat al-malāmatiyya* [in *al-Malāmatiyya wa'l-ṣūfiyya wa ahl al-futuwwa*, pages 86–120], ed. Abū al-'Alā al-'Afīfī, Cairo: Dār Iḥyā' al-Kutub al-'Arabiyya, 1364/1945.

Sulamī, Abū 'Abd al-Raḥmān Muḥammad ibn al-Ḥusayn, *Ṭabaqāt al-ṣūfiyya*, ed. Nūr al-Dīn Shurayba, Cairo: Maktaba al-Khānjī, 1406/1986 [1372/1953].

Sulamī, Abū 'Abd al-Raḥmān Muḥammad ibn al-Ḥusayn, *Tasavvufta Fütüvvet / Kitāb al-futuwwa*, ed. and trans. Süleyman Ateş, Ankara: Ankara Üniversitesi İlāhiyat Fakültesi Yayınları, 1977.

Sulamī, Abū 'Abd al-Raḥmān Muḥammad ibn al-Ḥusayn, *Tasavvufun Ana İlkeleri: Sülemī'nin Risaleleri*, ed. and trans. Süleyman Ateş, Ankara: Ankara Üniversitesi Basımevi, 1981.

Sulamī, Abū 'Abd al-Raḥmān Muḥammad ibn al-Ḥusayn, *Uṣūl al-malāmatiyya wa ghalaṭāt al-ṣūfiyya*, ed. 'Abd al-Fattāḥ Aḥmad al-Fāwī Maḥmūd, Cairo: Jāmi'a al-Qāhira, 1405/1980.

Sulamī, Abū 'Abd al-Raḥmān Muḥammad ibn al-Ḥusayn, and al-Ḥakīm al-Tirmidhī, *Three Early Sufi Texts*, trans. Nicholas Heer and Kenneth Honnerkamp, Louisville, KY: Fons Vitae, 2003.

Sviri, Sarah, 'Ḥakīm Tirmidhī and the *Malāmatī* Movement in Early Sufism', in *Classical Persian Sufism from Its Origins to Rumi*, ed. Leonard Lewisohn, London: Khaniqahi Nimatullahi Publications, 1993, 583–613.

Sviri, Sarah, 'The self and its transformation in Ṣūfism, with special reference to early literature', in *Self and Self-Transformation in the History of Religions*, ed. David Shulman and Guy G. Stroumsa, Oxford: Oxford University Press, 2002, 195–215.

Sviri, Sarah, 'Wa-rahbāniyyatan ibtadaʿūhā: an analysis of traditions concerning the origin and evaluation of Christian monasticism', *Jerusalem Studies in Arabic and Islam* 13 (1990): 195–208.

Ṭāhirī-ʿIrāqī, Aḥmad, 'Abū Saʿd-i Khargūshī', *Maʿārif* 15, no. 3 (1999): 5–33.

Tanūkhī, al-Muḥassin ibn ʿAlī, *The Table-Talk of a Mesopotamian Judge*, trans. D. S. Margoliouth, London: Royal Asiatic Society, 1922.

Taylor, Christopher Schurman, *In the Vicinity of the Righteous:* Ziyāra *and the Veneration of Muslim Saints in Late Medieval Egypt*, Leiden: Brill, 1999.

Tirmidhī, Muḥammad ibn ʿAlī al-Ḥakīm, *The Concept of Sainthood in Early Islamic Mysticism: Two Works by Ḥakīm al-Tirmidhī*, trans. John O'Kane and Bernd Radtke, Richmond, Surrey: Curzon, 1996.

Tirmidhī, Muḥammad ibn ʿAlī al-Ḥakīm, *Thalātha muṣannafāt li'l-Ḥakīm al-Tirmidhī: Kitāb sīrat al-awliyā', Jawāb masā'il allati sa'alahu ahl Sarakhs ʿanhā, Jawāb kitāb min al-Rayy*, ed. Bernd Radtke, Stuttgart: F. Steiner, 1992.

Tor, Deborah, 'Privatized jihad and public order in the pre-Seljuq period: the role of the *mutatawwiʿa*', *Iranian Studies* 38 (2005): 555–73.

Tornero, Emilio, 'A report on the publication of previously unedited works of Ibn Masarra', in *The Formation of al-Andalus, Part 2: Language, Religion, Culture and the Sciences*, ed. Maribel Fierro and Julio Samso, Aldershot, UK: Ashgate, 1998, 133–49.

Trimingham, J. Spencer, *The Sufi Orders in Islam*, Oxford: Oxford University Press, 1998.

ʿUnṣur al-Maʿālī, Kaykāvūs ibn Iskandar ibn Qābūs, *Qābūsnāma*, ed. Ghulām Ḥusayn Yūsufī, Tehran: Shirkat-i Intishārāt-i ʿIlmī va Farhangī, 1375/1996 [1345/1966].

Urvoy, Dominique, 'The *ʿulamā'* of al-Andalus', in *The Legacy of Muslim Spain*, ed. Salma Khadra Jayyusi, Leiden: Brill, 1994, 849–77.

Utas, Bo, 'The Munajat or Ilahi-Namah of ʿAbdu'llah Ansari', *Manuscripts of the Middle East* 3 (1988): 83–7.

Wild, Stefan, 'Jugglers and Fraudulent Sufis', in *Proceedings of the VIth Congress of Arabic and Islamic Studies, Visby 13–16 August, Stockholm 17–19 August, 1972*, ed. Frithiof Rundgren, Stockholm: Almqvist & Wiksell International, 1975, 58–63.

Index